European Solidarity in Times of Crisis

The euro crisis, several sovereign debt crises, the Great Recession, the refugee crisis, and Brexit have all challenged Europeans' willingness to show solidarity with other European citizens and member states of the European Union. *European Solidarity in Times of Crisis* provides a clear theoretical framework to understand European solidarity for the first time. It offers a systematic empirical approach to determine the strength and causes of European solidarity. The authors distinguish between four domains of solidarity and test a set of theoretically derived criteria with a unique data set to investigate European solidarity.

Based on a survey conducted in 13 EU member states in 2016, the empirical analysis leads to some unanticipated results. Europeans display a notably higher degree of solidarity than many politicians and social scientists have presumed so far. This especially applies to the support of people in need (welfare solidarity) and the reduction of territorial disparities between rich and poor EU countries (territorial solidarity), but also to the domain of fiscal solidarity (financial support of indebted EU countries). This optimistic view is less true for the domain of refugee solidarity. While citizens of western and southern EU countries accept the accommodation of refugees and their allocation between European countries, the majority of people in eastern European countries do not share this point of view.

The book will appeal to students and scholars in fields such as comparative sociology, political science, social policy and migration research, and European studies. It is also relevant to a non-academic audience interested in the development of the European project.

Jürgen Gerhards is Professor of Sociology at the Freie Universität Berlin. His research interests include comparative cultural sociology and sociology of European integration. His most recent publications include *Global Inequality in the Academic System: Effects of National and University Symbolic Capital on International Academic Mobility* (Higher Education, 2018, with S. Hans and D. Drewksi); *Social Class and Transnational Human Capital. How Upper and Middle Class Parents Prepare Their Children for Globalization* (Routledge, 2017, with S. Hans and S. Carlson); *European Citizenship and Social Integration* *in the European Union* (Routledge, 2015, with H. Lengfeld); *Transnational Linguistic Capital: Explaining English Proficiency in 27 Countries* (International Sociology, 2014); 'European Integration, Equality Rights and People's Beliefs' (*European Sociological Review*, 2013, with H. Lengfeld); 'From Hasan to Herbert: Name Giving Patterns of Immigrant Parents between Acculturation and Ethnic Maintenance' (*American Journal of Sociology*, 2009, with S. Hans); 'Free to Move? The Acceptance of Free Movement of Labour and Non-Discrimination among Citizens of Europe' (*European Societies*, 2008).

Holger Lengfeld is Professor of Sociology at Leipzig University and Research Fellow at the German Institute of Economic Research Berlin. His research focuses on social stratification, inequality, and European social integration. Among his publications are 'Does Physiological Distribution of Blood parameters in Children Depend on Socioeconomic Status? Results of a German Cross-sectional Study' (*BMJ Open*, 2018, with K. Rieger, M. Vogel, C. Engel, U. Ceglarek, K. Harms, U. Wurst, M. Richter, and W. Kiess); 'Drifting Apart or Converging? Grades of Non-traditional and Traditional Students over the Course of Their Studies' (*Higher Education*, 2017, with T. Brändle); 'Do European Citizens Support the Idea of a European Welfare State?' (*International Sociology*, 2016, with J. Gerhards and J. Häuberer); 'The Long Shadow of Occupation: Volunteering in Retirement' (*Rationality and Society*, 2016, with J. Ordemann); 'European Citizenship and Social Integration in the European Union' (Routledge, 2015, with J. Gerhards); 'The Growing Remit of the EU in Climate Change Policy and Citizens' Support across the Union' (*Journal of European Social Policy*, 2008, with J. Gerhards).

Zsófia S. Ignácz is a lecturer and researcher at the Institute of Sociology, Goethe Universität Frankfurt am Main, Germany. Her main research interests include social justice and methodological topics. Her most recent publications are 'The Remains of the Socialist Legacy: The Influence of Socialist Socialization on Attitudes toward Income Inequality' (*Societies*, 2018); 'Social Cohesion and Its Correlates' (*Comparative Sociology*, 2018, with J. Delhey, K. Boehnke, G. Dragolov, M. Larsen, J. Lorenz, and M. Koch); *Wage Distribution Fairness in Post-Socialist Countries* (Routledge, 2018); *Social Cohesion in the Western World* (Springer, 2016, with G. Dragolov, J. Lorenz, J. Delhey, K. Boehnke, and K. Unzicker).

Florian K. Kley is a researcher and lecturer at the Institute of Sociology, Leipzig University, Germany. Previously, he was a researcher in the HORIZON 2020-Project, *Solidarity in European Societies: Empowerment, Social Justice and Citizenship (SOLIDUS)* at the Chair for Societal Institutions and Social Change at the Institute of Sociology at Leipzig University. His main research fields are European social integration, social stratification research, and quantitative data analysis.

Could and should the EU become more solidaristic? This is a key question for all Europeans. To move beyond superficial answers, we need to clearly spell out the meaning of 'EU solidarity' and then tap citizens' orientations. This volume makes a fundamental step forward in this direction. It distinguishes between fiscal, territorial, welfare and refugee solidarity and finds a surprisingly high popular support for enhancing the 'caring' mission of the EU. The authors offer not only an innovative and rich analytical framework but also invigorating signals for all those who have not lost faith in the European project.

Maurizio Ferrera, *Professor of Political Science,*
Università degli Studi di Milano

I believe that the political elites – first and foremost the despondent social democratic parties – underestimate the disposition of their voters to engage themselves for projects reaching beyond narrow self-interest. The fact that this view isn't just a reflection of unfulfilled philosophical ideals can be seen in the most recent publication by the research group led by Jürgen Gerhards and Holger Lengfeld, who for years has pursued wide-ranging and intelligent comparative studies on solidarity in thirteen EU member states. They have not only found indicators for a shared European identity distinct from national identity, but also an unexpectedly high willingness to support European policies that would imply redistribution across national boundaries.

Jürgen Habermas, *Professor Emeritus of Philosophy,*
Goethe Universität Frankfurt am Main

European Solidarity in Times of Crisis is a superb contribution to the literature on the dynamics of social transformation in Europe and to the sociology of the European Union. At a time when nationalist populism is on the rise, it demonstrates that the vast majority of European Union citizens feel a strong sense of obligation toward other Europeans. Through rigorous and reader-friendly empirical analysis of a public opinion survey conducted in thirteen countries, Jürgen Gerhards and his co-authors correct the impression conveyed by the media of a European Union corroded by national egoism.

Juan Díez Medrano, *Professor of Sociology,*
Universidad Carlos III de Madrid

Remarkably, in a time of apparent nationalist renaissance this volume provides us with an optimistic message for European integration – Europe's citizens are actually much more solidary with citizens of other EU countries than many social scientists and politicians tend to presume. The data from thirteen countries show that Europe is a space of solidarity in terms of sharing wealth, income, and fiscal resources. Even if European solidarity is more problematic in terms of sharing refugees, and even if solidarity might generally be more conditional than these data suggest at first sight, this volume's message comes at the right time and its importance cannot be overestimated.

Hanspeter Kriesi, *Professor of Comparative Politics,*
European University Institute, Florence

Maximilian Priem is a data analyst at DIW Econ GmbH, Germany. Previously he worked as a researcher in the project *European Solidarity* at the Chair of Macrosociology at the Freie Universität Berlin. His main research interests include European sociology, inequality, and living conditions. His most recent publication is 'Everyone Happy: Living Standards in Germany 25 Years after Reunification' (*DIW Economic Bulletin*, 2014, with J. Schupp).

Routledge Advances in Sociology

For more information about this series, please visit www.routledge.com/Routledge-Advances-in-Sociology/book-series/SE0511

European Solidarity in Times of Crisis

Insights from a Thirteen-Country Survey

Jürgen Gerhards,
Holger Lengfeld,
Zsófia S. Ignácz, Florian K. Kley,
and Maximilian Priem

Routledge
Taylor & Francis Group

LONDON AND NEW YORK

First published 2020
by Routledge
2 Park Square, Milton Park, Abingdon, Oxon OX14 4RN

and by Routledge
605 Third Avenue, New York, NY 10017

First issued in paperback 2020

Routledge is an imprint of the Taylor & Francis Group, an informa business

This book was copyedited and partially translated by Roisin Cronin and Oliver S. White.

British Library Cataloguing-in-Publication Data
A catalogue record for this book is available from the British Library

Library of Congress Cataloging-in-Publication Data
A catalog record has been requested for this book

ISBN 13: 978-0-367-72709-3 (pbk)
ISBN 13: 978-0-367-25728-6 (hbk)

Typeset in Times New Roman
by Wearset Ltd, Boldon, Tyne and Wear

Contents

Figures

Tables

Acknowledgements

This book is a product of the joint venture between two research groups: (1) the international research project *Solidarity in Europe: Empowerment, Social Justice and Citizenship (SOLIDUS)* is funded by the European Commission through the Horizon2020 research programme (Grant Agreement n. 649489), and (2) the German DFG Research Unit Horizontal Europeanization funded by the Deutsche Forschungsgemeinschaft (DFG) (FOR 1539).

Many individuals and institutions contributed to this study. Foremost, we would like to mention the support of Marta Soler and Raul Ramos from the University of Barcelona for enabling the cooperation to take place. Additionally, we would also like to extend our gratitude to the members of the SOLIDUS partner institutions and the members of the DFG Research Unit for their constructive feedback throughout the development of the research project and book.

We would also like to thank Jürgen Hofrichter and Anja Simon from Kantar TNS (formerly known as TNS infratest dimap), the market research company which carried out the survey in the 13 countries, for their competent and reliable support and execution of the field survey. We thank Inga Ganzer for always being prepared to support the project with administrative assistance and with her editorial skills. Laura Schiller's work on the chapters has been invaluable in the last phase of the manuscript preparation. Furthermore, we thank our student assistants Inan Bostanci, Laura Einhorn, Lennart Selling, and Kilian Weil who supported our work in different stages of the project. Special thanks go to Roisin Cronin and Oliver S. White who copyedited those parts of the manuscript which were in English, and translated the parts originally composed in German.

We have received helpful comments on individual chapters from four anonymous reviewers, and indispensable feedback on various versions of the book and its chapters from Juan Díez Medrano, Martin Heidenreich, Ulrich Kohler, Christian Lahusen, Steffen Mau, and Michael Zürn.

Berlin/Leipzig, February 2019
Jürgen Gerhards
Holger Lengfeld
Zsófia S. Ignácz
Florian K. Kley
Maximilian Priem

Chapter 1

Introduction – European crises and the existence of European solidarity

1.1 Setting the stage

For a long time, it seemed as if the story of the European Union would be one of continual progression and enduring success. The number of member states has expanded from originally six to 28, widening the territorial dominion of the EU. The European Union's institutions have increasingly gained power at the cost of national institutions, as the policy areas where nation states no longer have exclusive authority have been expanded. In addition, the EU has become more democratic by strengthening the European Parliament and introducing the co-decision procedure, even if those who demand a democratisation of the EU are not yet satisfied with the European Parliament's power. In this way, a unified European legal and social space has been created, and the rudimentary foundations of a European society have been laid. Internal border controls have largely been abolished. Nowadays, all EU citizens have the right to settle and work in any member state, and many of them have made use of this new opportunity. The EU's promise that a single market will lead to more growth and prosperity has come true for many countries and for many, though not all, population segments.

In parallel with these developments, the narrative of a great success story was constructed. The EU's own institutions staged this narrative. It developed to the point where the narrative became hegemonic and was acknowledged by other actors. One such acknowledgement came in 2012 when the Norwegian Nobel Committee gave the European Union one of the most significant accolades in terms of symbolic capital: the Nobel Peace Prize. The EU, so the reasoning went, has not only increased the wellbeing of its members and their citizens and transformed old enmities into friendships, but has also made a crucial contribution to stabilising democracy in previously authoritarian countries. Furthermore, it is one of the few international institutions that has consistently and unabashedly upheld the banner of human rights.

However, the Nobel Peace Prize award came at a time when the pendulum of European integration had already started swinging in the opposite direction. Since 2010, the European Union has found itself in the greatest crisis since its emergence. In fact, the crisis is not just one but three separate crises: (1) the sovereign debt crisis of some member states, which almost led to a collapse of the euro, (2) the Great Recession, which was exacerbated by the sovereign debt crisis and led to negative growth rates and high employment rates, especially in southern European countries, and the (3) refugee crisis, triggered by the surge in refugees arriving from war-torn regions, especially from Syria. Undoubtedly, the European Union has experienced many crises throughout its history. But many observers agree that the recent crises are of a different quality and that the future of the EU is at stake. Within the last ten years, the number of political advocates who either want their country to leave the EU or at least reduce its authority and re-strengthen national sovereignty has dramatically increased. In many countries, Eurosceptic parties have become significantly more important. These include The Finns in Finland, UKIP in the UK, the People's Party in Denmark, Rassemblement National (formally known as Front National) in France, Geert Wilders' Party for Freedom in the Netherlands, the Alternative for Germany (AfD), the Freedom Party in Austria, the People's Party Our Slovakia, Attack in Bulgaria, Fidesz in Hungary, Lega in Italy, and Law and Justice in Poland. In some countries, Eurosceptic parties have even succeeded in entering government.

But there is more to it than that: the entire discourse about Europe has fundamentally changed. Recently, Eurosceptic positions have attained a hegemonic position in public debates. Their narrative draws on an interpretive frame including the following arguments: the process of European integration has gone too far. As the nation state is the true sovereign, sovereignty rights should be returned from EU institutions to the member states, borders between them should be controlled, the number of migrants coming from outside Europe should be reduced. 'We must return in Europe to the concept of nation states, because only capable institutions can guarantee democracy, freedom, and also cultural diversity. The cultural unification of Europe would be a dangerous development – it would mean degradation', as stated by Jaroslaw Kaczyński, former prime minister of Poland and current leader of the Law and Justice Party (PiS) in 2016 (ACRE 2016).

However, right-wing politicians like Kaczyński were not the only ones arguing that the nation state alone has the capacity to integrate citizens into a society *and* constitute a space of true solidarity. From the perspective of many conservative politicians, only nationals constitute a community, as they share a common history, speak the same language, and feel connected to each other. Only national communities form the basis for solidarity between citizens. Since a European community does not exist, the conditions for European solidarity do not exist. This is why every country should be responsible for itself and not expect or call for help from other EU countries.

In contrast, defenders of the European Union have been defensive. Few optimistic voices have been raised about the future of the EU. Along with the tireless EU Commission president Jean Claude Junker, President Emmanuel Macron of France has also advocated a deepening of the EU in order to overcome the crises:

We can no longer choose to turn inwards within national borders; this would be a collective disaster. We must not allow ourselves to be intimidated by the illusion of retreat. Only by refusing this lie will we be able to meet the demands of our time, its urgency, its seriousness. It is up to us, to you, to map out the route which ensures our future.... The route of rebuilding a sovereign, united and democratic Europe.

(Macron 2017)

However, Macron and other proponents of stronger European integration have been hesitant and vague about their concrete ideas regarding the future of Europe. They assume that the mood of the majority of citizens is anti-European at the moment. For this reason, they have left the debate to the Eurosceptics.

In their arguments, Eurosceptic politicians and activists have often referred to citizens' attitudes and preferences. They have claimed that from the citizens' perspective, European integration has gone too far, as the recent crises of the EU have shown. Citizens are against supporting crisis-affected countries such as Greece. They are also unlikely to willingly provide financial support for countries experiencing high unemployment such as Spain. Citizens particularly resist the refugee crisis: they do not want the EU to accept a large number of refugees, and they do not want the EU to decide on the distribution of refugees among the member states. According to such critics, acting against the will of the citizens is acting against the very foundation of democracy.

But are citizens really as critical of the EU's future as Eurosceptics suspect? Is it true that citizens reject European solidarity, a form of solidarity that goes beyond nation state containers and refers to solidarity with other (European) countries and their citizens? This book attempts to answer this question. It aims to provide a diagnosis of the EU's present situation and at the same time be an academic book; after all, it is a theory-driven empirical study applying descriptive and multivariate statistical analysis examining European solidarity in a systematic way.

Our starting point is the current situation of the European Union and the crises that the EU has had to face and to deal with over the last ten years. The question of the existence of European solidarity has played a central role in the sovereign debt crisis and the Great Recession, but also in the refugee crisis. In this book we systematically distinguish between four domains of European solidarity, which are related to the different crises: (1) *fiscal solidarity* is defined as citizens' willingness to financially support crisis-affected European countries; (2) *territorial solidarity* is the willingness to reduce wealth inequalities between EU countries, which have widened in the economic crisis; (3) *welfare solidarity* is citizens' willingness to support Europeans in need – the unemployed, sick, elderly, and poor – regardless of where they live in the EU. Finally, (4) *refugee solidarity* is citizens' willingness to grant asylum status to refugees entering the European Union (external solidarity) and to share the burden by allocating them among the member states (internal solidarity).

In general, we want to learn whether Europeans are ready to endorse extending solidarity to others (either other people or other countries) in the European space and whether they support the notion of solidarity. Thus, we conceptualise the domains of solidarity as generalised attitudes of citizens regarding the specific domain's subject. The book does not focus on the realisation of specific European policies.

For each domain of solidarity, we will determine whether European solidarity exists. To do this, we need to define criteria that help us to determine the strength of European solidarity. As we will argue in more detail in Chapter 2, we assume that European solidarity exists if four criteria are met. (1) The majority of all Europeans and a majority in each European country support the idea of European solidarity. (2) The EU constitutes a specific space of solidarity distinguishable from both global and national solidarity. (3) EU citizens are prepared to sacrifice resources in defence of European solidarity. (4) Social and political cleavages between proponents and opponents of European solidarity are not pronounced. For each of the four domains of solidarity, we examine whether or not the four criteria have been met.[1]

Our study is based on a large and unique population survey we carried out in 13 EU countries in the summer and autumn of 2016. The Transnational European Solidarity Survey (TESS) was conducted by public opinion poll company Kantar TNS, which has extensive experience in multi-national survey work. TESS includes countries from all EU regions: Austria, Cyprus, France, Germany, Greece, Hungary, Ireland, the Netherlands, Poland, Portugal, Spain, Slovakia, and Sweden. Overall, 12,500 interviews were conducted using the computer-aided telephone interview technique (CATI). TESS is the result of a fruitful cooperation between two research groups: *Solidarity in European Societies: Empowerment, Justice, and Solidarity (SOLIDUS)* funded by the EU's Horizon2020 research programme, and *Horizontal Europeanization*, a German research group supported by the German Science Foundation (DFG). The survey allows us to test empirically our theoretical concept of European solidarity.

1.2 Structure and main results of the book

In addition to this introduction, the book consists of six substantive chapters: a theoretical chapter, four empirical chapters each devoted to a specific domain of solidarity, and a concluding chapter. In the appendix we give detailed technical description of the survey and the methodology.

Chapter 2: Theoretical framework. A conceptual chapter precedes the empirical chapters. In this chapter we thoroughly elucidate the theoretical framework of our study and deal with existing literature on the topic of European solidarity. In the first part of Chapter 2, we describe the different crises the European Union has faced in the last ten years in more detail and explain how exactly they relate to the question of European solidarity. We systematically distinguish between the previously mentioned four domains of European solidarity (fiscal, territorial, welfare, and refugee solidarity). Public and academic debates use the terms solidarity in general and European solidarity in a particularly vague and diffused way. Therefore, we dedicate the second part of Chapter 2 to clarifying our understanding of the meaning of both concepts and connect our considerations to the terminology used by Max Weber. In the third section, we contrast the concept of European solidarity to national and global solidarity. We argue that the strength of European solidarity can be determined only in comparison to solidarity in other territorial spaces. The comparison with national solidarity is especially relevant, because the nation state has historically been the central institution of solidarity. The global realm is also relevant because globalisation processes have led to the idea that the entire world might become a space for solidarity. The difference between various realms of solidarity is related to a debate on solidarity within the field of political philosophy and to the question of how national, European, or global solidarity can be legitimised. We build on this debate between cosmopolitans and communitarians in the form of an excursus. We will return to this philosophical debate in the empirical chapters.

In the fourth section of Chapter 2, we elaborate on our multilevel concept of solidarity as has been briefly introduced above. We will explain in more detail why the following four criteria are meaningful for determining the strength of European solidarity. (1) The majority supports European solidarity. (2) Europe constitutes a space of solidarity in its own right. (3) EU citizens are ready to defend European solidarity. (4) Social and political cleavages between supporters and opponents of European solidarity are rather weak. We conclude the second chapter by explaining the data our study uses and the different methods of data analysis we deploy.

The four domains of solidarity structure the book in that there is a chapter dedicated to each domain. Each of the empirical chapters has almost the same structure. To start with, we work out the links between the European crisis and its relevance for the politicisation of the solidarity domains. We then apply our four criteria to determine the existence and strength of European solidarity based on our survey data.

We conclude Chapter 2 by discussing how our study relates to the existing literature. It is important to remember that we subsumed different domains of solidarity under one umbrella to our conceptualisation of European solidarity including a set of criteria to measure the strength of European solidarity. Thus, we cannot build solely upon one specific body of literature. Instead, our study intersects with topics and empirical studies from several research fields, where often, however, diverging terminology is applied. Both at the end of Chapter 2 and within each empirical chapter, we discuss the relevant findings. In this way, we situate the design and results of our study in relation to the state-of-the-art.

Chapter 3: Fiscal solidarity. To resolve the European debt crisis, the Eurozone countries have made a commitment to reciprocal, albeit limited, financial assistance to balance national budgets. In Chapter 3, we explore whether EU citizens support the general idea of providing financial support to European countries in desperate need. The results show that two-thirds of the respondents are in favour of giving emergency assistance to EU countries in crisis. Although there are country differences in approval levels, citizens from all 13 countries favour European fiscal solidarity. Furthermore, European solidarity is somewhat less prevalent than the support for troubled regions within the respondent's own nation state (83%), but it is considerably more prevalent than the support for non-EU countries in crisis (49%). This spatial ranking of fiscal solidarity is also confirmed when respondents are asked to decide whether a region within their own country, a different EU country, or a country outside of the EU should be helped first. Europe is thus undoubtedly a distinct space of solidarity.

On top of this, the research shows that European solidarity is resilient, thereby fulfilling a further criterion of European solidarity. More than half of all Europeans would be willing to provide financial assistance to countries in need from their own pocket in the form of an additional tax. We find that a majority of EU citizens would be willing to make a minimum contribution of at least half per cent from their own incomes in all countries except France.

Furthermore, we analysed whether, in spite of the great willingness to provide fiscal assistance, there are social (structural and cultural) cleavages that could lead to a politicisation of fiscal solidarity. This analysis reveals only a very weak indication for potential cleavages; these are most evident in citizens' political orientations but hardly at all between citizens and countries with different socioeconomic positions. Concerning political cleavages, our analysis shows that citizens who reject fiscal solidarity are at the same time more inclined to vote for politically right-wing Eurosceptic parties. However, the correlation is weak and is contingent on the citizens' socio-economic and cultural characteristics.

All in all, our analysis shows that EU citizens from the countries we surveyed are clearly in favour of the idea of fiscal solidarity in times of crisis.

Chapter 4: Territorial solidarity. The economic convergence process between eastern and western European member states has significantly slowed down as a consequence of the European economic crisis. In addition, the crisis has caused growing disparities between crisis-affected southern, Mediterranean countries and northern European countries. One possible solution to halt this divergence of economies is to establish long-term mechanisms for redistributing wealth between member states. Comparable redistribution policies are already present within many EU member states and even between member states, as regional development funds have led to a redistribution of wealth between countries. In this chapter, we investigate citizens' attitudes to permanently reducing wealth between rich and poor EU countries. Findings reveal that 71% of the respondents are prepared to reduce disparities between rich and poor EU countries. Even though citizens of the southern and eastern EU countries are more strongly in favour of territorial solidarity than those in western EU countries, the majority of citizens in each of the 13 surveyed countries support redistribution between EU countries. The degree of approval is only slightly below the support for reducing disparities between regions within respondents' own nation states and is distinctly higher than approval rates for reducing disparities between EU and non-EU countries. Hence, Europe constitutes a distinct space of solidarity.

Multivariate analysis shows that people who have higher incomes and live in countries with greater degree of prosperity are more likely to oppose a redistribution of wealth between European countries. However, these differences between proponents and opponents are relatively small. Furthermore, people who reject European territorial solidarity are more likely to come out in support for right-wing parties in national elections and are less likely to hold a global identity. Again, these associations are rather weak. In addition, we can only find a slight indication for possible political cleavages.

Thus, citizens' high acceptance rates and the low potential for politicisation indicate that long-term redistribution of wealth in Europe is substantially rooted in citizens' understandings of solidarity.

Chapter 5: Welfare solidarity. EU member states, and in particular southern European countries, experienced severe reductions in economic growth rates and rising unemployment due to the Great Recession. Social inequality within countries increased and the risk of not being able to secure a decent standard of living rose especially for the most vulnerable people in southern European societies. Against this backdrop, Chapter 5 examines two aspects of welfare solidarity. First, we focus on citizens' attitudes towards the EU's role in providing social security to EU citizens in need – the sick, the elderly, and the unemployed – and second, we analyse citizens' willingness to reduce inequalities between rich and poor citizens living across the EU. An overwhelming majority of respondents (between 78% and 90%) support the view that the European Union should guarantee access to health care for everyone as well as a decent standard of living for the elderly and for the unemployed living in the EU. Although national welfare state institutions remain the first choice for respondents, differences between these two territorial spaces are small. Differences in approval rates per country are also small, ranging from 97% approval in Cyprus to 79% in Germany. Additionally, a great majority of respondents – 80% – support redistributive measures at the European level, while 82% are in favour of reducing inequalities within the nation state. Again, Europe constitutes a specific space of solidarity.

Our analysis identifies rather significant social cleavages. However, these do not translate into strong political cleavages. We observe that members of affluent social groups are more likely to oppose welfare solidarity at the European level; the same applies to those positioning themselves on the political right. We also find that a country's economic situation deepens these cleavages: in richer countries, affluent individuals more strongly oppose European welfare solidarity. The correlations are considerably weaker for political cleavages, although opponents of European welfare solidarity are slightly more likely to vote for parties representing right-wing Eurosceptic perspectives.

All in all, we observe a high degree of support for European welfare solidarity in the 13 surveyed countries. While we show that European welfare solidarity generates social cleavages, this is counterbalanced by the high support rates for this idea. The findings demonstrate that Europeans want to strengthen a social Europe and view the EU as a potential actor, which can meet this target.

Chapter 6: Refugee solidarity. The numbers of people seeking asylum in Europe skyrocketed in the years between 2014 and 2016. This development plunged the European Union into a dual crisis. In this chapter, we investigate the extent of solidarity in the context of the refugee crisis and distinguish between two domains of solidarity. First, external solidarity relates to the willingness to grant protection to people who come from outside the EU and flee to it due to discrimination, persecution, or (civil) war in their home countries. Second, internal solidarity relates to the willingness of EU member states to share the burden of the refugee crisis between the member states equally.

As there are different reasons and motives for why refugees aim to enter the EU, we distinguish between different refugee groups. In total, 90% of Europeans are prepared to give people a transitory right to stay in the EU who have campaigned for human rights in their home country or who have fled from war. We observe a smaller acceptance rate for granting asylum to refugees who have been persecuted because of their Muslim faith and their homosexuality. However, the approval rates diverge greatly across the surveyed countries. Significantly fewer people express solidarity with asylum seekers in the post-socialist countries, but also in Greece and Cyprus, compared to western European countries. Again, this especially applies for refugees of the Muslim faith. Their acceptance is rejected by a majority in Poland, Hungary, Slovakia, and Cyprus.

Concerning the emergence of social and political cleavages, multivariate analysis shows that cultural factors play a greater role in explaining attitudinal differences than socio-economic characteristics. In particular, citizens holding right-wing political orientations and those with a strong sense of national identity tend to oppose the acceptance of asylum seekers. Countries with higher shares of anti-immigration parties in the parliament and countries who have experienced a loss of national sovereignty in the past tend to have more citizens who would refuse to grant asylum to refugees. Thus, social cleavages can be found within as well as between EU countries. We also find that these social cleavages translate into political cleavages: those opposing to grant asylum to refugees are more likely to vote for right-wing Eurosceptic parties.

A similar picture emerges when we analyse attitudes to internal solidarity. We measured the degree of internal solidarity by examining the citizens' views on whether each EU member state should be required to take in refugees. Nearly two-thirds of all respondents agreed with this suggestion. However, we found even greater differences between countries here than for external solidarity. While citizens in all western and southern European countries support the idea that each country should accept refugees, three quarters of Polish, Hungarian, and Slovakian citizens are against it. Our cleavage analysis shows that within the countries, citizens' political orientations and national identification primarily influence where they stand on this question. Furthermore, external and internal solidarity are closely tied to each other. A person who is against accepting refugees in Europe also tends to oppose an equitable allocation of refugees between the member states. Finally, we show that these cleavages have a high potential of becoming politicised. The more vehemently citizens reject internal solidarity, the higher the probability is that they will vote for right-wing Eurosceptic parties in the next election.

Of all the crises that the European Union has recently faced, the refugee crisis is the greatest challenge to European solidarity. Remarkably, the actions of member states' governments are congruent with the attitudes of the general populations in their countries. For example, the open attitudes of German and Swedish citizens reflect the open refugee policies of their respective governments, just as the broadly intolerant attitudes of Hungarians mirror the restrictive stance of the Hungarian government.

Chapter 7: Conclusion. In the concluding chapter we summarise our results, relate them to our theoretical framework, and discuss their meaning for the future of the European Union. Our analysis of a survey conducted in 13 EU countries reveals quite surprising findings. Overall, Europe's citizens exhibit a notably higher degree of solidarity with citizens of other EU countries and EU states than many social scientists and politicians, especially from the Eurosceptic camp, have presumed so far. This especially applies to support for people in need (welfare solidarity) and to the reduction of wealth inequalities between rich and poor European countries (territorial solidarity), but also to fiscal solidarity. On top of this, the research shows that European solidarity is more established than global solidarity. Even if citizens mostly prioritise national solidarity when it is opposed to European solidarity, it is evident that these spaces of solidarity are not in competition with one another but instead complement each other or are seen as a compensation for the weaknesses of nation state solidarity. Furthermore, we can show that the influence of social-structural and cultural characteristics on the citizens' attitudes towards solidarity is predominantly weak. Therefore, the emergence of strong social and political cleavages is rather improbable.

We also discuss two important limitations of our study. First, it is important to underline that refugee solidarity is exempt of our optimistic view on European solidarity, as the majority of citizens in Cyprus and the Visegrád countries (Poland, Slovakia, and Hungary) neither agree with taking Muslim refugees nor with the notion of fairly allocating refugees between European countries. Due to historical reasons, national identity and self-determination are highly salient in these countries. Citizens of these countries perceive the inflow of refugees and asylum seekers, especially those of the Muslim faith, as an affront to their culturally defined national identities. They reject any allocation of refugees across the EU on the grounds that it infringes their national sovereignty. Second, as our study surveyed citizens' generalised attitudes towards European solidarity but not their attitudes towards specific policies, we cannot draw direct conclusions from our results about concrete policy measures. We illustrate this limitation using the example of European welfare solidarity: although citizens support the general idea that the EU should protect vulnerable groups all over Europe, they are much more hesitant when it comes to building a European welfare system that would replace national welfare state institutions. We conclude that policies should use the tailwind that emanates from citizens' support for European solidarity. At the same time, it should implement low-threshold measures of European solidarity and avoid creating new institutions at the European level.

We further explore the meaning of our findings by referring to the debate on the reconfiguration of the political space through the emergence of a new cleavage structure. We distinguish four main camps: right-wing communitarians, left-wing cosmopolitans, left-wing communitarians, and right-wing cosmopolitans. We contrast each camp's understanding of European solidarity with our empirical findings and conclude that attitudes of European citizens mostly reflect a left-wing cosmopolitan take on European solidarity (with the exception of refugee solidarity in some of the member states). We argue that the prominence of the right-wing communitarians is strongly overestimated in current public debates, and we discuss two reasons why this might be the case. First, right-wing communitarian actors have succeeded in placing their issues on the agenda of the public debate (published opinion). However, they appear stronger than they – as measured by the public opinion – actually are. Second, many citizens do not support the right-wing communitarian camp in elections, not because they support its rejection of European solidarity but because they are dissatisfied with some political measures of *implementing* European solidarity.

In the concluding paragraphs of the chapter, we discuss three recommendations for EU policy makers. First, the EU and its member states should ensure that aid measures that operationalise European solidarity are not exploited by those who do not need them and make certain that they reach those for whom they are intended. Second, policy makers should ensure more fairness in burden sharing. The majority of citizens want those who are better off to be more involved in implementing solidarity than those who are socially weaker. Lastly, the EU should refrain from developing supranational institutions warranting European solidarity and should look for alternative solutions. However, all in all, our evidence provides encouragement to drive forward the European project and policy makers should have no fear regarding trends towards renationalisation.

Note

1 The book does not explicitly deal with the relationship between the four different domains of solidarity. The analysis would dilute the contemporary diagnostic character of this book. Therefore, we decided to tackle it in an upcoming journal article.

References

ACRE. 2016. 'Jaroslaw Kaczynski: The EU Must Reform or It Will Collapse'. Retrieved 18 February 2019 (www.acreurope.eu/item/jaroslaw_kaczynski_eu_must_reform_or_it_will_collapse).

Macron, Emmanuel. 2017. 'Initiative for Europe Speech by M. Emmanuel Macron, President of the French Republic'. Retrieved 18 February 2019 (www.diplomatie.gouv.fr/IMG/pdf/english_version_transcript_-_initiative_for_europe_-_speech_by_the_president_of_the_french_republic_cle8de628.pdf).

Chapter 2

Theoretical framework – conceptualising and understanding European solidarity

2.1 European crises and the issue of European solidarity

Since 2010 the European Union has found itself in the greatest crisis since its emergence. This crisis consists not of one but of three separate crises: (1) the euro and sovereign debt crisis, (2) the Great Recession, which was exacerbated by the sovereign debt crisis, and (3) the refugee crisis. In all three crises, the question of whether there is such a thing as European solidarity played a central role in two different ways. Some observers claimed that more European solidarity could be a way of overcoming the respective crises (Ferrera 2017). Measures of solidarity – either partly implemented or merely being discussed – include plans to financially support highly indebted EU countries, to introduce greater financial transfers between wealthy and poorer countries, to safeguard individuals from welfare risks across Europe, and finally, to take in refugees who are fleeing towards Europe and fairly distribute the costs between the EU member states. Yet the call for more European solidarity has also unleashed political resistance: it has mobilised actors opposed to European solidarity. In their view, solidarity should be confined to the nation state alone. In the following, we elaborate in more detail how exactly the different crises of the European Union relate to the question of European solidarity.

(1) The financial crisis began in 2008 with the banking crisis in the USA, which led to a massive devaluation of investment securities in European banks. In order to save the banks, states had to bail them out. This drove several EU member states into a massive sovereign debt crisis – predominantly states in southern Europe (Greece, Italy, Portugal, Spain, and Cyprus), but also including Ireland. These member states' high and, in some cases, still rising debts had already existed long before the crisis, however, with the advent of the crisis they acquired a new intensity. Additionally, the threat of bankruptcy in some countries endangered the euro altogether, because Eurozone countries are highly intertwined with one another. According to a dominant interpretation, the collapse of the euro would lead to high asset losses for the creditor countries and their banks, causing collateral damage to the economy. Economic recessions,

high unemployment, and social problems were likely consequences not just for the highly indebted crisis countries, but for Europe as a whole. German chancellor Angela Merkel hit the nail on the head in a speech to the German Bundestag on 19 May 2010: 'If the Euro fails, so does Europe' (Merkel 2010).

In response to this threat, the EU, in cooperation with the International Monetary Fund (IMF), attempted to avert the sovereign debt crises in some EU countries and thus stabilise the euro currency. Since the initial ad hoc financial assistance did not prove sufficient, various bailout funds were established by 2010. The loans in these bailout packages were intended to prevent countries from defaulting by financially supporting their national banks. At first, these funds were only temporary, such as the European Financial Stabilisation Mechanism, with a credit volume of €60 billion, and the European Financial Stability Facility (€440 billion). However, as it became clear that the problem was a long-term one, a permanent umbrella scheme, the European Stability Mechanism (ESM; at the time €500 billion), was introduced in 2013. This scheme lends money to member states in the Eurozone if their economic problems endanger the entire monetary union. These measures are quite extraordinary in financial terms. Aid of this magnitude had only been given between regions of a country in the past.

A consequence of these financial schemes is that all member states are liable for the debts of individual countries. Better-off countries and their citizens act as guarantors for other European countries in economic hardship. Some observers interpret financial assistance to other European countries as acts of European solidarity as they indicate that national actors are willing to help out other EU countries in emergencies. Others argue that these policies are only intended to stabilise banks and to avoid defaults on private loans given by bondholders, but are not meant to support ordinary people suffering from the crisis in the countries in question (e.g. Streeck 2014).

These policies to resolve the euro crisis have been the subject of heated debates. First, right-leaning parties in well-off EU countries have been especially critical. They are explicitly against fiscal assistance for member states in need. Solidarity, they argue, should be restricted to nation states. Election results show that these right-wing populist parties who oppose European financial assistance have been increasingly well received by voters. Using data from the European Election Study, Sara B. Hobolt and Catharine de Vries (2016b) have shown in a survey carried out in 28 EU countries that the increase in voting for Eurosceptic parties can be causally linked to the financial crisis. For those who vote for right-wing Eurosceptic parties, being expressly against fiscal transfers is a typical stance. In national elections across Europe after the sovereign debt crisis, Eurosceptic parties registered a significant growth in support, e.g. The Finns in Finland experienced success. There was a surge in support for the Front National in France, and also one for Geert Wilders' Party for Freedom in the Netherlands (Hobolt and Tilley 2016).

Second, while right-wing parties opposed European financial assistance and argued for their country to leave the EU or the Eurozone, there was also support for European fiscal solidarity. The Italian and French governments, to name just two examples, warned against the withdrawal of fiscally troubled countries from the Eurozone and expressed their solidarity with them instead (Rankin 2015). Emmanuel Macron, who was elected in the French presidential elections in May 2017, doubled down on his position that the 19 countries of the Eurozone should be brought closer together, in direct contrast to his adversary, Marine Le Pen. In his view, Eurozone members should give each other reciprocal help, arrange their own budget, and institutionalise a European finance minister, as well as a separate parliament (Birnbaum and Faiola 2017).

Taken together, the sovereign debt crisis and the different measures proposed to resolve the crisis reveal an underlying question, namely to what extent can countries in crisis expect help from wealthier countries. We regard the financial support for indebted member states by other member states as *European fiscal solidarity*.[1]

(2) The sovereign debt crisis is closely interlinked with the Great Recession, especially in the southern European countries. The economic crisis most severely affected those who were dependent on the welfare state: the unemployed, pensioners, the sick, members of the lower classes, and young people (see Heidenreich 2016). For instance, the unemployment rate in Greece went from 7.8% in 2008 up to a peak of 27.5% just five years later, before stabilising at 23.5% in 2016. A quite similar development took place in Spain, where unemployment rose from 8.2% in 2008 up to 26.1% by 2013 and remained at 19.6% in 2016 (Eurostat 2018).

The economic crisis hit countries with relatively underdeveloped welfare states harder than western European countries. For this reason, these social problems could not be resolved by using national welfare-state-based programmes. Citizens faced cuts to their pensions, poverty rates rose, and healthcare systems also faced heavy cuts. In this context, Martin Heidenreich (2016) spoke of a double dualisation, a twofold increase in social inequality. One aspect of this is that the geographical disparities between southern European Union countries and all others have increased; the other aspect is that inequality has risen within the troubled countries themselves.

The measures for combating the sovereign debt crisis intensified the economic crisis and the related social problems. The countries that were bailed out were forced to carry out sweeping reforms of their state budgets and economic structures in return for bailout loans from the EU Commission, the European Central Bank (ECB), and the IMF. These measures included tax hikes and the privatisation of state property in order to increase the state's income, job cuts for public sector employees, increases in working hours for civil servants, and cuts to the social budget, as well as restrictions on welfare state provisions to reduce the burden on the social state. These austerity measures were aimed to stop the countries' mountains of debt from increasing or even reducing them. They were also intended to boost economic growth. In the short term, however, these measures have only further worsened the lives of vulnerable people in these indebted countries, who were most exposed to the effects of the economic crisis.

In light of these social problems, it is hardly surprising that demands for European welfare policies are growing in some member states. These calls have mostly come from indebted countries' own governments and populations, but also from left-wing parties in wealthy creditor countries. The demands for European social policy were already in circulation long before the Great Recession, though they were certainly strengthened and popularised by it. In essence, these involve two different domains of European solidarity, which we define as (a) *territorial solidarity* and (b) *welfare solidarity*.

(a) Reducing the rate of inequality and wealth differences between member states was and remains the stated aim of the European Union. Indeed, in the run-up to the Great Recession, richer and poorer countries had begun to converge due to EU investment schemes for underdeveloped regions (Beckfield 2009, 2013). This progress was interrupted at the beginning of the 2010s. Since then, inequality between EU countries has again increased. In contrast to a nationally defined territorial solidarity, *European territorial solidarity* does not deal with the 'redistribution of wealth' between rich and poor regions in the same country, but rather *between rich and poor countries within the European Union*.

(b) A key task of national welfare states is to protect people who do not earn enough to cover their living expenses from wages alone. The people in question are predominantly those in each member state who are ill, unemployed, unfit for work, old, or poor. In contrast, the special aspect of *European welfare solidarity* is that EU countries take responsibility together for *individuals in need and living within the territory of the EU*, regardless of which EU member state these individuals belong to.

Whereas the demands for European fiscal aid have been successfully met, this does not apply to the political demands for a 'social Europe'. Redistribution schemes between poor and rich countries have not been embraced. However, the topic did become a subject of political debate, and strengthened Eurosceptic parties, albeit left-leaning parties (Hobolt and de Vries 2016b). Their accusations, directed at the creditor countries, were that they lacked genuine European solidarity, namely towards those who were especially affected by the decline in social and economic status, and that a solidarity that would lead to a strong rebalancing of territorial inequality between rich and poor countries had not emerged.

(3) The European Union was still struggling with the sovereign debt crisis, the euro crisis, and the related economic crisis, which itself led to numerous social problems, when in 2014 the next serious crisis struck. The refugee crisis cast further doubts on the existence and strength of European solidarity.

The lack of internal borders is a core characteristic of the European Union. All citizens are allowed to move freely within the territorial area of the EU member states. National borders and passport controls were moved to the external border of the European Union. Regulations for granting entrance to refugees and asylum seekers into the European Union were established in the Dublin

Convention in 1990, which has been amended several times and is referred to as the Dublin Regulation. The most important aspect of the regulation is that the state where an asylum seeker arrives has to carry out the necessary asylum procedures. However, since the great majority of asylum seekers come from Africa, Asia, and the Middle East, for geographical reasons, most of the new arrivals first set foot on European soil in the Mediterranean countries of Italy, Greece, and Spain. Correspondingly, these countries are responsible for first receiving refugees and also for undertaking the asylum process. From the beginning, the Dublin Regulation has led to an asymmetry: it has burdened the Mediterranean countries and benefited the continent's northern and inland countries, which are also generally wealthier. The issue of solidarity already loomed large before the refugee crisis because the southern states felt left in the lurch by their northern neighbours and therefore already complained of a lack of solidarity. The situation, however, intensified considerably between 2014 and 2016.

An already significant increase in the numbers of people seeking asylum was recorded in 2014; the numbers of people then skyrocketed to 1.4 million in 2015. In 2016, too, nearly one million applications for asylum were filed.[2] In 2015 and 2016, most of these people arrived in Greece. Due to the sudden increase, many of the asylum applicants were no longer registered in the country of arrival, but rather passed on directly to northern Europe along the Balkan route. This effectively did away with the Dublin Regulation. The result was that many countries re-erected their national border controls, primarily in inland countries most favoured by refugees. These developments plunged the European Union into a dual crisis, both of which are directly connected with the issue of solidarity.

(1) The refugee crisis has underlined the question of whether and when people fleeing from civil war or political persecution should be provided refuge in Europe. The EU and its member states have committed themselves to this form of international humanitarian solidarity to a greater extent than any other international organisation. All member states have signed the Geneva Convention, which ensures that all people who are persecuted in their home country based on their race, ethnic group, religion, nationality, or their political beliefs have the right to seek asylum in another country. However, the Geneva Convention does not apply to people who have to flee from their country due to a civil war, or war in general. The European Union has codified the subsidiary protection of these groups of people in a special directive, the Qualification Directive (European Parliament and European Council 2011). Through this, both refugees from war-torn areas and those who are members of politically persecuted groups have the right to access the EU.[3]

The refugee crisis and the political answers that have been given to it have led to a massive internal European conflict over the question of how firmly the EU should abide by its foreign affairs' guiding values and legal obligations, i.e. how dependable humanitarian solidarity with those seeking refuge or fleeing political persecution should be. Several member states' governments have stressed that there are limits to international solidarity due to the large number of refugees. Viktor Orbán, the prime minister of Hungary since 2010, is one of the most prominent advocates of this position. He has called for a U-turn regarding the international solidarity with refugees. In many of his statements from 2015 and 2016 he insisted that refugees pose serious danger to public security and embody major terror risk. Along with Polish and Slovakian governments, Orbán feared that predominantly Muslim refugees would be too foreign for national and European cultures. Such speculations have increased support for Orbán and his colleagues among other right-wing populist parties in Europe. Analyses of the European Parliament elections in 2014 and other recent national elections showed that the right-wing populist parties have increased their share of votes, with immigration proving to be one of the most important reasons for voting such parties (Hobolt and de Vries 2016b; Hobolt and Tilley 2016).

At the same time, however, there are other people who interpret the introduced European refugee policies as a departure from the EU's value-oriented foreign policy and as a termination of solidarity with people who are politically persecuted or threatened. In this context, the European Union is accused of doing too little to rescue refugees who risk their lives by making the perilous journey across the Mediterranean. The second point of criticism relates to the deal negotiated with Turkey in March 2016.[4] Critics accused the EU of not only abandoning its own values with the Turkey–EU deal, but also of violating international law. They argue that Turkey is not a law-abiding state, and is not a credible treaty partner, which would obey international law. In addition, they criticise that the agreement may impede refugees from reaching European territory to apply for asylum.

The influx of refugees since 2014 and the accompanying political debate have raised the question about the extent European citizens are prepared to grant asylum to people who are persecuted and seek refuge in Europe. We refer to the willingness to grant *non-European refugees humanitarian protection* as *external solidarity*.

(2) The refugee crisis has opened up a second question in relation to the concept of European solidarity. Just as governments of Mediterranean countries criticised that they were left alone by other EU countries in order to deal with the problem before the great migration wave in 2014–2016, northern countries made similar claims after refugees began to arrive directly in wealthier countries. Once they were affected themselves, they also started calling for more solidarity. Solidarity meant for them that the refugees and the costs of accommodating them should be more fairly spread out between member states; in line with this, they demanded the introduction of a quota. It was this particular proposal, however, that was rejected by other countries, especially those in Eastern Europe.[5] This conflict of interest persists up to the present, with both sides drawing on different understandings of solidarity. The governments who support a fair distribution of refugees suggest that the idea of European solidarity is in jeopardy. Their argument goes as follows: with the partial abolition of national borders and the creation of a common European external border, immigration by

those escaping destitution and persecution has also become a common European problem. As a result, the costs must be divided *in common* too. The opponents of a quota regulation emphasise their national sovereignty. For the eastern European member states who just regained their sovereignty in 1990, the distribution of refugees is not a decision for Europe but rather a national one. We term this dispute over the *distribution of refugees* as a dispute over European *internal solidarity*.

In sum, it can be said that the exponential rise in the number of refugees and the rash introduction of policies intended to solve this problem have led to considerable conflicts between the EU member states. In the process, the existence of European internal solidarity (i.e. distributing the burden between the countries) and of external solidarity (the readiness to receive persecuted individuals and refugees) has been called into question.

However, there is a fourth crisis of the EU, which we have not tackled so far. The United Kingdom, one of the most important EU member countries, is to leave the EU. This again poses a significant threat to the future of the European project. We interpret the UK's exit from the EU, a move that was decided on by the British public in a referendum on 23 June 2016, as a consequence of the crises outlined in the previous paragraphs and see here also a direct connection to the theme of our book on European solidarity. The British government and the British people have always emphasised the importance of their national sovereignty more strongly than other European countries. Correspondingly, the UK has had a special position in the EU. It is neither part of the Eurozone, nor the Schengen Area, and it has resisted further European integration in other policy areas.

It is therefore no wonder that the UK objected to the policies to manage the debt crisis and questioned the call for a European social policy to manage the fallout of the Great Recession, as they were both perceived as unreasonable demands for European solidarity, which would in turn inhibit national sovereignty. This applies all the more for the EU's refugee policies: the idea of a common European responsibility for asylum seekers collided with the idea of national self-determination. The rejection of various calls for solidarity ultimately contributed to the Brexit decision. Such conclusions are supported by analyses of the Brexit vote. There are indications that the most important topic for 'leave' voters was immigration. According to a survey taken the day after the referendum (Lord Ashcroft 2016), '[o]ne-third of Leave voters (33%) said that the main reason for their vote was that leaving the EU "offered the best chance for the UK to regain control over immigration and its own borders" '.[6] In a multivariate analysis that sought to explain the support for Brexit, Sara B. Hobolt (2016:1270) concluded: 'Individuals who thought Britain should have many fewer EU migrants were 32 percentage points more likely to vote for Brexit compared to those who wanted more migrants.' Indeed, the topic of immigration was already an important one in the UK, particularly as it pertained to EU immigrants from eastern European countries.[7]

However, in 2015 and 2016, the importance of immigration was enormously boosted, above all in the media. For example, there were extensive media reports on the refugee camp in an abandoned waste disposal site near Calais, also referred to as the 'Calais Jungle', where thousands of refugees were waiting to enter the UK via the Eurotunnel. It is assumed that the EU's policy of distributing the burden of the refugee crisis between member states, and its demands to accept larger numbers of refugees all impacted the outcome of the referendum.

Considering the discussions of the different EU crises, it is clear how extensive the EU's current difficulties are. Its future seems to be uncertain at the moment. The possible scenarios in the public debate range from a dissolution of the EU and a return to a Europe of nation states to calls for a strengthening and democratisation of European institutions.

The previous paragraphs have also shown that behind the concrete questions of how problems can be politically resolved or ameliorated lies a more general and profound question. This is the question of the strength of European solidarity, a form of solidarity that goes beyond nation state containers and reflects a solidarity with other (European) countries and their citizens. Unfortunately, we know very little about whether citizens support the idea of European solidarity. Correspondingly, the question of the existence, the strength, and the resilience of European solidarity is the primary focus of our study. More precisely: do the citizens of Europe support the idea that financially troubled countries should be supported by wealthier countries? To what extent are citizens prepared to reduce inequalities between poor and wealthy countries and to support those in need even if they live in other European countries? Lastly, do Europeans support the idea that people fleeing from civil war or political persecution should be given refuge in Europe and that the burden of managing the refugee crisis should be distributed between member states equally?

In Section 2.4, we will define a set of theoretically derived criteria on how to measure the strength of European solidarity and explain the data set and the statistical methods we have used. However, as the terms solidarity in general and European solidarity in particular are used in public and academic debates in such a vague and diffuse way, it makes sense to first clarify our understanding of the meaning of both concepts in more detail. Hence, we shall next explain the design of our study somewhat more precisely.

2.2 Defining solidarity: nailing jelly to the wall

Many authors have attempted to define the concept of solidarity. Most of them emphasised that the term is not uniformly used in the literature and that there are very different definitions with correspondingly different meanings, which have also changed over time (see Bayertz 1998; Bayertz and Boshammer 2008; Brunkhorst 1997; Cingolani 2015; Hechter 2001; Procacci 2001; Schulze 2010; Stjernø 2005; Thome 1998; Wildt 1998). The fact that the concept of solidarity is used in a relatively diffuse way is not a coincidence; there are, from our point of view, systematic reasons for this. Solidarity is not only a term used by scholars in various disciplines but is also frequently used in the political debate. In public communication, solidarity has the status of a value that actors refer to in order to justify and valorise their respective positions (Bayertz and Boshammer 2008; Stjernø 2005). When politicians say, for example, that it is a requirement of solidarity to accept refugees in Europe, they are declaring the acceptance of refugees to be a moral duty. Those who oppose the acceptance of refugees are at the same time criticised as immoral. The institutions of the European Union also frequently refer to the concept of solidarity as an important value without the meaning of solidarity being clear (Knodt and Tews 2017).

Precisely because the concept of solidarity is used in such a diffuse manner, we do not think it makes sense to repeat the many different definitions in the literature at this point. Instead, we have decided to embark on our own systematic path. We build on Max Weber's basic sociological terms. Weber did not define the concept of solidarity himself. However, his terminology is usually a good starting point for sociologists. The connection to Max Weber makes it possible to separate the definition of the term 'solidarity' from the question of what motives motivate people to act in solidarity.

(1) Solidaric action. Weber (1968:4) defined social action as the central term of sociology. He understood this to mean (a) the behaviour of an individual insofar as that individual attaches a subjective meaning to his/her behaviour and (b) takes account of the behaviour of others. We defined solidarity as a specific form of social behaviour, where the ego (the giver of solidarity) and the alter (the recipient of solidarity) refer to each other and the ego attaches a specific meaning to his/her behaviour. If we follow this assumption, then it would be more precise to use the term solidaric action instead of solidarity (see Thome 1998).[8]

Regarding Weber's logic of terms, solidaric action is a special category of social action. But what special characteristics make solidaric action distinguishable from other forms of social action? The ego as the giver of solidarity shows solidarity with the alter as the recipient of solidarity if the ego gives something to the alter and thus intends to support the alter. The 'gift' may consist of goods, money, the transfer of rights, or the signalling of affection and recognition, e.g. even by a simple pat on the back. Furthermore, it is typical for solidaric action that the ego is not forced to act in this way; the action is instead voluntary. This characteristic differentiates solidaric action from forced action. In this context, Jürgen Habermas (2013) distinguished solidaric obligations from legal obligations and thus makes an action's voluntary character a feature of solidarity. Finally, solidaric action is characterised by the fact that the relationship between the giver of solidarity and the recipient is not an exchange relationship regulated by a contract. In this respect, the ego cannot therefore expect that the alter will return the benefit received, e.g. by the payment of money.[9]

(2) Causes and motives for acting in solidarity. Many authors refer to the causes of and motives for solidarity when defining the concept. In doing so, they

make the causes of solidarity an integral part of its definition. In our view this is an unwise policy – quite apart from any specific case used when defining the concept of solidarity. The definition of a phenomenon and the question as to which factors determine the existence of a phenomenon are two very different issues, which should not be mixed. The most common cause that is equated or directly related to the definition of solidarity in the literature is the feeling of cohesion experienced by group members, e.g. Ulrich Steinvorth (2017:10) defined solidarity 'as a bond that makes up a "we"'. Kurt Bayertz and Susanne Boshammer (2008:1197) described the 'inner cohesion of a group' and the 'feeling of mutual solidarity among the group members' as a central characteristic of solidarity.[10]

It is empirically quite plausible that people who feel emotionally connected to specific others act more in solidarity towards these people than towards people with whom they do not feel affectively connected. Therefore, it is more likely that members of a family or people who like each other will help each other than people who do not meet these criteria. However, it seems advisable to us to distinguish the causes of a phenomenon from the definition of the phenomenon. An analytical distinction of this kind also makes it clear that people may have very different motivations for acting in solidarity.

In the systematisation of possible causes for solidaric action, we again draw on Max Weber's terminology. Weber (1968:24–5) distinguished between four types of social action: instrumentally rational (*zweckrational*), value-rational (*wertrational*), affectual, and traditional. Weber made clear that traditional action lies at the borderline of what could be called meaningful action as traditional action very often is a kind of ritualised, habitual behaviour. Therefore, we only differentiate between three types of solidaric action. The three types are ideal types. In reality, solidaric action is often simultaneously caused by different motives.

(a) Solidarity based on self-interest (instrumentally rational behaviour). An action is instrumentally rational when an actor pursues his or her own goals of action and in doing so rationally calculates the use of resources and the consequences of his or her actions. Solidaric action is instrumentally rational if the action benefits the giver of solidarity and not (just) the recipient of solidarity and if the action is motivated by this benefit. In this context, other authors have also talked about a self-serving solidarity (Mau 2008). In this sense, Émile Durkheim's (1933) idea of organic solidarity is also an instrumentally rationally motivated kind of solidarity. For him, it was the dominant type of solidarity in a modern society based on a division of labour. In a society based on a division of labour, the actors are interdependent. Accordingly, the ego helps the alter because the ego fears that the ego will experience disadvantages if it does not help the alter. The Marxist idea of class solidarity is also, at least in part, an instrumentally rational form of solidarity. The workers have similar interests and therefore form a 'social class in itself' and are, due to their similar interests, mutually supportive (Marx 1947/1955:195).

In the context of the sovereign debt crisis of some EU member states, the motive of self-serving solidarity also plays a role. The more well-performing countries probably also agreed to support the indebted countries because they feared that the single currency might collapse and damage their own national economies. For example, the German chancellor justified her support for Greece with the following argument: 'We must not do anything that could jeopardise the global upturn and then put Germany in danger again' (Handelsblatt 2011). Angela Merkel does not refer to a common bond with Greece, but to the possible damage that could also arise for Germany if Greece were to become insolvent. Territorial European solidarity may also be instrumentally rationally motivated. Wealthy EU countries can support poorer member states because they want to prevent people from moving from the poorer countries to their countries.

(b) Solidarity based on values (value-rational behaviour). According to Weber, a person is acting in a value-rational way if he/she orientates his/her actions towards central values. Since solidaric action is about a voluntary transfer of resources from the ego to the alter, justice as a value often plays a particular role. Persons who, for example, believe that inequality between rich and poor countries in Europe is not fair will probably argue in favour of European solidarity precisely for this reason. They do this without an affective attachment to the people in the poor countries and without expecting to benefit from this solidarity. On the contrary, purely value-based action leads to a willingness to show solidarity even if you experience disadvantages.

During the refugee crisis, a specific value-rational orientation also played an important role among those who were campaigning for the reception of refugees in Europe. Those who attach great importance to human rights, consider the case of so many refugees drowning in the Mediterranean Sea a scandal. From this point of view, the rescue of refugees and their acceptance in Europe is a value rationally justifiable action and is accordingly a moral duty. For those who do not feel bound by the idea of an equal fundamental right for all people or who feel less bound by it and who consider the rights of citizens of their own nation state to be more important than the rights of 'foreigners', the moral obligation to save refugees will certainly be much less relevant.[11]

(c) Solidarity based on affectual ties (affectual behaviour). Solidarity can also be motivated by the fact that the solidarity giver feels affectively bound to the recipient of solidarity and sees him/herself as connected to the solidarity recipient within a group. Nationalism research has shown how elites can succeed in creating 'imagined communities' (Anderson 1983) from nations, so that the citizens of a nation state understand themselves as a community and are therefore prepared to support each other. Military and paramilitary combat units consist of affectively closely tied members, who are often even willing to sacrifice their own lives for their 'comrades'. Social psychological research has also shown that the members of a football club are much more willing to help a person who is a fan of their own club (Levine et al. 2005). Émile Durkheim's (1933) concept of mechanical solidarity can also be interpreted as a kind of

affective solidarity. The members of a group have a common collective consciousness and thus act in solidarity. Marx's idea of class consciousness combined self-serving solidarity with an affectual solidarity. The 'social class in itself' holds together and is solidaric because its members have the same interests. Beyond the common interests, a social class for itself is in solidarity because its members are affectively bound to each other (Marx 1947/1955:195).

The European Union, too, particularly in times of crisis, invokes the community of Europeans to demand solidarity. In the Nobel Lecture of the EU, Herman Van Rompuy, president of the European Council, said that the EU and its citizens

> are working very hard to overcome the difficulties.... But there is more that guides us: the will to remain masters of our own destiny, a sense of togetherness, and in a way ... speaking to us from the centuries ... the idea of Europa [sic] itself.
>
> (European Union 2012)

In addition, Jean-Claude Juncker, president of the Commission, emphasised in his State of the Union speech that 'solidarity is the glue that keeps our Union together' (European Commission 2016).

In our empirical analysis, we will come back to the classification of the various motives for solidarity in two ways. On the one hand, we analyse who is in favour of and against European solidarity among the interviewed citizens in the 13 countries and examine how to explain their attitudes. It is possible to classify those factors that influence citizens' attitudes towards solidarity based on the three motives. For example, we interpret the fact that citizens from poorer countries are more in favour of territorial redistribution between poor and rich EU countries than citizens from richer countries as an instrumentally rationally motivated attitude, because citizens in poorer countries would benefit from redistribution. And when left-wing citizens speak out in favour of and right-wing citizens against a European welfare state, we attribute this to different value-rational orientations. Finally, affective attachment to communities also plays a role for the declaration of solidarity. People who feel strongly attached to their nation state will be less in favour of European solidarity than people who identify more strongly with Europe.

The various reasons for acting in solidarity are, however, still important for our analysis for a second reason. Action based on values or emotions is considerably more difficult to change than action motivated by instrumental-rational concerns and is also less amenable to compromise. People who are completely convinced, for example, of their religion and the corresponding values, will not easily be talked out of their beliefs and won over for compromises. If, for instance, a person is opposed to Muslims for Christian-religious reasons and does not want to grant asylum to persons of this religious affiliation, there will be little willingness to compromise with regard to legal regulations in the future.

The same applies to a strong affective bond with a community. For example, if you are emotionally very strongly bound to 'your' nation, then this connection is internalised. It will not dissolve overnight or be replaced by another link, for example, to Europe. The conditions for compromises are also rather unpromising when it comes to affectually motivated action.

The situation is different with regard to instrumentally rational action. People will change their behaviour if it is opportune and if a different action will bring more benefit than the original one. And the chances of reaching a compromise are also more favourable here. Vilhelm Aubert (1963) has distinguished between two conflict types: conflicts of interests and conflicts of values. In conflicts of interest, such as collective bargaining disputes, it is easier to reach a compromise because the goods at the heart of the dispute are divisible. The parties to the conflict agree to a compromise when both can improve their situation. 'A conflict of value is based upon a dissensus concerning the normative status of a social object' (Aubert 1963:29). Different value-rational views on an object are not easily negotiable and cannot simply be translated into compromises. If our analysis shows that the opponents of European solidarity are primarily value-rationally and affectually motivated, then these opponents will become much more deeply entrenched and much more likely to persevere than opponents who are instrumentally rationally motivated. We will include these considerations in our empirical chapters, but now we will return to our preliminary conceptual clarifications.

(3) Institutionalised solidarity and attitudes towards institutionalised solidarity. Institutionalised forms of solidaric action can be distinguished from direct forms of solidaric action. For the former, it is not individuals but collective actors or institutions that are the solidarity givers or recipients. The national welfare state is probably the best-known form of institutionalised solidarity. The state, as a collective actor, collects taxes, and uses them to reduce social inequalities or to support the unemployed. In this case, the solidarity giver is an institution and the recipients are individuals. But the solidarity giver is not the only actor that can be an institution; this may also apply to solidarity recipients. For example, the welfare state not only supports people in need but also impoverished regions within a country. And the countries of the EU were able to provide mutual financial support to each other in the sovereign debt crisis. In both cases, the recipients of solidarity and the givers of solidarity are not individuals but collective actors.[12]

In the case of institutionalised solidarity, the solidarity of citizens is not reflected in the fact that they directly support other citizens, but in their attitudes towards the institutionalised forms of solidarity. When citizens welcome and support an institutionalised form of solidarity, they are not acting in solidarity, but their attitudes are signs of solidarity. Accordingly, our study is not a study of solidaric actions but of citizens' attitudes towards solidaric actions. However, the 'theory of planned behaviour' (Ajzen 1991) and the 'theory of reasoned action' (Fishbein and Ajzen 1975) has shown in many studies that preferences for and attitudes towards certain behaviour have a strong influence on the intention to act; the intention to act in turn greatly influences the executed action.[13]

(4) The situation of the recipient of solidarity. We have made a distinction above between givers and recipients of solidarity. Recipients of solidarity – be they individuals or institutions – may find themselves in different social situations, which lead solidarity givers to show their solidarity. These include famines, earthquakes, health problems, or unemployment. Our epistemological interest is primarily aimed at defining European solidarity in the context of the crises of the European Union. As explained above, we distinguish between four types of problematic situations in which solidarity recipients can find themselves and which are therefore linked to different domains of solidarity. (a) *An EU member state's debt:* The debt crisis in some member states has raised the question of whether the people of Europe are prepared to support indebted countries. The solidarity givers and recipients are both institutions. The EU acts as a giver and certain EU countries as recipients of solidarity. (b) *Inequality between the countries of the EU:* There is a considerable disparity in wealth between EU member states, which was exacerbated by the economic crisis. This problem has raised the question of whether the citizens of Europe are prepared to support a financial rebalancing between poorer and well-performing EU countries. In this case, too, the recipients and givers of solidarity are not individuals but institutions. (c) *Neediness of people in other EU countries:* The economic crisis has hit those people who depend on welfare state benefits (unemployed, poor, sick, and elderly people) particularly hard and has increased inequality between rich and poor. Accordingly, we are interested in the question of whether the citizens of Europe are in favour of reducing inequality and whether they want to support needy people even if they are not citizens of their own country but citizens of other EU countries. In this case, the recipients of solidarity are people and not institutions. (d) *The refugee situation:* The refugee crisis has raised a double question of solidarity. To what extent are the citizens of Europe prepared to accept persecuted people in Europe and to what extent do they believe that the burdens should be distributed evenly between the EU member states? In the first case, the recipients of solidarity are individuals and in the second case they are EU member states.

2.3 The space of solidarity: national, European, and global solidarity

The recipients and givers of solidarity may not only face different emergencies, they may also be territorially situated in different locations. There are unemployed people in their own countries, in other European countries, but also in other regions of the world. Our research interest is to empirically determine the strength of European solidarity; recipients of solidarity are individuals living in another European country or other member states of the EU.[14] We understand Europe as the territorial space of the European Union. From a sociological point of view, however, it is crucial to note that this territorial space has been structured by the EU institutions and their policies, and that this is a specific social area. The strength of European solidarity can only reasonably be determined in comparison with other territorial and social spaces. Two alternative areas of solidarity are particularly important in this respect: the nation state and world society.

(1) The process of nation state building began in the eighteenth century and accelerated in the nineteenth and twentieth centuries. A nation state as a specific territorial and social space is characterised by several features (see Hobsbawm 1992). First, the state defines, secures, and controls the borders of its territory. Second, nation state building goes hand in hand with the creation of a nationwide administration, a national currency, and legal, tax, and educational systems. Third, and at a later historical date in western Europe, state rule reconnects to the will of the people it governs through the establishment of democracy. Fourth, and occurring historically later, a welfare state is established to promote social equality and to protect against unemployment, disability, illness, and age-related risks. Fifth, people living within the territory of a state become citizens of their state, enjoy the protection of the state, and have freedom of movement within its borders. And if it is a democratic state, they have the right to elect their government and can claim social welfare benefits from their (and only their) country. Finally, nation states are not only characterised by specific institutional features, but by a new type of community and a specific sense of belonging felt by their citizens (Anderson 1983).

(2) Against this backdrop, European integration can be seen as the emergence of a new territorial, institutional, and social space, which manifests itself first in the establishment and expansion of the different political institutions of the EU. The competences of the European institutions and their organisational power grew over time at the expense of national institutions. Second, European institutions are not just there for their own sake; they have created a common European social space including a customs union, a common market, and a common currency. Third, European integration has not only advanced the structural integration of the member states by increasing exchange between them; it has reframed the nation state's concept of citizenship (Gerhards and Lengfeld 2015). The idea of a nationally bounded freedom to move, settle, and work is being Europeanised and replaced by an idea where all citizens of Europe are regarded as equals, meaning that they can move, settle, and work in any EU member state. In addition, the freedom of movement rule includes several additional social rights, including, among other things, the entitlement to the same social security and tax benefits as national citizens. Finally, the EU guarantees a set of political rights for all EU citizens, particularly the right to vote and to stand as a candidate for municipal elections in the member state of residence. Step by step, the European Union has replaced the nation state concept of equality with the idea of a Europe-wide equality for all European citizens by establishing a European citizenship status consisting of equal economic, social, and political rights.

(3) The strength of European solidarity should, however, be determined not only in relation to national solidarity but also to global solidarity. The process of Europeanisation described in the last paragraph is itself embedded in a larger process of globalisation (Held et al. 1999). According to a research group at the ETH Zurich – who developed the KOF Index of Globalisation – globalisation includes three different dimensions: economic, political, and social globalisation (Dreher 2006). Whereas economic globalisation is measured by worldwide flows of trade and foreign direct investment and political globalisation by the degree of political cooperation (e.g. the number of embassies, international organisations, and treaties), social globalisation manifests itself in the worldwide spread of information, international personal and virtual contacts, and migration. Since the late 1970s, there has been an upward trend in globalisation in all three dimensions. The world has come closer together to the extent that some authors (Luhmann 1997; Meyer et al. 1997) consider it appropriate to speak of a world society. In addition to the emergence of a European social space due to the European integration process, a global social space has developed. Against this backdrop, the question arises of how strong support for European solidarity is not only in relation to national but also in relation to global solidarity.

Accordingly, we distinguish between three different territorial and social solidarity spaces, in which potential recipients of solidarity can be located: (1) citizens and institutions of their own country (national solidarity), (2) citizens and institutions of EU countries (European solidarity), and (3) citizens and countries outside the EU (global solidarity). In our empirical study, we have therefore not only studied the strength of European solidarity, but also that of national and global solidarity, as we will explain in more detail in the next section.

Excursus: the spaces of solidarity and the debate between cosmopolitans and communitarians

The distinction between different spaces of solidarity touches upon a philosophical debate on solidarity that we would like to explore in a little more detail in the form of an excursus. At the heart of the philosophical discussion, there is the question of the normative legitimacy of different spaces of solidarity and not the question of how much solidarity citizens show empirically. The reference point for evaluating different spaces of solidarity is usually social justice theory. Two schools can be distinguished: the cosmopolitans and communitarians. Within these two schools, there are many variations, which we cannot cover here. In our descriptions, we are guided by the work of Andrea Sangiovanni (2012, 2013, 2016), who has summarised the discussion in detail.

Cosmopolitans argue that support for people in need should not stop at any territorial border. They are therefore in favour of global solidarity (Pogge 2008). For example, if two people find themselves in a similar plight, the first person in their own country and the other person in a foreign country, then both have the same legitimate right to solidarity. The rationale for cosmopolitan global solidarity refers to the idea of equality of all people. Because all human beings are equal from birth and because the place of birth and thus the territory where they will grow up and probably spend their life is determined by pure coincidence, there is no legitimate reason to justify advantaging or disadvantaging people based on their territorial location. This principle of equal treatment applies not only to fundamental human rights, but also to the distribution of resources to people in need, that is, it also applies to an ethic of solidarity (Sangiovanni 2013).

The idea of cosmopolitan solidarity implies in turn that the actual interactions between people, the concentration and institutionalisation of interactions as manifested in the nation state, for example, should be irrelevant for the question of justice and solidarity. Accordingly, cosmopolitans criticise theories that assume solidarity should be bound to the existence of a social community, i.e. to network of interactions between people and a certain social space.

From the perspective of cosmopolitans, the institutionalisation of European solidarity is the first step in the right direction, because it is here that the national container is being broken open and extended towards the 'world'. All Europeans, and not just the citizens of a nation state, should be treated as equals, and everyone has an equal right to solidarity. This replaces national communitarianism with European communitarianism. This is to be welcomed, but it is not enough from the cosmopolitan point of view because solidarity should not stop at the borders of Europe either, but should embrace the citizens of all countries (Benhabib 2004).

With regard to our study, a cosmopolitan perspective leads to the following conclusions. National solidarity can claim the lowest legitimacy for itself and global solidarity the highest, while European solidarity can be located between the two poles.

Communitarians, by contrast, assume that there are not only empirically different boundaries of solidarity and thus different social spaces of solidarity but these spaces can also claim different legitimacy for themselves. Solidarity between people only arises when people are connected, when there is interaction between them, and when a system of norms and institutions and a feeling of *communitas* emerges on the basis of these interactions. Some communitarians assume that the state is needed to create a community (Nagel 2005). Depending on the density of the interactions and the strength of the community, solidarity will then also vary in intensity.

The argument that the extent of solidarity is linked to an existing community is in substance an empirical statement and not a normative justification. Yet, norms cannot be derived from empirical facts. In this respect, a normatively more plausible communitarian justification is, for instance, the one developed by Andrea Sangiovanni (2012, 2013; see also Singer 2016). He described his own position as 'reciprocity-based internationalism'. His core argument was as follows: the creation of communities, such as that of a family, a nation state, or the European Union, occurs for a specific purpose – people enter into relationships and interactions in order to produce collective goods. By being willing to produce such collective goods and by participating in their production, people acquire the right to be supported by the other members of the community if necessary. The claim to solidarity arises as a result of participation in the production of collective goods. Solidarity is therefore based on reciprocity. A legitimate claim to solidarity arises when people have participated in the production of collective goods (similar to Singer 2016). According to reciprocity-based internationalism, demands for social solidarity at all levels of governance can be understood as demands for a fair return in the mutual production of important collective goods (Sangiovanni 2013:217).

Sangiovanni applies this general principle to different communities. Thus, the modern nation state consists of institutions that guarantee internal and external securities and provide people with access to the labour market, education, and health care. Citizens of a country participate in the production of these collective goods, for instance by completing compulsory military service or being prepared to defend their country in the event of war and by being willing to obey the laws and to pay taxes so that the state can also guarantee the safety, education, and health of its citizens.

Sangiovanni interpreted European integration as a process of new community building with the aim of producing collective goods. Above all, the creation of a common European market and a single currency was carried out with the aim and promise of increasing the prosperity of all European citizens. At the same time, however, the risks have changed with the European integration process. For example, the European free movement of workers can lead to an increase in unemployment in some countries as a consequence of intra-European migration. Also, the introduction of the euro can lead to currency and economic crises. Since it is not known in advance how high such risks are and who will be particularly affected by the risks, the insurance principle of solidarity applies here too: all those who are involved in the project of integration and who have participated in its realisation have a right to solidarity in a 'case of accident', just as they are entitled to 'consume' the fruits of the collective property.

For our study, this argument leads to the following conclusion: despite globalisation and Europeanisation processes, the nation state remains the dominant space of interactions in the production of collective goods. It is therefore empirically reasonable to expect that national solidarity will be more pronounced than European or global solidarity. And since the European Union has a much denser network of interactions and institutions than the global world society, European solidarity will be stronger than global solidarity. From the point of view of communitarians, however, the empirically expected ranking of the three solidarity groups is also a normatively justified ranking. Citizens give more to the nation state than to the European Union, and they give more to the EU than to world society.

We will return to the briefly outlined discussion between cosmopolitans and communitarians when presenting our empirical results, and especially in the final chapter. However, the terms cosmopolitanism and communitarianism are not only used in the philosophical debate, but also in the social sciences to empiri-cally describe different population groups characterised by different attitudes and social characteristics. We will come back to this in more detail in the next section.

2.4 Criteria to determine the existence of European solidarity

Our study focuses on European citizens' attitudes towards European solidarity and not, for instance, on public discourses or on governments' or political parties' positions on European solidarity. Before we discuss how we can deter-mine the existence of European solidarity, let us briefly explain why analysing citizens' attitudes is important and what role such analysis plays in the political process. In pluralistic competitive parliamentary democracies, parties campaign to win electoral votes (Downs 1957; Hooghe and Marks 2009). It is likely that existing parties align themselves with citizens' attitudes and adjust to the prefer-ences of the general public (Page and Shapiro 1983). In this way, parties increase their chances of being elected and subsequently of forming a government.[15]

How can we determine whether and to what extent a European solidarity exists? We apply a set of criteria to determine the existence and strength of European solidarity. In applying this concept to questions on specific policies, we can infer generalized attitudes towards European solidarity. This allows us to identify the extent of European solidarity in each domain. The basis for this concept was developed in a previous study we conducted (Gerhards and Lengfeld 2015); in addition, we rely on the literature on citizens' attitudes towards different domains of solidarity, which we will discuss at the end of this chapter. The following aspects, which will then be applied to each of the domains of solidarity, are significant for the existence of a European solidarity.

(1) Double majority support from the population. In democracies, legitimacy is created, among other things, by the majority support for the citizens. The European Union is a federation of states as well as a federal state at once. Accordingly, Euro-pean citizens have two roles in the constitution of the European Union: their role as citizens of the European Union, and their role as citizens of their home nations (Habermas 2011:67). This dual status of citizenship is reflected in the arrangement of the European institutions, including the European Parliament and the Council of the European Union. From the point of view of democratic legitimacy, it is not sufficient that a European majority supports the idea of European solidarity. The majority in each individual member state has to be in favour of the idea of solid-arity as well. Only a double majority can ensure that the populations in individual member states will not feel overruled. For each of the four domains of solidarity (fiscal, welfare, territorial, and solidarity with refugees), we will test whether such a double majority is empirically verifiable.

(2) European solidarity in relation to national and global solidarity. Our epistemological interest is to determine the extent of European solidarity. As we

have argued in the last section the strength of European solidarity is, however, a relational measure, which can only be determined in comparison to other solidarity in territorial spaces. The comparison with national solidarity is especially relevant, because historically the nation state has been the central institution of solidarity and in many ways still is. Simultaneously, globalisation processes have contributed to not just Europe, but the entire world becoming a space of solidarity. We thereby differentiate between three different territorial spaces of solidarity: (a) solidarity between citizens and regions of the same nation state, (b) solidarity with citizens and states within the EU, and (c) solidarity with citizens and states of the world society (including people and states located outside of the EU). Empirically we have determined the strength of European solidarity for each domain in relation to national and global solidarity. We thus claim that an independent European space of solidarity exists if European solidarity is stronger than global solidarity. However, we do not expect European solidarity to be stronger than national solidarity. Due to the long history and influence of the nation state, this would not only be unrealistic but theoretically implausible. Citizens are, of course, not just Europeans but at the same time, and more importantly, (still) citizens of their nation states.

(3) The resilience of European solidarity. As explained above, our study does not analyse citizens' solidaric behaviour but their attitudes towards institutionalised solidarity. For example, we ask whether citizens of Europe support the idea that countries in a financial emergency should be supported by wealthier countries. However, citizens supporting institutionalised European solidarity are only indirectly affected by the cost of solidarity. This may lead to higher approval rates.[16] Therefore, we investigate whether citizens' attitudes towards European solidarity are resilient, meaning that citizens are ready to stand up for their beliefs.[17] We thus asked respondents whether they would be willing to pay higher taxes to bring about European solidarity.[18] We also examined the influence of the level of taxes on the willingness to act in solidarity.

(4) Social and political cleavages between supporters and opponents of European solidarity. It can be assumed that not all EU citizens support the idea of European solidarity to the same degree, so there will be differences on both the aggregate country level and the individual level. A crucial question is whether such differences occur randomly or whether they have social causes. If attitudes towards European solidarity on the one hand and socio-structural and cultural characteristics on the other overlap the likelihood that the opposing minority will politically mobilise increases. Opponents of European solidarity become a kind of social dynamite if they succeed in organising themselves, mobilising for their cause politically, and bringing their interests to bear in the political arena. We link these considerations to the theory of social and political cleavages (see Deegan-Krause 2006; Ferrera 2005; Grande and Kriesi 2015; Hutter, Grande, and Kriesi 2016; Kriesi et al. 2012).[19] In cases where specific attitudes coincide with respondents' structural and cultural characteristics, social cleavages are likely to emerge and the probability that disaffected minorities will become an

influential political force and constitute a political cleavage increases. Therefore, for European solidarity to exist, another condition has to be fulfilled: those who oppose European solidarity should not form the basis for strong cleavages. We investigate the likelihood of the emergence of cleavages in two steps – we do so separately for each domain of solidarity.

(4.1) Social cleavages. We analyse to what extent structural and cultural characteristics of the respondents and the countries they live in relate to the different domains of solidarity. We should note at this point that the question of how to explain differences in EU citizens' attitudes towards European solidarity is not identical to the question of whether social cleavages exist, as not all factors contributing to the formation of attitudes lead to politicisation. However, we have primary interest in characteristics that could lead to social cleavage and politicisation.

And a second note is needed at this point. Although we use causal rhetoric throughout the book, our analysis is no causal analysis in the narrowest sense. Unfortunately, we do not have panel data available, which would allow us to investigate causality in the change of measures over time. In addition, our focus is not how and why cleavages emerge, but simply whether or not they exist.

We distinguish between *structural characteristics* of individuals and countries, which may then lead to the emergence of structural cleavages and *cultural* features, which may lead to cultural cleavages. Certainly we must specify the set of variables that operationalize structural and cultural cleavages for each domain of solidarity separately. We will do this in the respective chapters. However, on a more general level we can formulate several assumptions, which we discuss in the following.

On the one hand, European solidarity may counter an individual's and a country's interests accruing from their socio-economic status. For example, those in a lower socio-economic position might fear that allowing refugees to enter the EU will lead to tougher labour market competition and thus to a decrease in wages. That is why such individuals will oppose solidarity with refugees. On the other hand, European solidarity may also be incompatible with respondents' cultural characteristics. Those with a strong affectual attachment to their nation, whose values contradict the idea of a European solidarity, or who are living in a country with a strongly protected national identity are more likely to oppose the idea of European solidarity.

The differentiation between socio-structural and cultural characteristics can also be related to Max Weber's classification of different forms of social action. As explained above, according to Max Weber, attitudes and social behaviour can be motivated by three different factors: self-interest, values, and affective attachment to a community. 'Self-interest' refers to the socio-structural position of an individual or a country, and affective attachment and values can be classified as cultural characteristics.

The distinction between socio-structural and cultural cleavages is more systematic in character and can be applied to different historical periods and societies. Most recent literature assumes that a new cleavage has emerged in the context of globalisation processes (Bornschier 2010; Börzel and Risse 2017; Grande and Kriesi 2015; Hooghe and Marks 2009, 2017; Hutter et al. 2016; Kriesi et al. 2012). There are many different concepts and terms to describe the two poles of this new cleavage (Hooghe and Marks 2017:11). However, all concepts use socio-structural and cultural characteristics to describe the two camps of the new cleavage. On the one side, there are people who consider globalisation processes to be a positive phenomenon and support the opening up of nation states. They want to grant people from other countries the same rights, they welcome migration, and they regard it as enriching for their country. On the other side, there are individuals who interpret the opening up of their own nation state as a threat. They believe that citizens from their own country are entitled to more rights than people from other countries. They oppose accepting migrants, and consider migration a threat to their own culture rather than an enrichment. Céline Teney, Onawa P. Lacewell, and Pieter de Wilde (2014) as well as Wolfgang Merkel and Onawa P. Lacewell (2013) have described the first group as cosmopolitans and the second as communitarians. In contrast to those engaging in the philosophical debate discussed above, the authors mentioned are not interested in justifying which position is the right one. Instead, they attempt to identify the two groups empirically.

Both groups are characterised by different socio-economic features and by different values and attachments towards different communities. Cosmopolitans generally possess higher education (Hakhverdian et al. 2013), are more internationally connected, and more attached to transnational communities (Helbling and Teney 2015). Communitarians have the opposite characteristics (i.e. low education, less internationally networked, more attached to the nation state).

We presume that the advocates of European solidarity are more likely to be cosmopolitans and will display similar cultural and socio-economic characteristics, while the opponents are characterised by typically communitarian features. In the empirical chapters, we will analyse whether there is a link between structural and cultural factors on the one hand and attitudes towards European solidarity on the other. The acceptance of refugees, for example, can lead to an increase in competition on a country's labour market, especially for low-skilled domestic workers. If refugees are interpreted as a threat to the socio-economic status of certain individuals, the probability that these citizens will advocate for their nation state and oppose solidarity with refugees rises. We thus assume that an individual's status as unemployed and also a country's unemployment rate will have a negative influence on attitudes of solidarity.

(4.2) Political cleavages. Structurally and culturally determined opponents of European solidarity become politically relevant when they actively express their political preferences rather than leaving them latent. One of the most important modes of expressing political preferences is by electing political parties, because governments emerge based on elections, which then determine a country's political future. Accordingly, our survey extracts information on which party the

respondent would vote for in the next (national) election. This allows us to analyse whether the opponents of European solidarity have preferences for specific parties and thus transfer their objectives into the political arena.

We will apply the criteria listed here to determine the existence and strength of European solidarity. To do so, we assess for each of the four domains of solidarity whether (a) the majority of EU citizens and the majority of people in each country is ready and willing to support European solidarity, (b) how strong European solidarity is relative to national and global solidarity, and (c) how resilient European solidarity is. Finally, we investigate (d) how the differences in attitudes of citizens can be explained, and whether structural and cultural cleavages manifest as voting intentions for particular parties.

2.5 Data and methods

Our study uses a specially developed social survey (the Transnational European Solidarity Survey, or TESS – see appendix for a more detailed description of our survey methodology). The survey was carried out in 13 EU countries between May and November 2016 by the opinion polling firm TNS Opinion and Social, which is also responsible for the Eurobarometer surveys. The countries included in the survey are Austria, Cyprus, France, Germany, Greece, Hungary, Ireland, the Netherlands, Poland, Portugal, Slovakia, Spain, and Sweden. Overall, 12,500 interviews were conducted. In 12 of the 13 countries, 1,000 telephone interviews (both landline and mobile) were conducted. In Cyprus, the sample was reduced somewhat to 500. Respondents were exclusively registered as national citizens aged 18 or older at the time of the survey. We are aware that it is not possible to reconstruct a complete picture of the willingness of citizens to engage in solidarity in all 28 EU countries based on data from only 13 countries. However, in order to sample the broadest spectrum of countries possible with regard to the above-described domains of solidarity, we systematically selected the 13 countries.

Unfortunately, telephone interviews may not exceed more than 25 to 30 minutes. These restrictions have led to trade-offs between delving deeper into certain aspects and gauging the whole picture of European solidarity and touching upon the domains slightly superficially. We decided to put our focus on the latter. Of course, we are aware of the drawbacks of this decision. For example, it would have been ideal to have more items to measure each domain of solidarity for reliability. But if we had asked more questions about one domain of solidarity, we probably would have had to forego the measurement of another domain.

When selecting countries we considered among other things, the following criteria: (a) whether the country in question was one that previously received (Cyprus, Ireland, Portugal, Spain) or currently receives (Greece) financial assistance in the euro crisis; (b) whether the country is a member of the currency union (including Austria, France, Germany, the Netherlands, Slovakia) or not

(Hungary, Poland, Sweden); (c) what welfare state regime the country has (i.e. liberal, social-democratic, conservative, mediterranean, post-socialist). Additionally, we considered how long they have been members of the European Union. While France, Germany, and the Netherlands were all founding members of the European Economic Community (EEC) in 1957, we also included the relatively new EU member states, such as Hungary, Poland, and Slovakia in our survey sample.

The data we have collected have the enormous advantage of being a primary data source. They allow us to test our theoretical concept of solidarity empirically, tailored exactly to our scientific needs. Accordingly, we posed several questions on European, national, and global solidarity for all solidarity domains. We measured the general agreement with statements regarding these domains of solidarity on a scale with four possible answers ranging from 'totally agree' to 'totally disagree'. Additionally, respondents had to say whether they would prioritise national, European, or global solidarity if they had to choose one. Finally, we surveyed the participants on whether they would be prepared to pay more tax for European solidarity. With this method, we test the resilience of European solidarity. Unfortunately, we could only ask the question regarding citizens' willingness to pay more tax in the domains of fiscal and welfare solidarity, because asking about solidarity domains would have exceeded the limits of our survey.

In order to identify structural and cultural cleavages, we considered factors on the individual and country level; only variables that are theoretically plausible are considered for the empirical analysis and included in the regression models. These include on the individual level not only education, income, and the social class position of a respondent but also cultural characteristics such as respondent's political orientation (left/right)[20] or identification with the nation state and Europe. On the country level, we took the unemployment rate, GDP per capita, and the number of immigrants living in a country into account.

In each chapter and for each domain of solidarity, we will specify which variables may impact the existence of cleavages. Our research design slightly deviates from the classical hypothesis testing approach, which states hypotheses first and examines them subsequently (e.g. Hobolt 2014), as we are primarily interested in identifying the existence of cleavages rather than explaining why they emerged.

A few words about how countries were treated in our analysis might be useful at this point. We treat countries as a unit consisting of a set of social characteristics (e.g. unemployment rate, GDP per capita). Such classifications of countries using these social categories do not do justice to their particular historical development paths. Historically oriented comparative social scientists have stressed the importance of historical, path-dependent developments of individual countries. These scholars criticised approaches that treat countries as a complex of variables (Mahoney 2004). In principle, we agree with this critique, but we believe that both methodologies are compatible. A systematic, comparative analysis (Bollen, Entwisle, and Alderson 1993) such as ours can develop a rough sketch of the differences between countries but cannot completely replace a historical approach with microanalyses of particular conditions. Our study will not take the developmental, historical paths of individual societies into account. Consequently, the explanatory power of our findings is limited.

The evaluation of the data consists primarily of a descriptive, mostly cross-national comparative analysis. We generally present the findings of the research in the form of easily visible charts and graphs. The analysis of political cleavages is, in contrast, a causal analysis. In order to determine the cleavages on the individual level, we use linear regression analysis. Since all the respondents are nested within their nations, and country-specific correlations could be biased, we calculate cluster-corrected standard errors in pooled OLS models. We are, however, also interested in determining the influence of macro-factors on preparedness for solidarity, such as the effects of the unemployment rate or the number of refugees already living in a country. To investigate this, we analysed how macro-factors affected the unstandardised coefficients of country dummies, due to the small number of countries available in the survey. Lastly, we carried out a two-step regression analysis to investigate the cross-level effects of macro-factors due to our sample size. As a first step, we estimate individual models for each country. As a second step, we then used the values of the country-specific unstandardised coefficients as dependent variables and checked for the extent to which their variance can be explained through macro variables in an OLS model. Even if this statistical analysis deals with relatively elaborate processes, we have attempted to portray it in a reader-friendly manner so a wider audience understands the analysis. The details on the methodology are provided in the book's appendix.

The four domains of solidarity (fiscal, territorial, welfare, and refugee solidarity) structure the composition of this book. There is a chapter dedicated to each domain of solidarity.

2.6 Situating our study and reviewing the literature

We conclude this chapter by discussing how our study relates to the existing literature. It is important to remember when conceptualising European solidarity that we subsumed different domains of solidarity under one umbrella. Thus, we could not build solely upon one specific body of literature. Instead, our study intersects with empirical studies from several research fields, which often use diverging terminology.

In the following, we will review the relevant literature and employ a twofold strategy to outline how our study relates to other empirical studies. On the one hand, we will focus on studies analysing attitudes towards topics that come close to the different domains of European solidarity (i.e. topics related to fiscal (Section 2.6.1), territorial (Section 2.6.2), welfare (Section 2.6.3), and refugee solidarity (Section 2.6.4)). On the other hand, we will expand our focus beyond these very concrete topics and explore empirical findings in related fields; these include citizens' attitudes towards EU integration, Euroscepticism, and identification with Europe (Section 2.6.5). We will restrict our review to those studies where the connection to the domains of European solidarity can be clearly identified.

2.6.1 European fiscal solidarity

The European sovereign debt crisis triggered a wide-ranging public debate on how to resolve the crisis. A vast literature emerged explaining and discussing the problems of and possible solutions to the crisis (among others Copelovitch, Frieden, and Walter 2016; Dyson 2017; Habermas 2012, 2015; Kulish and Castle 2011). Two strands of empirical research have emerged, which deal with the question of whether the general public is in favour of financially supporting EU member states in need. However, these strands differ in the research designs they apply: (1) one uses survey methodology to tap into citizens' attitudes towards fiscal solidarity, while (2) the other one relies on experimental research and aims to understand both the attitudes and behaviour of individuals in relations to European fiscal solidarity. In the following we elaborate on the findings of the two strands.

(1) A growing number of studies have used survey methodologies to analyse public opinion regarding financial support for states in need. These studies have sought to explain who is more supportive of giving financial assistance to countries in crisis. Those conducted shortly after the sovereign debt crisis reported relatively low support for European fiscal solidarity (Bechtel, Hainmueller, and Margalit 2014; Pew Research Center 2013), while more recent surveys have reported higher support levels. According to this latter group of studies, the majority of respondents are in favour of European fiscal solidarity (Díez Medrano et al. 2019; Lengfeld and Kroh 2016; Lengfeld, Schmidt, and Häuberer 2014). Furthermore, studies have identified that agreement with European fiscal solidarity is higher among citizens with higher socio-economic status as well as among those who exhibit cosmopolitan attitudes, identify with Europe, have a left-wing political orientation, and live in affluent countries (Bauhr and Charron 2018; Daniele and Geys 2015; Díez Medrano et al. 2019; Kleider and Stoeckel forthcoming; Kuhn, Solaz, and van Elsas 2017; Stoeckel and Kuhn 2018; Verhaegen 2018). These studies have the advantage of often covering a large number of countries. However, they have several shortcomings. First, many such studies investigated only a limited number of mechanisms explaining why individuals would help financially struggling countries. Second, the studies primarily focused on generalised attitudes towards European fiscal solidarity. Consequently, they could not explore the different aspects of fiscal solidarity: what type of austerity measures do citizens envisage demanding in exchange for financial support or how much are they willing to pay to support crisis-affected countries.

(2) The findings of studies applying (quasi-)experimental methods are also relevant to the domain of European fiscal solidarity. Experimental research has the advantage of measuring specific behaviour under varying conditions. Here, researchers have identified how citizens' behaviour and attitudes depend on the circumstances related to the crisis (Bechtel et al. 2014, 2017; Kuhn et al. 2017; Stoeckel and Kuhn 2018). Studies showed that the conditions and attributes of the financial support shape citizens' willingness to either pay out of their own taxes or to support such measures. These include which country is the receiving country, what kinds of austerity measures are proposed, or how extensive the contributions are. Yet, experimental designs can often only cover a small number of countries, and the data often cannot be generalised to the population as a whole due to the lack of representativeness. In contrast, we present findings for 13 countries in our study, where we have representative samples for the general population of each surveyed country.

We combine the advantages of both approaches and extend the framework of our previous empirical studies (Lengfeld 2015; Lengfeld and Kroh 2016; Lengfeld et al. 2014, 2015). Although our main focus is on presenting findings for generalised attitudes, we also investigate citizens' attitudes to the conditions and attributes of financial help for states in need. Additionally, with our data from 2016, we also contribute to the discussion on how citizens' attitudes develop over time by extending the time frame. Furthermore, by applying our strategy of comparing different spatial levels (national, European, and global fiscal solidarity), our work widens the scope for relative measurements of European fiscal solidarity. Furthermore, we discuss the results with reference to cleavage theory – we therefore consider a multitude of factors relevant for European fiscal solidarity.

2.6.2 European territorial solidarity

Since the financial and economic crisis in 2008, the north–south divide in living standards within EU member states has widened (Heidenreich 2016). To ameliorate this divide, the EU is pursuing a self-defined goal of achieving convergence among the states. Basically, it is applying a far-reaching and complex system of convergence policies, including measures for regional redistribution across the member states. However, these redistributive measures have been hotly debated. This is especially true in net-contributor states, where the issue of redistribution has been relevant in several public debates and electoral campaigns, such as the Brexit campaign of 2016. To our knowledge, no study has investigated citizens' attitudes to a system of redistribution, which aims at reducing wealth differences on the European level.

Because there is a lack of studies focusing on European territorial solidarity, our main arguments primarily stem from a study by Laia Balcells, José Fernández-Albertos, and Alexander Kuo (2015) that analysed individuals' preferences regarding support for redistribution between rich and poor regions in Spain. The mentioned authors found that a small majority of the respondents support regional redistribution. While they could not find effects of income level or unemployment status, the perceived economic situation of the respondent's region is negatively correlated with support for regional redistribution. Additionally, politically right-leaning individuals and those who highly identify with a subnational region, such as Catalonia, tended to be less supportive of such measures. Although the study is far-reaching, with the additional quasi-experimental setting, any single-country study has the disadvantage of lacking international comparison. Moreover, given that Spain has regions with distinctive aspirations for autonomy, which many other countries do not have, the case is exceptional in terms of analysing interregional transfers.

Going beyond studies with a regional focus on territorial redistribution, we also drew on analyses focusing on attitudes towards redistribution within welfare states (Alt and Iversen 2017; Jæger 2006; Kulin and Svallfors 2013; Svallfors 1997). In particular, we considered several of the mechanisms discussed in this field to understand what cleavages can emerge in regard to European territorial solidarity.

However, our study goes beyond the existing literature in several ways. First, we expand the research on regional territorial redistribution to encompass European territorial redistribution and explore tendencies in 13 European countries. Second, we compare attitudes towards subnational regional redistribution with attitudes on the European and global level.

2.6.3 European welfare solidarity

The Great Recession and the consequences of the sovereign debt crises have increased the proportions of individuals in vulnerable social positions. This has created a need for European welfare solidarity. We will again only focus on studies dealing with citizens' attitudes and disregard research focusing on the actual institutions of welfare states. In the following, we will describe empirical research investigating this domain in order to give an overview of the state of the field. Furthermore, we will expand our focus to discuss how we made use of the findings from the related field of national welfare state attitudes.

Only a limited number of projects have conceptualised European welfare solidarity in a similar manner to ours and focused on citizens' attitudes towards the notion of European social security and EU-wide redistribution (Baute et al. 2018a, 2018b; Ciornei and Recchi 2017; ESS Round 8: European Social Survey 2016; Gerhards, Lengfeld, and Häuberer 2016b). These studies all underlined the clear (albeit not overwhelming) support for European welfare solidarity, with some country variations. In particular, the most recent data from the European Social Survey (2016) show that respondents from Austria, Finland, the Netherlands, and the United Kingdom were divided evenly between those supporting and opposing an EU-wide social security scheme, while respondents from other surveyed countries were generally in favour of such a scheme. There are even fewer analyses exploring the relationship of European welfare solidarity with other social factors (Baute et al. 2018a; Ciornei and Recchi 2017). They demonstrated that the support for European welfare solidarity has both structural and cultural underpinnings. In particular, individuals from the lower social strata, those with strong European identity, and those with egalitarian values were more likely to support European welfare solidarity.

However, there are a number of issues with these studies. First, they were all either conducted prior to the Great Recession or shortly afterwards (Baute et al. 2018a, 2018b; Ciornei and Recchi 2017; ESS Round 8: European Social Survey 2016; Gerhards et al. 2016b). Second, in some cases, the country selection was rather limited (Baute et al. 2018a, 2018b; Ciornei and Recchi 2017; Gerhards et al. 2016b); the exception here was the European Social Survey, where the number of surveyed countries was greater than that of our own survey. However, our study goes beyond this previous work as we employ a multi-spatial approach, where attitudes are tapped at the national, European, and the global level.

Due to the limited literature, we also heavily relied on studies exploring attitudes towards the *national* welfare state, a research field that has been well-established since the beginning of the 1970s (for recent comprehensive reviews see Chung, Taylor-Gooby, and Leruth (2018); Svallfors (2012)). Our study benefited in numerous ways from this research. First, research focusing on welfare state attitudes conceives of welfare solidarity as a multidimensional concept (cf. Roosma, Gelissen, and van Oorschot 2013). The dimensions include the two traditional functions of the welfare state: (1) providing social security and social protection and (2) maintaining equality by redistribution. Mirroring this understanding, we also identify two subdomains of (European) welfare solidarity: (1) attitudes towards social security and (2) attitudes towards redistribution. Second, we utilise established items employed in cross-national surveys measuring attitudes towards *national* welfare state attitudes (items surveyed in the International Social Survey Program, European Social Survey, and World Value Survey) and adapt them for use at European level. We aspired to leave the wording as intact as possible for our own survey. Third, given the lack of studies that have explored the different mechanisms of European welfare solidarity, we adopt mechanisms already well known in this research field. In particular, we apply the arguments of self-interest theory within our framework regarding how individuals from socially vulnerable situations are more likely to support the welfare state (Gelissen 2000). But we also use the theoretical claims emphasising that political value orientations influence attitudes (Andreß and Heien 2001). Fourth, we also borrow from mechanisms described in studies focusing on welfare chauvinism, which have stressed that feelings of community and identity foster solidarity (Dallinger 2009; Mewes and Mau 2012).

2.6.4 External and internal (refugee) solidarity

The refugee crisis has triggered a variety of studies in the social sciences. Again, we will concentrate on studies that place an empirical focus on capturing citizens' attitudes and that are related to our two research questions: citizens' attitudes towards refugees and towards the allocation of refugees between EU member states.

(1) Studies dealing specifically with external solidarity and attitudes towards refugees or asylum seekers are rather rare. Since the surge of refugees entering Europe, reports based on public opinion polls have covered this subject (Dixon et al. 2017; Heath and Richards 2016; TENT 2017). These studies have given a descriptive overview of attitudes towards refugees but have a limited theoretical scope. The picture they have revealed is mixed. In general, individuals exhibited positive attitudes towards refugees, but refugees' socio-demographic characteristics played a major role in the degree of acceptance. Furthermore, average approval rates for refugees varied greatly between countries. The studies reported less positive attitudes in eastern European countries (e.g. Hungary). Of the few relevant scientific studies that are not merely descriptive, there are some studies specifically focusing on attitudes towards refugees that are legally eligible to seek asylum (Crawley, Drinkwater, and Kauser 2013; Gerhards, Hans, and Schupp 2016a). For instance, Gerhards and colleagues (2016a) found majority support for accepting these refugees in Germany. In contrast, Crawley and colleagues (2013) reported rising hostility towards refugees in the United Kingdom. Another empirical study by Bansak and colleagues (2016) investigated attitudes towards refugees and other migrants based on an online survey across 15 European countries. It explored what attributes of an asylum seeker prompted more acceptance of them. The study showed that individuals were more likely to attribute higher 'humanitarian deservingness' to persons with higher human capital and those from non-Muslim backgrounds.

Overall, most of the studies lacked a broader theoretical framework, which would enable them to interpret their findings in a meaningful way and to connect the results to the relevant literature. Additionally, the research designs are often not broad enough to examine how attitudes relate to respondents' socio-economic and cultural background or to draw conclusions about cross-cultural differences; this is because they rely on data from just one country.

As refugees and asylum seekers are a subpopulation of immigrants in general, we also referred to literature focusing on attitudes towards immigrants and migration (Ceobanu and Escandell 2010; Dempster and Hargrave 2017; Hainmueller and Hopkins 2014). Among other factors, when examining social cleavages, we took into account the effect that the level of education has on attitudes towards migrants (Bobo and Licari 1989; Card, Dustmann, and Preston 2012; Chandler and Tsai 2001; Citrin et al. 1997; Hainmueller and Hiscox 2007; Knutsen 2010) and considered the role of cultural factors such as political orientation, identity, and cultural attitudes (Ceobanu and Escandell 2008; Dixon et al.

2017; Ford and Lowles 2016; Nickerson and Louis 2008; Sides and Citrin 2007). We will discuss the studies from this vast literature in greater detail in Chapter 6.

When exploring external solidarity, we utilise a research design that also takes into account the different attributes of refugees coming to Europe. However, certain theoretical underpinnings guided us and hence we investigate how the characteristics of refugees that are codified in asylum treaties and laws influenced citizens' attitudes. Additionally, our study is based on telephone interviews instead of an online survey, which makes our results more reliable. Furthermore, we are not essentially interested in the mechanics behind attitude formation. Instead, we present a representative, contemporary diagnosis of external solidarity while emphasising socio-structural and country differences.

(2) Another issue that has become prominent in the context of the refugee crisis is the issue of allocating asylum seekers between the EU member states. Our concept of internal solidarity focuses on what citizens think about this issue of allocation. Here, the literature is much more limited. Relevant publications that provide empirical analyses of attitudes largely deal descriptively with the question. Such studies investigate general willingness to help other member states facing a high influx of refugees (Genschel and Hemerijck 2018) but also try to identify the optimal allocation scheme favoured by the public (Bansak, Hainmueller, and Hangartner 2017; de Vries and Hoffmann 2016). All such studies have found Europe-wide support for helping countries in crisis and support for a proportional allocation scheme, although not in all member states. Nevertheless, the literature is rather limited in scope. The studies only employed descriptive reporting and lack detailed analyses about the mechanism that could be relevant for explaining attitudes.

Therefore, our research on internal solidarity offers more in-depth analysis and a more detailed understanding than was done in previously published studies in two specific respects. We enquire about (a) what people think about the question of whether every country should accommodate refugees and (b) whether countries who do not accept enough refugees should pay compensation. In particular, we more closely examined the potential intra-European and social conflicts related to internal solidarity across 13 countries.

2.6.5 Public support for European integration, Euroscepticism, and identification with Europe

Finally, we will discuss studies dealing with topics related to European solidarity, namely studies exploring citizens' support for European integration, Euroscepticism, and identification with Europe. Empirically, most of these studies relied on Eurobarometer (EB) survey data. Although these topics somewhat overlap with those of our study on solidarity, there are some important differences. The distinction is clearest when we compare the specific formulation of the Eurobarometer questions with the item formulations used in our study.

In essence, we understand *support for European integration* as citizens' support for the political process of European integration. Consequently, *Euroscepticism* means the lack of such support (for an overview see Hobolt and de Vries 2016a). While past studies predominately focused on support for European integration (e.g. Gabel and Palmer 1995), recent studies have increasingly concentrated on Euroscepticism, with a special focus on identifying the opponents of European integration (e.g. Boomgaarden et al. 2011; de Vries 2018; Hobolt and de Vries 2016b; Hobolt and Wratil 2015; Hooghe 2007; Kuhn et al. 2016; Skinner 2013; Stoeckel 2013; van Elsas and van der Brug 2015). Yet, both types of analyses used the same Eurobarometer question, albeit they differ in which answer categories they focused on (Hobolt and de Vries 2016a). Studies operationalised support by examining whether respondents chose the statement 'Membership of my country in the European Union is a good thing.' In contrast, studies that analysed Euroscepticism focused on respondents that chose the answer category 'membership ... is a bad thing' (cf. European Commission 2017b).

If we compare how support for European integration and Euroscepticism is operationalised with our measurement of European solidarity, it is obvious that both types of attitudes conceptually differ from one another. Support for European integration means support for building up or strengthening a political regime above the national level. European solidarity, in contrast, relates to the willingness of citizens to support vulnerable others (individuals, groups, or organisations) who are located in other EU countries. It is plausible that those approving European solidarity will also support European integration. This hypothesis, however, is not part of our research design and will not be tested in the following chapters.[21]

A similar argument holds for those studies that have analysed citizens' *identification with* Europe (e.g. Agirdag, Phalet, and van Houtte 2016; Fligstein 2008; Fuchs and Schneider 2011; Risse 2010). In her recently published dissertation, Stefanie Bergbauer (2018) has summarised the latest research in this area. Based on numerous previous studies, Bergbauer distinguished between three different components of identification with Europe: citizens' self-categorisation as Europeans, their evaluations of their membership in the European collective, and their affective attachment to Europe and other Europeans. These components were measured by three different indicators from Eurobarometer data.[22] If we compare the concept of identification with Europe and its measurement with our concept of citizens' attitudes towards European solidarity and how we measure them, it is again clear that we are dealing with two very different things, conceptually and empirically. However, our analysis can be linked to these studies in the following way. As previously explained, there may be different reasons why people support European solidarity (see Section 2.2 for details). We distinguish between motives of solidarity based (a) on self-interest, (b) on values, and (c) on identification with a specific community. Hence, identification with Europe may be one of the reasons why people speak out for European solidarity. Accordingly, we take identification with Europe into account as an independent variable. We assume that the stronger the identification with Europe is, the more strongly citizens support European solidarity.[23]

Overall, both sets of studies (those analysing citizens' support for European integration and citizens' identification with Europe) have sought to identify and systematise factors that shape citizens' attitudes. Three major dimensions have proved to be important. Attitudes are influenced by the interests of respondents and the interests of the country where they live, by cultural factors, again, located at the individual and country level, and finally, by the frames and cues offered by political parties in the public debate. It would be beyond the scope of our literature review if we were to look more closely at each individual factor that can be assigned to the three dimensions. We assume, however, that the three dimensions that influence EU support and identification with Europe are also important in explaining people's attitudes towards European solidarity. Accordingly, in formulating hypotheses to explain citizens' attitudes to European solidarity in each chapter, we will refer to all three dimensions.

Notes

1 We will go into more detail on the exact meaning of the term solidarity in the later section of this chapter, and differentiate between various domains of solidarity in this context.
2 The causes for the rapid increase in the number of refugees between the years 2015 and 2016 will be discussed in more detail in Chapter 6.
3 The special protection that refugees from war-torn areas and those politically persecuted enjoy in the EU is embedded in the frame of European foreign policy. In contrast to other international organizations, European foreign policy has been established based on particular moral standards. The EU does not act alone in its own economic and political interests, but rather couples its engagement with support for democracy, judicial review, and the application of human rights. It campaigns to fight poverty in developing countries and to secure humanitarian aid in natural and man-made disasters. Empirical studies have provided evidence that these normatively bound guidelines are not just empty rhetoric but also indubitably influence the EU's concrete foreign policy (see Kreutz 2015).
4 In the agreement with the EU, Turkey made itself duty bound to, among other things, take back all people who were registered in Greece, but whose asylum applications were incomplete or without proper foundation. Furthermore, it obliges Turkey to take all necessary measures to prevent illegal immigration to Europe. Turkey receives financial support in return, which is supposed to be for the benefit of the refugees staying in Turkey. In addition, the negotiations for Turkey's membership in the EU were recommenced, and the visa-duty for Turkish citizens wanting to travel into the EU was lifted (European Commission 2017a).
5 This was how in September 2015 the Interior Ministers of the EU member states ruled, against the votes of Slovakia, Hungary, Czech Republic, and Romania, for 120,000 asylum seekers to be redistributed among these countries. Additionally, even the suggestion of making the countries that did not wish to take in any refugees at all pay compensation found no consensus. Some of the overruled countries appealed to the European Court of Justice against this decision. The opening hearing for the case was on 10 May 2017.

6 A survey conducted before the referendum reached a similar conclusion. In an open question, the people were supposed to name the most relevant topics that influenced their voting in the referendum. Researchers then created word clouds out of the submitted answers, giving the most frequently mentioned terms the largest font size. For leave voters the most commonly used term by far was 'immigration' (British Election Study 2016).

7 For example, at the start of the year 2016 the then British prime minister, David Cameron, suggested to the European Commission that the amount of child support for children of EU migrants who do not live in the same country as their parents should be matched with the amount paid in the country of origin.

8 Scholars (see Lindenberg 2006) referred to solidarity in the same breath as prosocial behaviour, altruism, and cooperative behaviour. The literature emphasizes the idea that solidarity occurs between individuals who are part of the same group (cf. Heyd 2007; Laitinen and Pessi 2015). Thus, the notion of group connectedness as a requisite characteristic sets the concept apart from other related terms. However, as we can see in the next sections, we take a formal definition of solidarity when investigating European solidarity, and therefore our formal definition of solidarity is not equipped to differentiate between all forms of prosocial behaviour, before highlighting the causes and motives driving solidarity (see next paragraph).

9 Some authors mentioned reciprocity as another characteristic that is constitutive for relationships of solidarity (Hondrich and Koch-Arzberger 1992). This means that not only is the ego in solidarity with the alter, but that the alter is also obligated to act in solidarity with the ego. It may well be that the ego expects the alter to help the ego as well if the ego is in an emergency. However, the fulfilment of this expectation is not legally enforceable. For these reasons, we do not think it makes sense to define reciprocity as a determining element of solidarity.

10 Juan Diéz Medrano, Irina Ciornei, and Fulya Apaydin (2019) have pointed out that in the English, German, and Turkish linguistic areas, solidarity is equated with the feeling of community, while in the Romanic languages solidarity means that one actor helps another. The authors followed the Romanic meaning of the term in their own definition. Among other things, they examined the influence of identification with a group on solidarity.

11 General *political values* are a particular type of value-rational belief. Political orientations provide an interpretive framework for the assessment of concrete policy issues. What is particularly important is the political-ideological orientation, i.e. the question of whether a person belongs to the left or the right spectrum (Fuchs and Klingemann 1990). In this respect, studies on attitudes towards welfare solidarity have shown that people with a right-wing orientation tend to be against the expansion of the welfare state while those with a more left-wing orientation are in favour of it (Gelissen 2000).

12 With regard to European solidarity, Irina Ciornei and Ettore Recchi (2017) made a similar distinction. If the beneficiaries are citizens, they use the term transnational solidarity. If, by contrast, the beneficiaries are the countries of the EU they speak of international solidarity. A similar conceptual differentiation can be found in Knodt and Tews (2017:51).

13 The seminal work of Fishbein and Ajzen (1975) on the theory of reasoned action (later expanded to the theory of planned behaviour) first described in detail how attitudes and behaviour are connected. There has been growing evidence that behaviour, in particular the intention to engage in a certain behaviour, is contingent on the individual's attitude (see Conner and Armitage 1998; Sheeran, Norman, and Orbell 1999). For a historical overview of theoretical developments, see Manstead (1996).

14 On the concept of European solidarity, see also the contributions from Stefanie Börner (2013), Irina Ciornei and Ettore Recchi (2017), Heinz Kleger and Thomas Mehlhausen (2013), Michèle Knodt and Anne Tews (2017), Wulf Loh and Stefan

Skupien (2016), Steffen Mau (2008), Malcolm Ross (2010), and Andrea Sangio-vanni (2013).

15 If, however, the party system proves to be unresponsive to the concerns of the citizens, this can result in the foundation of new political parties as has been demon-strated by the change in the political landscape in several European countries: new Eurosceptic parties have been formed in the context of the multiple European crises.

16 In addition, we can expect a high degree of support for specific values when these values are socially desirable. This is likely to be the case on the issue of solidarity, since the term 'solidarity' has a positive connotation.

17 The term resilience is used in both the natural and the social sciences and has very different meanings (Olsson et al. 2015). Mostly, resilience means the ability of a system, such as the ecological system or even an individual, to adapt to and to cope with stressful situations. In our context, we define resilience as the willingness of people to support European solidarity even when it becomes costly to them.

18 The survey questions on the willingness to pay taxes can be criticised for being just 'ordinary' survey questions, which neither reflect respondents' true intended actions adequately nor will they allow to reconstruct the underlying mechanism that can help to explain people's behaviour. We are aware that laboratory experiments would have been a better approach for such undertakings, ensuring a higher internal validity for causal inference. However, this would have come at the cost of reducing external validity and generalisability of our findings (Jackson and Cox 2013). Instead, we are primarily interested in representative results in order to formulate a diagnosis about the strength of European solidarity. Theoretically, we could have incorporated experi-ments in our survey in form of vignettes (or similar factorial surveys). However, the cognitive load of vignettes has been reported to be high in face-to-face and self-administered surveys (Sauer et al. 2011) and it can be expected that for telephone interviews it is even higher. Thus application of such experimental items would have extended the response time, and would have even increased the likelihood of respond-ent break-offs. This would have not only jeopardised the reliability of our answers, but would have resulted in forcing us to sacrifice survey items for at least one domain of solidarity (as we had a time constraint of half an hour for the interviews).

19 According to Kevin Deegan-Krause (2006) – and many other political scientists – a political cleavage exists, when three criteria are met at the same time: (1) attitudinal differences between citizens, (2) structural and cultural characteristics of citizens, which are related to the attitudinal differences, and (3) institutional differences, e.g. political parties who represent different groups of citizens. In our study, we will focus on the first two levels only. Although we will not be able to analyse the institutional settings of party systems in different European countries, we will take citizens' party preferences into account.

20 The left-right scale measures two different dimensions: people's political orientations towards economic redistribution and/or people's cultural orientation towards inclu-sion and exclusion. As Hainmueller and Hopkins (2014) have shown for the case of attitudes towards migrants, the left–right scale loads mainly on the cultural dimen-sion. Therefore, we assign the left–right orientation of respondents to the cultural cleavage.

21 However, we relate to this research stream by detecting political cleavages aggravated by solidarity issues. We treat the phenomenon of voting for a Eurosceptic party as a proxy for Euroscepticism. We assume that citizens who reject European solidarity are more inclined to vote for politically Eurosceptic parties than citizens supporting the notion of helping other Europeans in need. In our empirical analysis, we categorise parties as proposed by Sara Hobolt and Catherine de Vries (2016b) on two dimen-sions – hard and soft Eurosceptic positions – as well as on right- and left-wing polit-ical ideology. We thus extend the current literature by systematically analysing not

only the determinants of solidarity, but also their possible translation into Eurosceptic behaviour.

22 Self-categorisation is measured by the question: 'In the near future, do you see yourself as [Nationality] only; [Nationality] and European; European and [Nationality]; European only?' Evaluation is operationalised by the question: 'And would you say you are very proud, fairly proud, not very proud, not at all proud to be European?' Finally, citizens' attachment to Europe is operationalised by the question

> People may feel different degrees of attachment to their town or village, to their region, to their country or to Europe. Please tell me how attached you feel to Europe. Very attached, fairly attached, not very attached, not at all attached.

23 As time in telephone interviews is very limited, we had to focus on one component and one question of identification with Europe (see below).

References

Agirdag, Orhan, Karen Phalet, and Mieke van Houtte. 2016. 'European Identity as a Unifying Category: National vs. European Identification among Native and Immigrant Pupils'. *European Union Politics* 17(2):285–302.

Ajzen, Icek. 1991. 'The Theory of Planned Behavior'. *Organizational Behavior and Human Decision Processes* 50(2):179–211.

Alt, James, and Torben Iversen. 2017. 'Inequality, Labor Market Segmentation, and Preferences for Redistribution'. *American Journal of Political Science* 61(1):21–36.

Anderson, Benedict. 1983. *Imagined Communities: Reflections on the Origins and Spread of Nationalism*. London: Verso.

Andreß, Hans-Jürgen, and Thorsten Heien. 2001. 'Four Worlds of Welfare State Attitudes?: A Comparison of Germany, Norway, and the United States'. *European Sociological Review* 17(4):337–56.

Aubert, Vilhelm. 1963. 'Competition and Dissensus: Two Types of Conflict and of Conflict Resolution'. *Journal of Conflict Resolution* 7(1):26–42.

Balcells, Laia, José Fernández-Albertos, and Alexander Kuo. 2015. 'Preferences for Inter-regional Redistribution'. *Comparative Political Studies* 48(10):1318–51.

Bansak, Kirk, Jens Hainmueller, and Dominik Hangartner. 2016. 'How Economic, Humanitarian, and Religious Concerns Shape European Attitudes toward Asylum Seekers'. *Science* 354(6309):217–22.

Bansak, Kirk, Jens Hainmueller, and Dominik Hangartner. 2017. 'Europeans Support a Proportional Allocation of Asylum Seekers'. *Nature Human Behaviour* 1(133):1–6.

Bauhr, Monika, and Nicholas Charron. 2018. 'Why Support International Redistribution? Corruption and Public Support for Aid in the Eurozone'. *European Union Politics* 19(2):233–54.

Baute, Sharon, Bart Meuleman, Koen Abts, and Marc Swyngedouw. 2018a. 'European Integration as a Threat to Social Security: Another Source of Euroscepticism?' *European Union Politics* 5(1) (https://doi.org/10.1177/1465116517749769).

Baute, Sharon, Bart Meuleman, Koen Abts, and Marc Swyngedouw. 2018b. 'Measuring Attitudes towards Social Europe: A Multidimensional Approach'. *Social Indicators Research* 137(1):353–78.

Bayertz, Kurt, editor. 1998. *Suhrkamp-Taschenbuch Wissenschaft*, Vol. 1364, *Solidarität: Begriff und Problem [Solidarity: Notion and Problem]*. Frankfurt am Main: Suhrkamp.

Bayertz, Kurt, and Susanne Boshammer. 2008. 'Solidarität [Solidarity]'. Pp. 1197–201 in *Handbuch der politischen Philosophie und Sozialphilosophie*, edited by S. Gosepath, W. Hinsch, and B. Rössler. Berlin: De Gruyter.

Bechtel, Michael M., Jens Hainmueller, and Yotam Margalit. 2014. 'Preferences for International Redistribution: The Divide over the Eurozone Bailout.' *American Political Science Review* 28(4):835–56.

Bechtel, Michael M., Jens Hainmueller, and Yotam Margalit. 2017. 'Policy Design and Domestic Support for International Bailouts'. *European Journal of Political Research* 56(4):864–86.

Beckfield, Jason. 2009. 'Remapping Inequality in Europe: The Net Effect of Regional Integration on Total Income Inequality in the European Union'. *International Journal of Comparative Sociology* 50(5–6):486–509.

Beckfield, Jason. 2013. 'The End of Inequality in Europe?' *Current History* 3:94–9.

Benhabib, Seyla. 2004. *The Rights of Others: Aliens, Residents, and Citizens*. Cambridge: Cambridge University Press.

Bergbauer, Stephanie. 2018. *Explaining European Identity Formation: Citizens' Attachment from Maastricht Treaty to Crisis*. Cham: Springer International Publishing (http://dx.doi.org/10.1007/978-3-319-67708-8).

Birnbaum, Michael, and Anthony Faiola. 2017. 'Macron's Victory Buoys the European Union after a String of Setbacks'. *Washington Post*, 8 May. Retrieved 12 September 2018 (www.washingtonpost.com/world/europe/macrons-victory-buoys-the-european-union-after-a-string-of-setbacks/2017/05/08/bb83d12e-33ef-11e7-ab03-aa29f656f13e_story.html?utm_term=.8d4957b3f0f9).

Bobo, Lawrence, and Frederick C. Licari. 1989. 'Education and Political Tolerance: Testing the Effects of Cognitive Sophistication and Target Group Affect'. *Public Opinion Quarterly* 53(3):285–308.

Bollen, Kenneth A., Barbara Entwisle, and Arthur S. Alderson. 1993. 'Macrocomparative Research Methods'. *Annual Review of Sociology* 19(1):321–51.

Boomgaarden, Hajo G., Andreas R. T. Schuck, Matthijs Elenbaas, and Claes H. de Vreese. 2011. 'Mapping EU Attitudes: Conceptual and Empirical Dimensions of Euroscepticism and EU Support'. *European Union Politics* 12(2):241–66.

Börner, Stefanie. 2013. *Belonging, Solidarity and Expansion in Social Policy*. Basingstoke: Palgrave Macmillan.

Bornschier, Simon. 2010. 'The New Cultural Divide and the Two-dimensional Political Space in Western Europe'. *West European Politics* 33(3):419–44.

Börzel, Tanja A., and Thomas Risse. 2017. 'From the Euro to the Schengen Crises: European Integration Theories, Politicization, and Identity Politics'. *Journal of European Public Policy* 54(1):1–26.

British Election Study. 2016. 'What Mattered Most to You When Deciding How to Vote in the EU Referendum?' Retrieved 12 September 2018 (www.britishelectionstudy.com/bes-findings/what-mattered-most-to-you-when-deciding-how-to-vote-in-the-eu-referendum/#.WLaUBHpnHg0).

Brunkhorst, Hauke. 1997. *Solidarität unter Fremden [Solidarity among Strangers]*. Frankfurt am Main: Fischer.

Card, David, Christian Dustmann, and Ian Preston. 2012. 'Immigration, Wages, and Compositional Amenities'. *Journal of the European Economic Association* 10(1):78–119.

Ceobanu, Alin M., and Xavier Escandell. 2008. 'East is West? National Feelings and Anti-Immigrant Sentiment in Europe'. *Social Science Research* 37(4):1147–70.

Ceobanu, Alin M., and Xavier Escandell. 2010. 'Comparative Analyses of Public Attitudes toward Immigrants and Immigration Using Multinational Survey Data: A Review of Theories and Research'. *Annual Review of Sociology* 36(1):309–28.

Chandler, Charles R., and Yung-mei Tsai. 2001. 'Social Factors Influencing Immigration Attitudes: An Analysis of Data from the General Social Survey'. *The Social Science Journal* 38(2):177–88.

Chung, Heejung, Peter Taylor-Gooby, and Benjamin Leruth. 2018. 'Political Legitimacy and Welfare State Futures: Introduction'. *Social Policy and Administration* 52(4):835–46.

Cingolani, Patrick. 2015. 'Solidarity: History of the Concept'. Pp. 1–5 in *International Encyclopedia of the Social & Behavioral Sciences*, edited by J. D. Wright. 2nd edn. Amsterdam: Elsevier.

Ciornei, Irina, and Ettore Recchi. 2017. 'At the Source of European Solidarity: Assessing the Effects of Cross-border Practices and Political Attitudes'. *Journal of Common Market Studies* 55(3):468–85.

Citrin, Jack, Donald P. Green, Christopher Muste, and Cara Wong. 1997. 'Public Opinion toward Immigration Reform: The Role of Economic Motivations'. *The Journal of Politics* 59(3):858–81.

Conner, Mark, and Christopher J. Armitage. 1998. 'Extending the Theory of Planned Behavior: A Review and Avenues for Further Research'. *Journal of Applied Social Psychology* 28(15):1429–64.

Copelovitch, Mark, Jeffry Frieden, and Stefanie Walter. 2016. 'The Political Economy of the Euro Crisis'. *Comparative Political Studies* 49(7):811–40.

Crawley, Heaven, Stephen Drinkwater, and Rukhsana Kauser. 2013. 'Regional Variations in Attitudes towards Refugees: Evidence from Great Britain'. *IZA Working Paper* (7647). Retrieved 16 August 2018 (http://repec.iza.org/dp7647.pdf).

Dallinger, Ursula. 2009. *Die Solidarität der modernen Gesellschaft: Der Diskurs um rationale oder normative Ordnung in Sozialtheorie und Soziologie des Wohlfahrtsstaats [Solidarity in Modern Societies: The Discourse on Rational or Normative Order in Social Theory and Sociology of the Welfare State]*. Wiesbaden: VS Verlag für Sozialwissenschaften.

Daniele, Gianmarco, and Benny Geys. 2015. 'Public Support for European Fiscal Integration in Times of Crisis'. *Journal of European Public Policy* 22(5):650–70.

de Vries, Catherine E. 2018. *Euroscepticism and the Future of European Integration*. Oxford: Oxford University Press.

de Vries, Catherine E., and Isabell Hoffmann. 2016. 'Border Protection and Freedom of Movement: What People Expect of European Asylum and Migration Policies'. *Bertelsmann Stiftung, eupinions* 1.

Deegan-Krause, Kevin. 2006. 'New Dimensions of Political Cleavage'. In *Oxford Handbook of Political Behavior*, edited by R. J. Dalton and H.-D. Klingemann. Oxford and New York: Oxford University Press.

Dempster, Helen, and Karen Hargrave. 2017. 'Understanding Public Attitudes towards Refugees and Migrants'. *ODI & Chatham House Working Paper* (512). Retrieved 18 June 2018 (https://euagenda.eu/upload/publications/untitled-92767-ea.pdf).

Díez Medrano, Juan, Irina Ciornei, and Fulya Apaydin. 2019. 'Explaining Supranational Solidarity'. Pp. 137–70 in *Everyday Europe: Social Transnationalism in an Unsettled Continent*, edited by E. Recchi, A. Favell, F. Apaydin, R. Barbulescu, M. Braun, I. Ciornei, N. Cunningham, J. Díez Medrano, D. Duru, L. Hanquinet, J. S. Jensen, S. Pötzschke, D. Reimer, J. Salamonska, M. Savage, and A. Varela. Bristol: Policy Press.

Theoretical framework 49

Dixon, Tim, Hans-Jürgen Frieß, Emily Gray, Robert Grimm, Stephen Hawkins, Marc Helbling, Miriam Juan-Torres, Katja Kiefer, Daniela Kossatz, Nicoleta Negrea, Alexandra Schoen, Liane Stavenhagen, Vincent Wolff, and Armgard Zindler. 2017. 'Attitudes towards National Identity, Immigration, and Refugees in Germany'. Retrieved 12 September 2018 (www.thesocialchangeinitiative.org/new-research-reports-on-attitudes-to-migrants-in-germany-and-france/).

Downs, Anthony. 1957. *An Economic Theory of Democracy*. New York: Harper & Brothers.

Dreher, Axel. 2006. 'Does Globalization Affect Growth? Evidence from a New Index of Globalization'. *Applied Economics* 38(10):1091–110.

Durkheim, Émile. 1933. *The Division of Labor in Society*. New York: Free Press.

Dyson, Kenneth. 2017. 'Playing for High Stakes: The Eurozone Crisis'. Pp. 54–76 in *The European Union in Crisis*, edited by D. Dinan, N. Nugent, and W. E. Paterson. United Kingdom: Red Globe Press.

ESS Round 8: European Social Survey. 2016. *ESS-8 2018 Data file edition 2.0:* NSD – Norwegian Centre for Research Data. Retrieved 12 September 2018 (www.european-socialsurvey.org/data/conditions_of_use.html).

European Commission. 2016. 'State of the Union Address 2016: Towards a Better Europe – a Europe That Protects, Empowers and Defends'. Retrieved 12 September 2018 (http://europa.eu/rapid/press-release_SPEECH-16-3043_en.htm).

European Commission. 2017a. *Report from the Commission to the European Parliament, the European Council and the Council: Fifth Report on the Progress Made in the Implementation of the EU–Turkey Statement.* COM(2017) 204 final. Brussels: European Commission. Retrieved 13 June 2017 (https://ec.europa.eu/home-affairs/sites/homeaffairs/files/what-we-do/policies/european-agenda-migration/20170302_fifth_report_on_the_progress_made_in_the_implementation_of_the_eu-turkey_statement_en.pdf).

European Commission. 2017b. *Standard Eurobarometer 87 – Public Opinion in the European Union.* S2142_87_3_STD87_ENG. Brussels: European Commission. Retrieved 15 December 2017 (http://data.europa.eu/euodp/en/data/dataset/S2142_87_3_STD87_ENG).

European Parliament, and European Council. 2011. *Directive 2011/95/EU of the European Parliament and of the Council: On Standards for the Qualification of Third-country Nationals or Stateless Persons as Beneficiaries of International Protection, for a Uniform Status for Refugees or for Persons Eligible for Subsidiary Protection, and for the Content of the Protection Granted.* 2011/95/EU. Brussels/Strasbourg: European Parliament; European Council. Retrieved 6 June 2017 (http://data.europa.eu/eli/dir/2011/95/oj).

European Union. 2012. 'Nobel Lecture'. Retrieved 12 September 2018 (www.nobelprize.org/prizes/peace/2012/eu/26124-european-union-eu-nobel-lecture-2012/).

Eurostat. 2018. *Unemployment by Sex and Age (une_rt_a): Eurostat – Data Explorer.* Retrieved 18 April 2018 (http://appsso.eurostat.ec.europa.eu/nui/show.do?dataset=une_rt_a&lang=en).

Ferrera, Maurizio. 2005. *The Boundaries of Welfare: European Integration and the New Spatial Politics of Social Protection.* Oxford: Oxford University Press.

Ferrera, Maurizio. 2017. 'The Stein Rokkan Lecture 2016 Mission Impossible? Reconciling Economic and Social Europe after the Euro Crisis and Brexit'. *European Journal of Political Research* 56(1):3–22.

Fishbein, Martin, and Icek Ajzen. 1975. *Belief, Attitude, Intention, and Behavior: An Introduction to Theory and Research*. 4th edn. Reading, MA: Addison-Wesley.

Fligstein, Neil. 2008. *Euroclash: The EU, European Identity, and the Future of Europe*. Oxford: Oxford University Press (www.loc.gov/catdir/enhancements/fy0907/2008295 404-b.html).

Ford, Rob, and Nick Lowles. 2016. *Fear & Hope 2016: Race, Faith and Belonging in Today's England*. London: HOPE not hate. Retrieved 18 June 2018 (www.barrow-cadbury.org.uk/wp-content/uploads/2016/03/Fear-and-Hope-report-1.pdf).

Fuchs, Dieter, and Hans-Dieter Klingemann. 1990. 'The Left–Right Schema'. *Continuities in Political Action: A Longitudinal Study of Political Orientations in Three Western Democracies*:203–34.

Fuchs, Dieter, and Christian Schneider. 2011. 'Cultural Diversity, European Identity and Legitimacy of the EU: A Theoretical Framework'. Pp. 27–57 in *Studies in EU Reform and Enlargement, Cultural Diversity, European Identity and the Legitimacy of the EU*, edited by D. Fuchs and H.-D. Klingemann. Cheltenham: Edward Elgar.

Gabel, Matthew, and Harvey D. Palmer. 1995. 'Understanding Variation in Public Support for European Integration'. *European Journal of Political Research* 27(1):3–19.

Gelissen, John. 2000. 'Popular Support for Institutionalised Solidarity: A Comparison between European Welfare States'. *International Journal of Social Welfare* 9(4):285–300.

Genschel, Philipp, and Anton Hemerijck. 2018. *Solidarity in Europe*. Policy Brief. Issue 2018/01. Fiesole: EUI School of Transnational Governance: School of Transnational Governance (https://stateoftheunion.eui.eu/wp-content/uploads/sites/9/2018/05/Policy-Brief-Solidarity-in-Europe.pdf).

Gerhards, Jürgen, and Holger Lengfeld. 2015. *European Citizenship and Social Integration in the European Union*. London, New York: Routledge.

Gerhards, Jürgen, Silke Hans, and Jürgen Schupp. 2016a. 'Kant, das geltende Recht und die Einstellungen der Bürger zu Flüchtlingen und anderen Migranten'. [Kant, Existing Law and Attitudes of Citizens Towards Refugees and Other Migrants]. *Leviathan* 44(4):604–20.

Gerhards, Jürgen, Holger Lengfeld, and Julia Häuberer. 2016b. 'Do European Citizens Support the Idea of a European Welfare State?: Evidence from a Comparative Survey Conducted in Three EU Member States'. *International Sociology* 31(6):677–700.

Grande, Edgar, and Hanspeter Kriesi. 2015. 'The Restructuring of Political Conflict in Europe and the Politicization of European Integration'. Pp. 190–226 in *Contemporary European Politics, European Public Spheres: Politics Is Back*, edited by T. Risse. Cambridge: Cambridge University Press.

Habermas, Jürgen. 2011. *Zur Verfassung Europas. Ein Essay [On Europe's Constitution – An Essay]*. Frankfurt am Main: Suhrkamp.

Habermas, Jürgen. 2012. *The Crisis of the European Union: A Response*. Cambridge: Polity.

Habermas, Jürgen, editor. 2013. *Im Sog der Technokratie. Kleine Politische Schriften XII [The Lure of Technocracy – Short Political Writings XII]*. Berlin: Suhrkamp.

Habermas, Jürgen. 2015. 'Warum Merkels Griechenland-Politik ein Fehler ist [Why Merkel's Greece Policy Is a Mistake]'. *Süddeutsche Zeitung*, 22 June. Retrieved 11 September 2018 (www.sueddeutsche.de/wirtschaft/europa-sand-im-getriebe-1.2532119).

Hainmueller, Jens, and Michael J. Hiscox. 2007. 'Educated Preferences: Explaining Attitudes toward Immigration in Europe'. *International Organization* 61(2):399–442.

Hainmueller, Jens, and Daniel J. Hopkins. 2014. 'Public Attitudes toward Immigration'. *Annual Review of Political Science* 17:225–49.

Hakhverdian, Armen, Erika van Elsas, Wouter van der Brug, and Theresa Kuhn. 2013. 'Euroscepticism and Education: A Longitudinal Study of 12 EU Member States, 1973–2010'. *European Union Politics* 14(4):522–41.

Handelsblatt. 2011. 'Kanzlerin Merkel sieht Aufschwung gefährdet [Chancellor Merkel Sees Economic Recovery in Jeopardy]'. *Handelsblatt*, 11 June. Retrieved 11 September 2018 (www.handelsblatt.com/politik/deutschland/euro-schuldenkrise-kanzlerin-merkel-sieht-aufschwung-gefaehrdet/4277760.html).

Heath, Anthony, and Lindsay Richards. 2016. 'Attitudes towards Immigration and their Antecedents: Topline Results from Round 7 of the European Social Survey'. Retrieved 18 June 2018 (www.europeansocialsurvey.org/docs/findings/ESS7_toplines_issue_7_immigration.pdf).

Hechter, Michael. 2001. 'Sociology of Solidarity'. Pp. 14588–91 in *International Encyclopedia of the Social & Behavioral Sciences*, edited by N. J. Smelser and P. B. Baltes. Amsterdam: Elsevier.

Heidenreich, Martin. 2016. 'The Double Dualization of Inequality in Europe: Introduction'. Pp. 1–21 in *Exploring Inequality in Europe: Diverging Income and Employment Opportunities in the Crisis*, edited by M. Heidenreich. Cheltenham and Northampton, MA: Edward Elgar.

Helbling, Marc, and Céline Teney. 2015. 'The Cosmopolitan Elite in Germany: Transnationalism and Postmaterialism'. *Global Networks* 15(4):446–68.

Held, David, Anthony G. McGrew, David Goldblatt, and Jonathan Perraton. 1999. *Global Transformations: Politics, Economics and Culture*. Stanford, CA: Stanford University Press.

Heyd, David. 2007. 'Justice and Solidarity: The Contractarian Case against Global Justice'. *Journal of Social Philosophy* 38(1):112–30.

Hobolt, Sara B. 2014. 'Ever Closer or Ever Wider? Public Attitudes towards Further Enlargement and Integration in the European Union'. *Journal of European Public Policy* 21(5):664–80.

Hobolt, Sara B. 2016. 'The Brexit Vote: A Divided Nation, a Divided Continent'. *Journal of European Public Policy* 23(9):1259–77.

Hobolt, Sara B., and Catherine E. de Vries. 2016a. 'Public Support for European Integration'. *Annual Review of Political Science* 19(1):413–32.

Hobolt, Sara B., and Catherine E. de Vries. 2016b. 'Turning against the Union? The Impact of the Crisis on the Eurosceptic Vote in the 2014 European Parliament Elections'. *Electoral Studies* 44:504–14.

Hobolt, Sara B., and James Tilley. 2016. 'Fleeing the Centre: The Rise of Challenger Parties in the Aftermath of the Euro Crisis'. *West European Politics* 39(5):971–91.

Hobolt, Sara B., and Christopher Wratil. 2015. 'Public Opinion and the Crisis: The Dynamics of Support for the Euro'. *Journal of European Public Policy* 22(2):238–56.

Hobsbawm, Eric J. 1992. *Nations and Nationalism Since 1780: Programme, Myth, Reality*. Cambridge: Cambridge University Press.

Hondrich, Karl O., and Claudia Koch-Arzberger. 1992. *Solidarität in der modernen Gesellschaft [Solidarity in Modern Societies]*. Frankfurt am Main: Fischer-Taschenbuch-Verlag.

Hooghe, Liesbet. 2007. 'What Drives Euroskepticism?' *European Union Politics* 8(1):5–12.

Hooghe, Liesbet, and Gary Marks. 2009. 'A Postfunctionalist Theory of European Integration: From Permissive Consensus to Constraining Dissensus'. *British Journal of Political Science* 39(1):1–23.

Hooghe, Liesbet, and Gary Marks. 2017. 'Cleavage Theory Meets Europe's Crises: Lipset, Rokkan, and the Transnational Cleavage'. *Journal of European Public Policy* 1(1):1–27.

Hutter, Swen, Edgar Grande, and Hanspeter Kriesi, editors. 2016. *Politicising Europe: Integration and Mass Politics*. Cambridge: Cambridge University Press.

Jackson, Michelle, and D. R. Cox. 2013. 'The Principles of Experimental Design and Their Application in Sociology'. *Annual Review of Sociology* 39(1):27–49.

Jæger, Mads M. 2006. 'Welfare Regimes and Attitudes towards Redistribution: The Regime Hypothesis Revisited'. *European Sociological Review* 22(2):157–70.

Kleger, Heinz, and Thomas Mehlhausen. 2013. 'Unstrittig und doch umstritten – europäische Solidarität in der Eurokrise [Uncontroversial but Controversial – European Solidarity in the European Crisis]'. *Politische Vierteljahresschrift* 54(1):50–74.

Kleider, Hanna, and Florian Stoeckel. Forthcoming. 'The Politics of International Redistribution: Explaining Public Support for Fiscal Transfers in the EU'. *European Journal of Political Research* 89(5).

Knodt, Michèle, and Anne Tews. 2017. 'European Solidarity and Its Limits: Insights from Current Political Challenges'. Pp. 47–64 in *Solidarity in the European Union: A Fundamental Value in Crisis*, edited by A. Grimmel and S. My Giang. Cham: Springer International Publishing.

Knutsen, Oddbjørn. 2010. 'The Regional Cleavage in Western Europe: Can Social Composition, Value Orientations and Territorial Identities Explain the Impact of Region on Party Choice?' *West European Politics* 33(3):553–85.

Kreutz, Joakim. 2015. 'Human Rights, Geostrategy, and EU Foreign Policy, 1989–2008'. *International Organization* 69(01):195–217.

Kriesi, Hanspeter, Edgar Grande, Martin Dolezal, Marc Helbling, Dominic Höglinger, Swen Hutter, and Bruno Wüest. 2012. *Political Conflict in Western Europe*. Cambridge: Cambridge University Press.

Kuhn, Theresa, Hector Solaz, and Erika van Elsas. 2017. 'Practising What You Preach: How Cosmopolitanism Promotes Willingness to Redistribute Across the European Union'. *Journal of European Public Policy* 95(4):1–20.

Kuhn, Theresa, Erika van Elsas, Armen Hakhverdian, and Wouter van der Brug. 2016. 'An Ever Wider Gap in an Ever Closer Union: Rising Inequalities and Euroscepticism in 12 West European Democracies, 1975–2009'. *Socio-Economic Review* 14(1):27–45.

Kulin, J., and S. Svallfors. 2013. 'Class, Values, and Attitudes towards Redistribution: A European Comparison'. *European Sociological Review* 29(2):155–67.

Kulish, Nicholas, and Stephen Castle. 2011. 'Slovakia Rejects Euro Bailout'. *New York Times*, 11 October. Retrieved 11 September 2018 (www.nytimes.com/2011/10/12/world/europe/slovak-leader-vows-to-resign).

Laitinen, Arto, and Anne B. Pessi, editors. 2015. *Solidarity: Theory and Practice*. Lanham, MD: Lexington Books.

Lengfeld, Holger. 2015. 'Die Kosten der Hilfe: Europäische Fiskalkrise und die Bereitschaft der Deutschen zur Zahlung einer europäischen Solidaritätssteuer [The Costs of Assistance: European Fiscal Crisis and the Willingness of the Germans to Pay a European Solidarity Tax]'. Pp. 381–405 in *Empirische Kultursoziologie: Festschrift für Jürgen Gerhards zum 60. Geburtstag [Empirical Cultural Sociology: Commemorative Publication for Jürgen Gerhards on His 60th Birthday]*, edited by J. Rössel and J. Roose. Wiesbaden: Springer.

Lengfeld, Holger, and Martin Kroh. 2016. 'Solidarity with EU Countries in Crisis: Results of a 2015 Socio-Economic Panel (SOEP) Survey'. *DIW Economic Bulletin* 6(39):473–9.

Lengfeld, Holger, Sara Schmidt, and Julia Häuberer. 2014. 'Fiskalpolitische Solidarität in der Europäischen Union: Erste Befunde einer Umfrage 2012 aus Deutschland und Portugal [Fiscal Policy Solidarity in the European Union: Preliminary Findings from a 2012 Survey in Germany and Portugal]'. In *Vielfalt und Zusammenhalt: Verhandlungen des 36. Kongresses der Deutschen Gesellschaft für Soziologie in Bochum und Dortmund 2012 [Diversity and Cohesion: Negotiations of the 36th Congress of the German Sociological Association in Bochum and Dortmund 2012]*, edited by M. Löw. Frankfurt am Main: Campus-Verl.

Lengfeld, Holger, Sara Schmidt, and Julia Häuberer. 2015. 'Is There a European Solidarity? Attitudes towards Fiscal Assistance for Debt-ridden European Union Member States'. *Working Paper Series of the Department of Sociology at the University of Leipzig* (No. 67). Retrieved 11 September 2018 (http://papers.ssrn.com/sol3/papers.cfm?abstract_id=2597605).

Levine, Mark, Amy Prosser, David Evans, and Stephen Reicher. 2005. 'Identity and Emergency Intervention: How Social Group Membership and Inclusiveness of Group Boundaries Shape Helping Behavior'. *Personality & Social Psychology Bulletin* 31(4):443–53.

Lindenberg, Siegwart. 2006. 'Prosocial Behavior, Solidarity, and Framing Processes'. Pp. 23–44 in *Critical Issues in Social Justice, Solidarity and Prosocial Behavior: An Integration of Sociological and Psychological Perspectives*, edited by D. Fetchenhauer, A. L. Flache, A. P. Buunk, and S. Lindenberg. New York: Springer.

Loh, Wulf, and Stefan Skupien. 2016. 'Die EU als Solidargemeinschaft [The EU as Solidary Group]'. *Leviathan* 44(4):578–603.

Lord Ashcroft. 2016. 'How the United Kingdom Voted on Thursday … and Why'. Retrieved 12 September 2018 (http://lordashcroftpolls.com/2016/06/how-the-united-kingdom-voted-and-why/).

Luhmann, Niklas. 1997. *Die Gesellschaft der Gesellschaft [The Society of Society]*. Frankfurt am Main: Suhrkamp.

Mahoney, James. 2004. 'Comparative-historical Methodology'. *Annual Review of Sociology* 30(1):81–101.

Manstead, Anthony. 1996. 'Attitudes and Behaviour'. Pp. 3–29 in *Applied Social Psychology*, edited by G. R. Semin and K. Fiedler. Newbury Park, CA: SAGE Publications.

Marx, Karl. 1947/1955. *The Poverty of Philosophy*. Moscow: Progress Publishing.

Mau, Steffen. 2008. 'Europäische Solidaritäten [European Solidarities]'. *Aus Politik und Zeitgeschichte* 21:9–14.

Merkel, Angela. 2010. *Regierungserklärung von Bundeskanzlerin Merkel zu den Euro-Stabilisierungsmaßnahmen [Government Statement by Chancellor Merkel on the Euro Stabilization Measures]*. Berlin. Retrieved 29 March 2018 (www.bundesregierung.de/ContentArchiv/DE/Archiv17/Regierungserklaerung/2010/2010-05-19-merkel-erklaerung-eu-stabilisierungsmassnahmen.html).

Merkel, Wolfgang, and Onawa P. Lacewell. 2013. 'Value Shifts in European Societies: Clashes between Cosmopolitanism and Communitarianism'. Pp. 77–95 in *Progressive Politics after the Crash: Governing from the Left*, edited by O. Cramme, P. Diamond, and M. McTernan. London: Tauris.

Mewes, Jan, and Steffen Mau. 2012. 'Unraveling Working-class Welfare Chauvinism'. Pp. 119–57 in *Contested Welfare States: Welfare Attitudes in Europe and Beyond*, edited by S. Svallfors. Stanford, CA: Stanford University Press.

Meyer, John W., John Boli, George M. Thomas, and Francisco O. Ramirez. 1997. 'World Society and the Nation-state'. *American Journal of Sociology* 103(1):144–81.

Nagel, Thomas. 2005. 'The Problem of Global Justice'. *Philosophy & Public Affairs* 33(2):113–47.

Nickerson, Angela M., and Winnifred R. Louis. 2008. 'Nationality versus Humanity? Personality, Identity, and Norms in Relation to Attitudes toward Asylum Seekers'. *Journal of Applied Social Psychology* 38(3):796–817.

Olsson, Lennart, Anne Jerneck, Henrik Thoren, Johannes Persson, and David O'Byrne. 2015. 'Why Resilience Is Unappealing to Social Science: Theoretical and Empirical Investigations of the Scientific Use of Resilience'. *Science Advances* 1(4)e1400217.

Page, Benjamin I., and Robert Y. Shapiro. 1983. 'Effects of Public Opinion on Policy'. *American Political Science Review* 77(1):175–90.

Pew Research Center. 2013. 'The New Sick Man of Europe: The European Union: French Dispirited; Attitudes Diverge Sharply from Germans'. Retrieved 12 September 2018 (www.pewglobal.org/2013/05/13/the-new-sick-man-of-europe-the-european-union/).

Pogge, Thomas W. 2008. *World Poverty and Human Rights: Cosmopolitan Responsibilities and Reforms.* 2nd ed. London: Polity Press.

Procacci, Giovanna. 2001. 'Solidarity: History of the Concept'. Pp. 14585–8 in *International Encyclopedia of the Social & Behavioral Sciences*, edited by N. J. Smelser and P. B. Baltes. Amsterdam: Elsevier.

Rankin, Jennifer. 2015. 'Eurozone Crisis: Which Countries Are for or against Grexit'. *Guardian*, 12 July. Retrieved 12 September 2018 (www.theguardian.com/business/2015/jul/12/eurozone-crisis-which-countries-are-for-or-against-grexit).

Risse, Thomas. 2010. *A Community of Europeans?: Transnational Identities and Public Spheres.* Ithaca, NY: Cornell University Press.

Roosma, Femke, John Gelissen, and Wim van Oorschot. 2013. 'The Multidimensionality of Welfare State Attitudes: A European Cross-national Study'. *Social Indicators Research* 113(1):235–55.

Ross, Malcolm. 2010. 'Solidarity – a New Constitutional Paradigm for the EU?' Pp. 24–45 in *Promoting Solidarity in the European Union*, edited by M. Ross and Y. Borgmann-Prebil. Oxford: Oxford University Press.

Sangiovanni, Andrea. 2012. 'Solidarity in the European Union: Problems and Prospects'. Pp. 384–411 in *Philosophical Foundations of European Union Law*, edited by J. Dickson and P. Eleutheriadēs. Oxford: Oxford University Press.

Sangiovanni, Andrea. 2013. 'Solidarity in the European Union'. *Oxford Journal of Legal Studies* 33(2):213–41.

Sangiovanni, Andrea. 2016. 'Non-Discrimination, In-work Benefits, and Free Movement in the EU'. *European Journal of Political Theory* 16(2):143–63.

Sauer, Carsten, Katrin Auspurg, Thomas Hinz, and Stefan Liebig. 2011. 'The Application of Factorial Surveys in General Population Samples: The Effects of Respondent Age and Education on Response Times and Response Consistency'. *Survey Research Methods* 5(3):89–102.

Schulze, Michaela. 2010. 'Solidarität – Die Basis Gesellschaftlicher Kohäsion: [Solidarity – The Basis of Social Cohesion]'. Pp. 230–43 in *Sozialwissenschaften 2010, Fundamente sozialen Zusammenhalts: Mechanismen und Strukturen gesellschaftlicher Prozesse*, edited by M. Becker and R. Krätschmer-Hahn. Frankfurt am Main: Campus.

Sheeran, Paschal, Paul Norman, and Sheina Orbell. 1999. 'Evidence That Intentions Based on Attitudes Better Predict Behaviour Than Intentions Based on Subjective Norms'. *European Journal of Social Psychology* 29(2–3):403–6.

Sides, John, and Jack Citrin. 2007. 'European Opinion about Immigration: The Role of Identities, Interests and Information'. *British Journal of Political Science* 37(3):477–504.

Singer, Peter. 2016. *One World Now: The Ethics of Globalization.* 3rd edn. New Haven, CT: Yale University Press.

Skinner, Marianne S. 2013. 'Different Varieties of Euroscepticism? Conceptualizing and Explaining Euroscepticism in Western European Non-Member States'. *JCMS: Journal of Common Market Studies* 51(1):122–39.

Steinvorth, Ulrich. 2017. 'Applying the Idea of Solidarity to Europe'. Pp. 9–19 in *Solidarity in the European Union: A Fundamental Value in Crisis*, edited by A. Grimmel and S. My Giang. Cham: Springer International Publishing.

Stjernø, Steinar. 2005. *Solidarity in Europe: The History of an Idea.* Cambridge: Cambridge University Press.

Stoeckel, Florian. 2013. 'Ambivalent or Indifferent? Reconsidering the Structure of EU Public Opinion'. *European Union Politics* 14(1):23–45.

Stoeckel, Florian, and Theresa Kuhn. 2018. 'Mobilizing Citizens for Costly Policies: The Conditional Effect of Party Cues on Support for International Bailouts in the European Union'. *JCMS: Journal of Common Market Studies* 56(2):446–61.

Streeck, Wolfgang. 2014. *Buying Time: The Delayed Crisis of Democratic Capitalism.* London: Verso.

Svallfors, Stefan. 1997. 'Worlds of Welfare and Attitudes to Redistribution: A Comparison of Eight Western Nations'. *European Sociological Review* 13(3):283–304.

Svallfors, Stefan. 2012. 'Welfare States and Welfare Attitudes'. Pp. 1–24 in *Contested Welfare States: Welfare Attitudes in Europe and Beyond*, edited by S. Svallfors. Stanford, CA: Stanford University Press.

Teney, Céline, Onawa P. Lacewell, and Pieter de Wilde. 2014. 'Winners and Losers of Globalization in Europe: Attitudes and Ideologies'. *European Political Science Review* 6(4):575–95.

TENT. 2017. 'Public Perceptions of the Refugee Crisis: Year 2'. Retrieved 12 September 2018 (www.tent.org/wp-content/uploads/2017/11/Tent_GlobalReport_V6.pdf).

Thome, Helmut. 1998. 'Soziologie und Solidarität [Sociology and Solidarity]'. Pp. 217–62 in *Suhrkamp-Taschenbuch Wissenschaft*, Vol. 1364, *Solidarität: Begriff und Problem [Solidarity: Notion and Problem]*, edited by K. Bayertz. Frankfurt am Main: Suhrkamp.

van Elsas, Erika, and Wouter van der Brug. 2015. 'The Changing Relationship between Left–Right Ideology and Euroscepticism, 1973–2010'. *European Union Politics* 16(2):194–215.

Verhaegen, Soetkin. 2018. 'What to Expect from European Identity? Explaining Support for Solidarity in Times of Crisis'. *Comparative European Politics* 16(5):871–904.

Weber, Max. 1968. *Economy and Society: An Outline of Interpretive Sociology*, edited by G. Roth and C. Wittich. New York: Bedminster Press Incorporated.

Wildt, Andreas. 1998. 'Solidarität – Begriffsgeschichte und Definition Heute [Solidarity – Conceptual History and Its Contemporary Definition]'. Pp. 202–16 in *Suhrkamp-Taschenbuch Wissenschaft*, Vol. 1364, *Solidarität: Begriff und Problem [Solidarity: Notion and Problem]*, edited by K. Bayertz. Frankfurt am Main: Suhrkamp.

Chapter 3

Fiscal solidarity – supporting member states in financial need

3.1 The European sovereign debt

The European economic and financial crisis that began in 2008 brought several EU countries to the brink of default. This strongly affected southern European countries in particular, as they found it increasingly difficult to obtain the credit from the capital markets that they needed to finance their state expenditure. The origins of the European banking crisis, which gave rise to these financial problems, lay in the 2008 US financial crisis, as its shockwaves rippled over Europe. However, the actual causes of the European crisis go somewhat deeper. At the time of the crisis, European banks possessed large amounts of American housing bonds that the American debtors could no longer service. As a result, once these debtors went bust, affected EU countries were left with little choice but to prop up their own national banking systems. The financial condition of southern European countries rendered them incapable of doing this without external assistance; they were highly indebted before the crisis struck. As the need for fresh capital to save the national banks rose, southern European countries' credit ratings plummeted on the international capital markets. In consequence, the interest rates for long-term state loans skyrocketed. Figure 3.1 clearly depicts this development using certain selected countries as examples. Save for Cyprus, all the countries portrayed had the same interest rates for long-term state loans. From 2009, the gap between the interest rates faced by the indebted southern European countries and Ireland on the one hand, and the western European countries on the other, began to grow wider. This is what first led to Greece – and later to Ireland, Cyprus, Spain, and Portugal – being threatened with financial insolvency. The graph also shows just how far these countries' long-term interest rates diverged from the levels defined as within the criteria for Euro convergence.[1]

In response to this crisis, the EU introduced special measures in 2009; this involved issuing credit straight from the EU's own budget on an ad hoc basis in order to help balance the national budgets of the crisis-affected countries (Dyson 2017). Unfortunately, these initial measures were far from sufficient, as the sovereign debt crisis had already spread further and had begun to threaten the

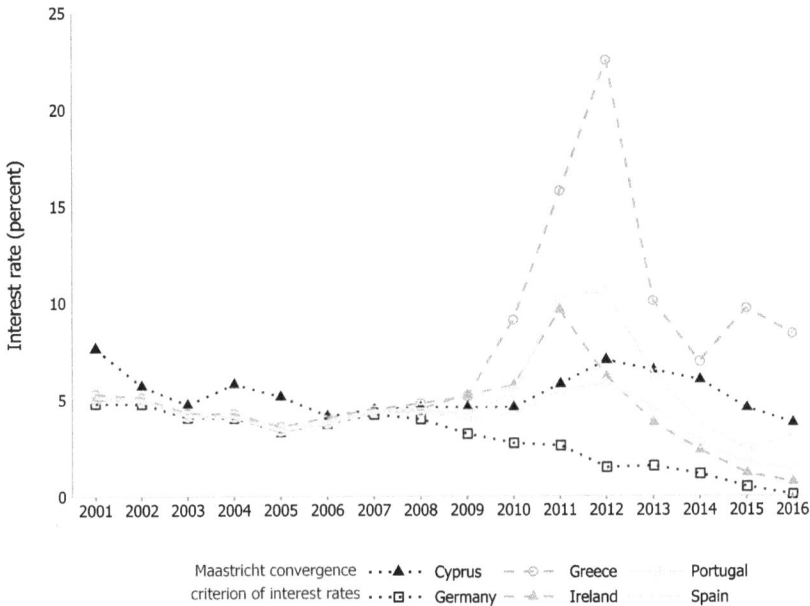

Figure 3.1 Development of bond yields for selected Eurozone countries (2001–2016).

Source: Eurostat (2017), own depiction.

stability of the common currency and of the entire Eurozone. As a result, EU member states and the International Monetary Fund (IMF) mutually decided to take the next step. This involved them establishing a temporary fiscal bailout fund in 2010, which they called the European Fiscal Stability Facility (EFSF). This bailout fund was intended to issue emergency loans with interest to all countries in the Eurozone that were threatened by acute state budgetary over-indebtedness. In so doing, the EU and IMF aimed to help the countries in question to meet the demands of their private and state creditors. On top of this, the debtor countries were to use these borrowed funds to stabilise their domestic banks and also initiate measures for restructuring their economies.[2] The greater part of these funds had to be raised by the member states of the Eurozone, with the IMF also making some contributions to make up the total amount.

In early 2011, alongside Greece and Ireland, Portugal too was now in need of assistance from the EFSF. It quickly became apparent that the initial sum of €440 billion would be insufficient, leading to the Eurozone countries enacting a new, permanent bailout package, the European Stability Mechanism (ESM). The purpose of the ESM is to stabilise Eurozone countries in the event of future debt crises. In addition to this mechanism, the European Central Bank (ECB) also decided to buy back the state debts of highly indebted countries from the capital market without any upper limitations. It thereby depressed interest rates on the capital market where these countries had procured their loans. In sum, the agreed measures led to Portugal, Ireland, Spain (which only received assistance to prop up its banking system), and Cyprus being able to exit from the bailout packages by 2016. At the time of our study, Greece was the only country continuing to receive financial assistance.

The agreed measures were, however, anything but politically uncontroversial. The Slovakian parliament was the first actor to vote against the expansion of the EFSF in 2011. Opponents of the EFSF argued that it would be unfair for Slovakia, the second poorest country in the Eurozone, to have to secure loans for countries like Greece and Portugal. These countries, so they said, were considerably wealthier than Slovakia and only had themselves to blame because they had brought this emergency upon themselves through lax fiscal policies (Kulish and Castle 2011).[3] Furthermore, in 2012, Finland announced that their solidarity with the bailed-out countries had its limits (SPIEGEL Online 2012a). The Finns then managed to negotiate special conditions to ensure that they could retain their deposits in the event of a financial default. The measures also received further criticism from other EU countries, who were concerned that the bailout policies would betray the principle that each member state is responsible for its own national budget. This, however, raised another conundrum, because if every country were responsible for itself and its own expenses alone, then there would be no European solidarity. In the national and European elections of 2014, right-wing populist and Eurosceptic political parties in many western European countries enjoyed a massive upswing in popularity; this was the case in Finland, France, the Netherlands, and Austria. These parties spoke out vociferously against the EU's bailout policies. In Germany, the Alternative für Deutschland (Alternative for Germany or AfD), which had only been founded in 2013, actually gained seats in the German and European parliament for the first time. This new political party had one demand at its core: that heavily indebted Greece should not receive financial support but should instead be forced to leave the Eurozone, because Germany and its citizens should not have to pick up the pieces for another country's own mismanagement.

Meanwhile, on the other side of the debate, there was also support for European fiscal solidarity. The Italian and French governments, to name just two, warned against the withdrawal of the bailed-out countries from the Eurozone and announced their solidarity (Rankin 2015). In 2017, the newly elected French president even went as far as to express his support for the institutionalisation of a European finance minister (Birnbaum and Faiola 2017). And from the academic world, Jürgen Habermas repeatedly argued that the European Monetary Union (EMU) had been lacking in fiscal solidarity since its inception. In this regard, he suggested that the European Central Bank's policy of buying back countries' debts was a step in the right direction (Habermas 2012, 2015).

The debate surrounding the bailout policies indicates just how the new financial institutions have led to political controversy. Even at the time of our survey in 2016, heavily indebted Greece was playing a central role in discussions, as the ECB and the IMF deliberated on whether they should remit a share of debt of this country (Theodoropoulou 2016). But away from these institutions, what do the peoples of Europe think about fiscal solidarity? Do they essentially support measures for emergency financial assistance; that is, do they support the idea that EU countries and their citizens should be supported in solidarity? Or are Europe's citizens more convinced that their own nation states represent the one truly legitimate space as far as fiscal solidarity is concerned?

The answers to these questions could be crucial in determining the future of the European integration process, for it is European citizens' collective belief in solidarity that could decide whether these politically determined measures will become a permanent part of a systematic consolidation of Europe in the medium term, or whether individual countries will withdraw from the union of cooperation. If Europeans do not consider the general idea of fiscal solidarity to be legitimate, then it is plausible that they will then withdraw their trust from their governments and potentially transfer it to Eurosceptic political parties instead.

To assess the willingness of citizens to show fiscal solidarity, we applied the set of criteria that we outlined in the first two chapters to this question. First, we measured the extent of fiscal solidarity with EU crisis countries and investigated whether a majority of citizens – both in total and in each of the surveyed countries – supported the idea of European solidarity. We then compared respondents' rates of willingness to display solidarity with people within their own nations with their solidarity with people from countries outside of Europe. Furthermore, in order to determine the resilience of European fiscal solidarity, we analysed how much of the financial burden European citizens were ready to share. Finally, we looked at individual willingness to establish a hypothetical European solidarity tax.

In contrast to the other domains of European solidarity explored in this book, we examined some additional aspects of the willingness to support fiscal solidarity in our survey.[4] We analysed which of the austerity measures EU citizens would be in favour of imposing on crisis-affected countries in return for financial assistance and which ones were particularly controversial. We expected European citizens' views on these austerity measures to differ widely.

Finally, we analysed whether social cleavages had emerged around the topic of European financial assistance and whether political cleavages are likely to develop in turn, assuming that citizens who reject the idea of fiscal solidarity will be more likely to vote in national elections for parties who claim to be opposed to further European integration.[5]

3.2 How strong is fiscal solidarity?

Can we expect the majority of Europe's citizens to favour fiscal solidarity with EU countries in crisis that need emergency assistance? There is an air of scepticism around this question for the following reasons: the spontaneous establishment of bailout packages marked a significant departure from the EU's previous policies on territorial redistribution. Within just a few years, the EU managed to radically alter its regime of redistribution by introducing policies such as the bailout packages and the ECB's purchasing of state debt titles. Before the financial crisis, the use of EU financial assistance to prop up individual Eurozone countries' budgets had been strictly forbidden and enforced expressly through the 'No Bailout' clause in Article 125 of the Treaty on the Functioning of the European Union (TFEU). Forming part of the monetary union's stability criteria, this article was intended to guarantee that nation states would be solely and exclusively responsible for their own household budgets and would manage their budgets with due care and prudence (Schelkle 2017:138–9). Even the exchange of bilateral assistance between member states was prohibited.

> 1.   The Union shall not be liable for or assume the commitments of central governments, regional, local or other public authorities, other bodies governed by public law, or public undertakings of any Member State, without prejudice to mutual financial guarantees for the joint execution of a specific project. A Member State shall not be liable for or assume the commitments of central governments, regional, local or other public authorities, other bodies governed by public law, or public undertakings of another Member State, without prejudice to mutual financial guarantees for the joint execution of a specific project.
>
> (European Union 2012: Article 125)

However, the bailout packages entailed a whole series of financial assistance measures that, according to many legal commentators, were in contravention of Article 125 of the TFEU.[6] To address this, Article 122 of the TFEU, according to which member states would be allowed to obtain financial assistance from the EU if they were gravely threatened by natural disasters or other extraordinary circumstances (e.g. a sudden shortfall in supply), was invoked when introducing the first bailout measures under the EFSF. In effect, the loans issued as part of the bailout packages functioned as subsidies. Because of this, the interest rates on them were significantly below the regular rates for government bonds that the countries in question would otherwise have had to pay on the capital market. Article 136 of the TFEU was later amended by adding a passage, according to which Eurozone countries were permitted to set up a stability mechanism 'to be activated if indispensable to safeguard the stability of the Euro area as a whole'.

  With that, the EU had completed a U-turn on its no-bailout imperative within just a few years. Even if the majority of Europeans were not aware of the details of these treaties, the break from the Eurozone's stability criteria that the bailout packages represented became a topic of intensive and critical media discussion in many EU countries. Assuming that EU citizens had been following these public discussions, many of them should have rejected the idea of European fiscal solidarity in our survey. Furthermore, we expected their understanding of fiscal solidarity in relation to the stability criteria to be restricted to their own nation states. That is, we assume that citizens in all countries would be in favour of supporting their own regions if they were to fall into financial difficulties but not necessarily other EU countries.

Compared to welfare solidarity, which concerns people in need (see Chapter 5), fiscal solidarity has several particular characteristics that led us to presume that this domain of solidarity would not really exist among European citizens. For one thing, the money does not go directly to individuals with clearly identifiable needs but rather into other countries' state budgets, that is, straight to big, faceless institutions. In addition, a sizeable portion of the money flows to insolvency-threatened banks as well as to anonymous creditors of the debt-ridden countries. This means that the immediate recipients of financial solidarity are not vulnerable citizens whom the average person can relate to, but impersonal institutions, many of which are regarded with a great deal of scepticism. Some authors argued that saving banks is, by definition, not in keeping with the definition of solidarity (e.g. Streeck 2014).

On top of all this, the structure of the bailed-out countries' creditors changed dramatically over the course of the crisis (Preunkert 2016). Whereas private creditors – mostly banks and institutional investors – provided the loans to the debtor countries at the beginning of the crisis, as it developed the proportion of public creditors grew ever greater. The ECB played a particular role in helping calm the capital markets with its ongoing, indefinite programme of purchasing state debts, beginning in 2012. By doing this, it also ensured that interest rates for new sovereign debts would also fall and stay low (Copelovitch, Frieden, and Walter 2016; Illing 2017:113–16). This meant, however, that the ECB, the member states, and their citizens would shoulder most of the risks and costs (Zettelmeyer, Trebesch, and Gulati 2013). This form of social integration, i.e. the transferring of responsibility to the European community, also happens to contradict the previously outlined concept of solidarity, whereby solidarity was confined to the nation state.

What conclusions can be drawn so far from the existing research, which used public opinion polls to answer the question of whether a European fiscal solidarity exists? The findings are somewhat contradictory. On the one hand, Eurobarometer surveys have shown that in the early days of the crisis in 2010 and 2011, just under half of all EU-27 citizens were in favour of providing financial assistance to bailed-out countries (Lengfeld, Schmidt, and Häuberer 2015). At the same time, however, studies also identified considerable differences in the results between the countries. For example, in 2011, three quarters of Luxembourgers approved of the use of financial assistance, while merely one quarter of all people in Slovenia approved. Eastern Europeans stood out especially as the most sceptical: in nine out of the 12 accession states from the 2004 and 2007 expansion phases, citizens rejected fiscal solidarity.

Nevertheless, surveys conducted by the Pew Research Center in 2013 came to some rather different conclusions (Pew Research Center 2013:70–1). According to these, there were no majorities in favour of European fiscal solidarity in the long-standing EU member states France and the United Kingdom. In contrast, in Italy, Spain, and Greece the approval rates lay between 60% and 80%, while in Poland and the Czech Republic over a half of respondents were in favour of solidarity. Yet, studies focusing only on individual countries also came to different conclusions. Michael M. Bechtel and colleagues (2014), for example, showed in an online survey that in 2012 only 28% of Germans were in favour of sending money to countries in crisis. In a population survey carried out in Denmark, Germany, Italy, Romania, Spain, and the United Kingdom in 2016, Juan Díez Medrano and colleagues (2019) asked whether respondents approved of 'pooling national state funds to help EU countries having difficulties in paying their debts' (ibid.:145). The results show a high degree of overall approval, but with higher rates recorded in Spain and Italy, and lower rates in Germany and the United Kingdom (ibid.). Holger Lengfeld and colleagues showed that around 50% of citizens eligible to vote in Germany were consistently in favour of bailout payments in several different surveys carried out between the years 2012 and 2015 (Lengfeld and Kroh 2016; Lengfeld, Schmidt, and Häuberer 2014). The cause for this enormous difference between the results of the two above-mentioned studies may lie in their respective methodologies. More precisely, it is possible that the self-selection of the participants in Michael M. Bechtel and colleagues' study (2014) may have led to a sample bias. On top of this, the inconsistent picture portrayed by these different studies may be linked to changes in opinion over time as several years have passed since 2011. We can assume that the initial scepticism of citizens in several EU countries has yielded to a more sympathetic stance in response to the construction of the new European crisis management strategy. We wish to ascertain whether this is true or not by utilising the TESS survey.

3.2.1 Citizens' general willingness to show fiscal solidarity

In our study, we differentiated between three spaces of fiscal solidarity. Financial assistance can be granted to: (1) regions in an emergency situation within the respondent's own country (national solidarity); (2) EU countries in an emergency situation (European solidarity); and (3) countries in an emergency situation that are not part of the EU (global solidarity).[7] We measured fiscal solidarity with the following four-point-scale items.[8]

We have learned in recent years that regions within countries as well as entire countries can fall into a severe debt crisis. Please tell me to what extent you agree or disagree with each of the following statements.

In times of crisis, the better off [NAME OF GENERAL REGION] in [NAME OF COUNTRY] should give financial help to other [NAME OF GENERAL REGION] facing severe economic difficulties.

> *In times of crisis, [NAME OF COUNTRY] should give financial help to other EU countries facing severe economic difficulties.*
> *In times of crisis, [NAME OF COUNTRY] should give financial help to other countries outside of the European Union facing severe economic difficulties.*

Figure 3.2 depicts the results for all the respondents. The answers are categorised according to their relative frequency, with answers that indicate approval appearing to the right of the central line and those indicating rejection to the left. The chart shows that two-thirds of the respondents supported financial assistance for crisis-affected countries. This finding unambiguously contradicts the sceptical hypothesis that we formulated above. More precisely, the approval level that we expected was considerably below the actual support level for emergency assistance handed out to regions within nation states (83%), but it was also significantly above what we expected for non-EU countries. Support for providing assistance to the latter group of countries fell just short of reaching a majority approval rate among the survey respondents (49%). Otherwise, the extent of agreement among our respondents generally fell as the size of the space of solidarity increased: the majority of respondents who approved of regional-level financial assistance 'completely' agreed with the proposition, while for the other

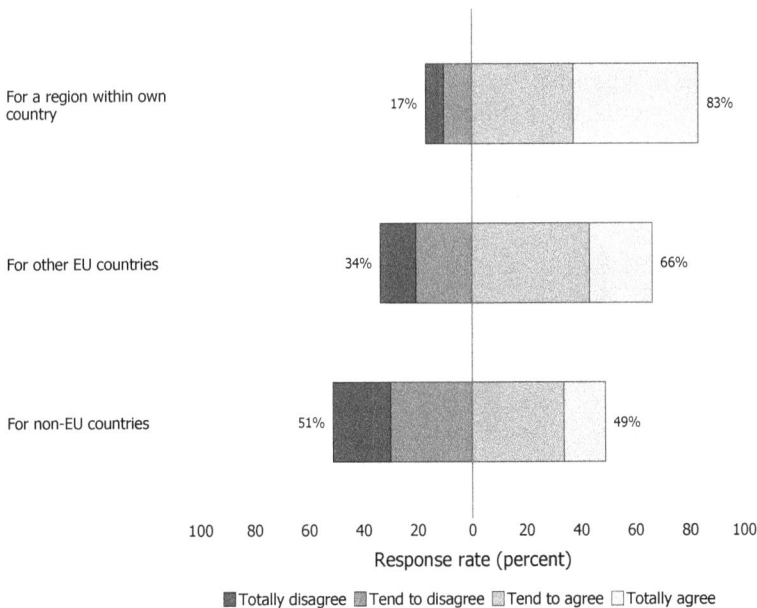

Figure 3.2 Response rates of the support for emergency assistance in times of crisis by recipient's spatial level.

Source: TESS 2016, own calculations.

two spaces, the majority of approving responses were given by people who selected 'tend to agree'.

The findings show that when it comes to fiscal solidarity, the nation state is indeed the space with the highest legitimacy, but surprisingly, the majority of European citizens also saw the EU as a legitimate space of solidarity. Contrary to our hypothesis, the citizens' support for solidarity did not conflict with the EU and IMF's institutional crisis management strategy. Nevertheless, solidarity only extended as far as the EU's external borders. This means that from the citizens' point of view the EU is a legitimate space of solidarity, albeit one that marks the external limit of solidarity.

How much did the willingness to express solidarity differ between our surveyed countries? As Figure 3.3 shows, the majority of citizens in every one of our 13 surveyed countries were in favour of European solidarity. This means that another one of our criteria for the existence of European solidarity is fulfilled: not only did the majority of all citizens across the EU support assistance for financially troubled countries in the EU; the majority of people in each country also agreed with this idea. The structure of legitimacy in all three spaces of solidarity for each country corresponded with the pooled results for all respondent shown in Figure 3.2: the nation state was perceived as the space with the greatest legitimacy, followed by other EU countries, and then by non-EU countries, which are at the back of the queue proverbially. Even Hungary and Slovakia, whose citizens rejected giving financial assistance as recently as in 2010 and 2011 (Lengfeld et al. 2015) agreed with these measures by a majority, albeit a small one. It is possible that a greater majority of these citizens acknowledged the advantages that the stabilisation of the Eurozone could provide for their own

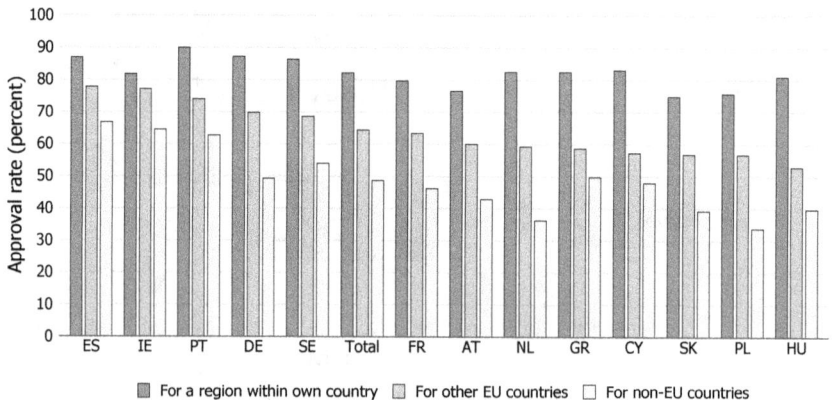

For a region within own country   For other EU countries   For non-EU countries

Figure 3.3 Average approval rates of the support for emergency assistance in times of crisis by recipient's spatial level by country.

Source: TESS 2016, own calculations.

countries. Whether this is the precise reason for the shift in attitudes, however, cannot be determined with certainty.

Let us now take a closer look at the individual countries. In three of the five countries, which received financial assistance (Spain, Ireland, and Portugal), approval rates were particularly high. These results are in line with previous research results (Díez Medrano et al. 2019; Pew Research Center 2013). We presume that this is due to citizens' instrumentally rational motives for financial assistance. Especially because their countries suffered through a crisis before and could potentially experience one again, it is in citizens' own interest to be able to receive financial assistance in the future (see Chapter 2). The high approval rates may also be the result of citizens taking a value-rational approach, i.e. their moral values motivate them to support financial assistance. They may be convinced that countries in crisis are entitled to help, having experienced the immediate consequences of the crisis themselves. However, this did not apply to Cyprus and Greece, who also received (and continue to receive) assistance from the EU. The approval rate for European fiscal solidarity reached just barely above 50% in these countries, possibly indicating an effect of the austerity policies imposed on them by the EU and the IMF, which hit Greece extremely hard (this will be explored in detail later on). While northern and western European countries stood out because they were the most in favour of this arrangement, the lowest approval rates were found in the three eastern European states in our sample.

At this point, we may draw an interim conclusion: our results so far have shown a surprisingly high rate of willingness to engage in European fiscal solidarity all-around. Even the differences between countries are low and thus show that neither the country's role in the sovereign debt crisis, nor its economic performance levels significantly influenced the attitudes of their citizens; we will return to this point again in Section 3.4.

There is one major weakness in our measurement of solidarity that critics might highlight, namely the problem of having respondents evaluate the three different items at the same time. This could lead to an overestimation of respondents' willingness to engage in solidarity within the European space, as they were not necessarily prompted to favour one space of solidarity over the others. We conducted a hypothetical experiment to make the approval rates clearer. Our hypothesis was that if all three spaces of solidarity were to undergo a crisis at the same time, with little available assistance, we could expect that the overwhelming majority of the citizens would opt in favour of giving assistance to their own nations first and foremost. At the same time, we could also assume that the difference in the willingness to express solidarity between EU and non-EU countries would be less pronounced.

We pre-emptively addressed these objections in the following way. In the TESS, we put our respondents into a decision-making situation. In this scenario, they were supposed to decide from their own perspective which of the three spaces they would help first in a crisis. This question was subdivided into two smaller ones. In the first part of the question, we asked where the citizen's first priority would lie; after that, we asked them to specify their second priority.[9] This decision-making thought experiment allowed us to rank the legitimacy of spaces of solidarity.

Assuming a decision about priority has to be made: in your opinion, where should financial support be provided to first ...

1.   *to a [GENERALREGIONNAME] within [COUNTRY].*
2.   *to another country in the European Union.*
3.   *to another country outside of the European Union.*

And where should it be provided to second?

1.   *to a [GENERALREGIONNAME] within [COUNTRY].*
2.   *to another country in the European Union.*
3.   *to another country outside of the European Union.*

Figure 3.4 shows the citizens' views on this question. The dark shaded bars indicate the space citizens prioritised first, while the lighter shaded bars stand for their second priority. The results show that in the event of a crisis, the overwhelming majority of EU citizens would choose to help the regions within their own country first. Only 7% of respondents opted for a country within the whole EU, and 9% for a country outside of the EU.

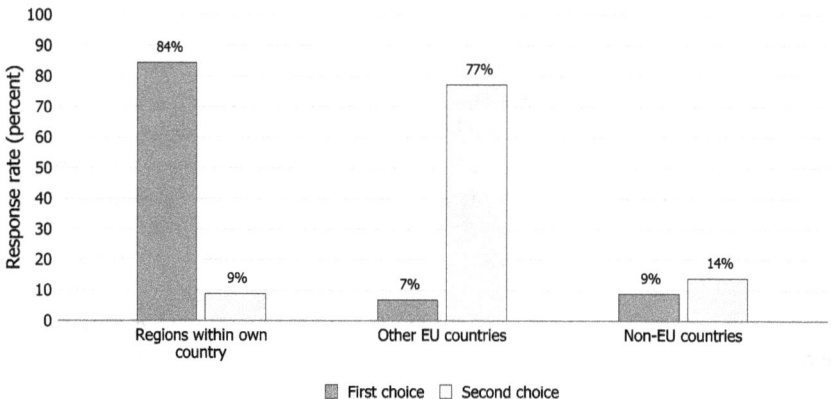

Figure 3.4 Response rates regarding who should receive emergency assistance first.

Source: TESS 2016, own calculations.

When we compare these responses to answers from Figure 3.2, it is striking that the willingness to prioritise EU countries first when expressing solidarity is significantly lower and does not differ from the levels of support for solidarity with non-EU countries. This means that, when push comes to shove, solidarity with the respondents' own nation remains supreme, even among those who would otherwise fundamentally support internal European solidarity. We conducted further analyses in which country-by-country differences were investigated (figure for the results not provided). This analysis shows that citizens of all countries agreed that in an emergency they would opt for 'the nation first'.[10] The percentage of those who would prioritise their own country first does not vary much between the peak rating of 88% in Poland, Portugal, and Spain and the lowest rating of 78% in Sweden, while the proportions of those who rate the European space as the first priority ranges between 3% (Spain) and 11% (the Netherlands).

Yet, in the second part of the scenario, where we asked respondents what space should be the second priority, the picture changed considerably. Here, the majority of respondents opted in favour of assisting crisis-affected EU countries. Only a small number of respondents took a purely cosmopolitan position of choosing to help countries outside of the EU. Through this, we can see that the respondents do seem to draw a line in their solidarity: from the citizens' point of view members of European society should also receive support from the wider community, with this precise version of community ending at the EU's external borders.

What does this result mean in light of the socio-philosophical debate sketched out in Chapter 2 between communitarians and cosmopolitans? While the cosmopolitans contend that, in its normative essence, solidarity is a universal phenomenon, the communitarians argue that solidarity should always be expressed in relation to a real, existing community. According to them, the more strongly established a community is, the more solidarity can be expected from members of this community. As the nation state persists as the social space with the thickest interactions between people in spite of processes of globalisation and Europeanisation, it seems perfectly legitimate from a communitarian point of view for national solidarity to be more pronounced than European or global solidarity. At the same time, the interactions of citizens in European Union territory are significantly thicker than the interconnectedness shared between the citizens and their nation states in the global space. Therefore, from a cosmopolitan perspective, it is normatively justifiable when citizens also wish to show more solidarity with their European neighbours. Nevertheless, empirical findings support the communitarian stance on the delimitations of solidarity. The nation state remains the definitive space of solidarity, which receives first priority from European citizens. However, from these citizens' perspectives, the EU does also represent a distinct space of solidarity that is clearly delimited from a world community.

3.2.2 The willingness to engage in country-specific fiscal solidarity

In our analysis so far, we have largely ignored the concrete conditions facing countries in need of financial assistance. These contextual conditions can, however, have an influence on attitudes towards solidarity too. After all, the countries that face economic crises are not abstract social constructs, but actual countries, which differ from one another in a plethora of distinctive respects.[11] It is not within the scope of this study to investigate the influence that these mani-fold contextual conditions have on attitudes towards fiscal solidarity. Instead, in this section we seek to determine whether and to what extent EU citizens differ-entiate between different countries on the question of who should receive support in a crisis. The answer to this question has some rather practical implications for policies. The more that citizens wish to exclude certain countries from European solidarity, the more conflict-laden the political ordeals these countries will face in times of crisis. We name this domain of solidarity *the willingness to engage in country-specific fiscal solidarity* (Lengfeld et al. 2014), bringing this study in conjunction with a previous one.

What do we know about the willingness to engage in country-specific fiscal solidarity so far? At the height of the sovereign debt crisis in 2012, Holger Lengfeld and colleagues collected data on the willingness to engage in country-specific fiscal solidarity in Germany and Portugal (Lengfeld et al. 2014, 2015). The participants were prompted to answer whether their own country should be required to give financial assistance to Ireland, Greece, Spain, Italy, and Portugal (only surveyed within Germany). The findings showed that more than 70% of the respondents from Portugal would allow assistance to be extended to all of the mentioned countries. Even the majority of German respondents were in favour of helping every country except Greece. In that case, only a mere 38% agreed to provide financial assistance. An experiment conducted in Germany by Michael M. Bechtel and colleagues (2017) in 2012 supports the findings. Here, too, participants differentiated between countries when determining which country should receive bailout payments. The study reported relatively high approval rates for supporting Ireland, Spain, and Italy (in order of degree of approval), but significantly lower rates for Greece. Nevertheless, both studies have several drawbacks: they have a limited number of surveyed countries but also a limited configura-tion of theoretical givers and recipients.

The selection of the countries, which the respondents were asked to assess, comprised 12 of our 13 surveyed countries in the TESS (France excluded) and also the United Kingdom.[12] To avoid respondent fatigue, we did not ask particip-ants to make an assessment of all 13 countries and instead provided each of them with six different countries respectively, among which two countries were selected from each of the three country groups. These countries were also sorted according to the rate at which they were affected by the euro crisis.[13]

The questions were formulated as follows (example for random respondent):

> *I will now read out a list of EU countries. Please tell me for each country whether or not it should receive financial support in times of crisis. What about ...?*
>
> ... *Greece?*
> ... *Ireland?*
> ... *Hungary?*
> ... *Slovakia?*
> ... *Austria?*
> ... *Sweden?*

In order to simplify the interpretation, we grouped the countries according to whether they belong to one of the 'old' western European EU countries (Ireland excluded), a former or current debtor country, or one of the 'new' eastern European EU countries. Figure 3.5 shows that across the whole sample (see 'total' column) the majority of respondents were in favour of supporting the specified countries in times of crisis. Moreover, we can see that there is in fact a rank order of willingness to engage in solidarity. Two-thirds of the respondents were willing to help crisis-affected countries or eastern European countries. In contrast, the willingness to express solidarity with the wealthier northern and western European countries was considerably lower. It is worth noting that when we broke down the answers by country (not depicted) the United Kingdom was the only country that the majority of respondents would not be willing to help. Because our surveys took place shortly before or after the EU referendum in the

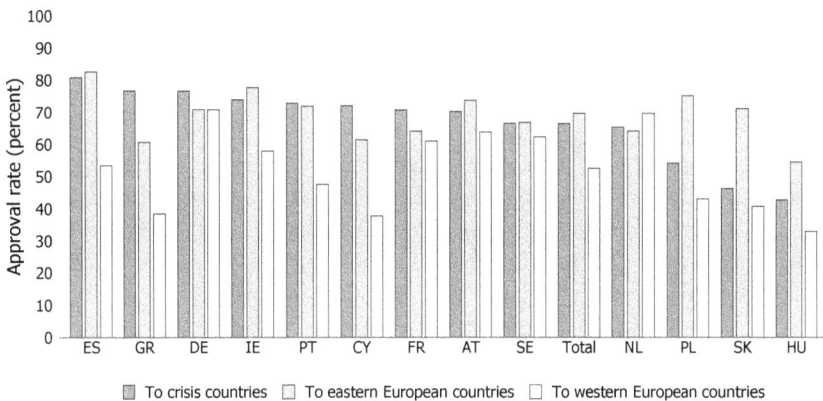

Figure 3.5 Average approval rates of emergency assistance to specific EU countries.

Source: TESS 2016, own calculations.

UK, we interpreted this result as an effect of the public discourse on Brexit. From the EU citizens' perspective, if a country's government allows its people to vote on leaving the EU, then this country should no longer be entitled to solidarity from the wider community.

What might motivate the viewpoints that allow citizens to determine which countries ought to be helped at all? Even without empirically measuring the different motives that we differentiated in Chapter 2, the results displayed in Figure 3.5 seem to correspond with the following interpretation: the attitudes of citizens from debtor countries and eastern European countries seemed to be determined by an underlying instrumentally rational motive. This was evident in countries' tendencies to more frequently show greater solidarity towards other countries that shared a similar economic situation as their own. The attitudes of western European citizens, on the other hand, seem to indicate an underlying value-rational motive, oriented around the principle of neediness. The more in need a country is, in their point of view, the greater support it will need. Indeed, there appeared to be two subtypes of needs: on one hand, the needs of a country due to a specific crisis (Ireland, Spain, Portugal, Greece, and Cyprus), and on the other hand, the neediness of a country due to its evidently low living standards, compared to the EU average (Slovakia, Poland, and Hungary).

Here, too, we can draw an interim conclusion: our analysis shows that EU citizens would support countries even if they are receiving EU assistance, are not acutely threatened by crises (Germany, the Netherlands, Austria, Slovakia), or are not members of the Eurozone (Poland, Sweden, Hungary). We interpret the difference between former debtor countries and non-crisis-affected countries as a consequence of the instrumentally rational orientation of European citizens. Those who have already experienced the effects of an economic crisis in their own country are far more receptive to external help, as this keeps them secure in the event of any other crises developing in future.

3.2.3 When solidarity comes at a price: citizens' individual readiness to pay

Showing solidarity with others can be considered costly and demanding. In the case of the European bailout packages there is a risk of defaulting on loans, with the consequences then striking the givers of solidarity or their community in general. However, the question regarding how and to what extent individual citizens would be willing to be directly involved in covering the costs remains open. If a country failed to repay its debts and the creditor country were to then stand in as guarantor for the granted securities, these debts would then substantially burden the national budget of the creditor country. The potential creditor country would then have less money available for its own expenses, investments, and debt-servicing requirements. It is difficult to predict in advance just how these budget restrictions would affect individual citizens exactly. It would be quite a different matter if all EU citizens were to directly finance assistance measures from their own taxes, assuming that they all have an income. Currently, there is no such direct burden on individual wealth endowments. A burden of this kind would, however, emerge if the European Union or the nation state were to raise taxes, with revenues ring-fenced for the financing of European bailout measures. Such a solidarity tax would not be a far stretch from what is already practised in reality, as this would resemble contributions that citizens in some states have to pay towards regional redistribution.[14]

Yet a European solidarity tax that would be assessed according to the rate of income exists only as a thought experiment. This would be a direct, earmarked tax with its contributions flowing into a European fund for combatting future debt crises. But would a majority of our respondents in our survey countries support such a tax? And how high a tax rate would they accept? It is clear that such a tax would directly place a heavy burden upon the population. But as we elucidated in Chapter 2, a further criterion for the existence of a European solidarity is that European citizens do not just verbally declare their non-binding commitment to solidarity, but that they are also willing to take on the costs this would entail. Therefore, we understand the sketched-out scenario as an effective test of individual solidarity.

Despite the optimistic picture that the findings in this chapter so far have painted, we do not believe that there are many other indications that the majority of EU citizens would accept a European solidarity tax. For one thing, taxes (particularly newly introduced ones) are a great social nuisance. In addition to perceiving them as taking money away from their own personal budgets, citizens do not know whether these compulsory payments will benefit them, even in the long term. Tax compliance research shows some indication that willingness to pay taxes depends, among other things, on citizens using and valuing the public good that their taxes finance (e.g. Alm and Torgler 2011; Torgler 2007). In this case, taxpayers are more prepared to state how much they truly value their incomes when assessing the tax base.

However, it is still unclear whether the contributor could expect returns on their payments in future in the event of there being an EU tax for emergency assistance. For some countries, it is highly improbable that they will ever experience a debt crisis themselves, while for others it is ever more likely. Because of the structure of their economies, northern and western European countries are very unlikely to face the same problems in future that the southern European countries have faced in the past. When considered from an instrumentally rational perspective, this means that citizens of western European creditor countries would be more likely to take a more critical position towards a solidarity tax than they would towards general and country-specific solidarity, as detailed in the preceding sections of this chapter. We also expected citizens of the three eastern European countries in our survey to object most strongly to the tax for the reason that 'The poor should not have to pay for the rich.' High rates of approval were only expected to occur in countries that have received EU bailout funds (Greece, Ireland, Portugal, and Cyprus) or in countries that would be among the beneficiaries of the solidarity tax due to their persistently high levels of debt and low rates of economic growth (Spain).[15]

There is one study that has used the idea of a solidarity tax in a manner comparable to our own.[16] In an online survey carried out in Germany in 2014, Florian Stoeckel and Theresa Kuhn (2018) asked respondents about the preferred degree of a solidarity tax if 'introduced to counteract economic imbalances in the EU'; respondents had to choose a value between 0.0% and 10.0% in their answer. The findings showed a mean value of 1.3%, although the number of respondents refusing to pay anything was not specified (see Stoeckel and Kuhn 2018, table A.3).

We measured the individual willingness to pay solidarity taxes as follows. We described a hypothetical situation of there being a European solidarity fund and then suggested three possible tax rates to them (3%, 2%, and 0.5%), which they would need to pay from their own personal monthly incomes.[17] To ensure respondents understood what we meant, we also attached an absolute minimum contribution (in national currencies) to go along with these tax rates.[18] The respondents were then required to state whether they agreed with paying the tax rate or minimum contribution in question (by answering yes or no). For example, the following question was posed to the Hungarian participants.

And now imagine the following situation. To fight against future debt crises, every Member State of the European Union has to contribute to a European solidarity fund. This money will only be used to fight economic crises in EU countries with severe financial problems. Would you personally be willing to pay 3% of your income, but at least 4,000 Forint per month to this fund?
  Yes.
  No.
  (Refuse to pay anything).
  And what about 2% of your income, but at least 2,500 Forint per month?
  Yes.
  No.
  (Refuse to pay anything).
  And what about 0.5% of your income, but at least 600 Forint per month?
  Yes.
  No.
  (Refuse to pay anything).

The first suggestion contained the tax rate of 3%. The lower tax rates were not proposed to respondents who accepted the highest tax rate, as lower tax rates inherently already include the highest tax rate. These respondents' answers were coded in the data set as if they had accepted each and every one of the tax rates. If the respondent rejected the proposed tax rate, the next lowest tax rate was then presented to them, with the same procedure repeated. This means that all the respondents were asked about the first tax rate but that not all of them were asked about the second and third tax rates.[19]

Figure 3.6 shows that, surprisingly, more than half of the respondents would accept at least one of the three tax rates (see left column). Of these, 34% of respondents said they would pay the highest given tax rate of 3%. Nineteen per cent of those surveyed were in favour of the lowest tax rate of 0.5%, and 8% were in favour of the tax of 2%. This result once again signifies an unexpectedly high degree of support for European fiscal solidarity. Indeed, it barely differs from the support recorded for the general willingness to engage in fiscal solidarity, which we saw in Figure 3.2 (with over 60% of those surveyed exhibiting this general solidarity). Nevertheless, this is just a scenario and not a prognosis of an actual willingness to pay. As there was no real initiative in the EU Commission or at the level of the EU Council to discuss such a tax at the time of this study, these findings ought to be interpreted with some caution.[20]

Figure 3.7 shows the acceptance rates for each country. The first notable statistic is the cumulative proportion of citizens who would be willing to pay one of the three tax rates. Apart from the French, a slight majority of whom rejected all the tax rates, and the Hungarians, who only just accepted any tax rate at all by a slight majority, in all other countries the majority of respondents were willing to

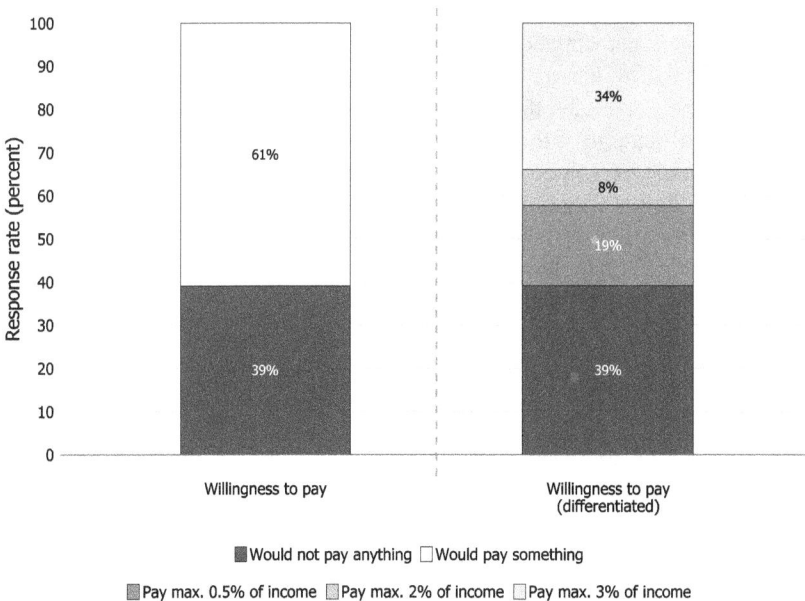

Figure 3.6 Individual willingness to pay into a solidarity fund for financial assistance.

Source: TESS 2016, own calculations.

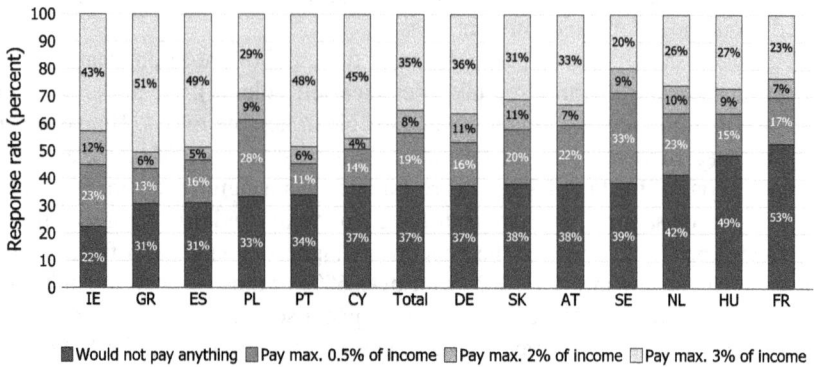

Figure 3.7 Individual willingness to pay into a solidarity fund for financial assistance by country.

Source: TESS 2016, own calculations.

pay. Nevertheless, it is evident that the willingness to pay was unequivocally highest in the (former) crisis countries. The five front-runners for willingness to pay are the five debtor countries, with only Poland ranking high on this metric and thus disrupting the pattern with its similarly above-average approval rates. Following on from our argument above, it seems that citizens' solidarity in debtor countries is motivated by instrumental rationality. Since future debt crises are more probable in their countries than in those of western and northern Europe, their appreciation of solidarity is thoroughly rational. Even the distribution of agreement to each of the tax rates underlines this interpretation. Hence, we find the highest approval rates for the willingness to pay 3% of income in the crisis-affected countries (43% to 51%). In contrast, for the four western and two other eastern European countries in the sample, we find no clear pattern that could be associated with any of the motives for willingness to engage in solidarity.

3.2.4 Austerity – what do citizens expect from the recipient countries?

Those who are prepared to help others in an emergency can expect certain reciprocal actions from them in return. One of these expected actions is for recipients to get back on their feet in the long run. This also applies to fiscal solidarity. In exchange for the loans they received, the bailed-out countries were required to fulfil certain conditions defined by the creditor countries. These conditions, known as austerity measures (Monastiriotis et al. 2013), were supposed to reduce the rate of national debt and deficit, allowing the economy to grow again. The specific policies to achieve this ranged from the privatisation of state assets, to the deregulation and flexibilisation of national (labour) markets. Likewise, they included downsizing public servants and cutting back on welfare state provisions (Schelkle 2017: chapter 6). The so-called troika (consisting of the EU Commission, the ECB, and the IMF) negotiated a separate austerity programme for each bailed-out country, with each programme containing concrete 'reform measures'.[21] Portugal, for example, requested help from the European Financial Stability Facility (EFSF) in early 2011. The austerity measures negotiated with Portugal consisted of, among other things, cutting spending in the education and health sectors, reducing the time limit allowed for obtaining unemployment benefits, slashing pensions, and flexibilising working time arrangements. In addition, there were also measures designed to reduce the number of employees in the public sector and raise tax yields (Council of the European Union 2011). Greece, Ireland, and Cyprus were also required to implement similar measures (Ladi 2014; Monastiriotis et al. 2013; Schelkle 2017: chapter 6).

A thorough discussion of the appropriateness of austerity measures – on whether they were fair and just or whether they caused more harm than good – is not within the remit of this chapter. We are more concerned with analysing citizens' attitudes towards austerity. We assume that these austerity measures are a central field of conflict between citizens of the creditor countries and the citizens of bailed-out countries. Large protests against austerity were staged in all the debtor countries by members of the general public, trade unions, and opposition parties, often in the form of general strikes.[22] Even the governments of the debtor countries, most notably Greece, opposed the implementation of austerity measures (Gerodimos 2013; Hardiman and Reagan 2013; Kriesi 2012; Rogers and Vasilopoulou 2012). Yet we know very little about what citizens in the Eurozone's creditor countries think about austerity measures. Using an experimental design, Michael M. Bechtel and colleagues (2017) surveyed German respondents who had to choose among bailout programmes with different conditions for the receiving country. While demanding reductions in public spending went along with a growing acceptance of a bailout programme, people more often rejected programmes that sought to reduce the number of workers in the public sector. Although citizens obviously distinguish between different austerity measures, the results must be interpreted with caution as the experiment was fielded in only one creditor country.

We presume that citizens from (potential) creditor countries adopted a stance directly opposed to citizens from debtor countries and supported the austerity measures in principle. One of their major motives could be the belief that it is each state's own responsibility to assist itself. By this logic, debtor countries should mobilise all the forces at their disposal in order to tackle the sovereign debt crisis, or to put it differently, solidarity should be extended to those who engage in efforts to become financially independent in the medium term in return for receiving financial assistance.

Nevertheless, it is important to consider that different actors in a society will be affected in various ways by the different measures. The cuts to welfare-state provision and the increases in value-added tax (VAT), for instance, affect the most socially vulnerable groups as well as parts of the middle classes most severely. In contrast, higher taxes on capital gains and property put a heavier load on companies and members of the upper classes. With cuts to public service expenditures and the privatisation of state companies, it is unclear whether this has led to growth in social inequality. However, if austerity measures were to impact social inequality, this could then lead to variations in citizens' willingness to support the measures based on how they and their social group have been affected. This means that, regardless of whether a citizen's country is affected by the sovereign debt crisis or not, their views on the different austerity measures could turn out to be quite divergent. For this reason, we assumed that attitudes towards some of the austerity measures related to the motives for solidarity that we outlined in the second chapter: solidarity out of self-interest, out of an affectual bond to a community, and out of value-rational motives. The question is, to what extent do the citizens share a grounded, value-rational principle of solidarity that is founded on an acknowledgement of the needs of the individual? Our assumption is that the more strongly citizens – particularly those from creditor countries – reject austerity measures, which affect the most vulnerable members of society more than other social groups or organisations, the more plausible is that their willingness to engage in fiscal solidarity is grounded on value rationality and on the principle of need, because the need principle states that the weakest in a society should not be made to carry a heavier burden.

In the TESS survey, we provided the respondents with a short list of austerity measures, which countries in crisis would be required to fulfil should they wish to receive financial assistance from the EU. The measures that we assumed would put more of a strain on the socially weaker groups were cuts to welfare spending and increases in VAT.[23] In contrast, the increases in property tax would predominantly affect the more socially affluent classes. Some of the other policies assessed by the respondents included the raising of the age for receiving a statutory pension and the reductions in the number of public servants.

> *There are certain measures countries in crisis have to take in order to get financial support from the European Union. Please tell me for each measure to what extent you agree or disagree that countries in crisis should take them in order to get financial support from the EU.*
>   *Increase value-added tax*
>   *Raise wealth tax*
>   *Cut social spending*
>   *Raise the retirement age*
>   *Reduce the number of employees in the public sector*
>   *(totally agree, tend to agree, tend to disagree, totally disagree)*

Figure 3.8 shows that just two of the five austerity measures had majority approval among the respondents. A significant majority of respondents were in

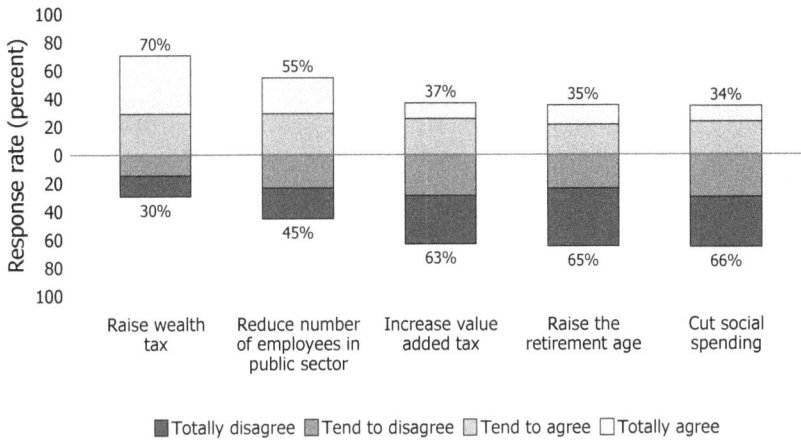

Figure 3.8 Response rates for conditions for receiving financial assistance.
Source: TESS 2016, own calculations.

favour of raising the wealth tax rate, while only a slight majority (55%) of the participants favoured cutting jobs in the public sector. Around two-thirds of citizens rejected cutting social welfare provision and raising VAT; note that these measures would disproportionately affect disadvantaged social groups. The evidence therefore indicates that citizens' willingness to engage in fiscal solidarity is based predominantly on value-rational motives. It appears that citizens are in favour of the stronger members of society – those who possess property – making a greater contribution to solving the crisis than those who are dependent on state help in crisis-affected countries, whatever the background.

The respondents in our survey also rejected the raising of the age for receiving a statutory pension. Although this measure does not directly contribute to the widening of social inequality, the citizens' hostile stance towards this policy is further indicative of value-rational motives. Elderly people are seen as one of the main groups of vulnerable people in society (as we will see in Chapter 5) and therefore we cannot expect and accept them to bear an extra load in the form of a deferred age of retirement.

What role does holding citizenship in a specific EU country play in forming attitudes towards austerity? In Figure 3.9 we broke down the participants' answers by country and charted their approval levels for two measures that have opposing effects on social inequality: specifically, cuts to social spending and the raising of taxes on wealth. We observed that citizens from the creditor countries and Sweden (which is not in the Eurozone) had the highest approval rates for raising the wealth tax, while the majority of citizens from the bailed-out countries uniformly rejected these measures. One exception is Ireland, whose citizens were also in favour of raising the wealth tax rate. The overall picture

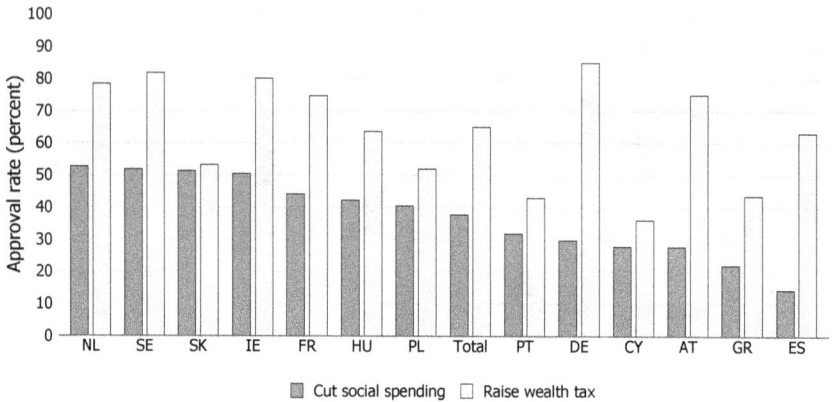

Figure 3.9 Average approval rates for selected conditions for receiving financial assistance by country.

Source: TESS 2016, own calculations.

looks quite different when we look at cuts to social provision. We discovered that the highest relative rates were in Sweden, the Netherlands, and France, but also in Slovakia and in the bailed-out country of Ireland. In contrast, more than 70% of German and Austrian respondents rejected cuts to social provision, with equally high or even higher rates of rejection found elsewhere in Spain, Greece, Portugal, and Cyprus. Upon comparing the results on both measures, it is apparent that citizens of southern European debtor countries make virtually no distinction between the measures, but rather reject both at an equally high rate instead. In the other countries, however, citizens make a clear distinction between the policies. The evidence partially supports the presumption that we expressed at the beginning of this section, according to which attitudes to austerity generally signal a split between European citizens. What is clear is that citizens from debtor countries generally reject demands for budget cuts. However, citizens of the other countries – both creditor countries and countries that are not in the Eurozone – clearly differ extensively in how they apply value-rational criteria to the issue of which measures can be expected of debtor countries.

3.3 Divided over European fiscal solidarity?

So far, our analysis has brought to light the surprisingly high degree of willingness to engage in solidarity in Europe, both within each country as well as across Europe as a whole. Citizens' willingness to meet the costs in the form of tax hikes also seems to be reflected in this accordingly. However, it does not suffice to simply determine solidarity on the basis of majority support alone, for underneath the apparently approving majority, there may be small, structurally homogenous minorities who stand in clear opposition to the majority while still supporting the notion of helping countries in crisis. These minorities may possess considerable potential for political mobilisation. Parties, interest groups, and social movements that reject European institutions for fiscal solidarity can appeal to these minorities and use them for their own political aims. The attitudes of opponents to solidarity can thus influence political movements and policies regarding crisis support. For these reasons, it is important that we investigate whether social and political cleavages have emerged between European citizens in terms of their willingness to engage in solidarity. In answering this question our research draws on the literature on social and political cleavages, which is largely based on the seminal works of Seymour M. Lipset and Stein Rokkan (1967). This debate has experienced a resurgence in recent years thanks to a series of studies that have investigated the impact of European integration and globalisation processes on the formation of new cleavages (Bornschier 2010; Börzel and Risse 2018; Gerhards and Lengfeld 2015; Grande and Kriesi 2015, 2016; Hooghe and Marks 2009, 2018; Hutter, Grande, and Kriesi 2016; Inglehart and Norris 2016; Kriesi et al. 2012). In the first two chapters of this book, we have already outlined the basic premises of cleavage theory and the terminological differences between social and political cleavages. We now apply them to examine fiscal solidarity's potential for conflict and politicisation. This occurs in several steps: in the first step, we will formulate some assumptions on the possible factors that can lead to the formation of social (structural and cultural) cleavages regarding European fiscal solidarity. We will then test these arguments in a multivariate analysis. In the final step, we will investigate whether social cleavages are translated into political cleavages by analysing how likely it is for attitudes on fiscal solidarity to influence citizens' voting behaviour. To what extent do supporters and opponents of fiscal solidarity support different political parties and fuel political conflict around European solidarity? Of particular interest is whether a person's refusal to support European countries in crisis goes hand in hand with them supporting any of the new, right-wing populist parties that have been formed in many EU countries in recent years and have enjoyed a substantial increase in popularity and votes since.

3.3.1 Structural cleavages

From our point of view, there are three different hypotheses on how a citizen's socio-economic status can influence support for European fiscal solidarity. Even if the three hypotheses contradict one another to some degree, one thing that they do share is their suggestion that citizens may be instrumentally rationally motivated – especially through economic incentives – when assessing questions of solidarity.

(1) In the research on attitudes towards redistribution and solidarity at the national level, the following argument is commonly made: people with a poor socio-economic status – i.e. people who belong to a lower social class, who have limited human capital at their disposal, who earn low incomes, or are unemployed – are more supportive of national solidarity than people in higher social

classes. The more socially vulnerable groups expect and hope that their national governments will act to improve national citizens' life opportunities. Furthermore, they themselves stand to gain from such solidarity measures (de Beer 2012; Edlund 2007; Ingensiep 2016). In case of international bailouts, however, research shows that people with a higher socio-economic status are more willing to support financial assistance for countries in crisis than citizens with a lower socio-economic status (effect of income; Bauhr and Charron 2018), effect of education (Bauhr and Charron 2018; Kleider and Stoeckel 2019; Kuhn, Solaz, and van Elsas 2018; Verhaegen 2018), and social class (Kleider and Stoeckel 2019; Kuhn et al. 2018). Studies investigating support for European integration found similar effects,[24] which can be explained by citizens' self-interest (Hobolt and de Vries 2016a:420): individuals who benefit from the EU and the liberalised market, such as more highly educated individuals in better positions, will more likely support European integration because they have a higher utility. Because of that, they may also be more interested in strengthening and helping other EU member states, as they may fear a weakening of the EU and the market, and hence of their own benefits. Following this argument, we expected people who are more socially disadvantaged to be more likely to oppose fiscal solidarity on both the national and the European level than people who are more affluent. We empirically verified this correlation by calculating the effect that *individual* socio-economic characteristics had on attitudes towards fiscal solidarity. If the hypothesis proves to be correct, then the indicators considered should be able to predict attitudes towards national and European solidarity in broadly the same way.

(2) Another perspective on the subject is that survey participants may not only have their personal socio-economic interests in mind when responding to such survey questions. On the question of European financial assistance, they may also consider the economic condition of their country: the less affluent a country is, the more its citizens will refuse fiscal transfers and argue that scarce resources should be used for national purposes first. From their point of view, solving other EU countries' debt crises is a secondary matter, because the welfare of their own country is their priority. This argument is supported by recent research. Using EES data from 2014, Theresa Kuhn and colleagues (2018) as well as Hanna Kleider and Florian Stoeckel (2019) have shown that fiscal support for European states in need is positively correlated with the affluence of the respondents' country. We tested this relationship empirically on the macro level by calculating the influence that a country's gross domestic product (GDP), its rate of indebtedness, and its status as either a net creditor or net recipient of assistance during the crisis had on attitudes towards fiscal solidarity.

(3) A third structural cleavage may result from the combined influence of an individual citizen's social standing and their country's overall standard of living. Socially deprived people from poorer, crisis-affected countries have experienced the harsh consequences of the sovereign debt crisis, as the crisis was often followed by severe cutbacks in the social programmes that these individuals are

reliant on. Hanna Kleider and Florian Stoeckel (2019) suggest that this experience may amplify the negative association between social status and support for EU transfers. The reverse can be expected to apply to economically well-off people living in wealthier – ergo (potential) creditor – countries. We expect them to be the most supportive of European solidarity. The third hypothesis that we formulate here is measured by calculating the interactions between the above-listed macro and micro variables.

To test these formulated hypotheses, we used a series of indicators in our analysis. We quantified individual socio-economic status by measuring the following statistics: (a) the education level of the respondent (none or primary education, secondary, and tertiary education); (b) the occupational class according to the class scheme plotted by Robert Erikson and John H. Goldthorpe (1992; with seven classes); (c) the respondent's disposable income (in euro and purchasing power parity, logarithmised); (d) employment status (employed, unemployed) at the time of the survey. To determine the country's standard of living in our analysis, we took GDP into account as a global measurement of societal wealth as well as the country's degree of indebtedness and its status in the sovereign debt crisis (did the country receive loans, provide loans, or neither of the two?).[25]

3.3.2 Cultural cleavages

Solidarity cannot simply be motivated by economic self-interest alone. As Chapter 2 describes, people's individual values and their emotional bond to a specific community can also have a profound influence. As different studies have shown, citizens' political beliefs represent an interpretive framework through which they can assess specific political events related to the European Union and its institutions, such as the bailout issue (among others, Bauhr and Charron 2018; Ciornei and Recci 2017; de Vries and Edwards 2009; Díez Medrano et al. 2019; Kleider and Stoeckel 2019; Fuchs and Klingemann 1990; Gerhards and Lengfeld 2015; Hooghe and Marks 2009; Hutter et al. 2016; Kuhn et al. 2018; Stoeckel and Kuhn 2018; Verhaegen 2018). Of special significance in this context is the political-ideological orientation of citizens and hence the question of whether they prefer to align themselves with the left or right wing of the political spectrum. In this respect, we assume that people who perceive themselves as conservative/right wing are more likely to see the nation state as the primary, and perhaps even the only, legitimate space of solidarity. Right-wing people are thereby more likely to regard crisis assistance as a threat to national sovereignty; they are thus more likely to reject European solidarity than people on the left or in the political centre-ground (Díez Medrano et al. 2019; Kuhn et al. 2018; Verhaegen 2018; evidence for Eurobonds is provided in Daniele and Geys 2015).[26] In contrast, people positioning themselves on the left wing of the spectrum will likely relate to ideas of equality, solidarity, socialism, and internationalism (Fuchs and Klingemann 1990); thus left-wing people are more likely to be strongly in favour of fiscal solidarity.[27] We gauged the political orientations of our respondents by means of a self-assessment whereby the respondents were asked to locate themselves on the left–right scale.

Furthermore, we assume that people who are emotionally bound to Europe and who identify themselves as Europeans will be more strongly in favour of European fiscal solidarity because they perceive Europe as a real community. Empirical research has proven this to be an important factor in explaining attitudes towards European fiscal solidarity as we measure it (Kuhn et al. 2018; Verhaegen 2018) but also for attitudes towards Eurobonds (Ciornei and Recchi 2017:10). The reverse also applies: people who feel exclusively connected to their own nation state and who thus identify with this space alone and reject Europe as a space of identity are more likely to be against European fiscal solidarity (Kleider and Stoeckel 2019; Kuhn and Stoeckel 2014; Verhaegen 2018). People with a purely cosmopolitan orientation who identify with a world society are a rather intriguing case. For this group, solidarity has no territorial bounds but rather depends entirely upon the neediness of the individual (Benhabib 2004; Pogge 2008; see also Chapter 2). In their survey of six countries, Juan Díez Medrano and colleagues (2019) showed that cosmopolitan orientations correlate positively with approval rates for the establishment of EU bailout funds. Recent studies analysing EES data from 2014 supported this finding (Bauhr and Charron 2018; Kleider and Stoeckel 2019). These results were further supported by research conducted by Theresa Kuhn and colleagues (2018). Using an experimental setting, they showed that participants holding attitudes related to cosmopolitanism were willing to spend more money to support other Europeans than other participants. Applied to the euro crisis, this means that cosmopolitans should see the overcoming of the aforementioned prohibition on emergency bailouts as a step in the right direction. The bailouts mark a break from the constraints of a hitherto, confined national solidarity, making it more feasible to extend solidarity to the whole world. Therefore, cosmopolitans should be more likely to be more in favour of European fiscal solidarity than people who claim a stronger national identity. Yet this step will likely not go far enough for cosmopolitans, because the access to European financial assistance does not extend to anywhere beyond the EU's external border. For that reason, we assumed that cosmopolitans would agree with fiscal solidarity to a lesser extent than those who identify foremost as Europeans. We measured the strength of citizens' bonds to different spatial units by asking them about the extent to which they identify with their nation state, Europe, and the world.

On the subject of political values, it is also plausible that the above-mentioned effects would be strengthened or weakened by countries' various contextual conditions. We might therefore expect that left-wing people who lived in wealthier countries – i.e. countries that had not experienced a debt crisis or had a low rate of indebtedness – to be likely to support the idea of European solidarity more strongly than people who shared the same disposition but lived in less well-off countries. The argument is that left-leaning citizens would prefer international redistribution, as their country has the socio-economic means to support others, while left-leaning people in poorer countries would prefer resources to be redistributed within their country rather than helping other countries in need. Empirical findings support this expectation, as they found a positive interaction of support for domestic redistribution – their measure for left–right political position – and the wealth of a country (Kleider and Stoeckel 2019:15).

3.3.3 Notes on methodology

To test our assumptions, we used the items on generalised willingness to engage in fiscal solidarity, which we are familiar with from Section 3.2. We used the indicators for structural cleavages outlined above as independent variables alongside other control variables, which we will describe in more detail below. Our guiding assumption is that the greater the effects of these predictors, the bigger the potential for conflict will be as a result of the gulf in attitudes between our survey participants.

In addition, we carried out an analysis that used the respondents' positions on subnational financial assistance as the dependent variable with the same predictors before comparing the direction of effects at both territorial levels (on the basis of the signs) and the proportion of the variances that are revealed. Through this, we observed whether the topic of European fiscal solidarity was more controversial and therefore more likely to lead to conflict than subnational fiscal solidarity.

In the following section, we utilise a multi-step analytical process. To keep the procedure as simple as possible, we considered the different item scales of different forms of solidarity as quasi-metric and thus employed the ordinary least square (OLS) regression method.[28] We investigated the factors that can influence the attitudes of citizens on two levels: the individual level and the aggregate level of all the countries. Furthermore, we checked the cross-level interactions between the two levels. In order to identify country-specific influencing factors, we used a two-step regression analysis (Bryan and Jenkins 2016) in which we first estimated regressions for country samples, before analysing the coefficients that result from these as dependent variables in the second step.[29]

In the first part of the causal analysis, we carried out OLS regressions in an incrementally expanding order of magnitude, with the aim of identifying factors among the entire European population that could explain the willingness to engage in fiscal solidarity on both the European and the national level. In doing this, we additionally controlled for participants' age, gender, number of children in the household, migration background, and their country of residence (these are the dummy variables). Since all the participants were nested in their respective countries, and given that observations within each country were therefore not independent of one another, we calculated cluster-adjusted standard errors in pooled OLS models.

In the second part of the causal analysis, we turned our attention to explaining country-by-country differences. Within the country samples, we had a sufficiently large number of individual cases in our sample. Yet, for the regressions on the macro level, we only had 13 countries. For the analysis, we first analysed the unstandardised coefficients for the countries' dummy variables, which were calculated in the individual regression models and controlled for by the covariates. From then on, we used these country dummy coefficients controlled for by individual characteristics as dependent variables. We depicted some specifically selected results in charts, which allowed us to clearly describe both the general correlation and the particularities specific to each country/country group. Additionally, we then calculated OLS regressions with the country dummy coefficients as the dependent variables and the contextual distinctions as explanatory factors in order to stochastically test the observable correlations. To keep the number of degrees of freedom as high as possible, we restricted ourselves to a maximum of two contextual features per model. In addition, we raise the alpha error to a level of 10% due to the low probability of the null hypothesis being rejected with such a low number of cases.

In the third step of the analysis, we ascertained the postulated cross-level interaction effects based on two-step regression models. We tested whether the individual variable effects vary between the countries and whether this variance is due to the contextual features that we previously considered. We first carried out OLS regressions for each country separately, considering all the above-named covariates on the individual level in the process. Through this, we obtained coefficients for every covariate in each respective country sample. The coefficients of individual variables were subsequently deployed as dependent variables in the model and clarified by considering country-specific features. This is in line with the basic idea behind the two-step approach, where 'the first level parameters across units are themselves the quantities to be accounted for by macro-level features' (Achen 2005:448). Because we treated the estimated coefficients of the country samples as dependent variables, we were able to determine the extent to which their variance can be attributed to the influence of macro variables in this procedure.

At this point, it is necessary to expand upon how we treat countries in our analysis. In this and in the other empirical chapters of the book, we treat countries as a unit consisting of a set of shared socio-economic characteristics (e.g. GDP per capita; government debt). However, by classifying countries based on these characteristics, we risk ignoring the specific historical development patterns of individual countries. Some comparative social sciences scholars have stressed the importance of the historical, path-dependent development of individual countries. These scholars criticise approaches that treat countries as a crude complex of variables (Mahoney 2004). We agree with this critique in principle, although we still believe that both methodologies are compatible. A systematic, comparative analysis such as ours can offer a rough sketch of the differences between countries, but they cannot replace a complete historical approach including microanalyses of particular conditions. Ultimately, we decided that our study would not take the historical developmental paths of individual societies into account and that, in consequence, the explanatory power of our findings will be limited.

3.3.4 Results on social cleavages

Table 3.1 displays the results on social cleavages between citizens at the overall European level. Let us first look at models M1 to M3, which gauged the willingness of citizens to engage in European solidarity at an incrementally expanding spatial scale. The first point to highlight is that, in contrast to the findings of studies using the EES we presented earlier (Bauhr and Charron 2018; Kleider and Stoeckel 2019; Kuhn et al. 2018; Verhaegen 2018), our findings showed that the socio-economic variables did not have a significant influence on willingness to engage in solidarity. Therefore, we can conclude that instrumentally rational motives hardly played a role in influencing citizens' views on fiscal solidarity. The single feature that did have an effect concerns people who completed secondary education. These people had a slightly lower willingness to engage in solidarity than those who completed tertiary education. Contrary to our predictions, there was no evident difference between those with just a primary education and those with a tertiary education. Also, as far as indicators of occupational class position were concerned, respondents in more basic employment positions (manual workers, low routine non-manual workers), and the self-employed tended to be more strongly against fiscal assistance than people with high-end careers. However, these effects were not significant. Only middle-to-upper-class professionals stood out as having a strikingly lower willingness to engage in solidarity. While these effects remained stable across all models, they were fundamentally not in line with what we expected. Both employed and economically inactive people were slightly more against solidarity than unemployed people (but the difference was not significant). Meanwhile, household incomes did not have an impact. The variance apparent in model M2 was still meagre at 4% and barely increased from the base model M1. Furthermore, Hanna Kleider and Florian Stoeckel (2019) have shown that the effect of left–right orientation on European fiscal solidarity is conditioned by respondents' class position. To test this for our sample, we conducted OLS regressions with interaction effects of education, class, unemployment, and income with political placement (not depicted). The effects were insignificant throughout.[30]

With respect to cultural orientations (M3) the results turned out somewhat differently. First, the dummy variables for political self-assessment do show the expected left–right effect: compared to those in the political centre, people on the left were more in favour of increasing the amount of assistance for crisis-affected countries, while those on the right were more against this. These results support the majority of the empirical findings we presented above (Díez Medrano et al. 2019; Kuhn et al. 2018; Verhaegen 2018). The same effect was evident when we factored in people's identification with the three social spaces: the nation state, the EU, and the world. People who felt a stronger affinity with

Table 3.1 Social cleavages regarding providing financial emergency assistance to EU countries and to regions within the nation state; individual level

	European Union		Nation	
	M1	M2	M3	M4
Control variables				
Sex (ref.: male)	−0.06 (0.04)	−0.05 (0.04)	−0.04 (0.04)	0.02 (0.03)
Age (by 10 years)	−0.01 (0.04)	−0.02 (0.04)	−0.01 (0.04)	0.02 (0.03)
Age (by 10 years, squared)	0.00 (0.00)	0.00 (0.00)	0.00 (0.00)	0.00 (0.00)
Household: number of children	−0.03* (0.01)	−0.03* (0.01)	−0.02 (0.01)	−0.01 (0.00)
Migration generation (ref.: no migration background)				
First generation	−0.07 (0.05)	−0.06 (0.05)	−0.06 (0.05)	−0.04 (0.03)
Second generation	−0.02 (0.08)	−0.02 (0.08)	−0.02 (0.07)	0.04 (0.05)
Structural cleavages				
Level of education (ref.: tertiary)				
Non or primary		−0.06 (0.05)	−0.01 (0.05)	−0.01 (0.06)
Secondary		−0.13** (0.04)	−0.06* (0.03)	0.02 (0.02)
Occupational class (ref.: upper class (I))				
Upper middle class (II)		−0.01 (0.02)	−0.02 (0.02)	0.03 (0.03)
Centre middle class (IIIa)		−0.09*** (0.02)	−0.08*** (0.02)	0.00 (0.02)
Lower middle class (V & VI)		−0.04 (0.05)	0.00 (0.05)	0.07 (0.04)
Self-employed (IVab & IVc)		−0.16 (0.08)	−0.12 (0.07)	−0.01 (0.06)
Routine non-manual (IIIb)		−0.05 (0.03)	−0.04 (0.03)	0.09* (0.03)
Unskilled manual workers & agriculture (VIIa & VIIb)		−0.02 (0.05)	0.00 (0.05)	0.11* (0.04)
Unemployed (ref.: employed)		0.02 (0.04)	0.03 (0.04)	0.06* (0.03)
Household income		0.01 (0.02)	−0.01 (0.01)	−0.01 (0.01)
Cultural cleavages				
Political placement (ref.: centre)				
Left			0.17*** (0.04)	0.11* (0.04)
Moderate left			0.22*** (0.04)	0.07 (0.04)
Moderate right			−0.06* (0.03)	−0.08*** (0.01)
Right			−0.20*** (0.04)	−0.12 (0.07)
Identity: national (ref.: no)			−0.10* (0.04)	0.10 (0.07)
Identity: European (ref.: no)			0.38*** (0.03)	0.08** (0.03)
Identity: global (ref.: no)			0.19*** (0.03)	0.10** (0.03)

Country differences

Country (ref.: Spain)								
Austria	-0.44***	(0.01)	-0.43***	(0.01)	-0.32***	(0.02)	-0.24***	(0.02)
Cyprus	-0.42***	(0.01)	-0.43***	(0.01)	-0.18***	(0.02)	0.11***	(0.02)
France	-0.41***	(0.01)	-0.40***	(0.01)	-0.29***	(0.02)	-0.15***	(0.02)
Germany	-0.25***	(0.01)	-0.26***	(0.02)	-0.16***	(0.02)	0.07**	(0.02)
Greece	-0.40***	(0.00)	-0.39***	(0.01)	-0.24***	(0.02)	0.02	(0.02)
Hungary	-0.65***	(0.01)	-0.63***	(0.02)	-0.48***	(0.03)	-0.06	(0.04)
Ireland	-0.15***	(0.01)	-0.15***	(0.02)	-0.00	(0.02)	-0.13***	(0.02)
The Netherlands	-0.42***	(0.01)	-0.43***	(0.02)	-0.25***	(0.02)	-0.02	(0.02)
Poland	-0.54***	(0.01)	-0.54***	(0.01)	-0.40***	(0.02)	-0.33***	(0.03)
Portugal	-0.09***	(0.00)	-0.08***	(0.01)	-0.00	(0.01)	0.21***	(0.02)
Slovakia	-0.54***	(0.00)	-0.52***	(0.02)	-0.35***	(0.03)	-0.16***	(0.04)
Sweden	-0.39***	(0.01)	-0.38***	(0.02)	-0.23***	(0.02)	-0.01	(0.02)
Constant	3.22***	(0.13)	3.27***	(0.15)	2.84***	(0.14)	2.98***	(0.12)
R^2	0.037		0.044		0.102		0.044	
AIC	25,177.1		25,114.8		24,548.3		23,500.7	

Source: TESS 2016, own calculations.

Notes

$n = 9,179$; Unstandardised coefficients from pooled OLS regression with robust standard errors (clustered by country). $^*p < 0.05$; $^{**}p < 0.01$; $^{***}p < 0.001$, standard errors in parentheses.

their national identity were more likely to reject European solidarity, whereas people who identified with Europe and the world were more strongly in favour of it. Both observations are in line with analyses from previous research (Kleider and Stoeckel 2019; Kuhn et al. 2018; Kuhn and Stoeckel 2014; Verhaegen 2018). The effect we found for global identity – i.e. that it is weaker than European identity – seems to match with our theoretical assumptions. Cosmopolitans do value European integration as a progressive step forward from the insularity of the nation state, but they still view a solidarity reserved exclusively for EU countries as one that does not go far enough.

Comparing the influence of structural factors and cultural ones, we found that attitudes to solidarity were not based on instrumentally rational motives but on value-rational ones (centring on left/right values); even if the effects altogether do not amount to much, these were associated with an individual's affectual connection to Europe. The country effects are depicted in the lower part of Table 3.1. Although the countries were only included in the regression for methodological reasons, they nonetheless confirm the findings of the descriptive analysis of the willingness to engage in solidarity provided in Section 3.2, this time controlling for participants' socio-economic and cultural features. Compared to Spain (the reference country), all the other countries indicate a lower willingness to engage in solidarity. In the eastern European countries, as well as in Greece and Cyprus, the levels of willingness to engage in solidarity differed the most from the levels found in Spain. Smaller differences could be found among all the western European countries, while citizens of the formerly bailed-out countries Ireland and Portugal had the smallest deviation from Spain's levels (in model M3, the coefficients became insignificant compared to the Spanish reference group).

Let us now compare the findings on European solidarity with those found for the subnational level (M4). The results show that the potential for conflict barely changed from one level to the other. The socio-economic indicators had a similarly weak influence on the willingness to engage in solidarity in both cases. Since the differences between the two spatial levels were low and the effects were weak, we presumed that the potential for politicisation was also similarly low for both the European and the national level. The same also applied to cultural cleavages. Right-wing people rejected financial assistance at the national level to a lesser extent than they did for the European level. The same effect was found among people who identified predominantly with their own nation. This result is plausible because, from the perspective of people who identify with their own country, redistribution on the subnational level is necessary for the integration of the national community. Therefore, this should take priority over transnational solidarity. Moreover, people who identified as European or as global citizens were also in favour of subnational assistance. Both groups ostensibly associated the nation with their understanding of solidarity through the concept of 'nested membership' (Faist 2001). Finally, an analysis of the impact of country citizenship showed that the differences in levels of European solidarity between the countries were slightly greater than they were for national solidarity, a finding which we already acknowledged in Figure 3.3. This means that the difference between the variance resolution rates on both levels can be significantly attributed to the country-by-country differences. Nevertheless, the variance resolution for European willingness to engage in solidarity was, at 10%, still very meagre.

There are grounds for criticising this analysis, as our dependent variable only reflected a general attitude towards solidarity but not a distinct behaviour. To check for this, we conducted an additional regression analysis to compare the effects on the attitude towards European fiscal solidarity with the question on the willingness to contribute to a fund.

From these results, we can draw the following conclusions: first, we have seen that the citizens from our surveyed countries have a great willingness to engage in fiscal solidarity with countries in crisis. Second, we found only a few signs of social cleavages emerging around this issue. This finding confirms the results that we produced in a study using Eurobarometer questionnaires from the years 2010 and 2011, when the crisis had not yet reached its peak (Lengfeld et al. 2015). The fact that we could barely find any social cleavages across all surveyed countries indicates that there is no single, cohesive conflict structure developing across all of Europe, but rather a plethora of country-specific factors, which are more important in determining whether somebody opposes European financial assistance.

Figure 3.10 displays the results of the selected macro analysis. The graph on the left shows that the willingness to engage in European fiscal solidarity as an aggregate measure on the European level (coefficients of country dummies) changes when a country's average gross domestic product (as of 2015 in

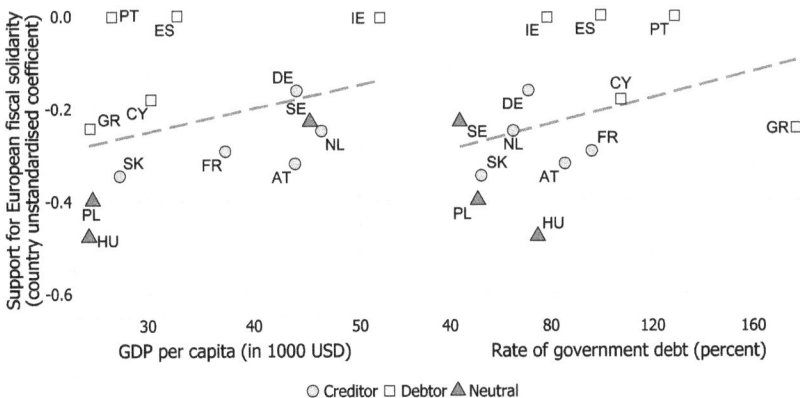

○ Creditor   □ Debtor   ▲ Neutral

Figure 3.10 Social cleavages regarding providing financial emergency assistance to EU countries; country level.

Source: TESS 2016, own calculations.

purchasing power parity) is adjusted upwards by one unit (1000 euros). From this point on, we paid extra attention to the individual countries and noted whether they were part of the Eurozone at the time of the crisis, and if so, whether they were creditor or debtor countries. The gradient does indeed show a positive correlation, though this correlation is not significantly different from the null hypothesis. The same result can be found on the right-hand graph for the relationship between the official rate of indebtedness (as a percentage of GDP) and the willingness to engage in solidarity. The effect of the correlation is not significant in either case.[31]

The only discernible magnitude of influence was the country's position in the crisis, which explained 62% of the variance between the countries. In both graphs, we see that the crisis-affected countries are situated substantially above the regression gradient. In contrast, the majority of Eurozone creditor countries and non-Eurozone countries are below the gradient. So, if there is any relevant social cleavage to be found at all, it likely exists (mostly) between the eastern European countries on the one side and the southern and western European countries on the other.[32]

Finally, we turn to the cross-level effects. We hypothesised that people with a low socio-economic status and those with left-wing convictions who live in poorer countries would be more strongly against European solidarity than their peers in affluent countries. Yet, we barely found any significant relationship with socio-economic status that supports our thesis, even when the four indicators (education, occupational class, household income, and unemployment) were factored in (not depicted). For political self-placement, we found an effect for left-wing people, who were more supportive in more affluent countries. Yet, this effect is rather weak; hence we assess this to be rather unimportant.

Our analysis leads us to two final conclusions. First, the probability of social cleavages emerging around the topic of European fiscal solidarity is rather low. No significant causal effect could be found between citizens' socio-economic status, either on the European level or on the nation state level. Instead, our analysis revealed the effects of political values and showed that the strength of identification with the nation state has weak effects on attitudes towards European solidarity. In addition, differences in living standards between EU countries were found to have no role in causing the polarisation of EU citizens on the topic of EU financial assistance. Even the prediction that impoverished people in rich EU countries would be the most opposed to European solidarity could not be verified in this study. This means that our criterion for the existence of European solidarity, the absence of strong social cleavages, has been fulfilled. This finding confirms the results from our descriptive analysis: citizens of EU countries are in favour of fiscal solidarity with their neighbouring EU countries to a high extent. Additionally, the propensity to give preference to European solidarity with the crisis-affected countries is socially structured in the same way as the willingness to engage in solidarity with crisis-affected regions within individual nation states. In this regard, fiscal solidarity appears to be a universal stance, which is structurally independent of spatial scale. It is only in the strength of conviction for solidarity that the two stances marginally differ from one another.

3.3.5 Results on political cleavages

Finally, we wish to examine the extent to which attitudes to European fiscal solidarity affect voting behaviour. Does rejecting European fiscal solidarity lead people to vote for a particular political party that represents these views in a general election and thus make European solidarity a relevant political issue? Opponents of European solidarity become politically relevant when they are given the opportunity to actively express their political preferences in the voting booth instead of lingering in the shadows. This question becomes relevant to the concept of the EU's politicisation, which is a matter of heated discussion among political scientists (see de Wilde 2011; Hooghe and Marks 2018; Rauh and Zürn 2014). The protagonists in this discussion presume that the permissive consensus has been broken and that citizens' tacit support for the European integration process is no longer a given. Such scholars invoke the continuous and increasing transfer of nation state competencies to EU institutions and the various European crises as some of the reasons for why the European integration process has become ever more controversial in recent years. We can also see how the EU has become increasingly politicised by analysing how the EU is depicted and debated in the mainstream media (Drewski 2015; Hutter et al. 2016; Risse 2014).[33] This politicisation is also evident in the founding and the increasing relevance of populist parties, who have found a substantial amount of public support by demanding an end to European integration or even campaigning for their country to fully exit the EU (Hobolt and de Vries 2016b; Hobolt and Tilley 2016).

In our investigation, however, we did not seek to analyse the politicisation of EU institutions, nor did we analyse the behaviour of political parties and the content of public discourse. We focused on asking whether citizens' negative attitudes towards European fiscal solidarity have led them to support parties in elections that explicitly position themselves against the new fiscal support system. We hypothesised that opponents of fiscal solidarity would be much more likely to vote for right-wing populist parties. Left-wing populist parties, however, have also historically campaigned against the EU's crisis management techniques and particularly against austerity policies, as shown by the examples of Podemos in Spain and Syriza in Greece. These parties act out of quite a different motive: namely, that European solidarity does not go far enough. Sara B. Hobolt and Catherine E. de Vries (2016b) have demonstrated this by using EES data from 2014. Their analysis shows that people who reject the idea of fiscal solidarity tend to vote for right-wing populist parties in the European elections. In contrast, support for fiscal solidarity does not go hand in hand with a stronger propensity to vote for left-wing populist parties.[34]

So what are the results of our analysis? To measure party preference, we asked the survey participants the following open question:

> *If the [NATIONALELECTION] were held tomorrow, which party would you vote for?*

Following the suggestion of Sara B. Hobolt and Catherine E. de Vries (2016b), we first grouped the parties named by our respondents according to how critical they were of the EU, its policies, and institutions into the following categories: moderate, weak (soft) Eurosceptic, and strong (hard) Eurosceptic. Additionally, we subdivided the soft and hard Eurosceptic parties along the ideological left–right scale into right- and left-wing parties respectively. Then for each of the four scale-points on the variable 'approval or rejection of fiscal solidarity', we calculated the probability of citizens voting for a moderate, soft left-wing, extreme left-wing, soft right-wing, or extreme right-wing Eurosceptic party, by using a multinomial logistic regression model. By applying this descriptive analytical procedure, we can understand how voting preferences change when the rate of agreement with fiscal solidarity increases by a single scale-point.

The results are shown in Figure 3.11. To make the results more comprehensible for the reader we decided to leave out voters who selected one of the moderate parties. Out of all those who outright rejected fiscal assistance measures (first dot in each figure) 1% of them stated they would vote for a left-wing, strongly Eurosceptic party and 4% had preferences for a left-wing, soft Eurosceptic party. However, 9% of these people would prefer a right-wing, soft Eurosceptic party, while even as much as 18% of respondents stated they would vote for a right-wing, strong Eurosceptic party. The remaining 69% of voters opted

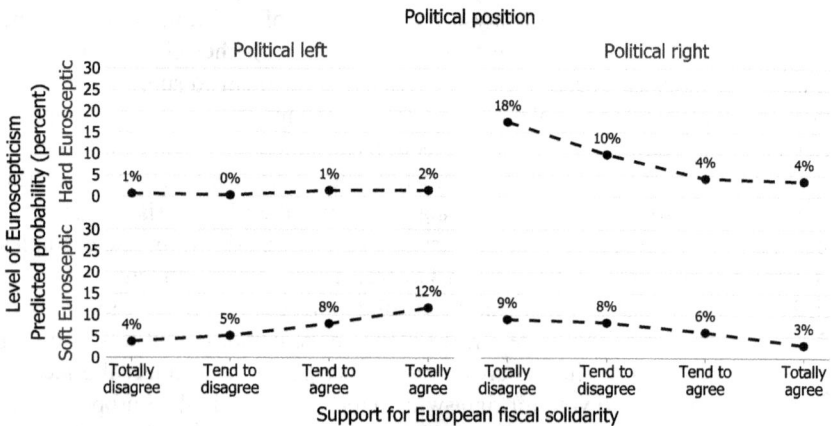

Figure 3.11 Support for European fiscal solidarity and political position of party voted for.

Source: TESS 2016, own calculations.

for a more moderate political party. It is evident that willingness to vote for right-wing parties, especially for ones with hard-line Eurosceptic views, is clearly pronounced among citizens who rejected European fiscal solidarity. This result persisted even when we controlled for other covariates in an additional multivariate regression. This means that the willingness to provide fiscal assistance to countries in crisis may become politically significant – albeit on a rather moderate level. Our analysis therefore supports findings from Sara B. Hobolt and Catherine E. de Vries (2016b). People who rejected rescuing indebted EU countries were more inclined to vote for right-wing Eurosceptic parties than citizens who support the idea of European fiscal solidarity.

Our analysis on social cleavages has shown that opponents of fiscal solidarity do not comprise a distinct, homogenous, socio-economic, or value-oriented group. Nevertheless, many of them are prepared to align their views with their voting behaviour, by supporting right-wing Eurosceptic parties. However, the results also show that the correlation between the rejection of European fiscal solidarity and the tendency to vote for a right-wing Eurosceptic party is rather weak. Even among citizens who are drawn to right-wing Eurosceptic parties, around half of them are still supportive of fiscal solidarity. We therefore conclude that it is not very likely that European fiscal solidarity will lead to the formation of strong political cleavages.

3.4 Conclusion

In this chapter, we sought to discover to what extent European citizens are willing to support EU member states that find themselves in serious financial difficulties. We termed this specific form of support 'fiscal solidarity', a domain of solidarity that is organised in considerable part by social institutions. We made theoretical assumptions that fiscal solidarity among European citizens would be a controversial issue as it contradicts the 'No Bailout' clause that had been in place across the EU for over two decades. Studies that investigated citizens' attitudes at the peak of the crisis between 2010 and 2012 also hinted at this contradiction. Our analysis, which was based on the 2016 TESS survey, deviated from these previous findings, although we consider our results to be more valid than those reached in preceding studies. Our investigation of European fiscal solidarity is much more extensive than previous ones in terms of the number of countries taken into account, and it also applies a comprehensive testing and measurement concept, which covers various societal spaces and examines citizens' willingness to pay for solidarity. Based on this understanding of solidarity and the way it is operationalised empirically, we have come to the following conclusions:

1   Two-thirds of citizens in the countries we investigated agreed with fiscal solidarity, while in each of the 13 surveyed countries, no majority rejected it. At the same time, citizens' willingness to help European crisis-affected

countries was admittedly lower than their willingness to help regions within their own nation state. Nevertheless, it was still significantly higher than for countries that are not part of the EU. Thus, our results show that without doubt, Europe constitutes a distinct space of solidarity. Furthermore, it is evident that citizens do not differentiate in their views between the different countries that require help to any significant degree. In light of the debate between cosmopolitanism and communitarianism outlined in Chapter 2, the conclusion suggests that in the case of fiscal solidarity, the majority of citizens are in favour of a European communitarianism that is limited to the EU's external borders.

2   On top of this, European solidarity seems to be resilient, thereby fulfilling a further criterion for measuring European solidarity. More than half of our respondents stated that they would be willing to make contributions to countries in need in the form of an extra tax. This result was evident in our analysis of a scenario in which our respondents had to decide on whether they would contribute to a European solidarity fund to combat economic crises. Nevertheless, the willingness to contribute varied substantially between the different countries, from its highest peak in countries where citizens had already experienced a crisis, specifically in southern European countries, to its lowest levels in the eastern and western European countries. Yet, in every country other than France, we still found a majority of people who would be willing to make a minimum contribution of at least 0.5% of their own incomes.

3   There have been numerous, intense political debates surrounding the notorious austerity measures, which debtor countries were forced to accept in return for EU assistance during the crisis. Nonetheless, the general population agreed with some of these policies, though not all of them. For example, over 70% of the respondents were in favour of wealthier people in the debtor countries making additional contributions towards the overcoming of the crisis, for instance through the raising of a wealth tax. At the same time, they stated that the weakest members of society in the debtor countries, i.e. those receiving benefits from the welfare state, ought to be exempt from the cuts, with two-thirds of respondents rejecting these specific measures. The only deviations from this otherwise unanimously held standpoint came from citizens living in several of the debtor countries, who rejected the majority of these austerity policies altogether.

4   By referring to the concept of social cleavages, we first searched for social (structural and cultural) cleavages between citizens and between the countries around the topic of European fiscal solidarity. On this issue, we found a very weak indication of potential cleavages emerging, which was most evident between groups of citizens with different political orientations but was barely evident at all between citizens and countries with different socio-economic positions. In relation to political cleavages, our analysis shows that citizens who rejected fiscal solidarity were, at the same time, more

inclined to vote for politically right-wing Eurosceptic parties. However, the correlations were weak and only loosely related to the citizens' socio-economic and cultural characteristics.

All in all, we reach a result that probably comes as quite a surprise to many political and scholarly commentators: European citizens from the 13 countries that we investigated were overwhelmingly and highly willing to support one another in the event of economic crises. This means that European citizens fundamentally perceive the general idea of cross-border fiscal solidarity as legitimate. However, the precise, real EU policies, bailout packages, and austerity measures that citizens are referring to cannot be deduced to their full extent from these findings. So in future, conflicts of interest on these issues and political clashes can be expected, just as there are today; such clashes that may indeed be regarded as the fruitful outcomes of a vibrant democracy in action.

Notes

1 The definition of the levels for convergence is declared in the TFEU Treaty Protocol No. 13. On the convergence criterion on interest rates:

> The criterion on the convergence of interest rates … shall mean that, observed over a period of one year before the examination, a Member State has had an average nominal long-term interest rate that does not exceed by more than two percentage points that of, at most, the three best performing Member States in terms of price stability. Interest rates shall be measured on the basis of long-term government bonds or comparable securities, taking into account differences in national definitions.
>
> (European Union 2012: Article 4)

2 At the same time, a second fund, the European Finance Stability Mechanism (EFSM) was established in 2010. The EFSM was a communal fund that allowed the European Commission to acquire a maximum of up to €20 billion from the capital markets. It was then allowed to lend this money to countries in crisis (including those outside of the Eurozone). The funds for the EFSM were financed directly from the EU budget.

3 At the time of establishing the EFSF in summer 2010, the Slovakian parliament had already temporarily refused to ratify the treaty, before eventually doing this once the parliament had been newly elected.

4 Hence, our explanations in this chapter also go further in depth than those in other chapters.

5 Although we use causal rhetoric throughout the book, our analysis is not a causal analysis in a narrow sense. For a strict causal analysis, a randomised trial (Hernán 2018) or panel data (Morgan and Winship 2015:363–91) would be more appropriate. Our cross-sectional survey data cannot be categorised as such. Nonetheless, we share the opinion of Miguel A. Hernán who argued that 'without causally explicit language, the means and ends of much observational research get hopelessly conflated' (2018:617).

6 Some people were nevertheless of the opinion that there was no contradiction between the regulations of the TFEU and the establishment of bailout packages (see, for example, the discussion in Ruffert 2011 and Tomkin 2013).

7 The first case corresponds to the logic of inland financial reimbursement. Here, the debtors of financial assistance are the wealthier regions within the same nation. In the

other two cases, we decided that the respondent's home country would be the assumed country from which the assistance originated. We decided to do this because this allowed us to make clear to the respondents that in extremely bad scenarios, such as the default on repayments of loans, the provision of assistance could give rise to costs that would then have to be paid by the citizens of the nation state. Our measurement was thus more sensitive to costs and more robust than it would have been if we had asked the respondents whether institutions such as the EU or the IMF ought to grant assistance without mentioning any particular conditions.

8   We based the phrasing of the questions and items on the formulations given in the above-cited Eurobarometer survey from 2011, as well as on some of our own studies (Lengfeld et al. 2014; Lengfeld and Kroh 2016). In the first item for each of the respondents' countries, we used the name of the largest regional area, such as 'Kraje' in Slovakia and 'Województwa' in Poland. In the second and third items, the name of the respondent's home country was used.

9   This question was asked of all the participants. The area respondents chose in response to the first part of the question could not be selected again in the second part of the question. They were, however, permitted to refuse to give an answer. Those who did not wish to give assistance to any of the three regions and who stated this to the interviewer were codified with the answer 'Nowhere'. Responses from people who were willing to provide assistance but did not wish to rank the areas in any order of priority were codified with the answer 'Everywhere equally/To both equally'. The rates for these two categories were 0.2% and 2.8% respectively. In the following section, however, we only consider the three pre-given answers.

10   In contrast to this, a comparably greater proportion of the participants who supported helping non-EU countries in Figure 3.2 seemed to stick to their cosmopolitan principles when put in the decision-making scenario.

11   These contextual conditions include the general criteria independent of the crisis such as the country size, the country's standard of living, cultural characteristics related to basic shared values like religion and democracy, and its history of conflict and/or cooperation. The crisis-relevant criteria include the extent to which the country was affected, the extent of the debts, the country's economic weight/relevance in the Eurozone and the EU internal market, the levels of compliance with European regulations, norm-compliance (corruption), the extent to which the country was responsible for the crisis situation, and the behaviour of the country's government during the crisis, e.g. the extent to which government and the populace have actively sought to overcome the crisis (through deficit reduction and austerity measures).

12   The original intention was to conduct the TESS in the United Kingdom as well, however, after our questionnaire had already been completed, we had to replace the UK with France for organisational purposes. This is why we gathered data on the respondents' attitudes on the United Kingdom as a potential aid-receiving country but did not do so for France.

13   We first created three country groups. Group 1 contained the crisis-affected countries that received financial assistance from the EU bailout funds EFSF and ESM in the period between 2011 and 2016: Cyprus, Greece, Ireland, and Portugal. Group 2 consisted of the group of eastern European countries – Hungary, Poland, and Slovakia – as well as Spain. These countries were less affected by the crisis than those in Group 1 (Spain was not subject to the EU and IMF's demands for budget cuts), and in European terms, they had a similarly low standard of living compared to the countries in Group 3. In this third group, there were the wealthy western European countries: Germany, Great Britain, the Netherlands, Austria, and Sweden. For each respondent, we randomly selected two countries from each group. That way, none of the respondents could end up assessing their own country. Ultimately, there were

between 4,536 (Austria) and 6,025 (Cyprus) possible answers provided for each country.

14 In Germany, every employed person pays a 'solidarity premium' of up to 5% of their income and capital gains tax. This tax has been used to support the development of East German states since the 1990s.

15 These assumptions are supported by two preceding studies. Our already-mentioned FSEU study showed that in 2012, 44% of Germans and 52% of Portuguese were willing to accept a 0.5% solidarity tax on individual income (Lengfeld 2015; Lengfeld et al. 2015). Using the same question formulation, we found that only 35% of the Germans who responded supported this solidarity tax in the German Socio-Economic Panel's (GSOEP) Innovation Sample questionnaire carried out in Germany in 2015 (Lengfeld and Kroh 2016). These differences indicate that individual willingness to pay in one of the main creditor countries, Germany, declined from its high point in the crisis in 2012 to 2015. In spite of using the same question formation, we obtained different results, which can be attributed to time effects and differences in the context in which the data was gathered. We shall return to this topic further in the chapter.

16 Michael M. Bechtel and colleagues (2017) also dealt with the question of the extent of payment in a recent study. They surveyed how much the citizens of Germany would be willing to contribute as a whole to a onetime bailout programme. In contrast, we are interested in a continuous payment directly from the citizens themselves.

17 We decided to steer clear of the term 'tax', since this strong term could have provoked a fundamentally negative stance among the interviewees. This may have so strongly affected the participants that they would not have paid any further attention to the concrete characteristics of the tax described subsequently in the assessment.

18 We did this for two reasons. First, the contributions were supposed to be noticeable, meaning also for people with very low incomes. Second, question formulations in which percentage amounts are named are suspected to be not very reliable. We presume that less-educated interviewees in particular would have some difficulties in assessing the actual financial consequences of the contribution to be paid. Furthermore, the relatively low absolute value of the tax rates (0.5%, 2%, or 3%) could have positively influenced approval for these suggestions. This is why we also named additional absolute minimum amounts, which were calculated as proportional values of the national average income. For each respondent's country, we calculated the median income before tax (in euro or in the country's own currency), determining the absolute value of the amount to be paid for each respective tax rate and incorporating it into the question.

19 Participants who had already stated that they would not be willing to make any contribution at all in the first scenario, regardless of how much, were coded by the interviewer as 'refuse to pay anything'. This prompt for the answer was not read out. If the respondent gave this answer in the first or second part of the question, then the interviewer skipped over the other parts of the question that followed. In total, 981 people gave the response 'refuse to pay anything' across all survey countries: 621 in the first part of the question, 236 in the second, and 124 in the third scenario. This constitutes 7.85% (unweighted) of the gross sample and 6.63% of the weighted subsample that was used here.

20 These results also deviated from our above-cited survey from 2012 (FSEU) and 2015 (GSOEP) despite a comparable sample and close to identical question design. It is possible that these results fluctuated between 2012, 2015, and 2016. We presume this to be a halo effect within the TESS survey, in which questions on solidarity take up far greater space than in the two other surveys. Unfortunately, we cannot say how great this methodological effect is in percentage terms.

21 For details see the European Commission's website on 'EU financial assistance' for the Eurozone countries Ireland, Greece, Portugal, Hungary, and Cyprus (http://ec.europa.eu/economy_finance/assistance_eu_ms/index_en.htm; retrieved July 15, 2016).

22 In relation to this, there also were repeated mass protests in Spain, Portugal, and Greece at the climax of the crisis in 2012 and 2013 (BBC 2013; SPIEGEL Online 2012b).

23 General VAT rises have socially unequal effects because they burden people with low household incomes more in relative terms than people with high household incomes. This does not apply for the general raising of the retirement age because in any case this does not tend to affect members of all classes at the same rate.

24 See the review by Sara B. Hobolt and Catherine E. de Vries (2016a) for a detailed overview of research and explanations.

25 Since all debtor countries have a higher standard of living than the eastern European countries, we presume that citizens of the latter countries would be more sceptical towards European solidarity. Nonetheless, this effect was expected to be somewhat slight. The descriptive analysis does indeed indicate that countries with the lowest living standards also tended to exhibit the lowest rates of agreement with European solidarity. Yet at the same time, more than half of the citizens appeared to be in favour of fiscal solidarity. The disparity in support for fiscal solidarity across all country levels is comparatively low at 25% (Spain is highest at 78% and Hungary is lowest at 53%). In addition to this comes the fact that the countries with the highest standard of living are not the most generous when it comes to showing solidarity but rather lie somewhere around mid-table.

26 Other studies have also come to contradictory conclusions. Both Holger Lengfeld and colleagues (2015) and Theresa Kuhn and Florian Stoeckel (2014) found on the basis of Eurobarometer surveys that political orientation had no significant effect on support for bailouts or coordinated European economic governance. In contrast, Monika Bauhr and Nicholas Charron (2018) found the lowest approval rates among people in the political centre. Hanna Kleider and Florian Stoeckel (2019) provided evidence that the effect of a voter's political viewpoint is in turn dependent on their class position.

27 It would still be quite plausible for these people to reject the bailout funding policies of the EU as an actual event, because as we have already detailed, these policies resulted in the giving of credit to banks and institutional investors, which ultimately worsened the situation of the socially disadvantaged in the crisis-affected countries due to subsequent demands for budget cutbacks. In any case, our analysis does not aim to appraise the EU's concrete policies and the institutions created during the crisis. For our study, the citizens' fundamental stances towards transnational fiscal solidarity in cases of economic crisis take priority.

28 Although we used an ordinal scale for this item, Geoff Norman (2010) has shown that treating Likert-like scales as continuous does not bias estimates. Additionally, Norman underlined that dichotomising data leads 'to a reduction in statistical power' (Norman 2010:628).

29 In addition, we calculated OLS regressions on the individual level with macro variables alongside hierarchical linear models (HLM). These calculations serve the additional purpose of validating the results from the two-step regressions. We only report these results in short excerpts. Although HLMs are commonplace and widely found in the research, we used these here merely as an additional test of the robustness of the results due to the complexity of the topic and the debate surrounding the presuppositions. The reason is that the validity of the results from HLMs are deemed unreliable as long as the number of cases on the higher level are below a certain critical mass. Mark L. Bryan and Stephen P. Jenkins, for example, concluded that HLMs require at

least 25 countries for the null hypothesis not to be rejected at a comparatively premature stage (2016:19–20). Since the 2016 TESS does not fulfil this requirement, as it
only comprises 13 countries, we carried out HLMs merely as a robustness test.

30 This may be due to a different operationalisation of left and right in the studies. Hanna
Kleider and Florian Stoeckel (2019) captured political orientation as agreement on
domestic redistribution. In comparison, we captured it as left–right self-assessment.

31 Additionally, we calculated further regressions with different indicators that measured
the country's living standards, the proportion of the national budget spent on the EU,
the country's rate of social inequality, and its poverty and unemployment rates (not
illustrated here). These results show that in countries that exhibited more economic
and social problems (generally the southern European countries), the acceptance of
solidarity was only slightly higher than in countries with less urgent social and economic problems. However, these correlations were either insignificant or, at best, displayed a very weak significance (around the 10% level).

32 On top of this, we analysed the impact of macro factors on attitudes towards subnational fiscal solidarity. The effects we discovered were all quite similar, running
consistently in the same direction, albeit weakly for the most part. This means, once
again, that citizens' interests and values do not prompt them to discriminate between
EU crisis countries and crisis regions in their own countries on the topic of solidarity.

33 Nevertheless, Edgar Grande and Hans-Peter Kriesi (2016) show in an examination of
five EU countries and Switzerland that in most of these countries right-wing populist
parties barely had any success in decisively influencing the public debate on whether
or not to support crisis-affected countries during the sovereign debt crisis.

34 In the European Election Study, fiscal solidarity was measured with an item that had
the exact same wording as the measurement from the TESS in 2016.

References

Achen, Christopher H. 2005. 'Two-step Hierarchical Estimation: Beyond Regression
Analysis'. *Political Analysis* 13:447–56.
Alm, James, and Benno Torgler. 2011. 'Do Ethics Matter? Tax Compliance and
Morality'. *Journal of Business Ethics* 101:635–51.
Bauhr, Monika, and Nicholas Charron. 2018. 'Why Support International Redistribution?
Corruption and Public Support for Aid in the Eurozone'. *European Union Politics*
19(2):233–54.
BBC. 2013. 'Eurozone Crisis: Portugal Protests against Austerity'. *bbc.com*, 2 March.
Retrieved 25 June 2017 (www.bbc.com/news/world-europe-21643853).
Bechtel, Michael M., Jens Hainmueller, and Yotam Margalit. 2014. 'Preferences for
International Redistribution: The Divide over the Eurozone Bailouts'. *American Polit-
ical Science Review* 58(4):835–56.
Bechtel, Michael M., Jens Hainmueller, and Yotam Margalit. 2017. 'Policy Design and
Domestic Support for International Bailouts'. *European Journal of Political Research*
56:864–86.
Benhabib, Seyla. 2004. *The Rights of Others: Aliens, Residents, and Citizens*. Cambridge:
Cambridge University Press.
Birnbaum, Michael, and Anthony Faiola. 2017. 'Macron's Victory Buoys the European
Union after a String of Setbacks'. *Washington Post*, 8 May. Retrieved 19 May 2017
(www.washingtonpost.com/world/europe/macrons-victory-buoys-the-european-union-
after-a-string-of-setbacks/2017/05/08/bb83d12e-33ef-11e7-ab03-aa29f656f13e_story.
html?utm_term=.8d4957b3f0f9).

Bornschier, Simon. 2010. 'The New Cultural Divide and the Two-dimensional Space in Western Europe'. *West European Politics* 33(3):419–44.

Börzel, Tanja A., and Thomas Risse. 2018. 'From the Euro to the Schengen Crisis: European Integration and Changing Identity Politics'. *Journal of European Public Policy* 25(1):83–108.

Bryan, Mark L., and Stephen P. Jenkins. 2016. 'Multilevel Modelling of Country Effects: A Cautionary Tale'. *European Sociological Review* 32(1):3–22.

Ciornei, Irina, and Ettore Recchi. 2017. 'At the Source of European Solidarity: Assessing the Effects of Cross-border Practices and Political Attitudes'. *Journal of Common Market Studies* 55(3):468–85.

Copelovitch, Mark, Jeffry Frieden, and Stefanie Walter. 2016. 'The Political Economy of the Euro Crisis'. *Comparative Political Studies* 49(7):811–40.

Council of the European Union. 2011. 'Council Implementing Decision of 30 May 2011 on Granting Union Financial Assistance to Portugal (2011/344/EU)'. *Official Journal of the European Union* L 159:88–92.

Daniele, Gianmarco, and Benny Geys. 2015. 'Public Support for European Fiscal Integration in Times of Crisis'. *Journal of European Public Policy* 22(5):650–70.

de Beer, Paul. 2012. 'Earnings and Income Inequality in the EU during the Crisis'. *International Labour Review* 151(4):313–31.

de Vries, Catherine E., and Erica E. Edwards. 2009. 'Taking Europe to its Extremes: Extremist Parties and Public Euroscepticism'. *Party Politics* 15(1):5–28.

de Wilde, Pieter. 2011. 'No Polity for Old Politics? A Framework for Analyzing the Politicization of European Integration'. *Journal of European Integration* 33(5):559–75.

Díez Medrano, Juan, Irina Ciornei, and Fulya Apaydin. 2019. 'Explaining Supranational Solidarity'. Pp. 137–70 in *Everyday Europe: Social Transnationalism in an Unsettled Continent*, edited by E. Recchi, A. Favell, F. Apaydin, R. Barbulescu, M. Braun, I. Ciornei, N. Cunningham, J. Díez Medrano, D. Duru, L. Hanquinet, J. S. Jensen, S. Pötzschke, D. Reimer, J. Salamonska, M. Savage, and A. Varela. Bristol: Policy Press.

Drewski, Daniel. 2015. 'Has There Been a European Public Discourse on the Euro Crisis? A Content Analysis of German and Spanish Newspaper Editorials'. *Javnost – The Public* 22(3):264–82.

Dyson, Kenneth. 2017. 'Playing for High Stakes: The Eurozone Crisis'. Pp. 54–76 in *The European Union in Crisis*, edited by D. Dinan, N. Nugent, and W. E. Paterson. London: Palgrave.

Edlund, Jonas. 2007. 'Class Conflicts and Institutional Feedback Effects in Liberal and Social Democratic Welfare Regimes'. Pp. 30–79 in *The Political Sociology of the Welfare State*, edited by S. Svallfors. Stanford, CA: Stanford University Press.

Erikson, Robert, and John H. Goldthorpe. 1992. *The Constant Flux: A Study of Class Mobility in Industrial Societies*. Oxford: Clarendon Press.

European Union. 2012. 'Consolidated Version of the Treaty on the Functioning of the European Union'. *Official Journal of the European Union* C 326:47–390.

Eurostat. 2017. *EMU Convergence Criterion Series – Annual Data (irt_lt_mcby_a): Eurostat – Data Explorer*. Retrieved 13 July 2017 (http://appsso.eurostat.ec.europa.eu/nui/show.do?dataset=irt_lt_mcby_a&lang=en).

Faist, Thomas. 2001. 'Social Citizenship in the European Union: Nested Membership'. *Journal of Common Market Studies* 39(1):37–58.

Fuchs, Dieter, and Hans-Dieter Klingemann. 1990. 'The Left Right Schema'. Pp. 203–34 in *Continuities in Political Action: A Longitudinal Study of Political Orientations in*

Three Western Democracies, edited by M. K. Jennings and J. van Deth. Berlin: de Gruyter.

Gerhards, Jürgen, and Holger Lengfeld. 2015. *European Citizenship and Social Integration in the European Union.* London: Routledge.

Gerodimos, Roman. 2013. 'Greece: Politics at the Crossroads'. *Political Insight* 4(1):16–19.

Grande, Edgar, and Hanspeter Kriesi. 2015. 'The Restructuring of Political Conflict in Europe and the Politicization of European Integration'. Pp. 190–226 in *European Public Spheres: Politics Is Back*, edited by T. Risse. Cambridge: Cambridge University Press.

Grande, Edgar, and Hanspeter Kriesi. 2016. 'The Euro Crisis: A Boost to the Politicisation of European Integration?' Pp. 240–76 in *Politicising Europe: Integration and Mass Politics*, edited by S. Hutter, E. Grande, and H. Kriesi. Cambridge: Cambridge University Press.

Habermas, Jürgen. 2012. *The Crisis of the European Union: A Response*. Cambridge: Polity Press.

Habermas, Jürgen. 2015. 'Warum Merkels Griechenland-Politik ein Fehler ist [Why Merkel's Greece Policy Is a Mistake]'. *Süddeutsche Zeitung*, 22 June. Retrieved 22 June 2015 (www.sueddeutsche.de/wirtschaft/europa-sand-im-getriebe-1.2532119).

Hardiman, Niamh, and Adian Reagan. 2013. 'The Politics of Austerity in Ireland'. *Intereconomics* 48(1):9–14.

Hernán, Miguel A. 2018. 'The C-word: Scientific Euphemisms Do Not Improve Causal Inference from Observational Data'. *American Journal of Public Health* 108(5):616–19.

Hobolt, Sara B., and Catherine E. de Vries 2016a. 'Public Support for European Integration'. *Annual Review of Political Science* 19:413–32.

Hobolt, Sara B., and Catherine E. de Vries. 2016b. 'Turning against the Union? The Impact of the Crisis on the Eurosceptic Vote in the 2014 European Parliament Elections'. *Electoral Studies* 44:504–14.

Hobolt, Sara B., and James Tilley. 2016. 'Fleeing the Centre: The Rise of Challenger Parties in the Aftermath of the Euro Crisis'. *West European Politics* 39(5):971–91.

Hooghe, Liesbet, and Gary Marks. 2009. 'A Postfunctionalist Theory of European Integration: From Permissive Consensus to Constraining Dissensus'. *British Journal of Political Science* 39(1):1–23.

Hooghe, Liesbet, and Gary Marks. 2018. 'Cleavage Theory Meets Europe's Crises: Lipset, Rokkan, and the Transnational Cleavage'. *Journal of European Public Policy* 25(1):109–35.

Hutter, Swen, Edgar Grande, and Hanspeter Kriesi. 2016. *Politicising Europe: Integration and Mass Politics.* Cambridge: Cambridge University Press.

Illing, Falk. 2017. *Die Eurokrise: Analyse der europäischen Strukturkrise [The Euro Crisis: Analysis of the European Structural Crisis].* 2nd edn. Wiesbaden: Springer VS.

Ingensiep, Cathrin. 2016. 'Determinants of Persistent Poverty: Do Institutional Factors Matter?' Pp. 48–67 in *Exploring Inequality in Europe: Diverging Income and Employment Opportunities in the Crisis*, edited by M. Heidenreich. Cheltenham: Palgrave.

Inglehart, Ronald, and Pippa Norris. 2016. *Trump, Brexit, and the Rise of Populism: Economic Have-nots and Cultural Backlash.* HKS Working Paper: RWP16–026.

Kleider, Hanna, and Florian Stoeckel. 2019. 'The Politics of International Redistribution: Explaining Public Support for Fiscal Transfers in the EU'. *European Journal of Political Research* 58:4–29.

Kriesi, Hanspeter. 2012. 'The Political Consequences of the Financial and Economic Crisis in Europe: Electoral Punishment and Popular Protest'. *Swiss Political Science Review* 18:518–22.

Kriesi, Hanspeter, Edgar Grande, Martin Dolezahl, Marc Helbling, Dominic Höglinger, Swen Hutter, and Bruno Wüst. 2012. *Political Conflict in Western Europe*. Cambridge and New York: Cambridge University Press.

Kuhn, Theresa, Hector Solaz, and Erica J. van Elsas. 2018. 'Practising What You Preach: How Cosmopolitanism Promotes Willingness to Redistribute Across the European Union'. *Journal of European Public Policy* 25(12):1759–78.

Kuhn, Theresa, and Florian Stoeckel. 2014. 'When European Integration Becomes Costly: The Euro Crisis and Public Support for European Economic Governance'. *Journal of European Public Policy* 21(4):624–41.

Kulish, Nicholas, and Stephen Castle. 2011. 'Slovakia Rejects Euro Bailout'. *New York Times*, 11 October. Retrieved 19 July 2017 (www.nytimes.com/2011/10/12/world/europe/slovak-leader-vows-to-resign-if-bailout-vote-fails.html).

Ladi, Stella. 2014. 'Austerity Politics and Administrative Reform: The Eurozone Crisis and Its Impact Upon Greek Public Administration'. *Comparative European Politics* 12(2):184–208.

Lengfeld, Holger. 2015. 'Die Kosten der Hilfe: Europäische Fiskalkrise und die Bereitschaft der Deutschen zur Zahlung einer europäischen Solidaritätssteuer [The Costs of Assistance: European Fiscal Crisis and the Willingness of the Germans to Pay a European Solidarity Tax]'. Pp. 381–405 in *Empirische Kultursoziologie: Festschrift für Jürgen Gerhards zum 60. Geburtstag [Empirical Cultural Sociology: Commemorative Publication for Jürgen Gerhards on His 60th Birthday]*, edited by J. Rössel and J. Roose. Wiesbaden: Springer VS.

Lengfeld, Holger, and Martin Kroh. 2016. 'Solidarity with EU Countries in Crisis: Results of a 2015 Socio-economic Panel (SOEP) Survey'. *DIW Economic Bulletin* 6(39):473–9.

Lengfeld, Holger, Sara Schmidt, and Julia Häuberer. 2014. 'Fiskalpolitische Solidarität in der Europäischen Union: Erste Befunde einer Umfrage 2012 aus Deutschland und Portugal [Fiscal Solidarity in the European Union: Preliminary Findings from a 2012 Survey in Germany and Portugal]'. In *Vielfalt und Zusammenhalt: Verhandlungen des 36. Kongresses der Deutschen Gesellschaft für Soziologie in Bochum und Dortmund 2012 [Diversity and Cohesion: Negotiations of the 36th Congress of the German Sociological Association in Bochum and Dortmund 2012]*, edited by M. Löw. Frankfurt am Main: Campus.

Lengfeld, Holger, Sara Schmidt, and Julia Häuberer. 2015. *Is There a European Solidarity? Attitudes towards Fiscal Assistance for Debt-ridden European Union Member States*. Working Paper Series of the Department of Sociology at the University of Leipzig, No. 67.

Lipset, Seymor M., and Stein Rokkan. 1967. 'Cleavage Structures, Party Systems and Voter Alignments: An Introduction'. Pp. 1–64 in *Party Systems and Voter Alignments: Cross-national Perspectives*, edited by S. M. Lipset and S. Rokkan. New York: Free Press.

Mahoney, James. 2004. 'Comparative-historical Methodology'. *Annual Review of Sociology* 30:81–101.

Monastiriotis, Vassilis, Niamh Hardiman, Aidan Regan, Chiara Goretti, Lucio Landi, J. Ignacio Conde-Ruiz, Carmen Marín, and Ricardo Cabral. 2013. 'Austerity Measures in

Crisis Countries – Results and Impact on Mid-term Development'. *Intereconomics* 48(1):4–32.

Morgan, Stephen L., and Christopher Winship. 2015. *Counterfactuals and Casual Inference: Methods and Principles for Social Research.* 2nd edn. New York: Cambridge University Press.

Norman, Geoff. 2010. 'Likert Scales, Levels of Measurement and the "Laws" of Statistics'. *Advances in Health Sciences Education* 15(5):625–32.

Pew Research Center. 2013. *The New Sick Man of Europe: The European Union: French Dispirited: Attitudes Diverge Sharply from Germans.* Retrieved 8 August 2018 (http://assets.pewresearch.org/wp-content/uploads/sites/2/2013/05/Pew-Research-Center-Global-Attitudes-Project-European-Union-Report-FINAL-FOR-PRINT-May-13-2013.pdf).

Pogge, Thomas. 2008. *World Poverty and Human Rights: Cosmopolitan Responsibilities and Reforms.* 2nd edn. London: Polity Press.

Preunkert, Jenny. 2016. 'The European Integration Process and the Social Consequences of the Eurozone Crisis'. Pp. 220–41 in *Exploring Inequality in Europe: Diverging Income and Employment Opportunities in the Crisis,* edited by M. Heidenreich. Cheltenham: Palgrave.

Rankin, Jennifer. 2015. 'Eurozone Crisis: Which Countries Are for or against Grexit'. *Guardian,* 12 July. Retrieved 20 July 2017 (www.theguardian.com/business/2015/jul/12/eurozone-crisis-which-countries-are-for-or-against-grexit).

Rauh, Christian, and Michael Zürn. 2014. 'Zur Politisierung der EU in der Krise [On the Politicisation of the EU during the Crisis]'. Pp. 121–45 in *Krise der europäischen Vergesellschaftung? Soziologische Perspektiven [Crisis of the European Socialization? Sociological Perspectives],* edited by M. Heidenreich. Wiesbaden: Springer VS.

Risse, Thomas, ed. 2014. *European Public Spheres: Politics Is Back.* Cambridge: Cambridge University Press.

Rogers, Chris, and Sofia Vasilopoulou. 2012. 'Making Sense of Greek Austerity'. *The Political Quarterly* 83(4):777–85.

Ruffert, Matthias. 2011. 'European Debt Crisis and European Union Law'. *Common Market Law Revue* 48:1777–806.

Schelkle, Waltraud. 2017. *The Political Economy of Monetary Solidarity: Understanding the Euro Experiment.* Oxford: Oxford University Press.

SPIEGEL Online. 2012a. 'SPIEGEL Interview with Finland's Finance Minister: "Our Solidarity Is Limited".' *SPIEGEL Online,* 24 July. Retrieved 19 July 2017 (www.spiegel.de/international/europe/finnish-finance-minister-defends-debt-agreements-with-spain-and-greece-a-846096.html).

SPIEGEL Online. 2012b. 'Autumn of Discontent: Turmoil over Austerity Hits Spain and Greece'. *SPIEGEL Online,* 26 September. Retrieved 25 June 2017 (www.spiegel.de/international/europe/protests-in-spain-and-strikes-in-greece-over-austerity-measures-a-858040.html).

Stoeckel, Florian, and Theresa Kuhn. 2018. 'Mobilizing Citizens for Costly Policies: The Conditional Effect of Party Cues on Support for International Bailouts in the European Union'. *Journal of Common Market Studies* 56(2):446–61.

Streeck, Wolfgang. 2014. *Buying Time: The Delayed Crisis of Democratic Capitalism.* London: Verso.

Theodoropoulou, Sotiria. 2016. 'What Solidarity in the Eurozone after the Greek Crisis of 2015?' Pp. 33–60 in *Social Policy in the European Union: State of Play 2016,* edited by B. Vanhercke, D. Natali, and D. Bouget. Brussels: European Trade Union Institute (ETUI).

Tomkin, Jonathan. 2013. 'Contradiction, Circumvention and Conceptual Gymnastics: The Impact of the Adoption of the ESM Treaty on the State of European Democracy'. *German Law Journal* 14(1):169–90.

Torgler, Benno. 2007. *Tax Compliance and Tax Morale*. Cheltenham: Edward Elgar.

Verhaegen, Soetkin. 2018. 'What to Expect from European Identity? Explaining Support for Solidarity in Times of Crisis'. *Comparative European Politics* 16(5):871–904.

Zettelmeyer, Jeromin, Christoph Trebesch, and Mitu Gulati. 2013. 'The Greek Debt Restructuring: An Autopsy'. *Economic Policy* 28(75):513–63.

Chapter 4

Territorial solidarity – reducing inequality

4.1 The development of territorial disparities in Europe after the crisis

The British government's decision in 2016 to leave the European Union represents a major turning point in the EU's development. From the 1950s up until Brexit, the EU expanded continually, from six to 28 states in total.[1] Nevertheless, most of the countries that joined after the 1970s were less wealthy than the founding members of the 1950s. The various rounds of enlargement since then have led to an increase in the disparities of wealth between member states. This wealth gap was especially widened due to the accession of eastern European states (and also Malta and Cyprus) in the expansions of 2004 and 2007. Even if it was unclear in the early 2000s whether these countries would be able to successfully integrate into the EU in an economic sense, in retrospect, the trend was positive overall (see Figure 4.1): until the onset of the financial crisis in 2008, economic disparities between states decreased at an ever-improving rate (European Central Bank 2015; Eurostat 2017). The growth of the post-socialist economies made a particular contribution to the acceleration of this convergence process.

However, after 2008, the financial and economic crisis changed how these disparities in wealth developed (Figure 4.1). More specifically, the northern and western countries maintained their lead, while the eastern European countries, after a short period of stagnation, continued the catching-up process. The southern European states, in contrast, slipped far behind. At the beginning of the crisis, their average economic power lay at 90% of the EU average, but from then on, it continually fell to a low of 78% by 2014; it has remained at this level ever since. This has resulted in a recurrent rise in inequalities in living standards, especially between the northern and southern member states (Heidenreich 2016:6).

It is the EU's declared aim to reduce disparities between member states and between different European regions and to improve the living standards of all EU citizens (European Committee of the Regions 2018:3).[2] The increase in territorial disparities since the crisis has re-opened the debate about whether the EU

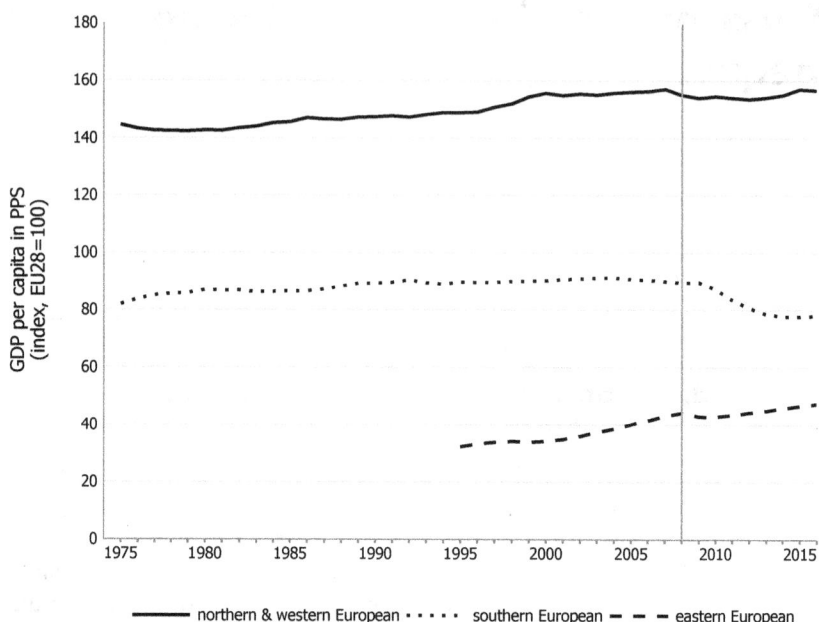

Figure 4.1 Development of GDP for selected EU country groups (1975–2016).
Source: World Bank (2017).

ought to have a stronger mandate to equalise differences in its citizens' living standards. As such, to name just a few examples, then German foreign minister Sigmar Gabriel demanded a strengthening of solidarity in the EU (SPEIGEL Online 2017). Similarly, French president Emmanuel Macron also advocated a common European budget and improved coordination of economic policy-making across EU member states in order to reduce disparities between countries. He suggested that the strong should help the weak: 'A monetary union does not exist without the sharing of the revenues! The stronger ones must help the weaker ones' (Süddeutsche Zeitung 2015).[3] The proposal to cut crisis-affected countries' deficits, which has been widely discussed in public, is also essentially a call for the redistribution of wealth between richer and poorer EU countries (Varoufakis 2015).

One way the EU could achieve greater equality in Europe would be to establish fiscal equalisation schemes between rich and poor member states. Therefore, we define *territorial solidarity* as compensating for economic disparities among territories (e.g. subnational regions or member states) by redistributing wealth between them. In contrast to other redistribution, such as interpersonal redistribution in the form of welfare solidarity (see Chapter 5), the resources are not redistributed among certain social groups within a certain geographical territory, e.g. the nation state, but within the territory as a whole. Territorial solidarity is not a recent invention but is, in fact, a practice long upheld at the nation state level of many EU member states (e.g. Austria, Germany, Portugal, or Spain; cf. OECD 2013:103). Its basic tenet goes as follows: the nation state ensures its social and territorial integration by providing citizens in all its regions similar living conditions. Therefore, the state supports regions that are worse off than others, for example, because of poorer economic output, lower tax receipts, or greater expenses (OECD 2013). Territorial solidarity within the nation state hence means the eradication of locational disadvantages, such as the lack of certain production factors that are important for a region's wealth generation; it also means establishing an equality of public service provision.

Yet, it is not only the nation state but also the EU that maintains policies of territorial solidarity, albeit via a different mechanism. Since the 1970s, the EU has sought to encourage economic cohesion among all its member states. Unlike policies for territorial redistribution of wealth within the nation state, the EU's cohesion policies served to increase the economic clout of weaker regions within EU countries and reduce the wealth gap between countries (Mau 2004:332). For this purpose, the EU's budget co-finances infrastructural projects, investments, and educational programmes. The EU's development funds are distributed according to the economic strength of certain regions and countries, so that the economically weakest receive the highest proportions of investment. In addition to directly supporting countries, the EU's cohesion policies for regions have indirectly led to the reduction of disparities between EU countries as well, since most of the EU's poorer regions tend to be located in the EU's poorest countries. The amount of funding dedicated to the EU's cohesion policies is considerable: it amounts to more than a third of the overall EU budget (European Commission 2016).

Thus, the idea of territorial solidarity, which re-emerged as an issue during the Great Recession, is well established in the EU. In certain member states, however, it has prompted an increasing political resistance, especially in the net contributor states (i.e. in the member states that contribute more to the EU budget than they receive).[4] Eurosceptic parties in Germany, the Netherlands (Financial Times 2014), and France (Wood 2017) predominantly see the EU's cohesion policies as a burden on their respective countries. In Great Britain too, then foreign secretary Boris Johnson referred to an imbalance imposed on his country, using it as justification for why they should leave the EU: 'We send the EU 350 million pounds a week. Let's fund our NHS [National Health System]. Vote leave. Let's take back control' (Henley 2016).[5]

In this context of growing economic disparities between different regions and EU member states, in this chapter we ask about EU citizens' positions on European territorial solidarity. As measures for redistributing resources frequently give rise to political conflicts, citizens' views on this question are of considerable importance for the EU's ongoing integration process. Our assumption is that the EU's position on future territorial solidarity will also be highly dependent on citizens' stances concerning this question. If they are in favour of reducing disparities between rich and poor EU countries, then the EU institutions could interpret this as permission to further expand the measures that have already been taken.

To answer the question of whether a genuine European territorial solidarity exists, we will apply the criteria introduced in Chapter 2. First, we will present the arguments for and against accepting territorial solidarity in the European space and compare them to what survey data have found (Section 4.2). In line with the previously defined criteria, we will investigate whether the majority of respondents think that long-term redistributive efforts that aim to reduce the gap in living standards between the rich and poor EU countries are desirable. The first condition for the existence of European solidarity would be fulfilled if citizens across all EU countries, as well as in each individual country, favoured redistributive policies within Europe, and if this rate of approval was higher than approval for territorial solidarity with countries outside of the EU. In the third section, we will explore whether opponents and advocates of European territorial solidarity are divided according to social cleavages; furthermore, we will analyse the extent to which attitudes towards European territorial solidarity can influence citizens' voting behaviour (political cleavages). The analysis in the third section will indicate how strongly contended the topic of territorial solidarity can be politically. The chapter is then rounded off with a short conclusion (Section 4.4).

4.2 How strong is European territorial solidarity?

What arguments suggest that EU citizens would be in favour of or against direct redistributive measures between European countries? The first argument concerns the particular historical development paths of nation states and their degree of social integration compared to the EU. Institutionalised redistribution has been taking place since the establishment of European nation states in the nineteenth century, almost exclusively among citizens of the same state within the boundaries of nation state territories. In many OECD and EU member states, regional redistribution policies are also an essential tool for balancing subnational regions' budgets today (OECD 2013:10). These policies predominantly serve the purpose of integrating nation states infrastructurally, administratively, and socially.

Why are we sceptical regarding citizens' attitudes to territorial solidarity on the European level? First, some authors have argued that the introduction of mechanisms for wealth redistribution is dependent on specific social and cultural prerequisites (for a summary, see Gerhards, Breuer, and Delius 2016; Gerhards and Lengfeld 2015). For people to accept redistribution measures, they need to view themselves as part of a community that is socially integrated. Social integration can be separated into two ideal forms: one *cultural* and one *civil* (Bruter

2005). A civil form of social integration mostly relies on members of a society sharing the same rights (Marshall 1983 [1949]). These preconditions are present to the greatest possible extent in nation states. In contrast, at the level of the EU they either do not exist or are only very weakly present. Even a superficial comparison shows that the rights and duties that Europeans share with one another are significantly weaker than the rights and duties of citizens from the same nation state. In an attempt to address this, EU citizens' rights were expanded through the introduction of European citizenship status (Maas 2007). What European citizenship status does is give people from other EU countries the fundamental right to migrate to all other EU countries and thereby participate in any of the other countries' prosperity (Gerhards and Lengfeld 2013, 2015). However, European citizenship status does not establish any right for redistribution between citizens who live and work in different countries in the EU.

In addition to this, in terms of culture, nation states are significantly stronger and more homogeneously integrated than the EU. Depending on the nation state, cultural similarity may variously relate to a common language, similar historical experiences leading to the formation of collective memory, and shared religion(s) and values. With regard to these aspects, the EU member states are considerably more integrated individually than the European Union is as a whole, as we have argued elsewhere (Gerhards et al. 2016). With regard to the EU, the best scenario, which could be envisaged, is that citizens' strong identification with the EU provides a precursor to European territorial solidarity. Whether this form of identification exists empirically, however, is open to debate (among others, Follesdal 2014; Risse 2010; Roose 2013).

For the above-mentioned reasons, we presumed that the bond of national solidarity between wealthy and needy regions, organised predominantly within the nation state, would be stronger than the bond between poorer and richer EU states.

There is another argument why citizens might be sceptical towards European territorial solidarity in a general sense. Territorial solidarity is a form of compensation that occurs between social spaces and not between certain groups of people. At the same time, the actual recipients of solidarity are not clearly defined. For those paying, it is unclear who will ultimately benefit from these redistributive measures. It could, therefore, result in a situation where not only poor people in poor countries benefit from redistribution between rich and poor countries, but rich people in poor countries too; this might occur if redistributive means were to go towards financing hospitals, schools, and roads. In addition, businesses, public corporations, or state institutions are often the direct beneficiaries of financial investments as part of territorial solidarity measures. Citizens could thus interpret territorial redistribution as a measure that benefits abstract bodies rather than citizens in need.

However, there are also arguments why citizens could favour long-term measures of territorial solidarity on the European level. For one, the state of political, legal, and economic integration of the EU is advanced enough for the emergence of such a solidarity. In the introductory section, we mentioned that mechanisms of territorial solidarity already exist on the EU level (Bachtler, Mendez, and Wishlade 2013). The EU grants resources from its own budget to regions and countries to encourage economic equalisation among member states.[6] This is stated in the EU's various founding documents, such as in the preamble of the Treaty on European Union: '[The Union] shall promote economic, social and territorial cohesion, and solidarity among Member States' (European Union 2012a, article 3(3); and similarly in article 174 of the Treaty on the Functioning of the EU (FTEU); European Union 2012b). The closing of the gap in living standards is thus an established component of the EU's cohesion policies and also of a vision of a unified Europe. For decades, the EU's budgetary policies have been formulated with this goal in mind, and this objective has been constantly pursued within the EU's integration process. The current system stipulates that member states provide resources through payments into the EU budget. In return, all member states receive different proportions of funding via redistributive measures. The EU hence does not exclusively support poorer member states but assists richer states as well. We presumed that both the existence of European redistributive mechanisms and the fact that all states are beneficiaries of these funds would bolster the approval rates for European territorial solidarity.

A further argument that could justify why European citizens ought to be in favour of European territorial solidarity relates to citizens' own self-interest. As redistribution means transforming resources from rich countries to poor countries, the latter become the real beneficiaries of territorial solidarity. We consequently assumed that citizens from the less economically developed countries, such as the eastern and southern European states, would endorse such redistributive policies. We wish to distinguish these direct utilitarian effects from indirect ones. Redistribution may not only be useful to those who receive aid but also to citizens of the countries that give aid. Georg Vobruba (1996) highlighted this, using the example of environmental pollution in countries from the former Soviet Union. He argued that development funds that went towards technical environmental protection for eastern European companies indirectly benefited western European citizens, as the emissions from eastern European industries also had a damaging effect in western Europe. Analogously, Georg Vobruba has argued that territorial redistribution benefiting the poorer EU countries also benefits citizens from the wealthier member states, as reducing gaps in living standards can also reduce the number of workers migrating from poorer to richer countries. This, in turn, diminishes the conflicts that arise as a result of new migration (Vobruba 1996:87–8). To this extent, it could be suggested that supporting poorer regions and their economies is a costly but attractive alternative to inter-European migration; indeed, this argument has gained force through the rising unemployment rates caused by the economic crisis in the southern European states.

From this, it follows that citizens' agreement with the basic premise of European territorial solidarity should vary across countries. We predicted that the direct effects of benefiting from territorial solidarity would lead to greater approval rates among citizens from poorer countries in eastern and southern Europe than the indirect effects would among citizens from the richer, western European countries. As the previously defined criterion for majority support also applies to the approval rates within any particular country, the question of country-by-country differences will likely play a special role here.

All in all, there are arguments both for and against a majority approval for European territorial solidarity. However, such theoretical reflections cannot tell us which of the arguments are more applicable. Nor can existing empirical research be of any use in this aspect. According to our knowledge, there is, to date, no empirical study that has investigated citizens' attitudes towards European territorial solidarity. While research in economics and political science has examined the already institutionalised forms of territorial solidarity in the EU, these studies have particularly focused on whether the current policies contribute towards the EU convergence process (see among others, Becker et al. 2012; Boldrin and Canova 2001; Dall'erba and Le Gallo 2008; Pellegrini et al. 2013).

In the TESS survey, citizens were asked their opinion on whether regional differences in wealth in Europe ought to be reduced. Drawing on the previously outlined concept of three spaces of solidarity, we presented the respondents with three statements on redistribution. These statements referred to givers and recipients that were either regions inside a nation state (national territorial solidarity, Statement 1), countries within the EU (European territorial solidarity; Statement 2), or states outside of Europe (global territorial solidarity; Statement 3).

There are differences between rich and poor regions in a country, between countries in Europe, and also between countries in the world. Please tell me to what extent you agree or disagree with the following statements.

(1) Differences between rich and poor [GENERALREGIONNAME]s in [COUNTRY] should be reduced, even if wealthier [GENERALREGION-NAME]s have to pay more.
(2) Differences between rich and poor countries in the EU should be reduced, even if wealthier countries in the European Union have to pay more.
(3) Differences between EU countries and poor countries outside of the EU should be reduced, even if EU countries have to pay more.

All three statements referred to a horizontal financial compensation system, through which each giver and recipient of solidarity was equal. Unlike in a vertical compensation scheme, in a horizontal scheme more highly situated redistribution institutions play no role. Such a formulation foregoes the problem of the respondents rejecting one of the respective *institutions* for redistribution, such as the EU or the national government.[7] Because reducing disparities is highly socially desired, we added a reminder of the possible costs that would arise through the redistributive policy. It should, therefore, have been clear to the participants that each form of solidarity had negative financial repercussions for richer states and regions.

Figure 4.2 shows the extent of all the participants' approval and rejection for each of the three statements. Obviously, measures reducing disparities between EU member states had high rates of acceptance among EU citizens. More than two-thirds of citizens (71%) supported this idea. Surprisingly, the rate of approval here was only marginally behind support for reducing wealth disparities between regions in one's own country (76%). In contrast, only a slight majority accepted territorial solidarity on the global level (53%). From the citizens' point of view, a global sphere of redistribution was therefore the most controversial. As far as the intensity of approval of respondents goes, the three spatial scales were almost indistinguishable from one another: the proportions of those who 'fully and completely' or 'tend to' reject or agree, were all very similar in both directions.

Thus, the majority of EU citizens see the European space as the legitimate space for compensating for wealth differences. In contrast to what we expected, the approval rate for European solidarity was close to the same level as that for national solidarity. Territorial solidarity is quite clearly no longer confined to the national container. Our data suggested that it was not inhibited by the fact that

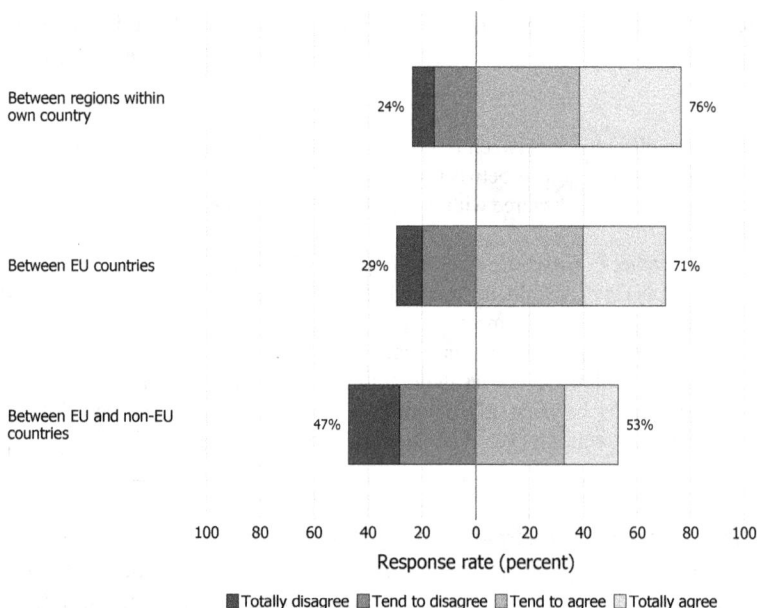

Figure 4.2 Response rates of the support for the reduction of territorial disparities by recipient's spatial level.

Source: TESS 2016, own calculations.

the EU is much less of a real perceived community than the nation state or by the fact that the recipients of redistributed aid are not individuals, but rather abstract institutions. At the same time, the much lower degree of approval for reducing global wealth disparities clearly indicates that territorial solidarity does have its spatial limits: only a slight majority was in favour of a worldwide system of redistribution. We can largely rule out the argument that attitudes towards reducing disparities between territorial entities were, to any extent, due to a general cosmopolitan motive among the participants.

How big were the differences between the countries? Figure 4.3 shows the average willingness to agree on territorial solidarity in each surveyed country for the three different spaces of solidarity.[8] The findings show that a majority of citizens from all countries supported solidarity on the European level. Hence, the data confirm a further criterion for the existence of European solidarity. Nevertheless, the approval rates varied by a margin of 35 percentage points, between 53% in the Netherlands and 88% in Spain. Majority approval was also found on the national level in all countries, albeit with a considerably smaller range. In contrast, for territorial solidarity on a global level, majority support was only found in seven of the 13 surveyed states.[9]

A look at the country-by-country differences reveals that we can empirically distinguish three different country groups when it comes to approval for European territorial solidarity. The highest approval rates were found in the Mediterranean countries, where European territorial solidarity approval ratings were found to be even higher than those for national territorial solidarity. The second group of countries displayed high approval ratings on average, and mostly comprised the eastern European member states. In these states, the willingness to engage in European territorial solidarity was marginally lower than in the

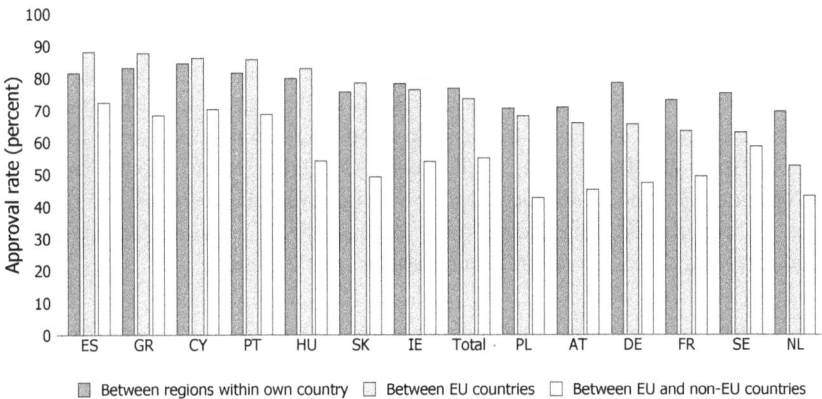

Figure 4.3 Average approval rates of the support for the reduction of territorial disparities by recipient's spatial level by country.

Source: TESS 2016, own calculations.

Mediterranean countries. However, we also found stable majorities here. Furthermore, we found higher approval rates for European territorial solidarity than for national solidarity in both Hungary and Slovakia. In the northern and western European countries (except for Ireland), agreement with European territorial solidarity was markedly lower than in the two aforementioned country groups.[10]

Thus, the prediction that citizens of less wealthy countries would be more likely to accept European territorial solidarity can only be partially confirmed. Indeed, citizens from economically stronger countries and from countries benefiting less from current redistribution policies in northern and western Europe were less supportive of European territorial solidarity than citizens from the Mediterranean countries. However, citizens from economically weak states from eastern Europe bucked this linear trend as they showed lower levels of approval than those in the relatively richer states from the south. The reason for this could lie in the different ways that these three groups had developed economically in the years prior to the survey. This, however, shows that beliefs in solidarity in the form of redistribution do not, or at least not predominantly, follow the motive of self-interest – if this were the case, citizens from the poorest countries would surely also be the biggest proponents of solidarity. In Section 4.3, the relation between economic power and attitudes towards solidarity is investigated in even greater detail.

Given these results, we see that the first of our criteria for establishing a European solidarity for the domain of territorial solidarity is met: there is a majority approval among all citizens, as well as among the citizens within each state. Furthermore, we found a strong approval for European territorial solidarity over a global one, which is a first sign that our second criterion may be fulfilled and also points to the existence of a *European communitarianism* (see Chapter 2).

To further check our criterion on the relation to national and global solidarity, we investigated whether this high willingness to agree with European territorial solidarity was also persistent. To get a sense of the strength of citizens' convictions, we put respondents into a fictional decision-making scenario about the space of solidarity. Similarly to Chapter 3, the respondents were asked which of the three spaces of solidarity they would choose first if they had to choose one. This question was followed up with one on what their second choice would be; the option they selected for the question was not available for selection a second time. A scenario like this allowed us to estimate what meaning each degree of solidarity would possess in direct comparison with the others.

(1) Assuming a decision about priority has to be made: in your opinion, where should the difference be reduced first?
  (a) Between rich and poor [GENERALREGIONNAME]s in [COUNTRY]
  (b) Between rich and poor countries in the European Union.
  (c) Between EU countries and poor countries outside of the European Union.

(2) And where should they be reduced second?
   (a) Between rich and poor [GENERALREGIONNAME]s in [COUNTRY]
   (b) Between rich and poor countries in the European Union.
   (c) Between EU countries and poor countries outside of the European Union.

The dark grey columns in Figure 4.4 show the prevalence, in percentage points, with which people list a particular space of solidarity as their first priority; the light grey columns show the space of solidarity that they gave as their second choice. More than half of the respondents prioritised reducing disparities between regions within their own country (57%). What is surprising is that, in this case, the European space of solidarity was only slightly more likely to be chosen ahead of the global space (25% vs 18%). It is only when we asked respondents to list their second priority that it became evident that the respondents prioritised Europe-wide solidarity over global solidarity (62% vs 16%). Citizens in general found that reducing wealth disparities between rich and poor regions in their own country was the most important by far. The bare majority who prioritised the national level indicated, however, that many citizens would be in favour of reducing disparities beyond their own borders. The European space represented the second most important scale of territorial redistribution. The criterion for a higher approval rate in favour of a European space of solidarity over a global one is thereby fulfilled and hence supports the existence of a *European communitarianism*.

Figure 4.5 shows that reducing disparities within respondents' own country took the first priority in all the surveyed countries. Nevertheless, there were some variances in the proportion of people selecting the European space as the

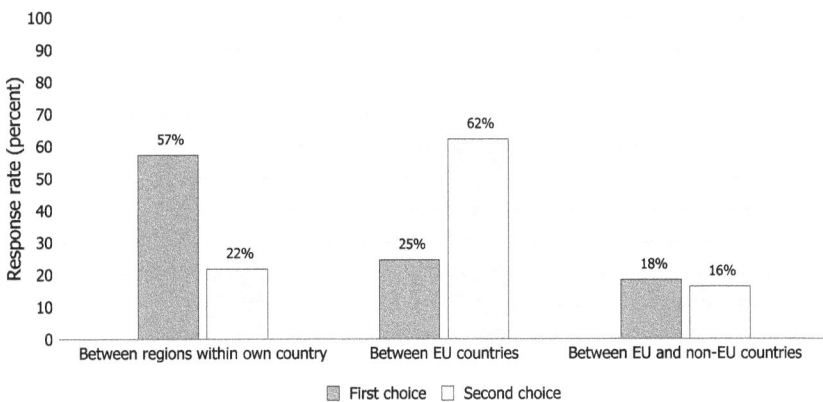

Figure 4.4 Response rates to where should disparities be first reduced.
Source: TESS 2016, own calculations.

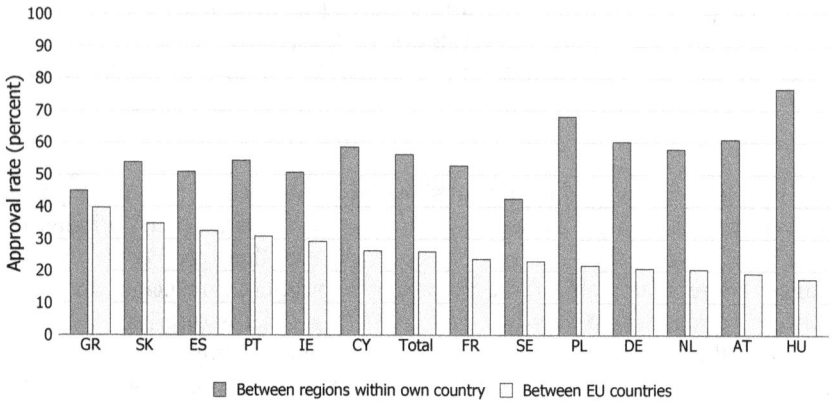

Figure 4.5 Response rates to where should disparities be first reduced by country.

Source: TESS 2016, own calculations.

first preference (the highest agreement with this category being in Greece, at 40%, and the lowest in Hungary at 17%). There was an even greater margin of difference between countries giving their own nation first preference (the highest rate is in Hungary, at 77%, and the lowest in Sweden, at 43%). In Greece and Sweden, no absolute majority could be found in favour of prioritising national territorial solidarity. Even if the quality of the answers on the decision-making question varied from state to state, a tendency towards a particular pattern can be recognised. Once again, the Mediterranean states displayed the strongest affinity with Europe. In contrast, northern and western European citizens chose their own nation as the first-choice space of solidarity more often. While France and Sweden slightly deviated from this pattern, they still remained below the overall average when all countries were ranked in order. Ireland, once again, represented an anomaly, as its citizens more often named Europe as the first-choice space of solidarity. The eastern European countries did not form a cohesive group on this matter.

To draw a short interim conclusion: among all the citizens, a large majority favours narrowing the economic disparities between EU member states through redistribution policies. In addition, a majority agrees with the idea of European territorial solidarity in each surveyed country. This result is especially noteworthy, as the survey items emphasised the negative consequences of territorial solidarity for the wealthier states.

Thus, our first criterion for proving the existence of European territorial solidarity is clearly met. Furthermore, willingness to support European territorial solidarity is much greater than support for global wealth-redistribution. Additionally, in some states, the perceived legitimacy of European territorial solidarity is stronger than support for the national solidarity system. Hence, another criterion, which points to the existence of a *European communitarianism*, is fulfilled. This is further underlined in the decision-making scenario. While the national space continues to be the most important space of solidarity for most of the respondents, European territorial solidarity is a clear second preference. The sometimes-large differences between countries indicates that participants' attitudes towards European solidarity are motivated by their own self-interest to a limited extent. Indeed, wealthier citizens from the northern and western European countries are less in favour of the idea of European redistribution of disparities. Some citizens from countries benefiting the most from development funds (i.e. the less-developed eastern European economies), however, express lower preferences for redistributive measures than southern European citizens, whose countries' economic performance lies below northern European countries, but above eastern European ones.

4.3 Divided over European territorial solidarity?

In the following section, we will first investigate whether there are certain social groups that reject European territorial solidarity and whether there is consequently a threat of creating social cleavages. Similarly to the chapter on fiscal solidarity, we will distinguish between two types of social cleavages. Structural cleavages are anchored in instrumentally rational motives, while cultural cleavages are affiliated with value-rational or affective motives. The two types of cleavages can influence political compromises in regard to territorial solidarity, as we already explained in detail in Chapter 2. Instrumentally rationally motivated conflicts are interest based and therefore offer more room for compromise in principle. In contrast, political conflicts stemming from value-rational and affective stances are much more difficult to resolve. In the following, we will determine which characteristics influence attitudes towards European territorial solidarity: that is, which (a) participant characteristics, (b) country characteristics, and (c) combinations of individual and country characteristics. We then test our expectations with the help of multivariate analytical procedures. After analysing whether both types of social cleavages are present, we will investigate whether these conflict lines translate into political cleavages. For this, we will analyse whether those who reject European territorial solidarity also express a special preference for Eurosceptic political parties.

4.3.1 Structural cleavages

(a) Based on studies on attitudes towards the national welfare state (cf. Alt and Iversen 2017; Jæger 2006; Linos and West 2003; Svallfors 1997), we expected that people with low socio-economic status would be more inclined to be in favour of redistribution between EU countries. According to these studies, people with low socio-economic status associated any form of redistribution with a shifting of resources from above to below; they would be the beneficiaries of these measures. As individual self-interest guides such orientations, we presumed that this motive also influences attitudes to (European) territorial solidarity.

Laia Balcells and colleagues (2015) have analysed citizens' attitudes towards territorial redistribution on a regional level in Spain, using original survey data from 2012. Yet, they could not find an effect of individual income or unemployment on supporting regional redistribution. As their research was restricted to the subnational level and to Spain, we expected that EU structural policy, in practice, could lead low-status people to favour European territorial solidarity. In particular, some EU projects explicitly target improving the labour market conditions of people from poor economic backgrounds. These measures are promoted in poor and rich countries alike through various schemes, such as the European Social Fund (ESF), which funds projects for basic education, further education, vocational training, and for reintegrating people into the job market.[11] Because people with low incomes are more likely to benefit from these measures than those on high incomes, the former group should have a more positive opinion on development funds. We assumed that people with low socioeconomic status would share this generalised view, and because of this, would generally display a positive stance towards European redistribution policies. We thus assumed that EU citizens were basically informed on how EU development funds promote labour market policies for the socially disadvantaged. However, since these measures are promoted regardless of a region's degree of wealth, we expected that European territorial solidarity would also be supported by socially disadvantaged people in wealthy countries. All in all, we expected a high degree of support for European territorial solidarity from less-educated people, lower-class individuals, the unemployed, and people with low incomes.[12]

(b) The descriptive analysis in the previous section has shown that willingness to support territorial solidarity varies greatly between countries. In this chapter's introduction, we already noted that wealthier countries make greater contributions to the structural and regional funds than poorer countries. This imbalance is further reinforced by contemporary redistribution policies. The EU allocates its development funds based on regions' relative economic situation by dividing regions into three groups: 'Less Developed Regions', 'Transition Regions', and 'More Developed Regions'. Each of these groups receives a precalculated amount of the total funds available. The amount decreases in inverse relation to the region's economic power.[13] Despite all regions being eligible for EU funding, both the financing and the payment system disadvantages wealthier member states. This situation has prompted many political conflicts in the past (the so-called 'net contributor debate'). Not only do wealthier member states have to contribute more into the EU budget, they also end up getting less in return.

Jan Delhey and Ulrich Kohler (2006) showed that EU citizens compare the state of living standards in their own country with that of other countries. We expected that citizens would also estimate whether their country is likely to profit from further European redistributive policies or not. Therefore, we assumed that respondents in richer countries would support European territorial solidarity to a lesser degree than those from poorer ones. Findings from the above-cited study from Laia Balcells and colleagues (2015) in Spain supported this assumption. Perceiving their region as being in a better economic position led respondents to offer significantly lower support for regional redistribution. We will refer to the gross domestic product (GDP) per capita to measure the wealth of each country (with one unit equalling €1,000 per person in 2015).[14]

Another factor to consider is a country's economic development. Regarding this, the recent economic and sovereign debt crisis affected the Mediterranean countries most severely. In these states, economic growth stopped or even declined; hence the populations might have perceived territorial solidarity as a safety net, which would prevent their country from falling further behind other countries. Correspondingly, we presumed that a high proportion of their citizens would support European territorial solidarity. In contrast, in the economically well-performing regions, especially in the eastern member states, the anticipation that the economy will further grow should lead to lower approval of European territorial solidarity. Therefore, we expected that a country's economic growth over the last few years would negatively correlate with its citizens' approval of territorial solidarity. We measured economic development by taking the relative development of real GDP since the onset of the economic crisis (in the period between 2008 and 2015).

(c) We previously assumed that citizens with low socio-economic status would be more in favour of European territorial solidarity than those with high social standing. However, we also expected this effect to vary according to a country's wealth. Especially in the poorer countries, people with lower education levels, those from lower social classes, the unemployed, or respondents from low-income households should support territorial solidarity more strongly than those with a similarly low social status in richer countries. Individuals with low socio-economic status in richer countries may fear that territorial solidarity would affect their disadvantaged situation even more: financial transfers related to European territorial solidarity from their country to others may result in cutbacks to transfers within their own nation state. From this, we expected individuals with low socio-economic status in economically powerful countries to exhibit lower approval rates for European territorial solidarity than their counterparts in poor countries.

For the interaction between the effects of socio-economic status and economic growth on attitudes towards European territorial solidarity, our assumption was similar. Nevertheless, we emphasised the attitudes of those with a low socio-economic background in countries undergoing an economic downturn. In these countries, unskilled workers or those working in low-skilled service sector careers are particularly at risk of losing their jobs in times of economic stagnation, or due to rationalisation measures, restructuring of enterprises, national austerity programmes, or structural adjustment measures. Therefore, we expected citizens with a low level of education, those working in low-income jobs, and those working in economically vulnerable sectors – especially routine non-manual and unskilled manual workers – to feel more insecure than people from other groups. As a result, they could see territorial redistribution transfers as a chance to secure better security and a greater set of options – such as new jobs and additional economic growth. Altogether, we expected that, in countries that had experienced a negative economic development path in recent years, people with low socio-economic status would more strongly approve of European territorial solidarity than those with a similar relative degree of socio-economic status from countries experiencing economic growth.

4.3.2 Cultural cleavages

(1) Citizens' cultural characteristics consist of many different elements, among other things their political value orientations. We assumed that left-wing individuals would be more in favour of financial equalisation on the European level than people who positioned themselves in the political centre or on the right, because redistribution sentiments are a core principle of leftist ideology. Voters who place themselves on the left thereby tend to support measures of welfare state redistribution more regularly than others (Jæger 2008). This has also been empirically proven for support for territorial redistribution in Spain (Balcells et al. 2015). We gauged respondents' political identities through a self-assessment question, asking the participants to place themselves on the left–right spectrum.

Another factor that might influence citizens' attitudes towards European territorial solidarity is whether citizens identify with specific territorial spaces. People who have an emotional bond predominantly to their nation state should support the redistribution of resources first and foremost among their national population. From their perspective, solidarity requires givers and recipients of resources to share the same cultural, linguistic, and historical background, which is traditionally ensured by the nation state (Teney, Lacewell, and de Wilde 2014; Zürn and de Wilde 2016). In their analysis of Catalans' attitudes towards regional redistribution, Laia Balcells and colleagues (2015) showed that this was also true for sub-national identities: citizens who identified as Catalans strongly rejected support for other regions. Based on this we assumed that people with a strong sense of national identity would more strongly oppose European territorial solidarity, while respondents who saw themselves as Europeans would support it. We also expected a positive effect among those who considered themselves to be world citizens. These individuals supported cosmopolitan goals of global equality, the openness of all societies, the universality of human rights, and for internationalism. To measure the affectual bond to different territorial spaces, the respondents were asked to state whether they identify with their nation, Europe, or the world.

(2) We also expect the degree of cultural cleavages to vary according to their country's economic situation. We assume that citizens from richer countries with

right-wing political orientations or a strong nation identity would oppose the notion European territorial solidarity more than those from poorer countries. While having right-wing orientations should also indicate support for nation state protectionism, the latter should also be in favour of limiting solidarity to their own country. However, since their country may potentially benefit from redistribution measures, their country's interest should soften the influence of their political orientation on their support for European territorial solidarity.

4.3.3 Results on social cleavages

Our methodological approach was identical to the one applied in Chapter 3 (see Section 3.3.3 'Notes on methodology' as well as the Appendix). We measured territorial solidarity by taking people's attitudes towards the redistribution of wealth disparities between countries (member states) on the European level. The analysis first focused on the individual level. In addition, we compared the influence of the theoretically grounded variables on attitudes towards national territorial solidarity.

In Table 4.1 we can see that the indicators for detecting structural cleavages had almost no significant effects on European territorial solidarity. Only the effect of income was statistically significant, albeit at a weak level. The negative effect of income remained stable even when controlling for cultural factors. Although there was a positive but weak significant effect for education, other structural cleavage factors, such as class position or labour market status did not correlate with attitudes towards European territorial solidarity. While this finding contrasts with research on attitudes towards welfare redistribution (Alt and Iversen 2017; Jæger 2006; Linos and West 2003; Svallfors 1997), it is in line with the results of Laia Balcells and colleagues (2015) for territorial redistribution in Spain. Thus, we did not find structural cleavages in regard to European territorial solidarity. The proportion of explained variance also supports this interpretation: compared to M1 (the model controlling only for contextual factors and other individual-level control variables), when we included indicators for social cleavages the explained variance only showed a marginal improvement in M2 (from 11.6% to 12.1%).

Cultural factors, in contrast, were more useful in explaining attitudes towards European territorial solidarity. Compared to people from the political centre, people on the moderate right were less supportive of European territorial solidarity, while people positioning themselves as moderate or radically left wing were more supportive of European territorial solidarity. This is in line with previous research on attitudes towards redistribution (Balcells et al. 2015; Jæger 2008). One noteworthy finding is that the effect of political orientation was not linear throughout. The rate of approval was, in fact, greatest among the strongly left wing. Conversely, people on the radical right did not differ significantly from the reference group in the political centre.[15] Furthermore, the results for the question concerning identification with the different territorial units (nation state,

Table 4.1 Social cleavages regarding reducing territorial disparities between EU countries and between regions within the nation state; individual level

	European Union			Nation
	M1	M2	M3	M4
Control variables				
Sex (ref.: male)	0.02 (0.02)	0.01 (0.02)	0.00 (0.02)	0.02 (0.02)
Age (by 10 years)	**0.11*** (0.04)	**0.11**** (0.03)	**0.11**** (0.03)	**0.13***** (0.03)
Age (by 10 years, squared)	-0.00 (0.00)	-0.00 (0.00)	-0.00 (0.00)	-0.01* (0.00)
Household: number of children	**-0.03*** (0.01)	**-0.04*** (0.01)	**-0.02*** (0.01)	**-0.04**** (0.01)
Migration generation (ref.: no migration background)				
First generation	0.01 (0.03)	0.01 (0.03)	0.01 (0.03)	0.02 (0.02)
Second generation	0.01 (0.04)	-0.00 (0.04)	0.00 (0.05)	0.03 (0.04)
Structural cleavages				
Level of education (ref.: tertiary)				
Non or primary		0.08 (0.05)	0.08 (0.05)	0.05 (0.05)
Secondary		0.02 (0.02)	**0.05*** (0.02)	0.05 (0.02)
Occupational class (ref.: upper class (I))				
Upper middle class (II)		0.02 (0.03)	0.01 (0.03)	0.04 (0.03)
Centre middle class (IIIa)		-0.04 (0.03)	-0.03 (0.02)	0.00 (0.02)
Lower middle class (V & VI)		0.02 (0.04)	0.02 (0.04)	0.08 (0.04)
Self-employed (IVab & IVc)		-0.11 (0.07)	-0.09 (0.06)	-0.05 (0.06)
Routine non-manual (IIIb)		0.01 (0.02)	0.00 (0.02)	0.05 (0.05)
Unskilled manual workers & agriculture (VIIa & VIIb)		0.02 (0.05)	0.02 (0.05)	0.06 (0.04)
Unemployed (ref.: employed)		0.05 (0.05)	0.04 (0.05)	-0.01 (0.04)
Household income		**-0.06***** (0.01)	**-0.06***** (0.01)	-0.03 (0.02)
Cultural cleavages				
Political placement (ref.: centre)				
Left			**0.33***** (0.06)	**0.19**** (0.05)
Moderate left			**0.22***** (0.03)	**0.17***** (0.03)
Moderate right			**-0.15***** (0.03)	**-0.13***** (0.03)
Right			-0.06 (0.06)	**-0.16*** (0.07)
Identity: national (ref.: no)			-0.03 (0.07)	0.02 (0.10)
Identity: European (ref.: no)			0.10 (0.05)	0.02 (0.02)
Identity: global (ref.: no)			**0.10***** (0.02)	**0.06*** (0.02)

Country differences

Country (ref.: Spain)

	Model 1		Model 2		Model 3		Model 4	
Austria	-0.65***	(0.01)	-0.62***	(0.01)	-0.53***	(0.02)	-0.34***	(0.02)
Cyprus	0.11***	(0.01)	0.11***	(0.01)	0.26***	(0.04)	0.21***	(0.02)
France	-0.61***	(0.01)	-0.59***	(0.01)	-0.52***	(0.02)	-0.31***	(0.02)
Germany	-0.63***	(0.01)	-0.59***	(0.01)	-0.51***	(0.02)	-0.13***	(0.02)
Greece	0.10***	(0.00)	0.09***	(0.01)	0.18***	(0.03)	0.13***	(0.02)
Hungary	-0.19***	(0.01)	-0.22***	(0.02)	-0.08*	(0.03)	-0.08*	(0.03)
Ireland	-0.37***	(0.01)	-0.35***	(0.01)	-0.23***	(0.03)	-0.14***	(0.02)
The Netherlands	-0.84***	(0.01)	-0.82***	(0.01)	-0.68***	(0.03)	-0.35***	(0.02)
Poland	-0.61***	(0.00)	-0.61***	(0.01)	-0.49***	(0.03)	-0.37***	(0.02)
Portugal	-0.02***	(0.00)	-0.05***	(0.01)	0.04*	(0.02)	0.01	(0.02)
Slovakia	-0.35***	(0.00)	-0.39***	(0.01)	-0.25***	(0.03)	-0.19***	(0.03)
Sweden	-0.67***	(0.01)	-0.63***	(0.01)	-0.51***	(0.03)	-0.09**	(0.02)
Constant	3.00***	(0.11)	3.42***	(0.11)	3.15***	(0.12)	2.85***	(0.13)
R^2	0.116		0.121		0.158		0.074	
AIC	23,210.4		23,174.4		22,782.4		23,527.0	

Source: TESS 2016, own calculations.

Notes

$n = 9,134$; Unstandardised coefficients from pooled OLS regression with robust standard errors (clustered by country), $*p < 0.05$; $**p < 0.01$; $***p < 0.001$, standard errors in parentheses.

European, and world) were interesting. Although the effects of national and European identity went in the expected direction, they were nonetheless very weak and insignificant. The influence of cosmopolitan identity alone was the only significant one. Those holding cosmopolitan world views tended to agree with European territorial solidarity. When we included cultural determinants, the explained variance increased from 12.1% in M2 to 15.8% in M3. This suggests that cultural cleavages were more relevant than structural cleavages for territorial solidarity.

The effects of the country dummies in the lower part of Table 4.1 largely confirm the findings from the descriptive analysis (Figure 4.2). The results from M3 show that when we controlled for individual variables, the highest approval rates for European territorial solidarity were found in the Mediterranean states,[16] followed by the eastern European countries. With the exception of Hungary and Portugal, all country effects were significant and differed from our reference country Spain. The lowest rates of approval continued to be found in the northern and western European states, with the highest average degree of rejection altogether in the Netherlands. Ireland was once again an exception in its regional grouping.

Finally, we compared the results from M3 with the results on attitudes towards national territorial solidarity in M4. In terms of structural variables, almost no difference was evident between the two models. One remarkable finding was that income had no statistical effect on the national level. The influence of cultural characteristics on people's attitudes only gave rise to minor differences as well. Identification with the nation state and Europe did not have any impact on attitudes towards national solidarity. The impact of a global identity pointed in the same negative direction, albeit the effect was only significant on the 5% level. With regard to political self-placement, we found a linear relationship for national redistribution policies (M4).

Moreover, the strength of the effects were significantly different from one another: the impact of political self-placement on attitudes towards European territorial solidarity was considerably stronger than its influence on attitudes towards national solidarity. This means that the potential for conflict on the European level is higher than on the national level. A comparison of the explained variance confirms this interpretation: the same set of covariates explained 7.4% of the variance for territorial solidarity within the nation state but 15.8% of the variance for the European space.

Both the descriptive and the multivariate analysis have shown that attitudes to European territorial solidarity were most strongly influenced by country factors. We wish to clarify which factors account for this using macro-level analysis. Figure 4.6 shows the effects of country characteristics on country-specific approval rates for European territorial solidarity. Two independent macro variables are portrayed on the horizontal axis of both graphs. On the left-hand side, there is the degree of wealth, and on the right, there is each country's economic growth rate. In both parts of the graph, the country coefficients from Table 4.1

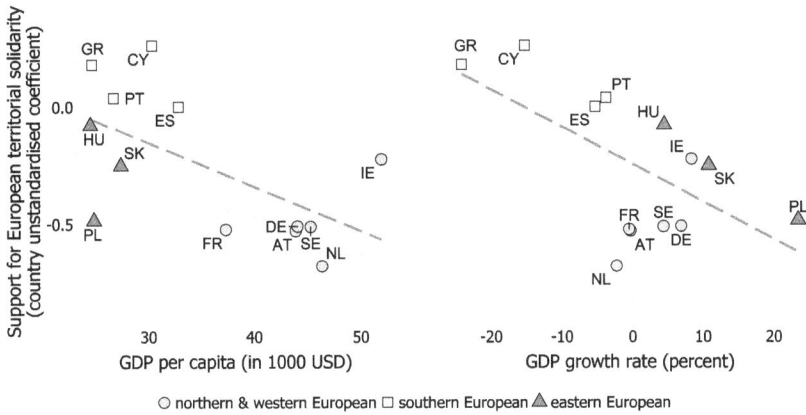

Figure 4.6 Social cleavages regarding reducing territorial disparities between EU countries; country level.

Source: TESS 2016, own calculations.

(Model 3) are portrayed on the vertical axis. Additionally, the countries are represented in accordance with the three regional groups – southern European, eastern European, and northern and western European states – through different symbols.

The results show that, in line with our expectations and previous research (Balcells et al. 2015), approval for territorial solidarity on the European level significantly declined as GDP rose. Nevertheless, there were some exceptions: the effect of the negative correlation was valid for the western and northern European states, but not for the southern and eastern European ones. Moreover, the countries from each of the three regions formed relatively homogeneous groups, with the exception of Ireland. Altogether, the findings confirmed our prediction that there would be a negative relationship between the degree of wealth of a citizen's country and the acceptance of territorial redistribution measures on the European level. Our hypothesis regarding the effects of economic growth was also confirmed. People from states with negative economic development – with the Mediterranean states leading the way – agreed with territorial solidarity to a greater extent than citizens with increasing economic growth, e.g. the post-socialist countries. Taking a look at the country groups, we see that the correlation was not valid for the northern and western European countries. Furthermore, the effects also remained stable when we included both macro variables in the same regression model,[17] or applied other analytical processes.[18]

In order to test whether the two country characteristics also influenced the impact of social cleavages on attitudes towards European territorial solidarity, we conducted cross-level analysis by means of a two-step regression (for methodological details, see Section 3.3.3 'Notes on methodology' in Chapter 3, as well as the Appendix). The regressions were calculated separately for each country in the first step. The country regressions show that the trends identified in the pooled analysis (Table 4.1) applied to each country individually. Moreover, the directions of the effects in country models were mostly identical. Therefore, the results from the cross-level analysis do not support our theoretical expectations. They show that a country's economic power does not moderate the effect of structural factors. As such, our expectation that those in a low socioeconomic situation in rich countries would be less in favour of European solidarity and citizens in a poor economic situation in countries with a declining economy would be more in favour (compared to their counterparts in rich countries or in countries with well-performing economies) cannot be confirmed. The second expectation concerning the cultural dimension also cannot be confirmed empirically. Contrary to what we predicted, right-wing people and those who identified with their nation from richer countries did not reject territorial solidarity to a greater extent. It is instead evident that left-wing people more strongly supported European territorial solidarity as the degree of wealth in their country rose. Finally, we found that the effect of European identity was strengthened by the country's economic power. The wealthier the country, the greater the effect of attachment to Europe on the support for territorial redistribution. Economic growth, in contrast, had little influence on the effects of structural or cultural cleavages. With the exception of an educational cross-level effect, which means that agreement with European territorial solidarity was higher among people with a lower level of education in countries with high economic growth (especially in Poland and Slovakia), we found no noticeable effects. In general, the cross-level effects were rather weak and predominantly not significant or only weakly so.

Overall, the analysis of social cleavages shows that there is no potential for a structural cleavage to emerge, and only a moderate one for a cultural cleavage. Regarding the cultural dimension, value-rational motives were decisive for whether citizens were for or against territorial redistribution in Europe. In combination with our descriptive findings, which showed a comfortable majority of 71% of the respondents supporting the idea of European fiscal solidarity, we do not expect a strong social cleavage to emerge at all, as agreement is high and not highly disputed among groups. However, the greatest differences are not within-country differences, but between-country ones, and these could only be partially explained by macro factors, while we did not find substantial cross-level effects.

4.3.4 Results on political cleavages

So far, our analysis has shown weak social cleavages regarding the question of territorial solidarity on the European level. In elections, citizens' resistance to or endorsement of European territorial solidarity may find its way into the political arena and may convert a social cleavage into a political one. In this section, we will test whether attitudes towards European territorial solidarity are related to specific voting behaviour and would likely lead to a preference for right-wing Eurosceptic parties.

In recent years, European territorial solidarity has become an issue in political debates and electoral campaigns. For example, the media coverage of Brexit has become all pervasive in the national and European public spheres. In the UK, this single issue even formed the basis for the founding of the UK Independence Party (UKIP) in the early 1990s, which had the specific political aim of leaving the EU for good.[19] This debate and its focus on the unequal conditions in the current redistribution system of the EU shows that the potential for conflict on European territorial solidarity is high. We therefore assumed that citizens who rejected European territorial solidarity would be more likely to vote for right-wing parties. In contrast, proponents of territorial solidarity would be more likely to vote for left-wing parties, which are more likely to support redistribution schemes in general for ideological reasons.

To measure respondents' (potential) voting behaviour, we asked them which party they would vote for in the next elections:

If the [NATIONALELECTION] were held tomorrow, which party would you vote for?

We followed the schema suggested by Sara Hobolt and Catherine de Vries (2016) for the classification of parties. According to this, parties not only differ by their political orientation on the left–right scale but also according to their strength regarding Eurosceptic orientation. So, Hobolt and de Vries distinguished between soft and hard Eurosceptic parties. As an initial analysis, we examined the proportion of voters from each of the party categories among the opponents and proponents of European territorial solidarity.

Figure 4.7 depicts the respondents' party preferences according to their degree of approval or rejection of European territorial solidarity. For each level of acceptance of European territorial solidarity, we depict the share of voters among each party group. To improve readability, the voters for moderate parties are not listed. The results show that attitudes towards European territorial solidarity neither influenced citizens' preferences for a hard Eurosceptic party from the left (upper left quadrant) nor for a moderate Eurosceptic party from the right (lower right quadrant). However – and in line with our expectations – the share of citizens voting for a hard Eurosceptic party from the right was highest among those who totally disagreed with European solidarity, and decreased continually in line with the rising degree of agreement with this domain of solidarity (upper right quadrant). In contrast, the share of those citizens voting for a left-wing, soft Eurosceptic party increased as the degree of agreement with European territorial solidarity rose (3% among those who 'totally disagree' to 1% who 'totally

Political position

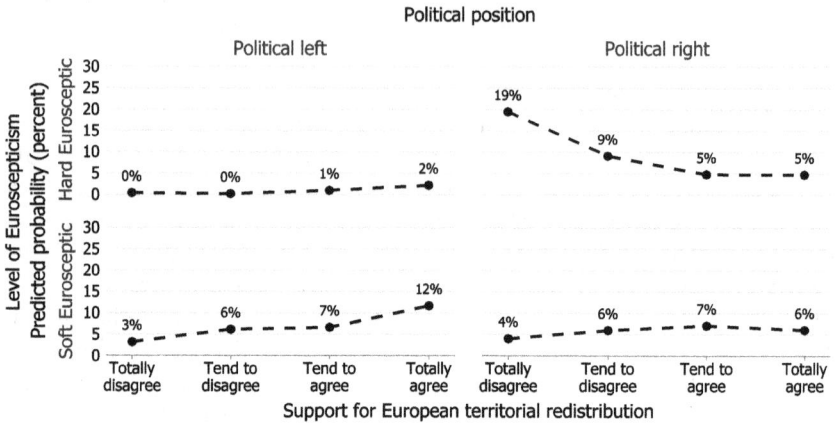

Figure 4.7 Support for European territorial solidarity and political position of party voted for.

Source: TESS 2016, own calculations.

agree'; lower left quadrant). Although these findings support our hypotheses, it should be underlined that the association between attitudes towards European territorial solidarity and party preference was rather weak.

In addition, it is important to consider that party preferences are influenced by many other factors. In a separate analysis, we tested whether the effect of attitudes towards European territorial solidarity on voting for a Eurosceptic party from the right still persisted when other factors were controlled for. Our analysis show that attitudes towards European territorial solidarity did not influence the propensity to vote for a right-wing Eurosceptic party when controlling for other variables. Thus, the effect depicted in the descriptive analysis was attributable to other factors determining people's voting decision.

In sum, our analysis on social and political cleavages comes to the following conclusions: the respondents' cultural attributes have an impact on their attitudes towards European territorial solidarity. Instrumentally rational motives only play a role insofar as they relate to the collective economic interests of respondents' national societies: citizens from wealthier countries and with lower rates of economic growth seem to fear that European territorial redistribution measures will endanger their country's wellbeing. In contrast, citizens from southern European crisis-affected countries, and also those from resurgent eastern European countries are likely to regard themselves as the beneficiaries of territorial solidarity and therefore are likely to support it. Our descriptive analysis already foreshadowed this latter finding. In contrast, citizens' individual social position – meaning their level of education, income, earnings status, and social class – has little impact on their approval for European solidarity, while cultural factors are rather important. Furthermore, our comparison of the national and European spheres of solidarity show that a European redistribution system is more controversial than a national one. Yet, our analysis also shows that these social cleavages do not translate into voting behaviour in the political arena, indicating that territorial solidarity will not threaten the process of European integration.

4.4 Conclusion on territorial solidarity

In this chapter, we focused on Europeans' attitudes towards reducing wealth disparities among EU member states. We call this domain of solidarity territorial solidarity. Measures of territorial redistribution exist not only within many nation states but also in the form of convergence policies within the EU. Redistribution might be a useful measure for achieving the EU's aim of generating economic convergence, especially at a time when the wealth gap within Europe is growing, particularly along the north–south axis. However, the EU's cohesion policies are a hotly contested political issue, in particular within the richer member states. Thus, we explored citizens' attitudes towards European territorial solidarity. Would they be willing to support transfers from richer to poorer countries within the EU? Guided by the criteria explained in Chapter 2, we analysed citizens' attitudes towards a European system of territorial redistribution. We reached the following conclusions:

1   More than two-thirds of the respondents support the idea of European territorial solidarity. The approval rate is only slightly lower than that for territorial solidarity within the nation state but it is higher than for global solidarity. At the same time, a majority of citizens support European territorial solidarity within all of the 13 survey countries. Therefore, our majority criterion is clearly met. If respondents had to make a decision on where disparities ought to be reduced first, more citizens would choose to reduce wealth disparities within the EU than on the worldwide level, also confirming our second criterion of a unique space of European solidarity.

2   Furthermore, the likelihood that social and political cleavages will emerge is rather low. While we could find almost no evidence for structural cleavages, there is some evidence for a cultural cleavage in regard to European territorial solidarity. The findings do show that European solidarity is contested in line with citizens' value-related motives. Yet, there are only some minor indications that attitudes towards European territorial solidarity have been transformed into the political arena, apart from the majority we found in favour of redistribution. Given the absence of cleavages, another criterion for the existence of European territorial solidarity is met.

3   Nevertheless, country differences play an important role. We identified three regional groups with similar attitudes towards European solidarity: there were high rates of acceptance in the Mediterranean countries, average acceptance levels in the eastern ones, and the lowest levels of acceptance in

the western and northern European countries. These group differences can be partially attributed to country differences in the wealth level and the rate of economic development.

Altogether, we found that the criteria for the existence of European territorial solidarity have been fulfilled. Contrary to our expectations, citizens' support for measures reducing territorial disparities is rather high. Thus, there seems to be some room for European political actors to develop new (or extend) existing policies in this field. Nevertheless, some important restrictions for further policy approaches must be noted. For one thing, the results show that the interests of all member states have to be taken into account, which is especially salient when combined with the net contributor debate and Brexit. The diverging approval levels for European territorial solidarity in the different member states indicate that enforcing a one-sided transfer system may result in further tensions within the EU or even mean the exit of countries from it altogether. Second, the empirical analysis presented here is based on citizens' general attitudes towards measures of regional redistribution. Even the observed high degree of approval does not mean unlimited or unconditional support for any kind of policy in this area. When it comes to imposing new policies or expanding the current cohesion policies of the EU, it is important for legislative institutions to be careful with further integration steps. As positive as the results may sound, the lack of empirical research highlights that we know little about public opinion in this area. Therefore, further research is needed to make sure that the policies implemented are appropriate.

Notes

1 The UK is the first country but not the first territory to have ever left the EU. Following a referendum carried out in 1982, Greenland also parted ways with the EU.
2 As a recent Eurobarometer poll has shown, 52% of the citizens mentioned 'comparable living standards' as the most helpful for Europe's future (European Commission 2017:467). Furthermore, this was the most often mentioned answer among several other items. Improving living standards obviously is also an important topic for the population.
3 Original quote: 'Eine Währungsunion ohne Finanzausgleich – das gibt es nicht! Die Starken müssen helfen.'
4 A balance sheet of the payments and donations made to member states can be found in the EU's Financial Report (European Commission 2016:82–3).
5 Another point of criticism is that it is empirically unclear whether the measures are at all responsible for producing the economic resurgence desired for its recipients. Some studies have indeed confirmed that the measures have had a positive impact on economic growth and the convergence process (see, among others, Becker, Egger, and von Ehrlich 2012; Pellegrini et al. 2013). Nevertheless, other studies have found no connection (see, among others, Boldrin and Canova 2001; Dall'erba and Le Gallo 2008). Guido Pellegrini and colleagues (2013) attribute the diverse results to poor data sets and the difficulty in isolating these economic measures from other influencing factors.

6 In the current phase from 2014 to 2020, development funds are granted through the 'European Structural and Investment Fund' (ESI) (European Parliament and Council of the European Union 2013c). The ESI comprises five special development funds.

   (1) The 'Cohesion Fund' (CF) serves the purpose of supporting the development of economically weaker countries (European Parliament and Council of the European Union 2013a).
   (2) The 'European Regional Development Fund' (ERDF) supports the development of economically weaker regions (European Parliament and Council of the European Union 2013b).
   (3) The 'European Social Fund' (ESF) supports projects in the areas of further education and integration into the job market (European Parliament and Council of the European Union 2013d).
   (4) The 'European Agricultural Fund for Rural Development' (EARFD) supports rural regions (European Parliament and Council of the European Union 2013e).
   (5) The 'European Maritime and Fisheries Fund' (EMFF) supports the maritime economy, fisheries, and coastal regions (European Parliament and Council of the European Union 2014).

7 In comparison to the EU's funding system, this scenario simplified the circumstances considerably. In the current system, the moneylenders were the EU countries, the official channels of redistribution were the EU institutions, and most of the recipients were subnational regions, countries, and projects within the regions.

8 The two alternative answers 'tend to agree' and 'totally agree' are aggregated to provide a better overview.

9 The great margin of difference (from 43% in Poland and the Netherlands to 72% in Spain) also indicates that global redistribution is clearly more controversial among European nations.

10 In Ireland, the approval rate with European territorial solidarity was higher than in the other northern and western European states. At the same time, support is lower than in other (former) crisis-affected countries in the Mediterranean region. This could be attributed to Ireland's specific condition at the time of the survey. Indeed, Ireland also received bailout measures during the European debt crisis. Yet, Ireland also counts as among the economically stronger European countries. We also assumed that the political situation in the neighbouring UK contributed to the high willingness to agree with European solidarity: it is possible that shortly before Brexit, the Irish survey participants felt urged to express their support for the EU by agreeing in the poll.

11 The goals of the ESF, however, encompass other areas of social inclusion as well: 'The ESF should improve employment opportunities, strengthen social inclusion, fight poverty, promote education, skills and life-long learning, and develop active, comprehensive and sustainable inclusion policies' (European Parliament and Council of the European Union 2013d).

12 A description of the variables can be found in the Appendix.

13 Nevertheless, the distribution of EU funds is still unequal: 'Less Developed Regions' (NUTS II regions with a GDP per capita that is lower than 75% of the country's average GDP) receive 52.45% of the total funding, 'Transition Regions' (GDP per capita between 75% and 90% of average GDP) receive 10.24%, and 'More Developed Regions' (GDP per capita larger than 90% of average GDP) receive 15.67% (European Parliament and Council of the European Union 2013c, articles 90 and 92). The rest of the funding is kept available for member states who are supported through the Cohesion Fund (meaning countries whose GDP per capita makes up less than 90% of the EU's average) and for the outermost regions (European Parliament and Council of the European Union 2013c, articles 90 and 92).

14 At this point, we concentrated on each country's degree of wealth and not their balance in terms of payments into and funds received from the EU Structural Fund. The reason for this is that a country's economic situation determines how much funding is allocated and where. It is also empirically evident that there is a high correlation between the two factors (Pearson's rank = 0.73 for 2015, according to our own calculations). Other than that, we expected citizens to have a more accurate idea of their country's relative economic standing in Europe than their country's balance of payments with the EU Structural Fund.

15 We do not know what the reason for this could be, especially since all individual effects concerning the participants' country of belonging are controlled for, thereby ruling out the possibility of composition effects.

16 The deviation from the sequential order in the descriptive analysis, however, cannot exclusively be attributed to the controls used for the individual variables. While we took a four-tier scale as a basis for the OLS regressions, the categories of agreement in the descriptive analysis of the country-by-country differences were cumulative. Therefore, the results from the multivariate analysis were also more strongly dependent on the polarisation of the types of answers, since these had a direct effect on calculating the overall average.

17 In addition, the explained variance for GDP and economic growth rate was rather high, 35.5% and 37.3% respectively. Just as noteworthy was that when both variables were taken into account in a model, the explained variance rose to 63.2%. This shows that the effects also functioned independently of one another.

18 The direction of the effects and their strengths were stable in both macro-level OLS regression models, as well as in hierarchical linear models. Only the pt values proved to be more conservative for the macro-level OLS regressions, while the random slope and random intercept models generally proved to be smaller.

19 While UKIP was a moderate party at the beginning, it became extremely right wing over time (for more details see Ford and Goodwin 2014).

References

Alt, James, and Torben Iversen. 2017. 'Inequality, Labor Market Segmentation, and Preferences for Redistribution'. *American Journal of Political Science* 61(1):21–36.

Bachtler, John, Carlos Mendez, and Fiona Wishlade. 2013. *EU Cohesion Policy and European Integration: The Dynamics of EU Budget and Regional Policy Reform.* Farnham and Burlington, VT: Ashgate.

Balcells, Laia, José Fernández-Albertos, and Alexander Kuo. 2015. 'Preferences for Inter-regional Redistribution'. *Comparative Political Studies* 48(10):1318–51.

Becker, Sascha O., Peter H. Egger, and Maximilian von Ehrlich. 2012. 'Too Much of a Good Thing? On the Growth Effects of the EU's Regional Policy'. *European Economic Review* 56(4):648–68.

Boldrin, Michele, and Fabio Canova. 2001. 'Inequality and Convergence in Europe's Regions: Reconsidering European Regional Policies'. *Economic Policy* 16(32):206–53.

Bruter, Michael. 2005. *Citizens of Europe? The Emergence of a Mass European Identity.* Basingstoke and New York [among others]: Palgrave Macmillan.

Dall'erba, Sandy, and Julie Le Gallo. 2008. 'Regional Convergence and the Impact of European Structural Funds over 1989–1999: A Spatial Econometric Analysis'. *Papers in Regional Science* 87(2):219–44.

Delhey, Jan, and Ulrich Kohler. 2006. 'From Nationally Bounded to Pan-European Inequalities? On the Importance of Foreign Countries as Reference Groups'. *European Sociological Review* 22(2):125–40.

European Central Bank. 2015. 'Real Convergence in the Euro Area: Evidence, Theory and Policy Implications'. *ECB Economic Bulletin* 5:30–45.

European Commission. 2016. *EU Budget 2015: Financial Report.* Retrieved 19 April 2017 (http://ec.europa.eu/budget/financialreport/2015/lib/financial_report_2015_en.pdf).

European Commission. 2017. *Special Eurobarometer 467: Future of Europe: Social Issues*. Retrieved 11 May 2018 (http://ec.europa.eu/commfrontoffice/publicopinion/index.cfm/ResultDoc/download/DocumentKy/80645).

European Committee of the Regions. 2018. *Reflecting on Europe: How Europe Is Perceived by People in Regions and Cities*. Retrieved 17 May 2018 (https://cor.europa.eu/Documents/Migrated/news/COR-17-070_report_EN-web.pdf).

European Parliament, and Council of the European Union. 2013a. 'Regulation 1300/2013 on the Cohesion Fund'. *Official Journal of the European Union* L 347:281–8.

European Parliament, and Council of the European Union. 2013b. 'Regulation 1301/2013 on the European Regional Development Fund and on Specific Provisions Concerning the Investment for Growth and Jobs'. *Official Journal of the European Union* L 347:289–302.

European Parliament, and Council of the European Union. 2013c. 'Regulation 1303/2013 Laying Down Common Provisions on the European Regional Development Fund, the European Social Fund, the Cohesion Fund, the European Agricultural Fund for Rural Development and the European Maritime and Fisheries Fund and Laying Down General Provisions on the European Regional Development Fund, the European Social Fund, the Cohesion Fund and the European Maritime and Fisheries Fund'. *Official Journal of the European Union* L 347:320–469.

European Parliament, and Council of the European Union. 2013d. 'Regulation 1304/2013 on the European Social Fund'. *Official Journal of the European Union* L 347:470–86.

European Parliament, and Council of the European Union. 2013e. 'Regulation 1305/2013 on Support for Rural Development by the European Agricultural Fund for Rural Development'. *Official Journal of the European Union* L 347:487–548.

European Parliament, and Council of the European Union. 2014. 'Regulation 508/2014 on the European Maritime and Fisheries Fund'. *Official Journal of the European Union* L 149:1–66.

European Union. 2012a. 'Consolidated Version of the Treaty on European Union'. *Official Journal of the European Union* C 326:13–45.

European Union. 2012b. 'Consolidated Version of the Treaty on the Functioning of the European Union'. *Official Journal of the European Union* C 326:47–390.

Eurostat. 2017. *Real GDP per Capita, Growth Rate and Totals (tsdec100): Eurostat – Tables, Graphs and Maps Interface (TGM)*. Retrieved 3 May 2017 (http://ec.europa.eu/eurostat/tgm/table.do?tab=table&init=1&language=en&pcode=tsdec100&plugin=1).

Financial Times. 2014. 'Wilders Makes His Case for "Nexit": Dutch Departure from EU Would Be Huge Leap in the Dark'. *Financial Times*, 6 February. Retrieved 9 January 2018 (www.ft.com/content/01f0161c-8f3a-11e3-9cb0-00144feab7de).

Follesdal, Andreas. 2014. 'Democracy, Identity and European Public Spheres'. Pp. 247–62 in *European Public Spheres: Politics Is Back*, edited by T. Risse. Cambridge: Cambridge University Press.

Ford, Robert, and Matthew Goodwin. 2014. 'Understanding UKIP: Identity, Social Change and the Left Behind'. *The Political Quarterly* 85(3):277–84.

Gerhards, Jürgen, Lars Breuer, and Anna Delius. 2016. *Kollektive Erinnerungen der europäischen Bürger im Kontext von Transnationalisierungsprozessen: Deutschland, Großbritannien, Polen und Spanien im Vergleich [Collective Memories of European Citizens in the Context of Processes of Transnationalisation: Germany, Great Britain, Poland, and Spain in Comparison]*. Wiesbaden: Springer VS.

Gerhards, Jürgen, and Holger Lengfeld. 2013. 'European Integration, Equality Rights and People's Beliefs: Evidence from Germany'. *European Sociological Review* 29(1):19–31.

Gerhards, Jürgen, and Holger Lengfeld. 2015. *European Citizenship and Social Integration in the European Union*. London: Routledge.

Heidenreich, Martin. 2016. 'Introduction: The Double Dualization of Inequality in Europe'. Pp. 1–21 in *Exploring Inequality in Europe: Diverging Income and Employment Opportunities in the Crisis*, edited by M. Heidenreich. Cheltenham and Northampton, MA: Edward Elgar.

Henley, Jon. 2016. 'Why Vote Leave's £350m Weekly EU Cost Claim Is Wrong'. *Guardian*, 10 June. Retrieved 3 May 2017 (www.theguardian.com/politics/reality-check/2016/may/23/does-the-eu-really-cost-the-uk-350m-a-week).

Hobolt, Sara B., and Catherine E. de Vries. 2016. 'Turning against the Union? The Impact of the Crisis on the Eurosceptic Vote in the 2014 European Parliament Elections'. *Electoral Studies* 44:504–14.

Jæger, Mads M. 2006. 'Welfare Regimes and Attitudes towards Redistribution: The Regime Hypothesis Revisited'. *European Sociological Review* 22(2):157–70.

Jæger, Mads M. 2008. 'Does Left-right Orientation Have a Causal Effect on Support for Redistribution? Causal Analysis with Cross-sectional Data Using Instrumental Variables'. *International Journal of Public Opinion Research* 20(3):363–74.

Linos, Katerina, and Martin West. 2003. 'Self-interest, Social Beliefs, and Attitudes to Redistribution: Re-addressing the Issue of Cross-national Variation'. *European Sociological Review* 19(4):393–409.

Maas, Willem. 2007. *Creating European Citizens*. Lanham, MD: Rowan & Littlefield.

Marshall, Thomas H. 1983 [1949]. *Class, Citizenship, and Social Development. Essays*. Westport, CT: Greenwood Press.

Mau, Steffen. 2004. 'Transnationale Transfers der EU-Regionalpolitik: Die institutionelle Bearbeitung eines verteilungspolitischen Problems [Transnational Transfers of EU Regional Policy: The Institutional Processing of a Distributional Problem]'. Pp. 331–60 in *Verteilungsprobleme und Gerechtigkeit in modernen Gesellschaften [Problems of Distribution and Justice in Modern Societies]*, edited by S. Liebig, H. Lengfeld, and S. Mau. Frankfurt am Main: Campus.

OECD. 2013. *Fiscal Federalism 2014: Making Decentralisation Work*. Paris: OECD Publishing.

Pellegrini, Guido, Flavia Terribile, Ornella Tarola, Teo Muccigrosso, and Federica Busillo. 2013. 'Measuring the Effects of European Regional Policy on Economic Growth: A Regression Discontinuity Approach'. *Papers in Regional Science* 92(1):217–33.

Risse, Thomas. 2010. *A Community of Europeans? Transnational Identities and Public Spheres*. Ithaca, NY: Cornell University Press.

Roose, Jochen. 2013. 'How European Is European Identification? Comparing Continental Identification in Europe and Beyond'. *Journal of Common Market Studies* 51(2):281–97.

SPIEGEL Online. 2017. 'It's the Stupid EU: German Campaign Turning into a Debate over Europe'. *Spiegel Online*, 10 April. Retrieved 25 July 2017 (www.spiegel.de /international/europe/german-election-2017-focuses-on-european-union-a-1142693. html).

Süddeutsche Zeitung. 2015. 'Emmanuel Macron im Interview: "Wir wollen eine Neu-gründung Europas" [Emmanuel Macron in an Interview: "We Want a Refoundation of Europe"]'. *Süddeutsche Zeitung*, 31 August. Retrieved 3 May 2017 (www.sueddeutsche. de/politik/emmanuel-macron-im-interview-wir-wollen-eine-neugruendung-europas-1.2628139).

Svallfors, Stefan. 1997. 'Worlds of Welfare and Attitudes to Redistribution: A Compari-son of Eight Western Nations'. *European Sociological Review* 13(3):283–304.

Teney, Céline, Onawa P. Lacewell, and Pieter de Wilde. 2014. 'Winners and Losers of Globalization in Europe: Attitudes and Ideologies'. *European Political Science Review* 6(4):575–95.

Varoufakis, Yanis. 2015. 'Germany Won't Spare Greek Pain – It Has an Interest in Breaking Us'. *Guardian*, 10 July. Retrieved 25 July 2017 (www.theguardian.com/ commentisfree/2015/jul/10/germany-greek-pain-debt-relief-grexit).

Vobruba, Georg. 1996. 'Self-interested Aid: Belated Modernization and Interwoven Inter-ests between East and West'. *Crime, Law & Social Change* 25:83–93.

Wood, Vincent. 2017. '"The Bloc WILL Obey": Marion Le Pen Claims EU Will Be Forced to Give France a Better Deal'. *Express*, 1 April. Retrieved 25 July 2017 (www. express.co.uk/news/world/786560/Marion-Mar-chal-Le-Pen-EU-France-Frexit-Referendum-David-Cameron-Marine-Front-National).

World Bank. 2017. *World Bank National Accounts Data, and OECD National Accounts Data Files: GDP Per Capita (Constant 2010 US$)*. Retrieved 20 September 2017 (https://data.worldbank.org/indicator/NY.GDP.PCAP.KD).

Zürn, Michael, and Pieter de Wilde. 2016. 'Debating Globalization: Cosmopolitanism and Communitarianism as Political Ideologies'. *Journal of Political Ideologies* 21(3):280–301.

Chapter 5

Welfare solidarity – supporting Europeans in need

5.1 European welfare states under pressure

During the Great Recession (2009ff.), European economies experienced severe declines in growth rates. Wage cuts, unemployment, and poverty greatly impacted European citizens' living conditions (Arpaia and Curci 2010; Duiella and Turrini 2014; Heidenreich 2016a; Jenkins et al. 2013b; Rueda 2014). However, these effects greatly differed between countries. In particular, southern European countries experienced higher unemployment rates than the stronger and more stable economies in western Europe. The latter group of economies bounced back from the crisis faster and returned to stability more successfully. Figure 5.1 depicts these trends for a selected number of countries included in the TESS survey, taking unemployment rates as an example. In contrast to Germany and France, Greece and Spain experienced an almost twofold increase in their unemployment rates. Additionally, unemployment rates in these countries took a considerably longer period of time to stabilise than those in other countries. In consequence, poverty rates rose (Diamond, Liddle, and Sage 2015). These increases were particularly large in countries worst affected by the crisis, but there was also substantial growth in poverty in some economically weak eastern European countries. For instance, in Greece the rate of material deprivation almost doubled within five years, from nearly 20% in 2007 to 37% in 2013 (Guio, Marlier, and Pomati 2017). Yet, affluent western countries did not experience comparable increases in relative deprivation rates, and in some eastern European countries that were less affected by the crisis (i.e. Poland, Slovakia), these rates even decreased.[1]

Without doubt, welfare systems in crisis-affected countries have had to deal with growing demands for welfare benefits. Social spending steadily increased in absolute terms in the past years, but also relative to GDP in many countries (OECD 2017). On top of this, the sovereign debt crisis has even worsened the situation, because debtor countries were required to curtail social spending as part of austerity measures during the bailout (Heins and de la Porte 2016; Taylor-Gooby, Leruth, and Chung 2017). So, in response, Greece, Portugal, and Ireland attempted to contain the relative growth of social spending in the years

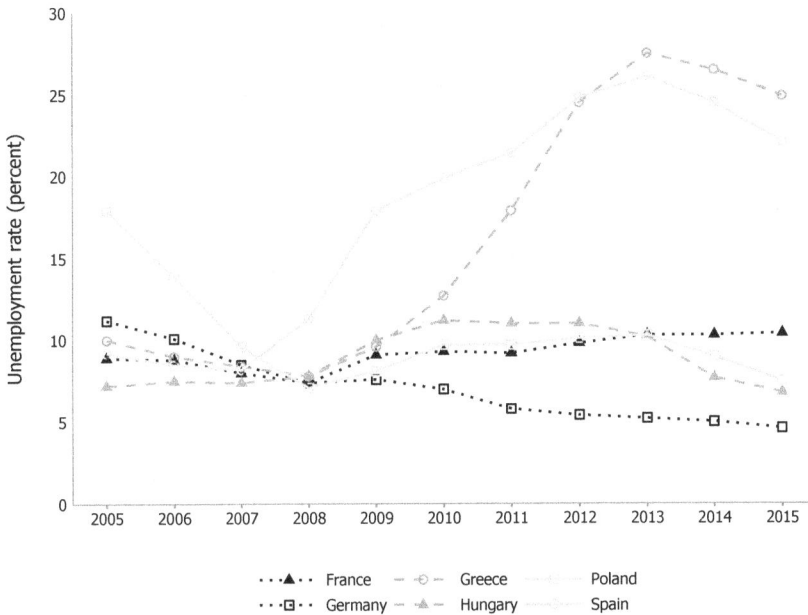

Figure 5.1 Unemployment rates in selected EU countries (2005–2015).
Source: Eurostat (2017), own depiction.

after the Great Recession, with mixed success. In general, the receipt of bailout loans was made conditional on enacting social spending cutbacks, i.e. reducing unemployment benefit and increasing the statuary retirement age (Heins and de la Porte 2016). These developments just added to the mounting pressure on welfare states. Overall, while demands for the welfare system to remain intact or even be strengthened persisted, the institutional efforts within countries aimed to dismantle the welfare state.

The European Union, however, was slow to react to these developments in its member states' social welfare policies. In contrast to the swift and direct responses in the domain of fiscal solidarity (see Chapter 3), the EU did not implement comparable measures to support Europeans in precarious economic situations. In fact, there were and are serious hurdles to overcome for the implementation of European social policy measures, as Stefan Leibfried has pointed out: 'There are no EU laws granting individual entitlement against Brussels, no direct taxes or contributions, no real funding of a "social budget" for such entitlements, and no significant Brussels welfare bureaucracy' (Leibfried 2015:264). The reasons for this relate to the EU's historical construction. As the EU was originally conceptualised as an economic cooperation (the European Economic Community), the integration process inaugurated by the Treaty of

Rome meant to keep welfare state policies separate from the integration of national polities (de Witte 2015).[2] However, as economic integration increased, this separation of market mechanisms and social policy became questionable (Leibfried 2015) and scholars began discussing how to enhance a 'social Europe' (cf. Vandenbroucke, Barnard, and Baere 2017). One of the biggest challenges for this, is the complexity of institutions at the supranational level (Ferrera 2017). Consequently, welfare policy remains under the jurisdiction of the member states, and even the Great Recession did not lead to the institutionalisation of European *welfare solidarity*.

Despite these legal restrictions, the European Union has nevertheless stepped up its engagement in social issues in the past years. For instance, in 2014 the Youth Employment Initiative (YEI) was launched as part of the European Social Fund (ESF). YEI aims to improve youth employment – one of the most serious social problems caused by the Great Recession and having long-term consequences for Europe's labour force. Its funds, however, are highly selective and only available in regions where youth unemployment exceeds 25% (European Parliament and Council of the European Union 2013). Initially, YEI's budget was €6.4 billion in total, but as of June 2017 the European Council and the Parliament had increased it (General Secretariat of the Council 2017) to €8.8 billion in total (European Commission 2019). The main recipients of the funding are young people from crisis-affected countries (Greece, Italy, Portugal) as well as from France. Additionally, the European Union has set aside approximately €83 billion to promote further labour market activation policies as part of the ESF, where the EU funds member states and their regions to finance projects.

Apart from the above-described measures, the European Union has not directly funded and promoted social policy in the past, instead emphasising respect for national sovereignty (Gerhards, Lengfeld, and Häuberer 2016:678). The European Pillar of Social Rights (EPSR), which was established in April 2017, seems to further reinforce the principle of national sovereignty. However, it also reiterates the notion that social issues in member states should be tackled together. In particular, the European Commission (2017b) has stressed that the European Union has responsibilities to protect its citizens from poverty and social exclusion. However, these statements are typically cautiously expressed and also underline the role of the nation state, stressing that the primary aim of a social Europe is to ensure harmonised labour market policies across all member states in agreement with national actors, i.e. not overstepping the principle of national sovereignty.

The social consequences of the Great Recession have nevertheless led to heated public debates in Europe regarding whether an explicit European social policy should be implemented. French president Emmanuel Macron has proposed a guaranteed minimum wage for every EU citizen that takes into account national economic differences; he has also encouraged a reduction of inequality in Europe (Macron 2017). Opponents of the implementation argue that a European social policy would violate the principle of subsidiarity and that responsibilities should remain solely at member state level. Economic leaders from well-developed welfare countries have been particularly opposed to this idea (Corti and Vesan 2017). They fear that a European social policy would mean taking on further financial burdens for social expenditures in member states with a poor welfare state. In contrast, proponents of a social Europe argue that 'social rights should not be just a pillar of the European Union; they must be their foundation and their priority, because there is no real European project without social justice'.[3] Despite these demands, in his State of the Union speech in September 2017, Jean-Claude Juncker (European Commission 2017c) offered reassurances that in the question of social matters, national sovereignty came first:

> National social systems will still remain diverse and separate for a long time. But at the very least, we should agree on a European Social Standards Union in which we have a common understanding of what is socially fair in our single market.

Nevertheless, the question of European social policy is a highly relevant and intensely debated topic: over 16,000 online replies and nearly 200 position papers were submitted during a broader consultation organised by the European Commission about the European Pillar of Social Rights alone.[4]

Against this backdrop, in this chapter we investigate whether EU citizens support the idea of a European welfare solidarity. Are citizens ready to extend the European project in the direction of a social Europe or do they respect the historical foundations of the European Union and prefer nation states to continue to have sole authority over social policy measures? If Europeans are strongly in favour of European welfare solidarity, this would suggest a demand for more integrative politics in the long term and would turn over a new leaf in the history of the European Union.

Before we delve into what the people think, we have to briefly address the concept of welfare solidarity. Welfare solidarity is a form of institutionalised solidarity that aims to support vulnerable individuals. If individuals support welfare solidarity, it means that they are ready to contribute to institutions providing such solidarity. It is useful to differentiate between the two subdomains, which constitute the two primary pillars of national welfare states: (1) protection against and compensation for social risks; e.g. the risk of being sick, the risk of being unemployed, the risk of becoming old, and the risk of becoming poor (Pettersen 1998), and (2) the reduction of social inequalities via redistributive policies (Roller 1998). As far as the first pillar is concerned, nation states have historically expanded the national social safety net in steps to include more and more types of life risks emerging from the labour market (Esping-Andersen 1990; Marshall 1949/1983). This first pillar became crucial during industrialisation at the end of the nineteenth century (Flora and Heidenheimer 1981). The second pillar is connected to one of the most important values in modern societies (Marshall 1949/1983; Roosma, Gelissen, and van Oorschot 2013). The first pillar is based on regulated redistribution via taxes or contributions. For the second pillar, states directly mitigate income differences between rich and poor people through progressive tax schemes and monetary funding programmes.

In this chapter, we will explore the domain of European welfare solidarity by focusing on its two subdomains (attitudes towards European social security and European redistribution). In the second section, we will first discuss arguments on whether or not Europeans support the idea of European welfare solidarity that involves (1) guaranteeing a European-wide social protection for the sick, elderly, and unemployed, and (2) seeking to reduce income differences between rich and poor Europeans. Then, we will present empirical findings and evaluate these findings based on our strategy for measuring the existence of European solidarity outlined in Chapter 2 of this book. To do so, we will compare the attitudes individuals express at the European level to attitudes at the national level.[5] Furthermore, we will report respondents' approval rates in regard to implementing a European-wide welfare system. In the fourth section of this chapter, we aim to theoretically and empirically identify social and political cleavages in relation to European welfare solidarity. According to our criteria, the presence of strong social cleavages and identifiable socials groups opposing European welfare solidarity would weaken the existence of European welfare solidarity. The fifth section concludes our results and addresses the question of political change to enhance the social dimension of Europe.

5.2 Is there an overwhelming majority for European welfare solidarity?

Are Europeans looking for strong European welfare solidarity or do they have concerns about social policies being extended to the European level and reject the notion? While there are several arguments that have predicted high support for European welfare solidarity, others strongly counter these. The first argument *for* European welfare solidarity emphasises that citizens view social security as a universal right, which allows everyone to have access to welfare state benefits when in need. As national welfare state policies are highly legitimated institutions (Dallinger 2010; Hemerijck 2004; Jæger 2006; Svallfors 2004), this support could be interpreted as representing a gradual spill-over from welfare solidarity being a societal norm to it becoming a basic and universal human right. Taking this into account, citizens could transfer this norm into a wider territorial context. Thus, support for European welfare solidarity may be a specific territorial application of this universal right. From this, it follows that everyone considering the European social space as a relevant territorial space for exercising this universal right would support the ideal of European welfare solidarity. This would apply to European communitarians, who think that European solidarity is a specific space of solidarity, which excludes those who are living outside of Europe. It would also include individuals with cosmopolitan leanings, for whom national borders are not relevant and who think in a global community.

The second argument emphasises how European welfare solidarity is contingent on the overall European integration process. This process has removed borders between member states to be obstacles in establishing social relationships due to two reasons (Beck and Grande 2007). First, because of transnational integration of institutions (Wobbe 2012), and second, as the result of horizontal, transnational social processes across member state borders (Delhey et al. 2014; Fligstein 2008). These transnational processes have led to greater cross-border cooperation and division of labour and have in turn generated a new transnational form of organic solidarity, of the kind we know from Durkheimian theory (Münch 2010). Thus, European (social) integration should likely produce European welfare solidarity.

Lastly, a re-interpretation of Thomas H. Marshall's (Marshall 1949/1983) evolutionary understanding of the development of civic rights suggests that European integration will likely generate an increased demand for European welfare solidarity. Marshall described how civil, political, and social rights were extended one after the other in the process of nation state building. European integration has mirrored this in the step-by-step expansion of Europeans' political, economic, and social rights (Gerhards and Lengfeld 2015; Mau 2005; Streeck 1995). Currently, EU citizens living abroad in another member state have the same access to national welfare benefits as citizens of the given member state. The next step in the integration process would be to commit to European welfare solidarity, where all Europeans are granted the same social rights across all member states. Thus, this argument suggests that support for European welfare solidarity might be an inevitable and path-dependent consequence of prior European integration processes. Additionally, we also expect there to be some regional differences in the support for European welfare solidarity. It is highly plausible that citizens from poorer countries could view European welfare solidarity as an answer to the deficits of their own national welfare states. Thus, there will be higher degree of support in these countries than in countries with extensive welfare provisions.

Despite the above-expressed arguments in favour of the existence of European welfare solidarity, some compelling arguments point in the opposite direction. One prime argument against the widespread acceptance of European welfare solidarity concerns the financial contribution of member states to introduce a harmonised European social policy (cf. Scharpf 2002). As citizens' attitudes reflect the logic of national decision makers and the collective interest of member states, countries' instrumental rationality may motivate citizens' attitudes to the topic. Following this rationale, we can expect resistance from citizens who think that European welfare solidarity would lead to an increase in expenditures by their home country (and therefore out of their own pockets). Such fears are likely to be grounded in experiences with the various 'bailout' packages, in which richer member states took on debt-ridden countries' economic burdens by offering debt guarantees. Analogously, in the case of European welfare solidarity, richer member states would eventually need to take on the financial burden attached to the social policy development for poorer member states. Thus, we expected to observe regional differences between countries, with individuals from economically well-off countries worrying about paying for social expenditures for Europeans living in other member states if they express welfare solidarity with other Europeans. Furthermore, they may fear a reduction of social standards along with the harmonisation of European welfare policies (Scharpf 2002). In contrast, citizens of poorer countries may fear that higher social standards will lead to less economic growth due to increasing unemployment.

What does research tell us about citizens' support for a European welfare solidarity? In general, we do not have much data about the degree of European welfare solidarity,[6] and the data we do have paint a mixed picture (cf. Baute et al. 2018). In recent years, scholarly work has demonstrated that the legitimacy of European welfare state policies has been quite stable. Some of the most recent information available about attitudes towards European welfare solidarity comes from a special Eurobarometer survey on the 'Future of Europe' conducted in the autumn of 2017 (European Commission 2017a). The reports highlighted how solidarity is an important keyword for Europeans in all member states. In particular, it underlined that Europeans were ready to have the European Union move in a direction where solidarity plays a larger role than individualistic approaches and stressed that societies in general should keep social equality and solidarity in their focus.

Another recent cross-national study conducted in 2015 complemented this finding (Vision Europe Summit Consortium 2015). The study showed that the majority of respondents in Belgium (84%), Finland (63%), France (86%), Germany (77%), Italy (73%), Poland (7%), Portugal (71%), and in the UK (70%) supported the notion that the EU should be the guarantor of minimum standards in social protection across Europe. Another recent publication from the European Social Survey (2016) showed that respondents from Austria, Finland, the Netherlands, and the United Kingdom were divided evenly between those supporting and opposing an EU-wide social security scheme, while respondents from other surveyed countries were generally in favour of such a scheme. This newer study mirrors the results of other past studies. In the Belgian National Election Study (BNES) of 2014, the majority of respondents favoured various policies supporting Europeans (Baute et al. 2018; Baute, Meuleman, and Abts 2019): child benefit (59%), minimum income benefits (59%), unemployment benefit (53%). Irina Ciornei and Ettore Recchi (2017) have also found similar results. They used Eurobarometer data from 2012 to look at whether Europeans thought it is important for the European Union to engage in social protection policies and whether it should help vulnerable individuals. On average, Europeans scored 8.1 on a scale from 1 to 10, where 10 means very important. This again demonstrates that European welfare solidarity is a prominent topic among Europeans.

Jürgen Gerhards and colleagues (2016) also reported comparable results based on the Europeanisation of Equality Survey (EES) from 2009. They showed that the majority of German (58%), Spanish (76%), and Polish (83%) citizens supported a European minimum wage. While the overall picture was favourable, the findings indicated that support varied strongly between countries. Ciornei and Recchi (2017) have found that the economic prosperity of a country is relevant for European welfare solidarity. Thus, these results suggest that countries' interests play a major role in determining the degree of European welfare state support. These observations also correspond with the findings from Genschel and Hemerijck (2018): respondents from net-contributor countries were much more reluctant to support member states with high unemployment rates.

Yet, these papers have several shortcomings. First, the empirical data for the studies were primarily collected before the Great Recession or shortly after (Baute et al. 2018; Ciornei and Recchi 2017; Gerhards et al. 2016). Moreover, studies conducted since the crisis have operationalised European welfare solidarity at a more abstract level (European Commission 2017a) or from the macroeconomic perspective of member states and not the perspective of Europeans (Genschel and Hemerijck 2018). So we have no in-depth evidence about the demand for European welfare solidarity since the crisis. Second, while two recent publications (Baute et al. 2018; Gerhards et al. 2016) have used similar conceptualisations and operationalisations to our own concept, their country selection is limited. Thus, our current knowledge about European welfare solidarity is rather fragmented and incomplete: we have a limited understanding of attitudes towards European social security, and the information we have about attitudes towards European redistribution is even more restricted. This makes the findings presented in the following especially important.

5.2.1 Attitudes towards social security for Europeans

What do citizens think about European social security? Should the European Union be responsible for guaranteeing social security to one of the three most vulnerable social groups in the EU: (1) the sick, (2) the elderly, (3) the unemployed?[7] Respondents were asked the following four-point-scale items:

People have different views on what the [NATIONAL] government should be responsible for. Please tell me for each of the following statements whether you totally agree, tend to agree, tend to disagree, or totally disagree.

The [NATIONAL] government should guarantee access to health care for everyone in [COUNTRY].

The [NATIONAL] government should guarantee a decent standard of living for the elderly in [COUNTRY].

The [NATIONAL] government should guarantee a decent standard of living for the unemployed in [COUNTRY].

Now please don't think about [COUNTRY], but about the European Union in Brussels and its responsibilities. Please tell me for each of the following statements whether you totally agree, tend to agree, tend to disagree, or totally disagree.

> *The European Union should guarantee access to health care for everyone in the EU.*
>
> *The European Union should guarantee a decent standard of living for the elderly in the EU.*
>
> *The European Union should guarantee a decent standard of living for the unemployed in the EU.*

Figure 5.2 depicts the aggregated responses to these questions pooled across countries. Clearly, an overwhelming majority of respondents believed that the European Union should be responsible for providing social security for people in need, irrespective of why they need this security. Focusing on the differences between the three social groups, there were minor variations in the responses. In total, 90% of respondents agreed that the European Union should be responsible for Europeans who are sick as well as for elderly Europeans. In contrast, only 77% of respondents supported the notion that the European Union should secure the standard of living of all unemployed Europeans. Despite the lower degree of agreement, the latter rate still exceeded two-thirds of the respondents.

When comparing the differences in attitudes towards social security at the European and the national level, we only observed marginally higher rates of agreement for the national level. The results for national welfare state attitudes were in line with previous research (Blekesaune and Quadagno 2003; Roosma, van Oorschot, and Gelissen 2014; Svallfors 2010). But what is more important for our research question is that approval on the two territorial levels did not distinctly differ from each other, underlining the high legitimacy of the idea of European solidarity.

We even observed high approval rates for European social security when we broke down responses by country (Figure 5.3). The majority of individuals were willing to support Europeans in need, albeit there was variation between the countries. One noteworthy finding is that the crisis-affected Mediterranean countries, which faced high unemployment rates in the aftermath of the crisis (Cyprus, Spain, Greece, Portugal), showed the highest approval rates, at 95% or more. This could indicate that citizens from these countries wanted the EU to solve their welfare issues. In contrast, countries less affected by the crisis exhibited significantly less agreement than the first group of countries (although the approval rates in these countries were still well over the 50% threshold). These extremely high rates could also suggest that structural and cultural cleavages between individuals may be relatively weak in this certain domain of European solidarity. We will explore this in the next section of the chapter.

In cross-country comparison, we can see that response rates were equally high or even higher in all countries for the national level. However, the discrepancy in approval rates between the two territorial levels (i.e. national and

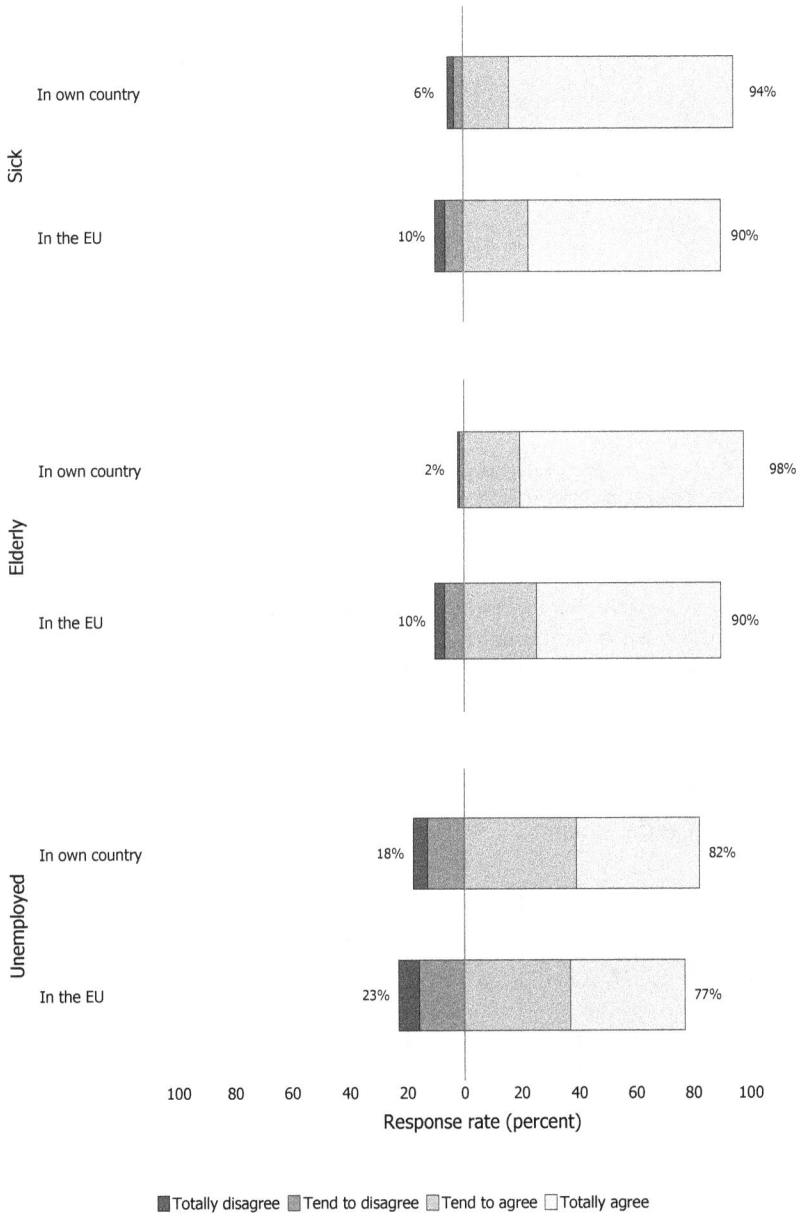

Figure 5.2 Response rates of social security for Europeans in need and citizens in need in own country.

Source: TESS 2016, own calculations.

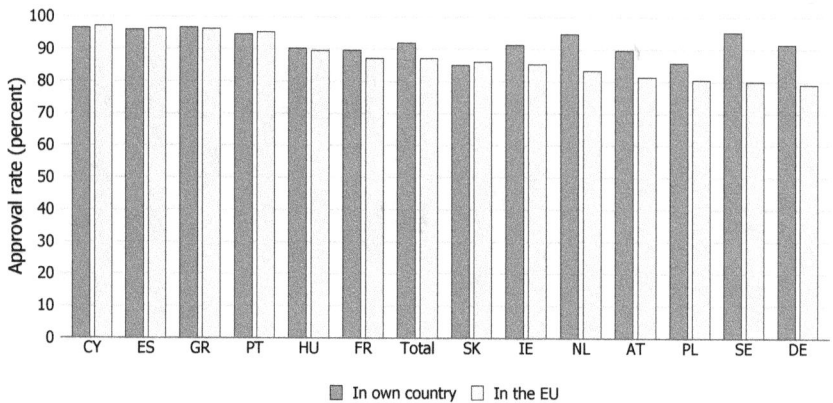

Figure 5.3 Average approval rates of social security for Europeans in need and citizens in need in own country by country.

Source: TESS 2016, own calculations.

European) was smallest in countries whose labour market had been badly affected by the crisis. For countries with lower than average support for European social security, the discrepancy was much higher.

5.2.2 Attitudes towards European redistribution

Similar to the first subdomain, we asked respondents to disclose to what degree inequalities should be redistributed in Europe and within their own country.[8]

People have different views on what the [NATIONAL] government should be responsible for. Please tell me for each of the following statements whether you totally agree, tend to agree, tend to disagree, or totally disagree.

The [NATIONAL] government should reduce income differences between the rich and poor in [COUNTRY].

Now please don't think about [COUNTRY], but about the European Union in Brussels and its responsibilities. Please tell me for each of the following statements whether you totally agree, tend to agree, tend to disagree, or totally disagree.

The European Union should reduce income differences between the rich and poor in the EU.

Figure 5.4 shows that a supermajority of citizens (80%) exhibited a strong positive preference for redistribution between rich and poor people on the European level. This rate is just slightly lower than the approval rates for

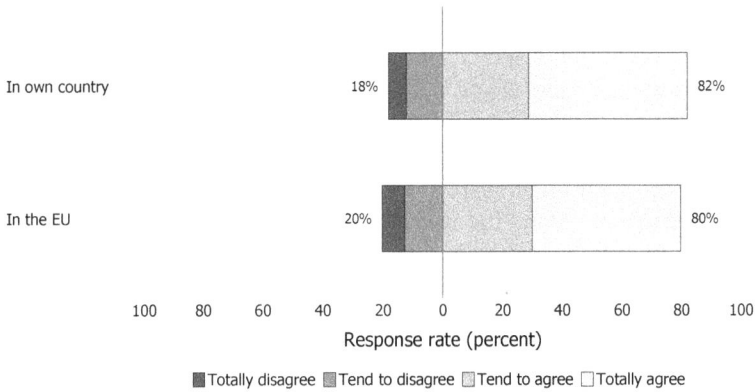

Figure 5.4 Response rates of redistribution between rich and poor Europeans and between rich and poor people in own country.

Source: TESS 2016, own calculations.

redistribution on the national level (82%). Dividing the responses by country (Figure 5.5), we found a supermajority for European redistribution in all countries. While in all countries, more than two-thirds of respondents agreed that the European Union should reduce inequalities between rich and poor Europeans, there were observable differences between the countries. Located at one end of the approval rates, we found Cyprus, which led the other countries by

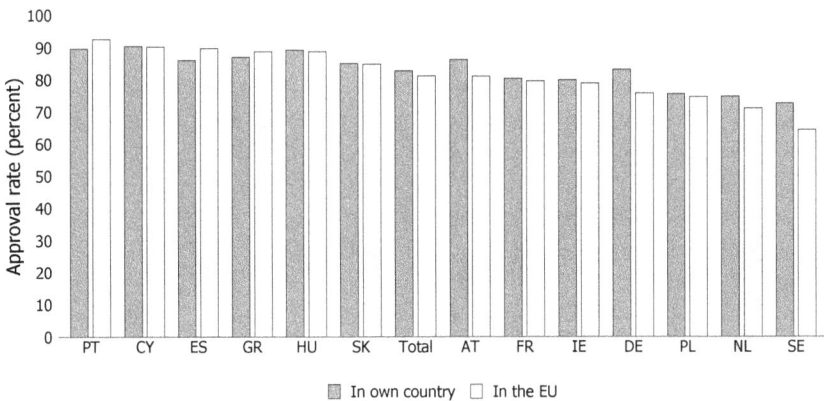

Figure 5.5 Average approval rates of redistribution between rich and poor Europeans and between rich and poor people in own country by country.

Source: TESS 2016, own calculations.

showing the highest support rates for European redistribution. In total, 93% of Cypriots agreed with the notion of European redistribution. In contrast, at the other end, we saw the lowest approval rates in the creditor countries. For example, Swedish respondents exhibited the lowest approval rates (64%). We found an interesting pattern in the gap between answers according to the national and the European level. Countries that struggled in the wake of the crisis had equal levels of support on the two territorial levels. What is more, they even had marginally higher levels of agreement with European redistribution than with national redistribution. In contrast, countries less affected by the crisis had a lower degree of approval for European redistribution than for national redistribution in general. In Sweden and Austria, the difference between national and European redistribution was the most pronounced; here, the differences between approval rates on the two territorial levels were even significant.

At this point, we can draw an interim conclusion: we find that results on both subdomains of welfare solidarity pass our first criterion of 'double majority'. First, the majority of respondents supported European social security and European redistribution across the whole sample. Second, the majority of individuals in all countries supported the notion of helping needy people on both subdomains. It is worth noting that the gap between the European and national level is more pronounced than for the subdomain of European social security. Thus, these first descriptive results reinforce the existence of European welfare solidarity.[9]

Despite these positive initial results, it is difficult to determine whether the huge support for European social security and for European redistribution truly refers to European boundaries, or whether it is simply a variation of a cosmopolitan disposition. If the latter were the case, it would suggest that European solidarity is nothing more than global solidarity applied coincidently to a European frame. To clarify this point, we again asked respondents to identify their territorial priority (national, European, or global) about where should people in need be helped first; this is what we did in the previous chapters of the book. By so doing, we forced respondents to clearly state their territorial preferences. For historical reasons, we expected respondents to put national priorities first. If the majority of respondents gave the national level first priority and the European level second priority, this would indicate that European welfare solidarity is a territorial space of solidarity of its own and distinct from other domains of transnational solidarity, i.e. global solidarity. And if the most common response was to prioritise Europeans in need against the other two options (i.e. own country and other countries outside of Europe), this would be a very clear sign for the existence of European welfare solidarity. In contrast, if respondents ranked global action as their first priority or second, it would suggest that the previously observed strong European welfare state is in fact a consequence of cosmopolitism.

There are people in need not only in [COUNTRY] and in the EU, but all over the world. Assuming a decision about priority has to be made: in your opinion, where should people in need be helped first?

(1) *In [COUNTRY].*
(2) *In other countries in the European Union.*
(3) *In other countries outside of the European Union.*

And where should they be helped second?

(1) *In [COUNTRY].*
(2) *In other countries in the European Union.*
(3) *In other countries outside of the European Union.*

Figure 5.6 depicts the responses for the first and second choices to the above-stated questions. The majority of individuals chose to support people in need in their own country first (57% of respondents in total). Only 15% of respondents picked other Europeans in need first, while nearly every third respondent (29%) prioritised helping individuals from countries outside of the EU. However, the responses for both the national and European level stood out when we compared them to the results for direct questions about solidarity (Figures 5.2 and 5.4). First, there was a very low share of respondents prioritising Europe over other territorial units, despite the high support rates for European social security and European redistribution in previous figures. Second, while helping fellow countrymen was the most popular first priority for respondents in Figure 5.6, the support still barely exceeded the majority threshold. This was significantly less compared to the extremely high support in Figures 5.2 and 5.4. This relatively low rate of respondents in favour of national solidarity (57%) and the high rate of respondents (29%) who wished to extend help to those outside of Europe first indicates that EU citizens do not want to automatically replace nation state welfare systems with European welfare measures. What is particularly interesting is that we observed a relatively high variation across countries (not depicted). Citizens from better-off countries had a lower tendency to choose their own country first than those from economically weaker countries. Furthermore, in those well-off countries, respondents also chose to help individuals outside of Europe as their first priority more than respondents from poor-performing economies. Put differently: we found that respondents from economies that had overcome the Great Recession without huge problems (Germany, Sweden, Poland) were less likely to support their fellow citizens in need as the first priority and would rather offer help to individuals from outside of Europe. Overall, these results suggest that respondents may understand social security as a universal right. From this, it follows that European welfare solidarity may be a consequence of cosmopolitism and does not constitute a social space on its own.

Investigating respondents' second priority provides more information about the existence of European welfare solidarity. For the majority of respondents (62%), their second choice was clearly to help Europeans in need. Thus, two-thirds of respondents gave second priority to their fellow *European* citizens. Nearly one fifth of the respondents (21%) picked helping their fellow citizens second, while a slightly lower proportion of respondents (18%) chose to help individuals outside of the EU as a second priority. The cross-country difference (not depicted) was insignificant for choosing Europe as a second category: only Greek and Portuguese respondents showed slightly lower rates. On the other hand, there was a larger variance for choosing the nation or regions outside of Europe as the territorial unit in which to support individuals.

The analysis has so far painted a mixed picture: extending help to Europeans is clearly not a first priority for most citizens, but is still important enough to be of second priority to the majority. Do such results indicate that European welfare solidarity is only a variant of cosmopolitan-driven solidarity? Do they possibly suggest that Europe does not constitute a social space of its own?

To clear up our concerns related to this, we additionally looked at detailed response patterns given to the first and second priority questions combined (not depicted). The patterns clearly showed that a majority (75%) of respondents would extend help to Europeans either as a first or second priority. In contrast, only one fourth of respondents omitted the European social space in their responses. This suggests that only a small minority did not consider Europe a relevant social space container.

From the six response patterns possible, most response patterns (46%) fell into the category in which respondents chose to help their fellow citizens first and then other Europeans second. Thus, a large proportion of respondents acknowledged the European social space for solidarity, which could indicate the presence of European communitarianism among respondents. The second largest group of respondents (at 14.5%) were those who first would help individuals from outside of Europe and then aid other Europeans second. This finding implicitly suggests that respondents could have considered the general socio-economic circumstances of countries outside of Europe when picturing people in need and could have considered Europe a safe haven and not a place where people needed the most support. Such responses reflect a cosmopolitan stance, according to which Europe is considered a smaller unit of the world. Furthermore, and more importantly, Europe still comes between world and nation state, thus is a relevant boundary for many respondents with cosmopolitan dispositions. This fits with our previous assumption and observation that social security is seen as a universal right extended to Europeans. The reasons behind such patterns are many, and indeed these patterns are worth more detailed analysis. Unfortunately, the scope of this volume does not allow us to delve more deeply into this topic.

Overall, our findings show that Europe was nevertheless a reference point for respondents, which resonates well with our quest to assess the prevalence of European welfare solidarity. The findings imply that although citizens favour the

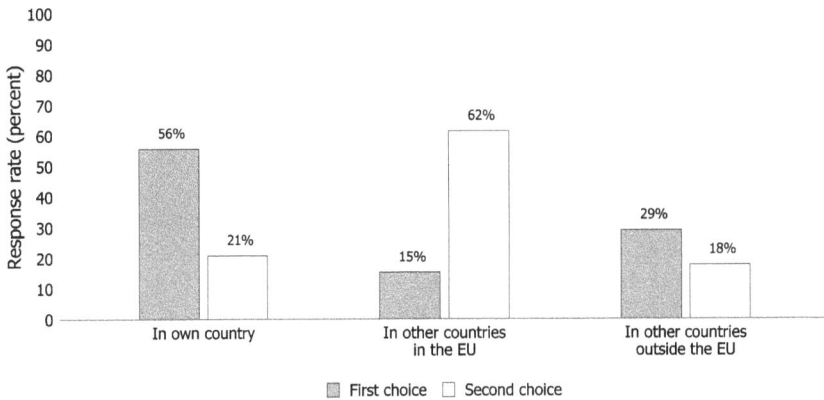

Figure 5.6 Response rates to where should people in need be helped first.
Source: TESS 2016, own calculations.

nation state as their first institutional choice for providing social security and reducing inequalities between rich and poor, they also agree that the EU should play a strong role in providing welfare to all Europeans in need. The results also suggest that European welfare solidarity is a phenomenon different from national and global welfare solidarity for almost the majority of individuals. Thus, the second criterion for the existence of European solidarity is fulfilled. This means we have found further indications that European welfare solidarity is a relevant concept in the European social sphere. The results for this set of questions are in line with our previous findings and indicate the existence of European welfare solidarity. Furthermore, the results suggest the emergence of a new form of Europe-centred communitarianism through European integration. This ultimately is positive feedback with regards to European integration.

5.3 Attitudes towards a European welfare system

Despite the positive findings on the two subdomains of European welfare solidarity, Europeans can still be reluctant to expand these principles and norms as institutional measures at a European level. In the previous section, we focused on generalised attitudes towards welfare solidarity. Thus, the items did not address the methods needed to bring about European social security or European-level redistribution. Current legal circumstances facilitate primarily harmonisation measures of various kinds with little obligations from the member states: these might range from open methods of coordination (OMC) to closer cooperation (cf. Scharpf 2002). While the convergence of the national welfare systems to a European model is empirically unlikely (e.g. Alsasua, Bilbao-Ubillos, and Olaskoaga 2007; Avdeyeva 2006), we went the extra mile and asked respondents about the institutionalisation of a European welfare system, i.e. developing a supranational institution responsible for protecting Europeans from the social risks and the consequences of high inequalities in European countries, where national sovereignty is restricted considerably. Thus, we put European welfare solidarity to the test by focusing on the support for implementing a supranational European welfare system. Does European welfare solidarity have as much traction as our initial findings suggest?

There are several reasons why support rates for implementing a European welfare system may not match the rates for the two subdomains discussed above. It is well known that national welfare systems differ according to their risk coverage, social benefits, financing principles, and interconnections to other key social institutions, especially the family, the labour market, and the education system (Arundel and Lennartz 2017; Aspalter 2017; Biegert 2017; Hantrais 2000:21; Hemerijck 2004, 2013; Leibfried and Pierson 1995; Thelen 2014; van Kersbergen and Vis 2015). Given that constructing a universal European welfare system would lead to a massive reorganisation of the national welfare state, citizens may interpret this as a threat to their current individual welfare status, regardless of the degree of security and social benefits a national system already provides. Thus, they may view the adoption as involving huge costs due to fundamental changes at the national level (de Swaan 1992; Leibfried and Pierson 1999). We therefore expect citizens from both richer and poorer EU countries to reject the institutionalisation of a European welfare state. While citizens of poorer countries may fear that higher social standards lead to less economic growth due to increasing unemployment, citizens living in economically well-performing countries may fear a reduction of social standards linked to a unified European welfare policy (Scharpf 2002).

However, empirical evidence from two survey studies does not support this assumption. Using EES 2009 data, Gerhards and colleagues (2016) found that in Germany a majority of respondents (53%) opposed a uniform European social welfare system, while in the poorer EU countries of Spain and Poland a majority of citizens welcomed it (69% and 79% respectively). A similar reluctance was also found among the Belgian respondents studied by Sharon Baute and colleagues (2018): 52% of Belgians were against a general European welfare system according to BNES 2014 data. Thus, we expected individuals to be less supportive of the introduction of a uniform European welfare state than they were of the two subdomains listed above.

In the TESS survey, we asked respondents about their support for the concrete implementation of a European welfare system. The wording of the item is the following:[10]

> *Please think now about the possibility of a social welfare system in the EU and tell me for the following proposition to what extent you agree or disagree.*
>
> *There should be a uniform social welfare system for everyone in the EU, even if this leads to an increase in taxes and social spending in [COUNTRY].*

In this item, we integrated the potential costs of a European social welfare system by indicating that the introduction of a European welfare system would mean an increase in taxes. Consequently, the question directly tested the financial pressure European welfare solidarity can endure. Additionally, it also complements the previous two sets of questions, which focused on attitudes towards social security and redistribution. Furthermore, this question also served as a test of legitimacy for the European Social Pillar recently introduced and discussed in the first part of the chapter.[11]

Figure 5.7 shows the approval rates for a uniform European welfare system. Overall, the majority of respondents (57%) supported the idea of a European welfare system, while 43% opposed it. However, there was considerable range of responses across the surveyed countries (Figure 5.8). As expected, support for the implementation of a uniform European welfare system was generally lower than and could not be compared to the previous results in regard to the two sub-domains of welfare solidarity. Approval rates for the item were considerably

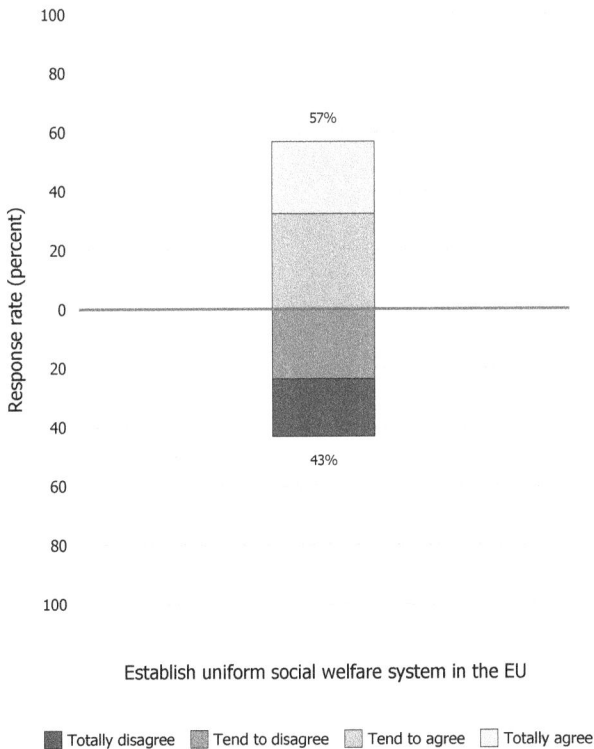

Establish uniform social welfare system in the EU

■ Totally disagree   ▨ Tend to disagree   ▨ Tend to agree   □ Totally agree

Figure 5.7 Response rates of the support of a uniform European welfare system.

Source: TESS 2016, own calculations.

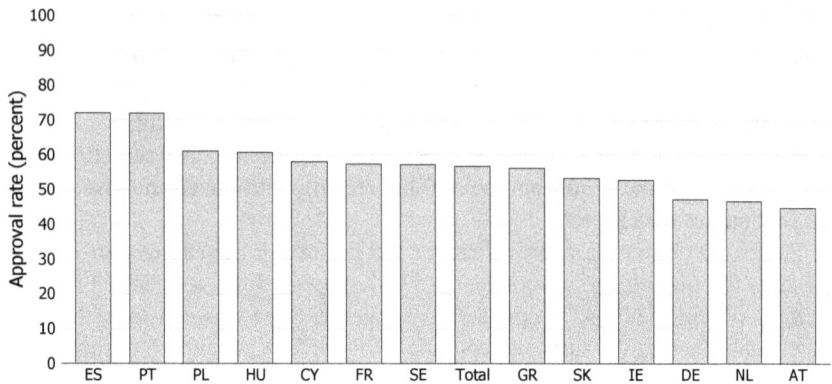

Figure 5.8 Approval rates of the support of a uniform European welfare system by country.

Source: TESS 2016, own calculations.

lower (almost 30 percentage points) than support for the two subdomains. Here, we observed the first signs of weakness in European welfare solidarity: when broken down by country, three countries (Austria, Germany, and the Netherlands) did not meet the 50% threshold. Thus, European welfare solidarity might be less robust than we previously anticipated, and the social integration of the European Union may still have a distance to go. Portugal and Spain exhibited significantly higher approval rates than the other countries, with 72% of respondents supporting the notion of a uniform European welfare system in both. In contrast, only the minority of individuals in Austria, Germany, and the Netherlands supported the notion of a European welfare system. Furthermore, these results indicated that the country's degree of social welfare affects citizens' approval of a European welfare system. For example, all of the countries where respondents were reluctant about it fall in the category of conservative welfare states.

We will discuss the political implications of the difference in support rates for a European welfare system and European welfare solidarity in the conclusion of this chapter.

5.4 Emerging social cleavages for European welfare solidarity?

As in the previous chapters, we now examine whether there are any social groups emerging that can potentially impede or promote policies to implement European welfare solidarity. Building on the work of Lipset and Rokkan (1967) and more recent work discussing social cleavages (Hooghe and Marks 2017), we reasoned that structurally or culturally homogenous groups opposing European solidarity could organise politically and could present obstacles to decision makers seeking to foster European solidarity. The main task of this section is to assess the prevalence of social and political cleavages for European welfare solidarity. This happens in two steps. First, based on the literature and by using multivariate analysis, we searched for any social cleavages behind opposing European welfare solidarity.[12] Second, we empirically investigated whether attitudes towards European welfare solidarity generated political cleavages.

5.4.1 Structural cleavages

We can identify structural cleavages in relation to European welfare solidarity if social groups form on the basis of common self-interest to support or to oppose European welfare solidarity. Typically, the guiding principle underlying self-interest is instrumental rationality and the goal of economic gain. We thus expected an individual's structural position to influence his/her support for European welfare solidarity.

(1) Vulnerable groups are strongly reliant on social protection provided by the welfare state. Research on national welfare state attitudes has demonstrated that members of such groups favour social welfare systems (Andreß and Heien 2001; Blekesaune and Quadagno 2003; Cnaan et al. 1993; Edlund 2007; Gelissen 2000; Häusermann, Kurer, and Schwander 2016; Jæger 2006). During the Great Recession, young people, individuals from migration backgrounds, and the low educated, were seen as outsiders in the labour market and were therefore the most prominent representatives of citizens reliant on welfare state provisions. Additionally, although women counted among the relative winners of the crisis if we look at the unemployment rate (Heidenreich 2015, 2016c), they still faced difficulties with long-term unemployment (Heidenreich 2016c) and in general *perceived* their risk of unemployment higher than it really was (Heidenreich 2016b). These social groups, and not affluent individuals, can be seen as the direct beneficiaries of the introduction of Europe-wide social policies and main supporters. In contrast, we expected affluent individuals to have little interest in supporting European welfare solidarity. This argument has also been confirmed by recent studies focusing on explaining attitudes towards European social security (Baute et al. 2019; Ciornei and Recchi 2017).[13] Altogether, we expect to see the same tendencies at the national and the European level, as self-interest and instrumental rationality should be the underlying mechanisms. We tested our assumptions by looking at how individuals' socio-economic characteristics influenced attitudes towards welfare solidarity.

We furthermore expect these structural cleavages to be more pronounced for European redistribution than for European social security. Redistribution policies not only lift individuals out of poverty (i.e. out of vulnerable life situations) by giving them subsidies, but also directly implement an income/wealth ceiling for the richest members of society by taxing them. Thus, individuals in rich households and those who are members of the upper social classes should have less inclination to support redistribution. At the same time, individuals who have an unfavourable labour market position (i.e. the unemployed), and those who do not possess much human capital (i.e. those with low levels of education) should favour European redistribution.

(2) Second, the situation of an individual's country can also play a role in how citizens relate to European welfare solidarity. In particular, in times of crisis, individuals are exceptionally aware of their own country's hardship. In this specific case, the Great Recession was the hardship. National welfare states faced the twofold burden of shielding their citizens from the effects of the Great Recession and maintaining national fiscal equilibrium (for details, see Chapters 3 and 4). Citizens from countries that struggled to maintain a welfare state are likely to be aware that European-level social policy could be a viable option. Supporting these arguments, Brian Burgoon (2009) found indication that European-level social policy was supported by respondents who lived in countries with poorly performing welfare systems. Genschel and Hemerijck (2018) also found that citizens were more open to the general notion of EU member states supporting countries struggling with high unemployment if they were from countries directly benefiting from such measures.[14] Thus, we can expect individuals from countries with low unemployment rates and low income inequalities (which are indicators that the national welfare state is performing relatively well) to be more likely to oppose European welfare solidarity. In contrast, individuals from countries with growing inequalities may support European social security and redistribution in the hope that some of the burdens of their national welfare state would be pooled at the European level. We expect them to welcome the notion of European welfare solidarity, as the European Union constitutes an economic safe haven when nation states are in turmoil. Accordingly, to maximise their own utility, we expect individuals from these countries in search of plausible alternatives on the European level to be willing to legitimise European welfare solidarity. We evaluated these assumptions in a macro-level analysis. More specifically, we looked at macro-structural indicators such as the unemployment rate and level of income inequalities and how they influenced attitudes towards European welfare solidarity.

(3) Lastly, we expect the interplay between a country's prosperity and an individual's socio-economic position to impact on citizens' attitudes towards European welfare solidarity. In economically well-performing countries, affluent individuals may be more reluctant to share their resources across Europe, as it does not serve their interests. By contrast, we expected a country's poor economic situation to have an overall negative effect on its citizens, which could relativise the interest differences within societies, making the structural cleavages weaker in countries in debt. Vulnerable individuals in both well-off economies and struggling economies would welcome a European safety net. Those from a well-off economy should welcome it, because it provides an extra buffer, while those from struggling economies should favour it, because it is a more reliable form of security than their social security system. To test these assumptions,

we interacted the macro-structural indicators for economic prosperity with indicators for socio-economic indicators in the empirical implementation.

In order to determine whether structural cleavages have emerged in relation to European welfare solidarity, we utilised indicators for respondents' socio-economic status for individual effects in our analysis. Thus, we investigated the effects of the following indicators on attitudes towards European welfare solidarity: respondents' education level, their occupational class position, their (equalised) household income, and their unemployment status at the time of the survey. At the country level, we investigated the effects of unemployment rates, the degree of inequalities, and the degree of social spending on European welfare solidarity. In order to measure the impact of the Great Recession on attitudes we considered the effects of changes in GDP growth between 2008 and 2015 on European welfare solidarity, the effect of changes in unemployment rates since the crisis, and whether the country needed financial assistance after the crisis.

5.4.2 Cultural cleavages

We assumed that attitudes towards European welfare solidarity may be related to three value orientations: (a) political value orientation, (b) distributive justice orientation, and (c) territorial attachment and identification.

(1) Historically, left-wing citizens have been more likely to support universalistic, redistributive policies, while individuals with right-wing orientation have been conservative, and opposed welfare state provision (Gelissen 2000). Since redistribution is typically one of the hallmarks of left-wing parties, they have often claimed to be the frontrunners for redistribution. As this mechanism addresses general principles associated with welfare states, we expect these dispositions to carry over to the European level. However, the results of research focusing on the European level have been mixed. Berg (2007) showed that right-wing individuals were slightly more likely to prefer transferring social policy decisions to the European level. In contrast, Gerhards and colleagues (2016) found that left-wing individuals were more likely to support the notion of a European welfare state, as did findings published by Baute and colleagues (2019) and Ciornei and Recchi (2017). We expect right-wing individuals to be more likely to reject European welfare solidarity, while citizens with left-wing political orientations are more likely to support the notion. We measured political orientations using the established ten-point left–right political scale (Lo, Proksch, and Gschwend 2013).

(2) Justice principles constitute citizens' preferences for a certain distribution logic. There is a general consensus among social scientists that there are three main types of justice principles (Deutsch 1985; Miller 1999): equality, equity, and need. Furthermore, there is the implicit assumption that 'need' is a core principle for welfare states (Arts and Gelissen 2001). The need principle states that share of goods should be distributed such that everyone's basic needs are met. Based on these considerations, we assume that people who did not adhere to the

need principle oppose the idea of European welfare solidarity.[15] We operationalised attitudes towards justice by asking respondents whether income should
cover the basic needs of everyone in society.

(3) Territorial attachment and the sense of connectedness to fellow (national
or European) citizens may also determine support for or opposition to European
welfare solidarity. Studies have shown that collective identity at a national level
leads to strong emotional ties to the in-group, which then fosters (national) solidarity (Gelissen 2000; Mayhew 1971).[16] This affective attachment is to encourage
individuals to support measures that help the members of the community to
become better off, as this also serves the well-being of the community. In fact,
collective identity serves as the basis for solidarity (Dallinger 2009), as a strong
collective identity is essential for solidarity according to this perspective. The
mechanism of welfare chauvinism also supports this latter argument. Welfare
chauvinism refers to how individuals are only willing to share goods with those
who they consider to be part of their own community (Mewes and Mau 2012;
Reeskens and van Oorschot 2012). Originally, work on welfare chauvinism
described how natives were reluctant to share their pooled resources with foreigners in national social systems because they did not feel that foreigners had
contributed enough to pooling the resources and they did not consider foreigners
part of their community. Adapting this argument to the context of European
welfare solidarity means assuming that the presence of welfare chauvinism can
undermine European welfare solidarity. Studies have so far confirmed the close
and negative relation between national identification and attitudes towards European welfare solidarity (Baute et al. 2019; Berg 2007; Ciornei and Recchi 2017;
Gerhards et al. 2016; Mau 2005). On the flipside, if individuals consider the
European Union a European community, they should support it. Hence, we
expect individuals who primarily make sense of the world based on national
containers and identify with their nation state to oppose European welfare solidarity. Conversely, individuals identifying with Europe (and the European Union
as a European community) and/or as a citizen of the world should strongly
favour European welfare solidarity.[17] We measured territorial attachment by
asking respondents whether they felt European, and whether they identified with
their nation state (i.e. thought of themselves as a national of their country).

(4) We consider whether the country's structural situation of a country aggra-
vates the gap between cultural cleavages. Cross-level interactions can help shed
light on whether support for European welfare solidarity is a form of European
communitarianism or cosmopolitanism. A lack of cross-level interactions in the
effect of European identity would indicate that European cosmopolitanism is
more likely to be at the heart of European welfare solidarity, as it would suggest
that a country's prosperity does not influence the value foundation of European
welfare solidarity. However, if identification with Europe led to less support for
European welfare solidarity in economically well-performing countries, this
would suggest that self-interest is a prime driver behind it. Similarly, if we see
that those identifying with their own country from weak economies still

supported European welfare solidarity, then this would be a clear indication that self-interest is a prominent indicator. Lastly, given the ideological foundation of left- and right-wing political orientations, we expect individuals in affluent countries with right-wing stances to more strongly oppose European welfare solidarity, as their value orientations make opposition more likely and, on top of that, it would also be in their country's interest. Such findings would have important consequences for the existence of European welfare solidarity. Namely, it would indicate that European welfare solidarity is circumstantial and not an overarching Europe-wide cultural gap.

We undertook the same analytical steps as in the previous empirical chapters.[18] Namely, our analytical approach was threefold. We first looked at whether structural and cultural cleavages were present on the individual level (and controlled for country context, as well as other individual factors). And we also contrasted whether the same mechanisms played a role for attitudes at the national level. If we found that the cleavages were more pronounced for the European level, this would also indicate a potential for the politicisation of European welfare solidarity. We then moved on to explain country differences in regard to European welfare solidarity. We concluded the empirical analysis by looking at whether country differences aggravated social and structural cleavages. Generally positive values would mean a positive association with European welfare solidarity, while a negative relation means a decrease in the support for European welfare solidarity.

5.4.3 Results on social cleavages

Table 5.1 shows how individual-level characteristics affect the first subdomain of European welfare solidarity, attitudes towards European social security. The first three columns show effects on European-level attitudes, while the last column in the table presents the complete model for national-level attitudes. The individual-level explanatory variables are divided into three different groups: control variables, indicators for structural cleavages, and indicators for cultural cleavages. Overall, the comparison of the models shows that the effects of the individual characteristics were relatively stable. This indicates that the chosen variables were independent of one another (and that there is no multicollinearity). First, we observed that self-interest played a prominent role in structural cleavages. Affluent individuals were less likely to support European social security solidarity, whereas members of vulnerable social groups were more likely to be in favour. So, citizens with tertiary degrees were less likely to support European social security compared to those with only primary or secondary education. The division between graduates of tertiary education and secondary school graduates was more robust, while, interestingly, the divide between primary and tertiary was only marginal. There was also a very clear class divide in attitudes. As far as attitudes towards European social security were concerned, self-employed people's attitudes were on par with those of

Table 5.1 Social cleavages regarding providing social security to people in the EU and within the nation state; individual level

	European Union				Nation			
	M1		M2		M3		M4	
Control variables								
Sex (ref.: male)	0.11***	(0.02)	0.09***	(0.01)	0.08***	(0.01)	0.04*	(0.01)
Age (by 10 years)	-0.02	(0.02)	0.00	(0.02)	-0.01	(0.02)	0.01	(0.02)
Age (by 10 years, squared)	0.00*	(0.00)	0.00	(0.00)	0.00	(0.00)	-0.00	(0.00)
Household: number of children	-0.02	(0.01)	-0.02	(0.01)	-0.01	(0.01)	-0.01*	(0.00)
Structural cleavages								
Level of education (ref.: tertiary)								
Non or primary			0.11	(0.06)	0.10	(0.06)	-0.02	(0.04)
Secondary			0.09***	(0.02)	0.10***	(0.02)	0.02	(0.01)
Occupational class (ref.: upper class (I))								
Upper middle class (II)			0.04*	(0.01)	0.03	(0.02)	0.00	(0.01)
Centre middle class (IIIa)			-0.01	(0.02)	-0.00	(0.02)	-0.00	(0.01)
Lower middle class (V & VI)			0.10***	(0.02)	0.09**	(0.02)	0.02	(0.01)
Self-employed (IVab & IVc)			-0.04	(0.04)	-0.02	(0.04)	-0.00	(0.03)
Routine non-manual (IIIb)			0.08*	(0.03)	0.07	(0.03)	0.00	(0.01)
Unskilled manual workers & agriculture (VIIa & VIIb)			0.08*	(0.03)	0.07*	(0.03)	0.02	(0.02)
Unemployed (ref.: employed)			0.06	(0.03)	0.05	(0.03)	0.09***	(0.02)
Household income			-0.08***	(0.02)	-0.07**	(0.02)	-0.03**	(0.01)
Cultural cleavages								
Political placement (ref.: centre)								
Left					0.16***	(0.04)	0.14**	(0.03)
Moderate left					0.08***	(0.02)	0.07**	(0.02)
Moderate right					-0.10***	(0.02)	-0.05***	(0.01)
Right					-0.05	(0.03)	-0.06	(0.03)
Justice: basic needs					0.23***	(0.02)	0.17***	(0.02)
Identity: national (ref.: no)					-0.04	(0.03)	-0.03	(0.02)
Identity: European (ref.: no)					0.06*	(0.02)	0.02	(0.01)
Country differences								
Country (ref.: Spain)								
Austria	-0.56***	(0.00)	-0.52***	(0.01)	-0.48***	(0.01)	-0.21***	(0.01)
Cyprus	0.10***	(0.00)	0.12***	(0.00)	0.19***	(0.02)	0.15***	(0.01)

France	-0.44***	(0.01)	-0.41***	(0.01)	-0.36***	(0.01)	-0.26***	(0.01)
Germany	-0.56***	(0.00)	-0.49***	(0.01)	-0.48***	(0.02)	-0.13***	(0.01)
Greece	0.05***	(0.00)	0.04**	(0.01)	0.09***	(0.02)	0.12***	(0.01)
Hungary	-0.36***	(0.01)	-0.41***	(0.02)	-0.34***	(0.02)	-0.16***	(0.02)
Ireland	-0.41***	(0.01)	-0.38***	(0.01)	-0.29***	(0.02)	-0.13***	(0.01)
The Netherlands	-0.54***	(0.01)	-0.50***	(0.01)	-0.40***	(0.02)	-0.12***	(0.01)
Poland	-0.61***	(0.00)	-0.61***	(0.01)	-0.46***	(0.02)	-0.30***	(0.02)
Portugal	-0.03***	(0.00)	-0.07***	(0.01)	-0.04**	(0.01)	-0.00	(0.01)
Slovakia	-0.33***	(0.00)	-0.38***	(0.02)	-0.32***	(0.02)	-0.29***	(0.01)
Sweden	-0.57***	(0.01)	-0.52***	(0.01)	-0.43***	(0.02)	0.04**	(0.01)
Constant	3.67***	(0.06)	4.10***	(0.11)	3.10***	(0.11)	3.20***	(0.12)
R^2	0.127		0.152		0.220		0.195	
AIC	18,619.0		18,362.3		17,566.1		10,800.3	

Source: TESS 2016, own calculations.

Notes

$n = 9,493$; Unstandardised coefficients from pooled OLS regression with robust standard errors (clustered by country). $^*p < 0.05$; $^{**}p < 0.01$; $^{***}p < 0.001$, standard errors in parentheses.

individuals from the upper classes; both groups were more likely to reject it. In contrast, members of all other (lower) classes were more in favour of European social security than the aforementioned two employment classes. Similarly, there was also a negative effect of household income: individuals living in high-income households tended to reject European social security.

Second, cultural factors also played an important role in the support for European social security. Individuals who were politically left wing supported the idea of European social security to a higher degree than respondents who located themselves in the centre or at the right-wing side of the political value orientation scale. Furthermore, the more individuals believed society should be organised based on the justice principle of need, the more they also favoured European social security. This latter factor was one of the strongest predictors for attitudes towards European social security. This indicates that cultural cleavages are prominent factors when accounting for the variance in attitudes towards European social security.

For the subdomain of European social security, only territorial attachment to Europe affected the approval rates, while identification with a nation state did not have a significant effect. Thus, individuals who had a territorial attachment to Europe were more likely to support European social security.

Finally, in the analysis we also considered whether social cleavages for European social security were comparable with the social cleavages for attitudes to national social security. The predictive value of indicators was, without exception, stronger on the European level. This suggests that cleavages in regard to European social security were more likely to be formed on the European level, because individual differences were more likely to separate respondents from one another here. This is also an indication that the question of European social security may be a topic for political mobilisation on the European level. Furthermore, while the weaker results may seem disappointing for readers well accustomed to strong individual differences in welfare state attitudes (Jæger 2006; Svallfors 2004), these results could be an indication that, on the national level, social security aims are now a norm in nation states and not something up for political debate.

Table 5.2 shows the results of the regression analysis for the second subdomain of European welfare solidarity. For European redistribution, we also detected structural cleavages; affluent individuals tended to oppose European redistribution to a larger degree than others. Individuals with a secondary education supported European redistribution to a higher degree than university graduates. Individuals in the lower classes (lower middle, routine non-manual, unskilled, and agricultural workers) were also more in favour of European redistribution than the upper classes, and so were the unemployed and those from lower-income households. Cultural cleavages were also present in respect to European redistribution. Individuals who located themselves politically on the right wing opposed the idea of European redistribution. Additionally, European identity did not have a significant effect on attitudes towards European redistribution. Instead, national identity proved to be relevant: those who had a strong national identity more strongly rejected European redistribution. A comparison of predictors for attitudes for national and European redistribution shows that cleavages are already present on the national level. What is more, structural cleavages were more pronounced for national-level attitudes. This indicates that income inequality and redistribution still aren't settled topics even in the national arena, let alone on a European platform.

Overall, attitudes towards European social security were less strongly divided along social class lines than attitudes towards European redistribution. European identity was decisive for support for European social security, while national identity influenced the support for European redistribution. It is also noteworthy that the justice principle of need was the strongest predictor for European social security, while for European redistribution household income was the most prominent one.

Looking ahead to country differences and foreshadowing the results that we found in the macro-level analysis in the next step, we observed significant country differences in regard to European welfare solidarity when looking at the coefficients for country dummies in Tables 5.1 and 5.2. In both subdomains, individuals from economically well-performing countries – i.e. countries less affected by the Great Recession – rejected the notion of European welfare solidarity (in particular Germany and post-socialist Poland). In contrast, respondents from debt-ridden countries were more in favour of European welfare solidarity. Can we explain these country differences systematically? This is the task of the macro-level analysis.

Moving on to the second step of the analysis, we investigated whether European welfare solidarity has the potential to create cleavages between member states. We assessed whether the social circumstances of a country influenced what respondents thought about European welfare solidarity. If we found higher support rates in countries with growing social problems, this may be a clear indication that structural cleavages on the macro level could emerge. Empirically, we used the unstandardised regression coefficients of the countries in the full model (M3) and contrasted them with macro-structural variables. Several structural features of the countries had a significant effect on the country differences for both subdomains. Figure 5.9 and 5.10 depict the selected effects most important for the previous argument. The graphs portray the values for each country along a selected macro-structural variable and the unstandardised coefficient of the country dummy. For both subdomains, the lower the inequality and the lower the unemployment rate, the more strongly citizens object to European welfare solidarity. What is also notable in the country differences is that attitudes in post-socialist countries did not significantly differ from those in western Europe, and that these did not represent one unified and distinct group of countries (contrary to what Chapter 2 suggested).

In the third step of the analysis, we looked at whether the cleavages observed between countries widened the cleavages on the individual level. Overall, the

Table 5.2 Social cleavages regarding redistribution of income between people in the EU and in nation states; individual level

	European Union				Nation			
	M1		M2		M3		M4	
Control variables								
Sex (ref.: male)	0.13***	(0.02)	0.10***	(0.02)	0.08***	(0.01)	0.09***	(0.01)
Age (by 10 years)	0.05	(0.03)	0.07	(0.03)	0.06	(0.04)	0.02	(0.03)
Age (by 10 years, squared)	−0.00	(0.00)	−0.00	(0.00)	−0.00	(0.00)	0.00	(0.00)
Household: number of kids	−0.04	(0.02)	−0.04*	(0.02)	−0.03	(0.02)	−0.03	(0.01)
Structural cleavages								
Level of education (ref.: tertiary)								
Non or primary			0.11	(0.08)	0.09	(0.08)	0.12	(0.06)
Secondary			0.13***	(0.02)	0.14***	(0.02)	0.13***	(0.01)
Occupational class (ref.: upper class (I))								
Upper middle class (II)			0.07**	(0.02)	0.06*	(0.02)	0.06*	(0.02)
Centre middle class (IIIa)			0.04*	(0.01)	0.04**	(0.01)	0.03*	(0.02)
Lower middle class (V & VI)			0.16***	(0.02)	0.15***	(0.02)	0.12***	(0.03)
Self-employed (IVab & IVc)			0.01	(0.05)	0.04	(0.04)	0.08	(0.04)
Routine non-manual (IIIb)			0.13**	(0.03)	0.10**	(0.03)	0.08***	(0.02)
Unskilled manual workers & agriculture (VIIa & VIIb)			0.18***	(0.04)	0.17**	(0.04)	0.10	(0.06)
Unemployed (ref.: employed)			0.09	(0.05)	0.07	(0.05)	0.05	(0.03)
Household income			−0.14***	(0.02)	−0.12***	(0.02)	−0.08**	(0.01)
Cultural cleavages								
Political placement (ref.: centre)								
Left					0.23**	(0.06)	0.26***	(0.06)
Moderate left					0.14***	(0.03)	0.23***	(0.04)
Moderate right					−0.15***	(0.04)	−0.18***	(0.04)
Right					−0.12	(0.08)	−0.17*	(0.06)
Justice: basic needs					0.35***	(0.01)	0.30***	(0.01)
Identity: national (Ref.: No)					−0.10*	(0.03)	−0.03	(0.03)
Identity: European (Ref.: No)					0.04	(0.02)	−0.03	(0.03)
Country differences								
Country (Ref.: Spain)								
Austria	−0.35***	(0.01)	−0.29***	(0.01)	−0.24***	(0.02)	−0.05***	(0.01)

Cyprus	−0.00	(0.00)	0.03***	(0.00)	0.12***	(0.02)	0.24***	(0.02)
France	−0.38***	(0.01)	−0.33***	(0.01)	−0.25***	(0.01)	−0.14***	(0.01)
Germany	−0.44***	(0.01)	−0.35***	(0.02)	−0.33***	(0.02)	−0.03*	(0.01)
Greece	0.01***	(0.00)	−0.02	(0.01)	0.06**	(0.02)	0.13***	(0.01)
Hungary	−0.06***	(0.01)	−0.15***	(0.02)	−0.03	(0.03)	0.24***	(0.03)
Ireland	−0.34***	(0.01)	−0.30***	(0.01)	−0.17***	(0.02)	0.00	(0.02)
The Netherlands	−0.63***	(0.01)	−0.57***	(0.01)	−0.43***	(0.02)	−0.23***	(0.02)
Poland	−0.57***	(0.01)	−0.58***	(0.01)	−0.34***	(0.03)	−0.21***	(0.03)
Portugal	0.10***	(0.00)	0.04**	(0.01)	0.11***	(0.02)	0.15***	(0.01)
Slovakia	−0.13***	(0.01)	−0.23***	(0.02)	−0.12***	(0.02)	−0.01	(0.02)
Sweden	−0.70***	(0.01)	−0.63***	(0.01)	−0.50***	(0.02)	−0.22***	(0.02)
Constant	3.22***	(0.10)	4.01***	(0.13)	2.56***	(0.12)	2.45***	(0.10)
R²	0.081		0.112		0.198		0.171	
AIC	24,865.4		24,560.6		23,617.3		22,930.2	

Source: TESS 2016, own calculations.

Notes
$n = 9,350$: Unstandardised coefficients from pooled OLS regression with robust standard errors (clustered by country), *$p < 0.05$; **$p < 0.01$; ***$p < 0.001$, standard errors in parentheses.

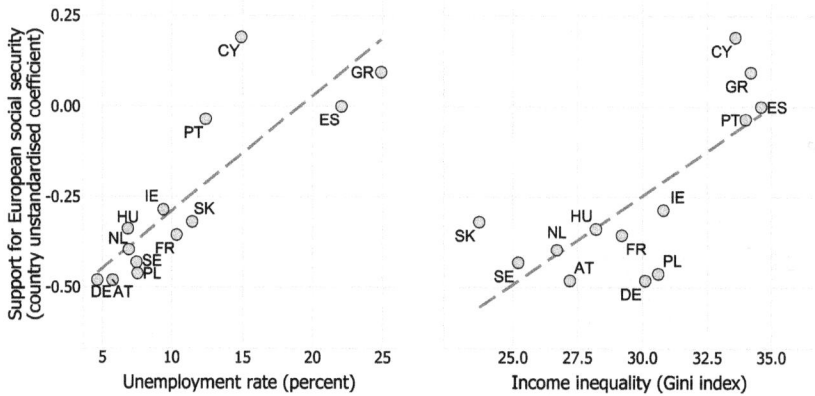

Figure 5.9 Social cleavages regarding providing social security to people in the EU and within the nation state; country level.

Source: TESS 2016, own calculations.

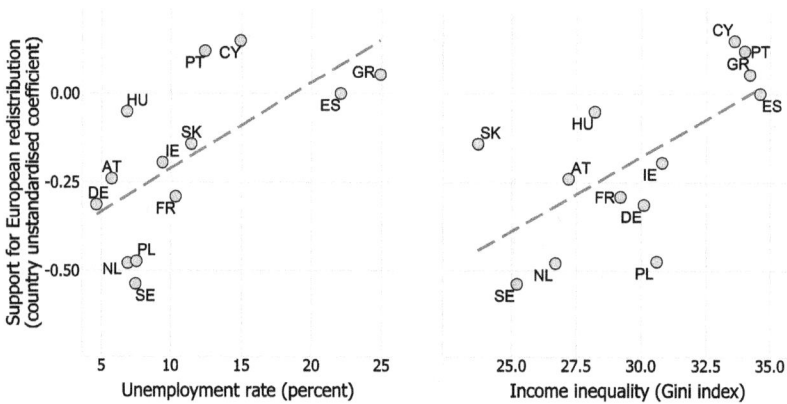

Figure 5.10 Social cleavages regarding redistribution of income between people in EU countries and in nation states; country level.

Source: TESS 2016, own calculations.

empirical results largely matched our expectations. Affluent individuals in economically well-performing countries rejected European welfare solidarity to a larger degree than affluent individuals in economically struggling countries. In countries with a high unemployment rate, the effect of household income was negligible, while in countries with a low unemployment rate household income had a strong negative effect. This indicates that the richer the country, the more likely individuals in richer households were to dismiss the notion of European welfare solidarity.

Further results illustrated how macro-structural circumstances foster links between personal circumstances and European welfare solidarity on the individual level. Specifically, for attitudes towards European social security in economically stable, prospering societies, the structural cleavage between citizens holding different educational credentials was more pronounced than in poorer countries. For attitudes towards European redistribution, we observed similar divides. In countries with low unemployment rates, the upper classes were considerably more negative about the notion of European redistribution, while in countries with high unemployment rates, the attitudes of the lower classes (i.e. the unskilled and manual workers) closed in to the opinions of the upper classes.

As far as cultural cleavages were concerned, we found some politically relevant outcomes. On the one hand, in both subdomains of European welfare solidarity, the difference between individuals with (moderate) left and (moderate) right-wing political orientations deepened the wealthier a society was. Empirically, we observed this in two ways. First, as a country's economic productivity increased, the gap between left-leaning and centrist individuals widened: the higher the GDP, the greater the support for European welfare solidarity among left-wing individuals. Second, the better a country's economic performance, the more strongly right-wing individuals rejected European welfare solidarity. It is further important to mention that the effect of political extremism (both for left and right wingers) was not affected by prosperity in the country, indicating that political extremism may be more grounded in deep-running beliefs in better-performing economies. We observed similar tendencies in the rate of social spending. The higher the rate of social spending in a country, the more likely right-wing radicals opposed European welfare solidarity. On the other hand, we also found that the predictive value of identity (both European and national) was contingent on how well a country was performing economically. In particular, in rich countries, individuals with national territorial attachment rejected European welfare solidarity, while in poor countries they were clearly in favour of European welfare solidarity. The latter may arise because rich people in poor countries see the European Union as a way of unburdening their country's national budget; this may overwrite their nationalistic views. Lastly, an individual's attachment to Europe only translated into strong support for European welfare solidarity in prospering countries.

All in all, the analysis provides us with three main conclusions. First, social cleavages exist both within member states and between member states. Second, the potential opponents of European welfare solidarity are affluent individuals from affluent countries, as well as nationalists from affluent countries. Third, the supporters of European welfare solidarity are either from economically struggling countries or individuals with a strong European identity in prospering countries.

These results call into question whether the fourth criterion for the existence of a European solidarity in this domain can be confirmed. However, given the high response rates, we do not consider the cleavages we observed to be a severe threat to European solidarity as they primarily occur at a high degree of approval of European solidarity. Any attitudinal differences indicating social cleavages primarily arose between the answer categories 'totally agree' and 'somewhat agree' of the scales used in the survey. Thus, the substantial meaning of the observed cleavages is that certain social groups support European welfare solidarity even more than others.

5.4.4 Results on political cleavages

The final step of this chapter is to explore whether attitudes to solidarity serve as a basis for political cleavages. If the findings show that citizens opposing European welfare solidarity would be willing to express their views by voting for a Eurosceptic party in national elections, this may indicate upcoming obstacles for the European Commission in its quest to strengthen the social dimension of Europe. But does an individual's opinion about European welfare solidarity guide their voting choices, and if so, who will individuals cast their vote for?

For all, we expect an individual's stance towards European welfare solidarity to be relevant for party partisanship, because European issues have become a relevant topic in (European) political campaigns since the Great Recession and they are no longer second order to national issues (Hobolt and de Vries 2016). We assume political parties would take up issues that reflected the concerns of their voters (or at least this should be an employed strategy), because a large component of democratic legitimacy is that 'citizens' normative preferences must eventually be translated into social policy' (de Witte 2015:54). In line with the arguments raised in the previous chapters, two main types of parties advocate against ideals of European welfare solidarity: (1) Eurosceptic parties, which advocate for extensive national sovereignty, and (2) parties with an economically liberal and right-wing understanding of the European community, which also opposed the European Pillar for Social Rights. Thus, we expected the opponents of European welfare solidarity to be more likely to vote for parties on the right, as well as parties who expressed Eurosceptic views.

In the following, we explain potential voting behaviour with our indicators measuring European welfare solidarity. To do so, we again relied on the party preference indicator used in the previous chapters:

> *If the [NATIONALELECTION] were held tomorrow, which party would you vote for?*

We once again captured potential voting behaviour by taking national parties, which we then categorised by their degree of Euroscepticism and their placement on the left–right wing spectrum based on Hobolt and de Vries (2016).

Based on this, we conducted bivariate multinomial logistic regressions for both subdomains of European welfare solidarity.

Figures 5.11 and 5.12 show the predicted probabilities corresponding with the regression analyses. They depict the changes in the probability of voting for a left- or right-wing, soft or hard Eurosceptic party based on the parties' support for European welfare solidarity. In both subdomains, there was only a weak

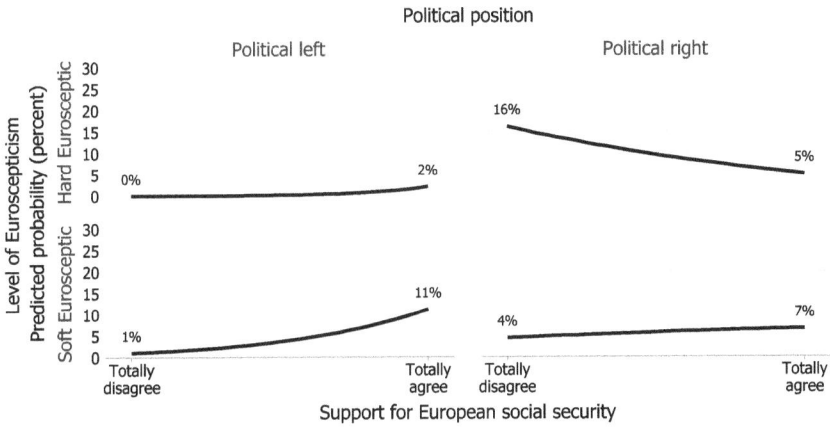

Figure 5.11 Support for European social security and political position of party voted for.

Source: TESS 2016, own calculations.

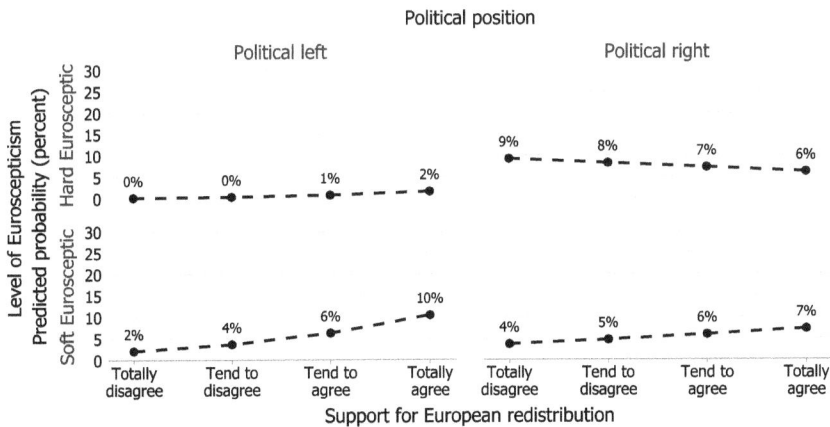

Figure 5.12 Support for European redistribution and political position of party voted for.

Source: TESS 2016, own calculations.

connection between European welfare solidarity and voting behaviour. The effect of European welfare solidarity is no longer significant when controlling for other explanatory factors. On the other hand, despite the weak association, clear tendencies emerged, which are also consistent with the findings of previous chapters in this volume.

In detail, this meant that, in both subdomains, rejecting European welfare solidarity increased the chances of voting for a right-wing Eurosceptic party. For all other party orientations, rejecting European welfare solidarity decreased the chances of voting for that party. Overall, a more distinct connection with attitudes towards European social security was evident than for attitudes to European redistribution. In the subdomain of European social security, there was a decrease in the predicted probability slope for right-wing Eurosceptic party voting. In total, 16% of those completely opposing such measures were willing to vote for a right-wing hard Eurosceptic party. In contrast, among those fully supporting such European measures, the probability fell by one-third: only 5% would vote for such a party in their own country. In all other types of parties, the relationship was positive: the more individuals supported European social security, the more likely they were to support parties from a given party family type. This positive connection is particularly clearly illustrated in the left-bottom graph of Figure 5.11. Here, the share of individuals voting for a left-wing Eurosceptic party increased from 1% to 11% when looking at those who are opponents of European social security measures and those who are proponents.

Taken altogether, results provide some indications that only the combination of (hard) Euroscepticism and right-wing orientations could endanger European welfare solidarity, while voting for a left-wing Eurosceptic party is not connected to European welfare solidarity. However, even among the strongest opponents of the European welfare solidarity, Eurosceptic right-wing voters are still a minority. In addition, the opponents and supporters of European welfare solidarity are affiliated with a broad spectrum of parties; thus, no political party can truly claim to be the 'warriors' of European welfare solidarity. In sum, we conclude that the question of European welfare solidarity has only weak or no potential to become politicised.

5.5 Conclusion on European welfare solidarity

In this chapter, we explored to what degree Europeans supported the notion that all Europeans should have access to social security as well as whether they endorsed redistribution between the rich and the poor people across the EU and want a uniform European welfare state. Our study investigated European welfare solidarity in much greater detail than previous studies. Consequently, we were able to show that there is an extremely high approval rate for European welfare solidarity, based on our test concept we introduced in Chapter 2. Additionally, thanks to cleavage analysis, we determined that self-interest-related, value, and affect-related drivers also lay behind this support. In a systematic overview below, we summarise three out of the four[19] criteria for the existence of European welfare solidarity.

1   In both subdomains of European welfare solidarity we observed an absolute majority in favour of European welfare solidarity across the 13 European countries, as well as an absolute majority within each country.
2   We confirmed that European welfare solidarity represents a separate spatial sphere compared to both national and global welfare solidarity. The support for European welfare solidarity was weaker than for national welfare solidarity, but it still had priority over global welfare solidarity for a large proportion of respondents. On the other hand, we also found indication that support for European welfare solidarity was prevalent among both cosmopolitans and European communitarians.
3   We identified social cleavages in relation to European welfare solidarity. Members of affluent social groups were more likely to oppose welfare solidarity on the European level, as well as those who positioned themselves on the political right. We also found that the economic situation of countries deepened these cleavages: in richer countries, affluent individuals more strongly opposed European welfare solidarity.
4   However, researchers should be cautious of overestimating the existence of cleavages on European welfare solidarity. Given the very high support rate for European welfare solidarity and the fact that social cleavages primarily occurred between those who totally and somewhat support European welfare solidarity, we do not expect the cleavages to severely undermine European welfare solidarity. In addition, we only found weak indications that support for European welfare solidarity created political cleavages. In particular, opponents of European welfare solidarity were likely to vote for parties representing right-wing and hard Eurosceptic positions.

What are the potential implications of our findings for policy makers and the future of the European integration process in the field of social policy? On the one hand, our results showed that an overwhelming majority of Europeans support the idea that the European Union should guarantee access to health care as well as a decent standard of living for the elderly and the unemployed. These results provide support for those politicians who want to deepen the European integration process and build a social Europe.

However, this conclusion cannot be directly drawn from our results. The items in our questionnaire measured *general* attitudes towards Europe-wide responsibility for people in need and towards reducing the degree of inequality. Our analysis has also shown that citizens were much more sceptical of attempts to institutionalise a European welfare state; such efforts will face resistance, especially from the more affluent social groups, the political right, and richer EU countries. Thus, support for a supranational welfare state does not automatically follow from European welfare solidarity.

But there are various non-supranational policy tools that could be used. For instance, the EU Commission could draft appropriate directives urging member states to adequately protect vulnerable groups. Such measures would still be implemented in the nation states. Another example of a European directive on social policy that would leave the responsibility for implementation at the national level would be the EU-wide minimum wage that Emmanuel Macron prominently mentioned in his Sorbonne address. The establishment of funds, on the other hand, could be a different tool to generate European welfare solidarity and constitute the 'golden mean' between European and national responsibilities (Weber 2017). In these scenarios, the historically emerging national social security systems would still remain the key instrument for the distribution of resources and would not be replaced by a new supranational system for all Europeans.

Lastly, we would like to stress the potential consequences of our findings related to structural cleavages. Vulnerable social groups and citizens from economically weaker countries are more in favour of European welfare solidarity than affluent individuals and citizens from affluent countries. Thus, affluent people, who are the main beneficiaries of European integration and the main supporters of the European project, oppose European welfare solidarity (i.e. an indicator for European integration). This ultimately threatens the future of the European project. Such structural cleavages pose a moderate threat to European integration. So, while our results indicate that European welfare solidarity is a widespread and accepted norm in European societies, it is important to continue to foster this domain of European solidarity.

Notes

1 While the increase in income inequalities is not so clearly linked to the Great Recession, Jenkins and colleagues (2013a) have suggested that there are many other, more serious long-term consequences of the Great Recession. These include the translation of health risks of being unemployed into health inequalities over time (Karanikolos et al. 2013; Mladovsky et al. 2012; Quaglio et al. 2013). Moreover, the continuing loss of income due to employment also put personal pensions at risk, and could even have structural consequences for the pension system.
2 Social policy provisions were already included in the Treaty of Rome of 1957, but they were of marginal importance (Verschraegen, Vanhercke, and Verpoorten 2011). These issues became more prominent after the mid-1980s in the political discourse (see for a historical overview of social policy Leibfried 2015.
3 Jordi Solé, MEP, at the European Parliament debate on A European Pillar of Social Rights on 19 January 2017.
4 Reported by Marianne Thyssen [CD&V, BE], commissioner for employment, social affairs, skills and labour mobility, during the EP session on 19 January 2017.
5 In contrast to the previous two chapters, we did not integrate the global spatial level into our investigation, because of the strong nation state nature of welfare solidarity and the lack of conceptual clarity on the global level.
6 There is also a set of papers that analysed European welfare solidarity to some extent, but their focus is on the question of sovereignty and the degree of decision making

instead of the degree of European welfare solidarity per se (Berg 2007; European Commission 2017a; Mau 2005). Since the crisis, the majority of citizens in most of the member states have been open to a higher degree of harmonisation of social security measures and welfare systems (European Commission 2017a).

7 We modelled questions after survey items measuring attitudes towards national social security in well-established public opinion polls (ESS Round 4: European Social Survey 2016; ISSP Research Group 1999). However, we adapted the question and also applied it to the territorial level of the European Union. The wording of the questions was identical at the two territorial levels; there was an essential difference only in the territorial framing.

8 Again, the items were based on established survey questionnaire items (ESS Round 4: European Social Survey 2016; ISSP Research Group 1999).

9 We did not have the opportunity to ask individuals about their priorities about where inequalities should be reduced first: on the national, European, and global level. Such a question would have served to verify that preferences towards European redistribution mean something different than global redistribution.

10 The item was a stand-alone item in our survey and was developed by our research team. A similar question was poised in the Europeanisation of Equality Survey (EES) in 2009 for a smaller number of countries (ESS Round 4: European Social Survey 2016).

11 Readers should note that there is no national- or global-level equivalent of the question. At the time of the item's construction, we abandoned the notion of surveying attitudes towards the national welfare system, as that would be beyond the scope of the project and the responses from such a large variety of countries with different national welfare systems would have influenced the interpretability of the response.

12 Although we use causal rhetoric throughout the book, our analysis is not a causal analysis in the narrow sense of the term. For a strict causal analysis, a randomised trial (Hernán 2018) or panel data (Morgan and Winship 2015:363–91) would be more appropriate. Unfortunately, our cross-sectional survey data cannot be categorized as such. Nonetheless, we share the opinion of Miguel A. Hernán who argues that 'without casually explicit language, the means and ends of much observational research get hopelessly conflated' (Hernán 2018:617).

13 Previous studies have also presented counterarguments and have explained why vulnerable individuals would oppose European welfare solidarity. The rationale is that self-interest, in fact, leads vulnerable groups to reject European-level social policy, because they fear that it will mean less benefits for them (Berg 2007; Gerhards et al. 2016; Mau 2005). However, their empirical findings did not support this counterargument. On the one hand, Berg (2007) using the Swedish SOM study from 2004 showed that people from lower occupational classes (i.e. blue collar workers) were more likely to support European-level social policy than those from higher classes. On the other hand, neither Mau (2005) using Eurobarometer data from 2000 nor Gerhards et al. (2016), with data from EES, found indication for this structural cleavage.

14 However, and in contrast to the mentioned studies, Ciornei and Recchi (2017) did not find indication that a country's situation in the crisis per se was relevant.

15 It is important to note, however, that we excluded the justice principles from the predictors of the subdomain of attitudes towards European redistribution, because the question of redistribution is inherently closely related to distributive justice principles, and the problem of statistical endogeneity arises. Thus, we expected respondents' support for European social security to increase in line with their adherence to the need principle.

16 This rationale is similar to the arguments used by van Oorschot (2006, 2008) to justify why individuals are in favour of informal solidarity ('deservingness' in other terms).

17 Such a positive relation may arise due to both the existence of *European* communitarianism, but also due to cosmopolitism. Unearthing the roots of such a relation requires a detailed analysis of territorial attachment to Europe and the world, but due to space limitations we could not undertake such an analysis.
18 See Appendix for details on our methodology.
19 The criterion of resilience could not be tested reliably in this domain.

References

Alsasua, Jesús, Javier Bilbao-Ubillos, and Jon Olaskoaga. 2007. 'The EU Integration Process and the Convergence of Social Protection Benefits at National Level'. *International Journal of Social Welfare* 16(4):297–306.

Andreß, Hans-Jürgen, and Thorsten Heien. 2001. 'Four Worlds of Welfare State Attitudes?: A Comparison of Germany, Norway, and the United States'. *European Sociological Review* 17(4):337–56.

Arpaia, Alfonso, and Nicola Curci. 2010. *EU Labour Market Behaviour during the Great Recession*. Brussels: European Commission, Directorate-General for Economic and Financial Affairs. Retrieved 8 September 2017 (https://mpra.ub.uni-muenchen.de/22393/).

Arts, Wil, and John Gelissen. 2001. 'Welfare States, Solidarity and Justice Principles: Does the Type Really Matter?' *Acta Sociologica* 44(4):283–99.

Arundel, Rowan, and Christian Lennartz. 2017. 'Returning to the Parental Home: Boomerang Moves of Younger Adults and the Welfare Regime Context'. *Journal of European Social Policy* 27(3):276–94.

Aspalter, Christian. 2017. 'Welfare Regime Analysis: 30 Years in the Making'. *International Social Work* 4(1):1–13.

Avdeyeva, Olga. 2006. 'In Support of Mothers' Employment: Limits to Policy Convergence in the EU?' *International Journal of Social Welfare* 15(1):37–49.

Baute, Sharon, Bart Meuleman, Koen Abts, and Marc Swyngedouw. 2018. 'Measuring Attitudes towards Social Europe: A Multidimensional Approach'. *Social Indicators Research* 137(1):353–78.

Baute, Sharon, Bart Meuleman, and Koen Abts. 2019. 'Welfare State Attitudes and Support for Social Europe: Spillover or Obstacle?' *Journal of Social Policy* 2(1):127–45.

Beck, Ulrich, and Edgar Grande. 2007. *Cosmopolitan Europe*. Cambridge: Polity Press.

Berg, Linda. 2007. *Multi-level Europeans: The Influence of Territorial Attachments on Political Trust and Welfare Attitudes*. Department of Political Science Statsvetenskapliga institutionen.

Biegert, Thomas. 2017. 'Welfare Benefits and Unemployment in Affluent Democracies: The Moderating Role of the Institutional Insider/Outsider Divide'. *American Sociological Review* 82(5):1037–64.

Blekesaune, Morten, and Jill Quadagno. 2003. 'Public Attitudes toward Welfare State Policies: A Comparative Analysis of 24 Nations'. *European Sociological Review* 19(5):415–27.

Burgoon, Brian. 2009. 'Social Nation and Social Europe'. *European Union Politics* 10(4):427–55.

Ciornei, Irina, and Ettore Recchi. 2017. 'At the Source of European Solidarity: Assessing the Effects of Cross-border Practices and Political Attitudes'. *Journal of Common Market Studies* 55(3):468–85.

Cnaan, Ram, Yeheskel Hasenfeld, Avital Cnaan, and Jane Rafferty. 1993. 'Cross-cultural Comparison of Attitudes toward Welfare-state Programs: Path Analysis with Log-linear Models'. *Social Indicators Research* 29(2):123–52.

Corti, Francesco, and Patrik Vesan. 2017. *Numerous Tensions Stand in the Way of Agreement on the European Social Pillar*. Brussels: Progressive Post.

Dallinger, Ursula. 2009. *Die Solidarität der modernen Gesellschaft: Der Diskurs um rationale oder normative Ordnung in Sozialtheorie und Soziologie des Wohlfahrtsstaats [Solidarity in Modern Societies: The Discourse on Rational or Normative Order in Social Theory and Sociology of the Welfare State]*. Wiesbaden: VS Verlag für Sozialwissenschaften.

Dallinger, Ursula. 2010. 'Public Support for Redistribution: What Explains Cross-national Differences?' *Journal of European Social Policy* 20(4):333–49.

de Swaan, Abram. 1992. 'Perspectives for Transnational Social Policy'. *Government and Opposition* 27(1):33–51.

de Witte, Floris. 2015. *Justice in the EU: The Emergence of Transnational Solidarity*. Oxford: Oxford University Press.

Delhey, Jan, Emanuel Deutschmann, Timo Graf, and Katharina Richter. 2014. 'Measuring the Europeanization of Everyday Life: Three New Indices and an Empirical Application'. *European Societies* 16(3):355–77.

Deutsch, Morton. 1985. *Distributive Justice: A Social-psychological Perspective*. New Haven, CT: Yale University Press.

Diamond, Patrick, Roger Liddle, and Daniel Sage. 2015. *The Social Reality of Europe after the Crisis: Trends, Challenges and Responses*. London: Rowman & Littlefield.

Duiella, Matteo, and Alessandro Turrini. 2014. *Poverty Developments in the EU after the Crisis: A Look at Main Drivers*. Issue 31, May 2014. Brussels: European Commission.

Edlund, Jonas. 2007. 'Class Conflicts and Institutional Feedback Effects in Liberal and Social Democratic Welfare Regimes'. Pp. 30–79 in *The Political Sociology of the Welfare State*, edited by S. Svallfors. Stanford, CA: Stanford University Press.

Esping-Andersen, Gøsta. 1990. *The Three Worlds of Welfare Capitalism*. Princeton, NJ: Princeton University Press.

ESS Round 4: European Social Survey. 2016. *ESS-4 2008 Documentation Report. Edition 5.4*. Bergen. Retrieved 12 September 2018 (www.europeansocialsurvey.org/data/conditions_of_use.html).

European Commission. 2017a. *Future of Europe: Report.* Special Eurobarometer. No. 467. Brussels.

European Commission. 2017b. *Communication from the Commission to the European Parliament, the Council, the European Economic and Social Committee and the Committee of the Regions: Establishing a European Pillar of Social Rights*. COM(2017) 250. Brussels.

European Commission. 2017c. *President Jean-Claude Juncker's State of the Union Address 2017*. European Commission Press Release Database. Retrieved 23 April 2019 (http://europa.eu/rapid/press-release_SPEECH-17-3165_en.htm).

European Commission. 2019. 'Youth Employment Initiative (YEI)'. Retrieved 19 February 2019 (https://ec.europa.eu/social/main.jsp?catId=1176).

European Parliament, and Council of the European Union. 2013. *Regulation (EU) No. 1304/2013 of the European Parliament and of the Council: of 17 December 2013 on the European Social Fund and Repealing Council Regulation (EC) No. 1081/2006*. Luxembourg: Publications Office of the European Union. Retrieved 4 October 2017 (http://eur-lex.europa.eu/legal-content/en/TXT/?uri=CELEX%3A32013R1304).

Ferrera, Maurizio. 2017. 'The European Social Union: A Missing but Necessary "Political Good".' Pp. 47–67 in *A European Social Union after the Crisis*, edited by F. Vandenbroucke, C. Barnard, and G. de Baere. Cambridge: Cambridge University Press.

Fligstein, Neil. 2008. *Euroclash: The EU, European Identity, and the Future of Europe.* Oxford: Oxford University Press.

Flora, Peter, and Arnold J. Heidenheimer. 1981. 'The Historical Core and Changing Boundaries of the Welfare State'. Pp. 17–34 in *The Development of Welfare States in Europe and America*, edited by P. Flora and A. J. Heidenheimer. New Brunswick, NJ: Transaction Books.

Gelissen, John. 2000. 'Popular Support for Institutionalised Solidarity: A Comparison between European Welfare States'. *International Journal of Social Welfare* 9(4):285–300.

General Secretariat of the Council. 2017. *2018 EU Budget Adopted (Press Release: 710/17).* Brussels. Retrieved 12 September 2018 (www.consilium.europa.eu/en/press/press-releases/2017/11/30/2018-eu-budget-adopted/).

Genschel, Philipp, and Anton Hemerijck. 2018. *Solidarity in Europe.* Policy Brief. Issue 2018/01. Fiesole: EUI School of Transnational Governance: School of Transnational Governance. Retrieved 10 January 2019 (https://stateoftheunion.eui.eu/wp-content/uploads/sites/9/2018/05/Policy-Brief-Solidarity-in-Europe.pdf).

Gerhards, Jürgen, and Holger Lengfeld. 2015. *European Citizenship and Social Integration in the European Union.* London and New York: Routledge.

Gerhards, Jürgen, Holger Lengfeld, and Julia Häuberer. 2016. 'Do European Citizens Support the Idea of a European Welfare State?: Evidence from a Comparative Survey Conducted in Three EU Member States'. *International Sociology* 31(6):677–700.

Guio, Anne-Catherine, Eric Marlier, and Marco Pomati. 2017. 'Evolution of Material Deprivation over Time: The Impact of the Great Recession in EU Countries'. Pp. 367–83 in *Theme, Monitoring Social Inclusion in Europe*, edited by A. B. Atkinson, A.-C. Guio, and E. Marlière. Luxembourg: Publications Office of the European Union.

Hantrais, Linda. 2000. *Social Policy in the European Union.* Basingstoke: Macmillan.

Häusermann, Silja, Thomas Kurer, and Hanna Schwander. 2016. 'Sharing the Risk? Households, Labor Market Vulnerability, and Social Policy Preferences in Western Europe'. *The Journal of Politics* 78(4):1045–60.

Heidenreich, Martin. 2015. 'The End of the Honeymoon: The Increasing Differentiation of (Long-term) Unemployment Risks in Europe'. *Journal of European Social Policy* 25(4):393–413.

Heidenreich, Martin. 2016a. 'The Europeanization of Income Inequality before and during the Eurozone Crisis: Inter-, Supra-, and Transnational Perspectives'. Pp. 22–47 in *Exploring Inequality in Europe: Diverging Income and Employment Opportunities in the Crisis*, edited by M. Heidenreich. Cheltenham and Northampton, MA: Edward Elgar.

Heidenreich, Martin. 2016b. 'The Segmentation of the European Labour Market – the Evolution of Short- and Long-term Unemployment Risks during the Eurozone Crisis'. Pp. 70–106 in *Exploring Inequality in Europe: Diverging Income and Employment Opportunities in the Crisis*, edited by M. Heidenreich. Cheltenham and Northampton, MA: Edward Elgar.

Heidenreich, Martin. 2016c. 'Women as the Relative Winners of the Eurozone Crisis? Female Employment Opportunities between Austerity, Inclusion and Dualization'.

Pp. 107–38 in *Exploring Inequality in Europe: Diverging Income and Employment Opportunities in the Crisis*, edited by M. Heidenreich. Cheltenham and Northampton, MA: Edward Elgar.

Heins, Elke, and Caroline de la Porte. 2016. 'Depleted European Social Models Following the Crisis: Towards a Brighter Future?' Pp. 207–21 in *The Sovereign Debt Crisis, the EU and Welfare State Reform*, edited by C. de la Porte and E. Heins. London: Palgrave Macmillan.

Hemerijck, Anton. 2004. 'Beyond the Double Bind of Social Europe'. Pp. 89–123 in *Work & Society*, Vol. 47, *A European Social Citizenship?: Preconditions for Future Policies from a Historical Perspective*, edited by L. Magnusson and B. Strath. Brussels: Lang.

Hemerijck, Anton. 2013. *Changing Welfare States*. Oxford: Oxford University Press.

Hernán, Miguel A. 2018. 'The C-Word: Scientific Euphemisms Do Not Improve Causal Inference from Observational Data'. *American Journal of Public Health* 108(5):616–19.

Hobolt, Sara B., and Catherine E. de Vries. 2016. 'Turning against the Union? The Impact of the Crisis on the Eurosceptic Vote in the 2014 European Parliament Elections'. *Electoral Studies* 44:504–14.

Hooghe, Liesbet, and Gary Marks. 2017. 'Cleavage Theory Meets Europe's Crises: Lipset, Rokkan, and the Transnational Cleavage'. *Journal of European Public Policy* 1(1):1–27.

ISSP Research Group. 1999. 'International Social Survey Programme: Role of Government 3 – ISSP 1996'. Retrieved 27 June 2017 (https://dbk.gesis.org/dbksearch/SDesc2.asp?ll=10&notabs=&af=&nf=&search=ISSP&search2=&db=E&no=2900).

Jæger, Mads M. 2006. 'Welfare Regimes and Attitudes towards Redistribution: The Regime Hypothesis Revisited'. *European Sociological Review* 22(2):157–70.

Jenkins, Stephen P., Andrea Brandolini, John Micklewright, and Brian Nolan. 2013a. 'Scope, Review of Approaches, and Evidence from the Past'. Pp. 1–32 in *Reports for the Fondazione Rodolfo DeBenedetti, The Great Recession and the Distribution of Household Income*, edited by S. P. Jenkins, A. Brandolini, J. Micklewright, and B. Nolan. Oxford: Oxford University Press.

Jenkins, Stephen P., Andrea Brandolini, John Micklewright, and Brian Nolan. 2013b. 'The Great Recession and its Consequences for Household Income in 21 Countries'. Pp. 33–89 in *Reports for the Fondazione Rodolfo DeBenedetti, The Great Recession and the Distribution of Household Income*, edited by S. P. Jenkins, A. Brandolini, J. Micklewright, and B. Nolan. Oxford: Oxford University Press.

Karanikolos, Marina, Philipa Mladovsky, Jonathan Cylus, Sarah Thomson, Sanjay Basu, David Stuckler, Johan P. Mackenbach, and Martin McKee. 2013. 'Financial Crisis, Austerity, and Health in Europe'. *The Lancet* 381(9874):1323–31.

Leibfried, Stephan. 2015. 'Social Policy: Left to the Judges and the Markets?' Pp. 263–92 in *The new European Union series, Policy-Making in the European Union*, edited by H. Wallace. 7th edn. Oxford: Oxford University Press.

Leibfried, Stephan, and Paul Pierson, editors. 1995. *European Social Policy: Between Fragmentation and Integration*. Washington, DC: Brookings Institution.

Leibfried, Stephan, and Paul Pierson. 1999. 'European Social Policy'. *ZeS-Arbeitspapier* (15):5–48.

Lipset, Seymour M., and Stein Rokkan. 1967. *Party Systems and Voter Alignments: Crossnational Perspectives*. New York: The Free Press.

Lo, James, Sven-Oliver Proksch, and Thomas Gschwend. 2013. 'A Common Left-right Scale for Voters and Parties in Europe'. *Political Analysis* (1):1–19.

Macron, Emmanuel. 2017. 'Initiative pour l'Europe: Discours d'Emmanuel Macron pour une Europe souveraine, unie, démocratique [Initiative for Europe: Speech by Emmanuel Macron for a Sovereign, United, Democratic Europe]'. Retrieved 22 August 2018 (www. elysee.fr/declarations/article/initiative-pour-l-europe-discours-d-emmanuel-macron-pour-une-europe-souveraine-unie-democratique/).

Marshall, Thomas H. 1949/1983. *Class, Citizenship, and Social Development. Essays.* Westport, CT: Greenwood Press.

Mau, Steffen. 2005. 'Democratic Demand for a Social Europe? Preferences of the European Citizenry'. *International Journal of Social Welfare* (14):76–85.

Mayhew, Leon. 1971. *Society: Institutions and Activity.* Glenview, IL: Scott, Foresman.

Mewes, Jan, and Steffen Mau. 2012. 'Unraveling Working-class Welfare Chauvinism'. Pp. 119–57 in *Contested Welfare States: Welfare Attitudes in Europe and Beyond*, edited by S. Svallfors. Stanford, CA: Stanford University Press.

Miller, David. 1999. *Principles of Social Justice.* Cambridge, MA: Harvard University Press.

Mladovsky, Philipa, Divya Srivastava, Jonathan Cylus, Marina Karanikolos, Tamás Eve-tovits, Sarah Thomson, and Martin McKee. 2012. 'Health Policy Responses to the Financial Crisis in Europe'. Retrieved 12 September 2018 (www.lenus.ie/hse/bitstream/10147/267834/1/e96643.pdf).

Morgan, Stephen L., and Christopher Winship. 2015. *Counterfactuals and Causal Inference: Methods and Principles for Social Research.* New York: Cambridge University Press.

Münch, Richard. 2010. *European Governmentality: The Liberal Drift of Multilevel Governance.* London: Routledge.

OECD. 2017. 'Youth Unemployment Rate'. Retrieved 20 February 2019 (https://data.oecd.org/unemp/youth-unemployment-rate.htm).

Pettersen, Per A. 1998. 'The Welfare State: The Security Dimension'. Pp. 198–232 in *The Scope of Government*, edited by O. Borre and E. Scarbrough. Oxford and New York: Oxford University Press.

Quaglio, Gianluca, Theodoros Karapiperis, Lieve van Woensel, Elleke Arnold, and David McDaid. 2013. 'Austerity and Health in Europe'. *Health Policy* 113(1–2):13–19.

Reeskens, Tim, and Wim van Oorschot. 2012. 'Disentangling the "New Liberal Dilemma": On the Relation between General Welfare Redistribution Preferences and Welfare Chauvinism'. *International Journal of Comparative Sociology* 53(2):120–39.

Roller, Edeltraud. 1998. 'The Welfare State: The Equality Dimension'. Pp. 165–96 in *The Scope of Government*, edited by O. Borre and E. Scarbrough. Oxford and New York: Oxford University Press.

Roosma, Femke, John Gelissen, and Wim van Oorschot. 2013. 'The Multidimensionality of Welfare State Attitudes: A European Cross-National Study'. *Social Indicators Research* 113(1):235–55.

Roosma, Femke, Wim van Oorschot, and John Gelissen. 2014. 'The Preferred Role and Perceived Performance of the Welfare State: European Welfare Attitudes from a Multi-dimensional Perspective'. *Social Science Research* 44:200–10.

Rueda, David. 2014. 'Dualization, Crisis and the Welfare State'. *Socio-Economic Review* 12(2):381–407.

Scharpf, Fritz. 2002. 'The European Social Model'. *Journal of Common Market Studies* 40(4):645–70.

Streeck, Wolfgang. 1995. 'From Market Making to State Building?: Reflections on the Political Economy of European Social Policy'. Pp. 389–431 in *European Social Policy: Between Fragmentation and Integration*, edited by S. Leibfried and P. Pierson. Washington, DC: Brookings Institution.

Svallfors, Stefan. 2004. 'Class, Attitudes and the Welfare State: Sweden in Comparative Perspective'. *Social Policy and Administration* 38(2):119–38.

Svallfors, Stefan. 2010. 'Public Attitudes'. Pp. 241–51 in *The Oxford Handbook of the Welfare State*, edited by F. Castles, S. Leibfried, J. Lewis, H. Obinger, and C. Pierson. Oxford: Oxford University Press.

Taylor-Gooby, Peter, Benjamin Leruth, and Heejung Chung. 2017. 'The Context: How European Welfare States Have Responded to Post-industrialism, Ageing Populations, and Populist Nationalism'. Pp. 1–26 in *After Austerity: Welfare State Transformation in Europe after the Great Recession*, edited by P. Taylor-Gooby, B. Leruth, and H. Chung. Oxford: Oxford University Press.

Thelen, Kathleen. 2014. *Varieties of Liberalization and the New Politics of Social Solidarity*. Cambridge: Cambridge University Press.

van Kersbergen, Kees, and Barbara Vis. 2015. *Comparative Welfare State Politics: Development, Opportunities, and Reform*. Cambridge: Cambridge University Press.

van Oorschot, Wim. 2006. 'Making the Difference in Social Europe: Deservingness Perception among Citizens of European Welfare States'. *Journal of European Social Policy* 16(1):23–42.

van Oorschot, Wim. 2008. 'Solidarity towards Immigrants in European Welfare States'. *International Journal of Social Welfare* 17(1):3–14.

Vandenbroucke, Frank, Catherine Barnard, and Geert de Baere, editors. 2017. *A European Social Union after the Crisis*. Cambridge: Cambridge University Press.

Verschraegen, Gert, Bart Vanhercke, and Rika Verpoorten. 2011. 'The European Social Fund and Domestic Activation Policies: Europeanization Mechanisms'. *Journal of European Social Policy* 21(1):55–72.

Vision Europe Summit Consortium. 2015. *Welfare State Reforms – Mapping Citizens' Opinion: An Opinion Survey in Eight European Countries*. Gütersloh: Bertelsmann Foundation. Retrieved 12 September 2018 (www.vision-europe-summit.eu/survey).

Weber, Enzo. 2017. 'European Unemployment Insurance: Finding the Golden Mean'. Retrieved 12 February 2019 (www.iab-forum.de/en/european-unemployment-insurance-finding-the-golden-mean/).

Wobbe, Theresa. 2012. 'Die "Europäische Union" als transnationale Vergesellschaftung: Eine inklusionstheoretische Sicht [The "European Union" as Transnational Vergesellschaftung: An Inclusion Theory View]'. Pp. 169–81 in *SpringerLink: Bücher, Transnationale Vergesellschaftungen: Verhandlungen des 35. Kongresses der Deutschen Gesellschaft für Soziologie in Frankfurt am Main 2010*, edited by H.-G. Soeffner. Wiesbaden: Springer VS.

Chapter 6

Refugee solidarity – coping with high numbers of asylum seekers

6.1 The two faces of the European refugee crisis

Since 2015, the rising number of refugees has seriously tested European countries, particularly the states at the end of the Balkan route, which took in more than 700,000 people in need of protection – a number far above the European average (European Commission 2015). Several changes in various push and pull factors led to this sudden and substantial increase in the number of asylum seekers. The most significant factors that pushed people to abandon their home countries were the escalation of the civil war in Syria and the cuts to resources in the Lebanese and Jordanian refugee camps. One of the most important pull factors was the general willingness of European states to take in refugees. Other factors included the opportunity that emerged due to the suspension of asylum seeker registration on the EU's external border, which encouraged and allowed refugees to move on, for the most part unhindered, towards the wealthier western and northern EU member states. German policies were no less of a contributing factor to this continued upsurge in migration, especially with statements by German chancellor Angela Merkel proclaiming her country's preparedness to accept refugees.

These shifts resulted in a near quintupling of the number of people seeking asylum in the EU annually in 2015. In 2016, too, more than a million people applied for asylum in the EU, as illustrated in Figure 6.1. The stark increase in refugees unleashed a controversial public debate in EU member states over whether and to what extent they should be prepared to take in refugees, even if their claims for asylum had been legally tested in advance.

The rise in the number of refugees did not just trigger a debate on whether countries should take in refugees, but also on how they should be allocated among EU countries. The Dublin Regulation, which governs refugees' access to Europe, states that asylum seekers have a duty to complete the asylum process in the first EU country they reach. This regulation placed a particularly heavy burden on the Mediterranean coastal countries, as the majority of refugees have to travel over the Mediterranean Sea to reach the EU. In contrast, the EU member states in the northern and central parts of the continent had barely been

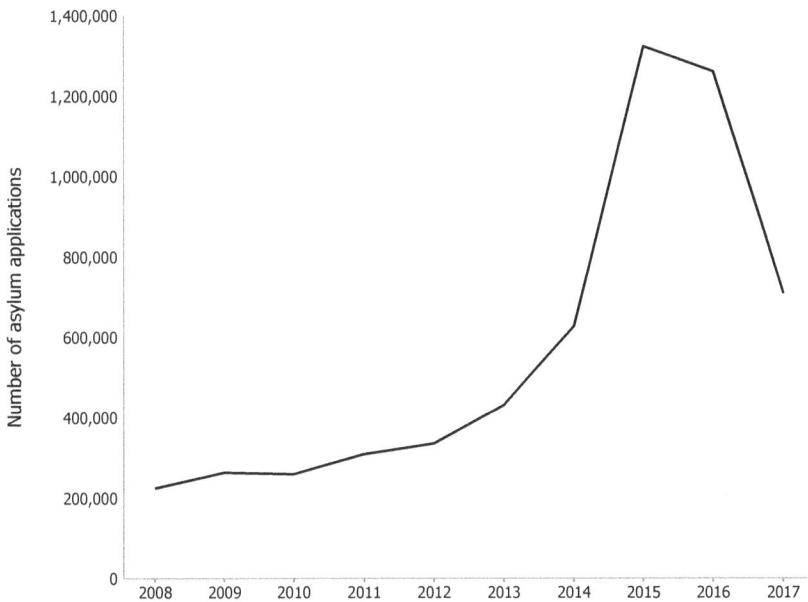

Figure 6.1 Asylum applications in all countries of the Dublin Treaty (2008–2017).

Source: Eurostat (2018), own depiction.

affected by the influx of refugees prior to 2014. The increase in the number of refugees since then, however, meant that Mediterranean countries, and Greece in particular, were incapable of registering all refugees properly. As a consequence, many refugees took the chance to journey further on to western and northern Europe, at which point these countries were suddenly confronted with a sharp rise in asylum seekers too. Figure 6.2 shows the unequal allocation of asylum seekers across EU countries during the height of the crisis between 2014 and 2016.

In addition to Hungary, which was a transit country, the most asylum applications per inhabitant were made in the wealthier states of Sweden, Austria, and Germany, followed by the Mediterranean states such as Malta and Cyprus. The lowest numbers of asylum applications were recorded in the eastern European countries as well as in Spain and Portugal. The countries that bore the greatest burden subsequently made demands for a fairer refugee allocation scheme among all member states. However, the EU's efforts to establish a legally binding quota for the allocation of refugees (European Council 2015) was opposed resolutely by several member states.

The developments summarised above raise two questions: (1) to what extent are European citizens prepared to grant asylum to people who have been

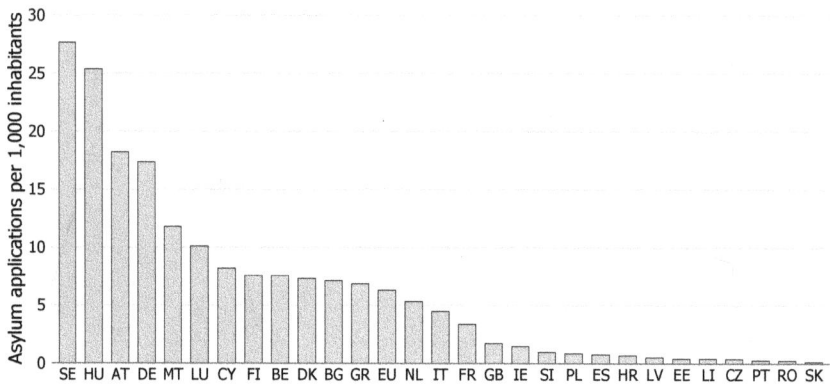

Figure 6.2 Asylum applications per thousand inhabitants by country (2014–2016).

Source: Eurostat (2017a, 2017b), own depiction.

persecuted and are seeking sanctuary in Europe; and (2) to what extent do European citizens support the idea of sharing the burden of refugee immigration equally between member states, e.g. by refugees being fairly allocated among the countries? We termed the willingness to offer humanitarian protection to refugees coming from *outside* of Europe 'external solidarity'. We described support for sharing the burden more equally and fairly across member states as 'internal solidarity'. Before we present our analysis of citizens' attitudes to the subject, we will first describe the political debates and legal regulations that are connected with both of these domains of solidarity in greater detail.

(1) More than any other international organisation, the EU and its member states have legally committed themselves to offering shelter for asylum seekers. Both refugees fleeing from (civil) war and people who are fleeing persecution based on their race, religion, sexual orientation, or political convictions enjoy the right to seek asylum in Europe. The EU member states have legally expressed their commitment to offering asylum by signing the Geneva Convention on Refugees as well as the Directive on Standards for the Qualification of Third-Country Nationals or Stateless Persons as Beneficiaries of International Protection (European Parliament and European Council 2011). At the same time, European refugee policies are embedded within a special understanding of foreign policy that is not solely based on interest but also on values. Empirical studies have shown that European foreign policy – in contrast to that of other countries, like China (Tseng and Krog 2014) – is not only driven by economic and security-based interests but also by humanitarian considerations (Kreutz 2015).

The refugee crisis has put the European Union's commitment to a foreign policy emphasising humanitarian values under substantial pressure. Even at the beginning of the refugee crisis, several European heads of government emphasised Europe's moral duty to help refugees. These included German chancellor Angela Merkel, who decided to allow Syrian refugees a direct passage to Germany without any elaborate screening process. However, facing the high and ever-rising number of asylum applicants, an increasing number of European politicians started to advocate for the rejection of the previous guidelines for European foreign policy and hence called for limits to be established regarding solidarity with refugees. For example, Austrian interior minister Johanna Mikl-Leitner called for the building of a 'Fortress of Europe' in response to numerous illegal border crossings (Newsweek 2015). Hungarian prime minister Victor Orbán unambiguously communicated his position in an interview on Hungarian TV when he said 'At the same time, one must make it most definitely clear that we will not permit – at least as long as I am the Prime Minister and as long is this government exists – Hungary becoming the target of immigrants' (Index.hu 2015).

An agreement signed between the EU and Turkey in early 2016 eventually reduced the number of refugees coming to Europe significantly (European Commission 2017a). In this treaty, Turkey committed itself to taking back any refugees who had illegally crossed the Turkey–EU border. In return, the EU countries agreed to take in a sizeable contingent of recognised Syrian refugees from Turkish refugee camps.

Critics of the Turkey–EU deal, and especially non-governmental organisations like Amnesty International, referred to the moral standards that the EU had set for itself. They accused the EU of contravening its own values and international law by signing the Turkey–EU deal. They also added that asylum seekers no longer even had the possibility to apply for asylum in Europe because they were unable to reach its territory in the first place. A further criticism stated that the Turkey–EU deal would only divert refugees onto a much more dangerous route from North Africa across the Mediterranean. For these reasons, critics have held the EU responsible for the rise in the number of drowned migrants in the Mediterranean Sea (UNHCR 2017). They favour the establishment of a legal asylum route to Europe, a policy proposal that has garnered support from some of the functionaries from EU institutions. For example, in an opinion published in an official advisory report, an advocate general at the European Court of Justice (ECJ), Paolo Mengozzi, pleaded for EU countries to start issuing visas to refugees from their own embassies provided that the refugees have some form of proof showing that their lives may be in danger or that they are under threat of torture in their home country:

> It is crucial in my view that, at a time when borders are closing and walls are being built, member states do not dodge the responsibilities that they follow from EU law, or if you will allow me to put it so, their EU law and our EU law.
>
> (Mengozzi 2017)[1]

(2) Yet, it is not only the question of how much solidarity Europe ought to show people who seek protection from persecution that has become a politicised issue during the refugee crisis; so, too, has the issue of the uneven allocation of refugees among member states. In response to this, Jean-Claude Juncker expressed his support for more solidarity with countries that are under strain from the refugee crisis, stating 'If a country makes an extraordinary effort, it must be recognised for this' (Juncker 2015). At the same time, he criticised member states that refused to take in refugees because these policies 'harm [their] neighbours and damage European solidarity'. Seeking to achieve more just allocation, Juncker made a recommendation to the Council of the European Union that refugees who had already entered the EU be allocated following a strict allocation formula. The European Council only accepted this suggestion with a qualifying majority; three Visegrád countries, Hungary, Slovakia, and the Czech Republic, as well as Romania all voted against this motion. In addition, Hungary and Slovakia instituted proceedings against this decision at the European Court of Justice. The disputes between the EU countries and the fact that up until September 2017 only 29,000 refugees from Greece had been transferred to other EU countries, clearly show that no consensus had been reached between the EU national governments regarding the allocation of refugees.

Our study, in contrast, draws on the perspectives of EU citizens and their views on these issues. Do they insist that the European Union should take in refugees and thus fulfil their legal commitments? Additionally, do they think all EU countries should play an equal part in overcoming this crisis?

First, we will investigate the citizens' attitudes towards external solidarity by differentiating between five different groups of refugees: people who are fleeing from war or civil unrest, people who advocate for human rights, people who are persecuted because of their homosexuality, people who are persecuted in their home country because of their Christian beliefs, and people who are persecuted for their Muslim beliefs. Just as in the previous chapters, we wish to test whether there is a majority of EU citizens in favour of taking in refugees and also whether there are strong social cleavages evident between the supporters and opponents of solidarity with refugees. We also wish to determine whether opponents of European external solidarity would be more inclined to vote for Eurosceptic political parties. We will take the same approach when analysing the attitudes of citizens towards internal solidarity. We surveyed the opinions of citizens regarding two proposals for the fair allocation of the burden of the refugee crisis between member states: (1) all EU countries should be bound by duty to take in refugees, and (2) countries that are not willing to do this should be required to pay compensation in return.

6.2 How strong is European solidarity with refugees?

What arguments suggest that (1) EU citizens would be in favour of taking in refugees and (2) what arguments suggest the opposite? (3) Furthermore, can we also expect the rate of agreement to differ between the EU countries and with regard to the type of refugees accepted?

(1) As already explained, member states imposed high moral standards on themselves by signing international and European legislative acts. The signing of the European Consensus on Humanitarian Aid in 2007 only placed more emphasis on this commitment (European Parliament et al. 2008). Regarding their Common Foreign and Security Policy (CFSP), the EU has also committed itself to promoting and adhering to basic human rights and the values of humanism.[2] This moral commitment is institutionally expressed in, among other things, the European Community Humanitarian Aid Office (ECHO), through which the EU finances humanitarian interventions and aid programmes worldwide. The humanitarian aid of the member states and ECHO's budget combined add up to more financial resources than any other international institution or country in the world (Lattimer and Swithern 2016). Annually, more than 120 million people in 90 countries benefit from this form of support.

The readiness to offer a safe haven in Europe to victims of political persecution or to people who have had their homes destroyed due to civil war forms part of the idea of a humanitarian value-oriented foreign policy. As explained above, these principles have been legally enshrined in the EU through the signing of the Geneva Convention on Refugees and the 2011 Directive on Standards for the Qualification of Third-Country Nationals or Stateless Persons as Beneficiaries of International Protection. As the protection of refugees remains a defining aspect of the European Union's self-image, we presumed that the majority of its citizens would also support the principles of a humanitarian foreign policy and taking in refugees.

(2) However, the pillars of a European humanitarian foreign policy had not been challenged up until 2015. In this respect, we assumed that there had been a permissive consensus in place regarding taking in and supporting refugees (Hooghe and Marks 2009), but that this consensus had never been confronted with a concrete event prior to the crisis in 2015, given that the number of refugees to Europe had remained at a relatively low and manageable level. As the number of refugees migrating to Europe surged, this properly tested governments' and citizens' willingness to show solidarity for the first time. The EU and several of its member states reacted to the new situation by changing their asylum policies. The Turkey–EU deal and the intensification of border control around the Mediterranean region implemented since then are both intended to make it more difficult for refugees to reach Europe and apply for asylum there. If we presume that governments' policies are an expression of their voters' demands, then this change in asylum policy could indicate that most citizens were not prepared to welcome in refugees. Challenged by the sheer number of refugees, EU citizens revealed the true extent of their solidarity.

(3) The hypothesis formulated in the last paragraph, namely that a majority of citizens would reject the taking-in of refugees if they experienced the

real-life consequences of the refugee crisis, can be further broken down into two parts and specified respectively. First, public discourse has concentrated predominantly on one particular group of refugees, specifically those with Muslim backgrounds. The government of Slovakia declared, for example, that they would only be prepared to take in refugees if they were Christian. A representative of the Slovakian Ministry of Internal Affairs justified this position by arguing 'We could take 800 Muslims, but we don't have any mosques in Slovakia, so how can Muslims be integrated if they are not going to like it here?' (BBC 2015). The Slovakian president, Robert Fico, has also stated his scepticism on integrating non-Christian refugees into Slovakian society (Associated Press: Dailymail 2016). Meanwhile, Hungary's prime minister, Viktor Orbán, has constructed links between Muslim refugees and an increased threat of Islamic terrorism, using this to justify the fortification of Hungary's eastern border when stating that migration is 'the Trojan Horse of terrorism' (Wintour 2017). A European survey from the Pew Research Center also showed that in the aftermath of the terror attacks in Paris, Nice, and Brussels, Europeans grew more afraid that the increasing number of refugees would raise the threat of terror attacks (Pew Research Center 2016). Thus, we expected citizens' views to differ depending on the particular refugee group concerned and we predicted that citizens' willingness to take in refugees would be markedly lower when refugees of Muslim religious background were specifically highlighted.

Second, our description of the political debate on the taking-in of refugees has clarified the point that there is currently no consensus on a common asylum policy between EU member states. The governments of the Visegrád countries in particular have spoken out against both taking in refugees and any sort of equal allocation of them among member states. If we assume that governments reflect the opinions of their citizens, then we could expect stark differences between citizens from different countries in terms of their approval rates on granting refugees asylum. Approval for taking in refugees should be notably lower in the eastern European countries within our sample than in the other surveyed countries. Another point relates to the history of the Eastern Bloc countries: it was just 30 years ago when these countries obtained state sovereignty again, and ever since, they have been going through a sort of national renaissance. Ivan Krăstev's book *After Europe* (2017) makes a very similar argument. In contrast to Western countries, Eastern European nations have been dominated by supranational powers that restricted their national sovereignty for over 100 years. In combination with other socio-economic factors, such as the ongoing 'brain drain' since EU accession, this has led to a cultural east–west divide on cosmopolitan topics such as immigration. Krăstev describes this divide as a 'clash of solidarities'. In this context, taking in foreigners has often been interpreted as a threat to national cultures. Accordingly, this led us to assume that the rejection of refugees would be distinctly pronounced in these countries.

At this point, before we analyse citizens' attitudes towards taking in refugees via our survey, we will summarise the results of various previous studies on this subject. Jürgen Gerhards, Silke Hans, and Jürgen Schupp (2016) analysed approval rates for accepting refugees, in the process distinguishing between different groups. On average, more than two-thirds of all the respondents were in favour of refugees having the right to stay. This study only considered Germany; there is no evidence for whether the approval rate is similarly high in other EU countries. The study also provided evidence that approval rates were quite different for various refugee groups. A significant majority of 81% was prepared to offer asylum to people fleeing from war, but when refugees of Muslim religious background were specified, only 51% of those surveyed were in favour of taking them in. Kirk Bansak, Jens Hainmueller, and Dominik Hargartner (2016) have come to very similar results.[3]

6.2.1 European citizens' attitudes towards refugees

As mentioned in the introduction, we differentiated in our survey between different groups of refugees. We gathered data on whether respondents would be in favour of granting people permission to remain in the EU on one of the following grounds: (a) they were persecuted for campaigning for human rights, (b) they were persecuted for their homosexuality, (c) they were persecuted for belonging to a Christian or Muslim religious minority, or (d) they had had to abandon their country due to war or civil unrest. This enabled us to capture the attitudes of citizens towards those who would potentially be granted asylum via the Geneva Convention (a to c) and the European Directive on Standards for the Qualification of Third-Country Nationals or Stateless Persons (d). Following the insights of studies mentioned above, we additionally distinguished between refugees from Christian and Muslim religious backgrounds within the category of people who were persecuted because of their religious beliefs. Differentiating between refugees according to diverse motives for fleeing allowed us to determine both the general willingness to accept refugees as well as whether there were particular concerns accepting refugees with certain characteristics. We modelled the questions on those used in one of the preceding studies by Jürgen Gerhards and colleagues (2016).

The right of abode is a universal human right. Therefore, in contrast to the other domains of solidarity analysed in the previous chapters, it made no sense to differentiate the questions on the right to stay according to different territorial spaces. Correspondingly, we were also unable to differentiate between different spaces of solidarity in this chapter as we did in the other chapters. We determined citizens' attitudes using a four-level Likert-type scale. The possible answer categories were 'totally agree', 'tend to agree', 'tend to disagree', and 'totally disagree', and the questions were:

> People have different reasons for coming to the European Union. Please tell me to what extent you agree or disagree with granting the right to stay for people who ...
> ... are persecuted because they campaign for human rights.
> ... are persecuted because they belong to a Christian minority.
> ... suffer from a war.
> ... are persecuted because they are homosexuals.
> ... are persecuted because they belong to a Muslim minority.

Figure 6.3 shows the opinions of all the respondents towards accepting refugees according to their reasons for seeking asylum. In addition, we calculated an index from the items to summarise the citizens' readiness to grant asylum to refugees in general.[4] Affirmative answers are displayed right of the vertical line marking 0% and negative answers are left. On average, 81% of citizens were in favour of refugees being granted the right to remain in the EU. Thus, our hypothesis that a majority of citizens would reject accepting refugees upon experiencing the refugee crisis in reality was not confirmed.

At the same time, the results show that the approval rates varied according to the reason for seeking asylum. The respondents were especially united on the acceptance of war refugees (90%), persecuted human rights activists (89%), and members of Christian minority groups (83%). Respondents were less prepared to accept refugees who have been persecuted due to their homosexuality (76%) or their Muslim beliefs (67%). Nevertheless, in all cases, more than two-thirds of those surveyed were in favour of offering refugees the right to remain in the EU. The differences found in the approval rates between the various reasons for seeking asylum corresponded with the figures given from a similar study that was carried out exclusively in Germany (Gerhards et al. 2016).[5] Furthermore, the finding that citizens were less willing to take in refugees from a Muslim background than other groups matched the findings from another study by Kirk Bansak and colleagues (2016); it also corresponded with our predictions formulated above. Altogether, the high approval rates give the first indication that the first criterion for the existence of a European solidarity is fulfilled. For the general population of the EU at least, the above-formulated hypothesis that the real experience of the refugee crisis would cause our respondents to reject refugees could not be confirmed.

The results presented in Figure 6.4 show that, in all 13 surveyed countries, most of the citizens supported the refugees' right to stay. With this, the first criterion for the existence of a European solidarity is fulfilled. Not only are a majority of all EU citizens willing to show solidarity with refugees but also a majority of respondents within each of the separate member states. Simultaneously, the sometimes-stark differences between the countries demand special attention. While the approval rates in Germany, Spain, and Sweden were as high as 87%, we found dramatically lower levels of approval in the eastern and southern European states.

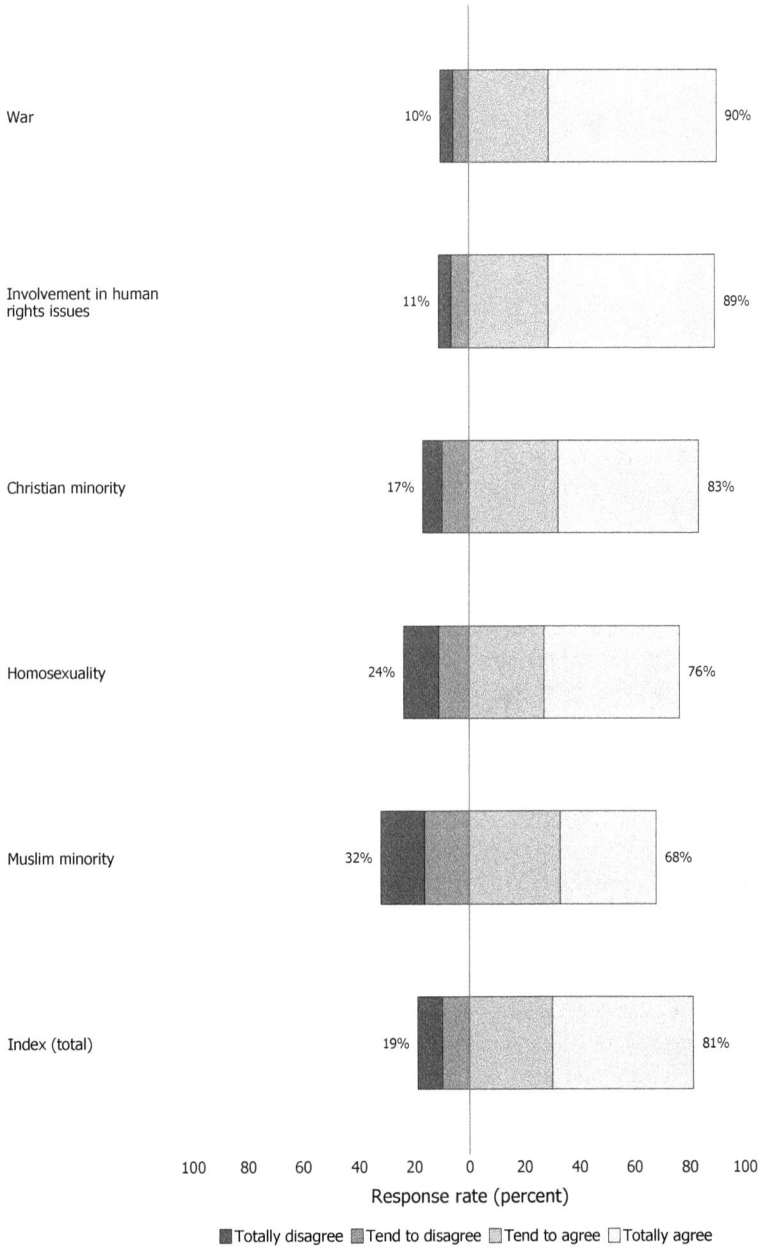

War 10% 90%

Involvement in human
rights issues 11% 89%

Christian minority 17% 83%

Homosexuality 24% 76%

Muslim minority 32% 68%

Index (total) 19% 81%

100 80 60 40 20 0 20 40 60 80 100
Response rate (percent)

■ Totally disagree ▨ Tend to disagree ▨ Tend to agree ☐ Totally agree

Figure 6.3 Response rates about granting refugees the right to stay.
Source: TESS 2016, own calculations.

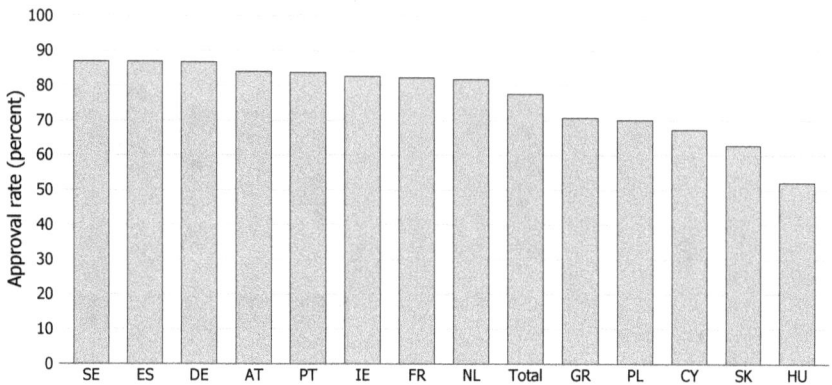

Figure 6.4 Average approval rates about granting refugees the right to stay by country.

Source: TESS 2016, own calculations.

Above all, the relatively low rates for the eastern European states corresponded with our outlined predictions. Drawing on the theory of Max Weber, we distinguished between three general motives for solidarity: solidarity based on self-interest, on moral values, and on affectual ties. If we follow the instrumentally rational argument, then the willingness to accept refugees should be lower in economically weaker countries than in wealthier societies, as taking in refugees places an additional burden on them, which poorer countries are less capable of bearing. Yet, the empirical results showed diverse forms and extents of solidarity in crisis-affected countries. The self-interest argument therefore seemed to be insufficient for explaining the country-by-country differences. The other two motives, in contrast, appeared to be more plausible, particularly in explaining the lower levels of solidarity displayed primarily in Poland, Slovakia, and Hungary. Here, we expected the strong affective bonds to the nation and Christian-oriented values to be of particular importance. As elucidated above, post-socialist countries are in the special situation whereby they have only relatively recently managed to regain full state sovereignty after the collapse of the Soviet Union. National identity and affectual connection to the nation state thus play a more significant role in these countries. The flipside of this is the defence of one's national identity from foreigners who are perceived as a threat.

Added to this, there is a second motive relating to a population's specific religious and moral value orientations. In Poland, Slovakia, and Hungary especially, references to Christian religious values are enormously significant in the construction of national identity.[6] The acceptance of people, who are thought to have other religious and secular values, such as Muslim refugees or homosexual refugees, may pose a cultural threat in the eyes of many citizens from these

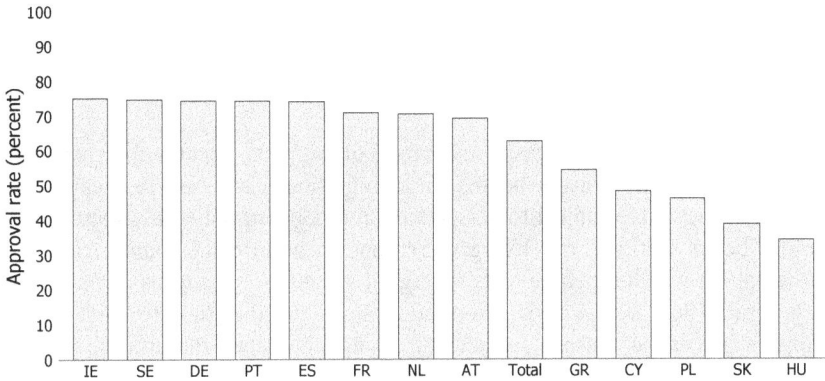

Figure 6.5 Average approval rates about granting Muslim refugees the right to stay by country.

Source: TESS 2016, own calculations.

countries (Ceobanu and Escandell 2008). Our data supported this argument (Figure 6.5). The approval rates for Muslims and homosexuals were lower across all countries than those for other groups of refugees, especially in Cyprus (48%), Poland (46%), Slovakia (46%), and Hungary (34%).[7]

At this point, we may draw a first interim conclusion. All in all, it is evident that both the majority of all EU citizens as well as the majority of citizens in each country were ready and willing to take in refugees seeking protection in Europe. The EU principles for the right of asylum are therefore shared by its citizens, even though EU citizens have experienced a substantial rise in the number of refugees. With this, the first criterion for the existence of a European solidarity as formulated in Chapter 2 is fulfilled. In this regard, the double majority approval is astonishing, especially when we consider how emotionally charged and controversial the public discourse on refugees has been in many EU countries.

Nevertheless, the extent of solidarity shown towards refugees varied between the individual surveyed countries, and extremely so in some parts. The post-socialist countries of Poland, Slovakia, and Hungary in particular exhibited a much lower rate of approval, although they still had overall majority approval rates for all groups of refugees. If there was any resistance displayed, it was predominantly against Muslim refugees. Here, there was no majority approval rate in four of our surveyed countries.

6.2.2 United in solidarity with refugees?

Up to this point, our analysis has shown a great deal of approval for the acceptance of refugees in Europe, even if not all groups of refugees receive the same degree of support. Yet despite this high degree of acceptance, the minority of citizens who reject refugees can carry great political weight if they have similar structural and cultural traits. In this respect, we drew on the theory of social cleavages, the basic premises of which have already been described in Chapter 2 and the other empirical chapters.

Refugees represent one specific subgroup of migrants, because they have particular reasons and motives behind their migration. They had to escape their country as they were subject to persecution and not simply because they wished to find better working and living conditions in a different country. Little is known about whether people have diverging attitudes on refugees and migrants in general. There is also little information about whether (and to what extent) refugees' particular reasons for seeking asylum influence the attitude towards them. A study conducted by Kirk Bansak, Jens Hainmueller, and Dominik Hangartner (2016) investigated what specific kinds of refugees citizens would be willing to take in. Their results indicated that the reason behind migration only played a limited role.

Since refugees were only partially perceived as a special group of migrants, we could draw on hypotheses formulated in the research literature that have investigated people's general attitudes towards migrants. A detailed overview of this literature is provided in the exemplary works of Alin M. Ceobanu and Xavier Escandell (2010), Helen Dempster and Karen Hargrave (2017), and Jens Hainmueller and Daniel J. Hopkins (2014).

Similar to the previous chapters, we will first establish how a respondent's characteristics (on the individual level) correlate with attitudes towards refugees. We will then do the same for country characteristics (macro level) and then examine the interplay of these two characteristics combined (cross-level effects). Finally, we will investigate whether groups who display a lack of solidarity with refugees also have a higher propensity to vote for Eurosceptic political parties, thus signifying the translation of social cleavages into political ones.[8]

6.2.3 Structural cleavages

(1) Many studies of attitudes towards migrants have related their findings to threat theory (Blalock 1967; Callens, Meuleman, and Valentova 2015; Ceobanu and Escandell 2010; Schlueter and Scheepers 2010). Such studies presumed that native citizens perceive migrants and foreigners first and foremost as competitors for scarce resources. On average, refugees have less education and poor language skills compared to the local population. They are hence dependent on state welfare provisions and will likely put pressure on less high-skilled parts of the job market. At this point, competition occurs between migrants and foreigners on the one side, and those who are similarly dependent on state benefits to a higher than average extent or who perform low-skilled jobs on the other. Thus, we expected that citizens who could be classified as in the lower echelons of the national income brackets, in low-skilled vocations, or as dependent on state

benefits to be specifically inclined to reject the right of refugees to remain in the EU. In order to check this hypothetical connection, we factored the following structural conditions of our survey participants into our empirical analysis: occupational class, job-market status (employed/unemployed), equivalent household income, and degree of education. A further structural variable was the respondent's own migration background, as first-generation migrants in particular tend to find themselves in the lower socio-economic reaches of society (OECD 2008). For this reason, we expected these people to also perceive the new arrival of refugees as a threat to their own structural position in society.

The respondent's degree of education has proven to be an exceptionally good predictor of their perspective on migrants. Indeed, previous studies have shown that people who are less educated and less skilled tend to be noticeably more negatively predisposed to migrants (Bobo and Licari 1989; Card, Dustmann, and Preston 2012; Chandler and Tsai 2001; Citrin et al. 1997; Hainmueller and Hiscox 2007). A high education level can influence a person's views on refugees in two regards: on the one hand, education is a form of human capital that eases access to loftier positions in the job market, so, accordingly, people with a higher education should feel less threatened economically. On the other hand, participating in higher education should lead to a greater degree of cognitive mobilisation, a deeper knowledge of the wider world, and a higher acceptance of foreign cultures. For these reasons, more highly educated people should be more receptive towards new arrivals from abroad (Knutsen 2010; Merkel 2017).

(2) Yet, individuals' attitudes towards immigrants and refugees are not only shaped by personal circumstances but also by concerns about their country and therefore by their country's attributes (Hatton 2016). At the country level, the threat theory also formed the basis for formulating hypotheses and selecting variables. We predicted that people would be more likely to perceive refugees as a threat to their socio-economic status if they lived in a country where the welfare state does not adequately protect citizens from the risks of the market, e.g. in the event of job loss. This form of welfare state protection against the risks of the market was labelled by Gøsta Esping-Andersen as *decommodification* (1990:22). We expected that solidarity with refugees would be lower in countries with a lower decommodification level. However, the degree of decommodification is difficult to measure.[9] To do so, we needed the robust and easily accessible proxy of the share of social spending of each country's GDP, even if that was not perfect. We thus calculated the correlation between a country's decommodification and attitudes towards external solidarity using the social state quota (the relation between social state expenditures and national GDP). As social spending is higher in richer countries than in poorer countries, we additionally tested these hypotheses while controlling for each country's respective economic performance.

(3) In the previous chapters, we also made it clear that countries' contextual factors not only have effects on their citizens' attitudes but also on the size of certain effects on the individual level. For example, we predicted that

high-income people living in poorer EU countries would be more likely to be in favour of European welfare than high-income people from richer countries. In the case of external solidarity, we expected there to be a quite similar interaction effect between a country's characteristics and the respondent's position within the structure of their society, specifically with regard to attitudes towards refugees. Thus, we theorised that people who had very few resources at their disposal (i.e. income, education, social class position) would be more likely to feel threatened by immigration if they belonged to a country with a weakly developed welfare state than people in the same situation but in a country with an established welfare state.

The above-formulated hypotheses presupposed that socio-economically vulnerable people from any given country would perceive the influx of refugees as a threat. Such an interpretation of the circumstances, however, could be dependent on the manner of the public discourse and the examples political parties bring to this debate. The strength and regularity with which political parties in a country deployed xenophobic rhetoric and defined immigration as a threat should in turn determine the likelihood of people feeling threatened by refugees. This hypothesis was confirmed in a study undertaken by Daniel J. Hopkins (2010). He determined that an actual growth in the number of migrants within a person's living environment only impacted their attention towards migrants if migration was frequently discussed in the public discourse.[10] Therefore, we expected there to be a strong structural split particularly in countries where right-wing populist parties had established a firm footing, and hence where their xenophobic rhetoric was more strongly represented in the national discourses.[11]

6.2.4 Cultural cleavages

The opposition to the influx of refugees cannot be only attributed to an individual's structural characteristics, but also to cultural ones. Cultural factors have a special significance when cleavages emerge in post-industrial societies (Pappi 2005), and this phenomenon applies especially to attitudes towards migrants (Dixon et al. 2017; Ford and Lowles 2016; Hainmueller and Hopkins 2014).

(1) Many citizens' basic political orientations can be projected onto a left–right political scale. As left-wing ideologies are more connected with ideas of equality, solidarity, and internationalism (Fuchs and Klingemann 1989), we assumed that people who identified themselves as left wing would be more strongly in favour of taking in refugees than people from the political centre. Meanwhile, we expected the exact inverse for right-wing people's stances on refugees. Among other things, the idea that citizens should enjoy privileges not enjoyed by non-citizens forms one part of the multiple ideas that constitute right-wing ideologies (Nickerson and Louis 2008; Sides and Citrin 2007).

In addition, we hypothesised that a person's attitudes towards refugees would not only be impacted by their political orientation but also by their general stances towards foreigners. There are people who perceive migrants' ways of life, values, and skills as an enrichment for their country and its culture. This group may be described as 'cultural cosmopolitans'. Yet there are also people who reject this notion and see migrants as a threat to their own way of life: these people can be described as 'cultural communitarians'. To measure these general-ised standpoints towards immigrants, we asked the following question in our survey: 'Please tell me to what extent you agree or disagree with the following statement: Cultural life in [COUNTRY] is generally enriched by people coming to live here from other countries.' By taking into account the findings from research on prejudice, we expected that people who disagreed with this state-ment would also show less solidarity towards refugees (Gerhards and Lengfeld 2015:86; Ivarsflaten 2005).

We argued that attitudes towards solidarity should also be influenced by peo-ple's affectual ties to the nation state and other collectives in Chapter 2. This relationship should also apply to solidarity towards refugees: people who exclu-sively identify with their nation state should be far more likely to be sceptical towards refugees than people who understand themselves as Europeans or as world citizens. For cosmopolitan people, it goes without saying that solidarity knows no borders and that refugees should thus be included within the com-munity of solidarity. National communitarians stand in direct opposition to cos-mopolitans, as they feel predominantly connected to the community of their own nation. According to our hypotheses, these people should be more inclined to reject refugees' right to stay. Tanja Börzel and Thomas Risse reached a similar conclusion in their analysis of the most recent EU crises (Börzel and Risse 2017). Whereas the financial crisis was a regulatory conflict, the refugee crisis was a cultural conflict between 'us' and 'the others' that activated some citizens' affectual ties to their nation. In our study, we measured these affectual ties via the question of whether the respondent identified exclusively with his/her nation.[12]

(2) However, attitudes towards refugees are not only influenced by individual political orientations and values but also by the culture of the country in which the citizen and their political views and values are embedded. Regarding atti-tudes towards refugees, we considered two cultural characteristics especially rel-evant: the strength of parties that are hostile to migrants in a country and the country's historical experience of the loss of national sovereignty.

In the previous section, we emphasised that refugees can be identified as a threat to national culture and wealth. When interpreting current affairs, citizens draw on the explanations provided in the national public discourse. Most impor-tantly, political parties, the government, and social movements structure interpreta-tions on topics by communicating their political opinions. This process of analysing and interpreting political topics is also known as *cueing* in the political-science literature (Gilens and Murakawa 2002; Green, Palmquist, and Schickler 2002; Hooghe and Marks 2005). Using the example of the 'EU integration' topic, Leonard Ray (2003) as well as Gary Marks and Marco R. Steenbergen (2004) have shown that cues from elites have a strong effect on citizens' attitudes. Moreover, Marco R. Steenbergen and colleagues (2007) have provided evidence that the effect of cueing was stronger for extremist parties than it is for mainstream parties, as extremist parties for the most part tend to represent a certain opinion on a single issue.

The refugee crisis has unquestionably been the cause of a highly controversial debate between political parties within and between European countries. While in Germany, for example, the government and other actors propagated their welcoming culture (*Willkommenskultur*) to refugees (Czymara and Schmidt-Catran 2017), the Hungarian government took an explicitly dismissive stance and initiated media campaigns that warned against the alleged dangers of immigration (Kallius, Monterescu, and Rajaram 2016). We accordingly expected that the more the political elites and parties operated using xenophobic rhetoric, the more likely it was that people would view the migration of refugees as a threat.

As we were not in a position to carry out a media analysis in the countries we investigated, we could only coarsely measure the postulated relationship empirically. We determined the strength of the xenophobic discourse in a country by measuring the proportion of votes in the most recent general elections for parties that were unequivocally against migration and refugees. The greater these parties' representation in their respective parliaments, the greater their influence on public discourse and in turn on voters. Studies by Moshe Semyonov and colleagues (2006) and by Andrea Bohman (2011) have indicated the existence of a relation between the expression of reservations against foreigners and the presence of politically influential right-wing populist parties.

There is a second cultural factor at the macro level that could potentially influence attitudes towards refugees. In this regard, we drew on evidence from our descriptive analysis, which demonstrated that the eastern European approval rates for taking in refugees were below the overall European average. We attributed this finding to the fact that post-socialist states had only managed to regain their complete national sovereignty after the downfall of the Soviet Union, and that this caused a markedly strong affectual bond with the nation state to develop in these countries. Thus, we attempted to systematically prove this theorised relationship by drawing on a theory designed by Wesley Hiers, Thomas Soehl, and Andreas Wimmer (2017). These authors invented an index based on the 'historical, geopolitical fate' of nations. The index incorporates a country's historical experiences of shocks, such as the loss of national sovereignty, the loss of a part of the state territory, as well as external and internal conflicts. Every nation is ascribed an index score according to the intensity and extent of the experience, varying on a scale of zero to six.[13] Scoring 0–1 means that there was low geopolitical threat; 4–6 means there was high geopolitical threat. Due to their recent histories, the post-socialist states in particular occupied the upper end of the scale. Using the index, Wesley Hiers and colleagues (2017) were able to explain attitudes towards migrants. We also used the index in our analysis and expected that the approval rates for taking in refugees in countries with a high ranking on the loss-of-sovereignty index would be lower than the approval rates in countries that boast a long, uninterrupted history of state sovereignty.

(3) When considering the weight of the impact that we have just outlined, we assumed an additional interaction effect between the individual and the macro level. We theorised that right-wing people, or those who exhibited a strong sense of national identity, who lived in a country that has an instable national identity as a result of historical sovereignty crises would be more likely to reject refugees than people who, despite possessing the same individual characteristics, lived in a country with a long uninterrupted history of nation state sovereignty.

6.2.5 Comments on the methodological procedure

We applied an identical methodology to that of previous chapters to test our hypotheses. Citizens' attitudes towards refugees' right to asylum constituted the dependent variable in all regression analyses. Using the data we gathered on people's attitudes towards different refugee groups, we managed to construct an index out of the different questions as explained above.

In the first part of the causal analysis, we analysed the individual level on its own and carried out incrementally extended OLS regressions in order to deter-mine whether an individual's structural and cultural characteristics explained attitudes towards refugees. We controlled for respondents' age, gender, and nationality (dummy variables) and lastly, for the respondent's degree of contact with foreigners. The use of the latter variables is in need of some explanation. Research on attitudes towards migrants has established via the contact hypo-thesis that people who had more regular contact with foreigners empathised with their situation more. Based on this, we expected a more positive point of view towards migrants and also towards refugees among those with more contact with foreigners (Allport 1979; Callens et al. 2015; Pettigrew and Tropp 2008; Schlue-ter and Wagner 2008). However, note that 'contact with foreigners' is not a suit-able basis for politicisation. As we had a special interest in identifying cleavages in our investigation, we accounted for the contact hypotheses by treating the appropriate variables as control variables.

In the second part of the causal analysis, we will seek to explain country-by-country differences, and in doing so use a process familiar from the previous chapters (see Section 3.3.3 'Notes on methodology' in Chapter 3).

6.2.6 Results on the social cleavages of external solidarity

Table 6.1 depicts the results from the regression analysis, which were done incrementally in the three models. Model M1 is the base model with only control variables. The results show that women exhibited a greater willingness to engage in solidarity than men and also confirm the contact hypothesis: people who were in regular contact with foreigners within their own country displayed more solid-arity towards refugees. Finally, the effects of the individual country variables

Table 6.1 Social cleavages regarding granting refugees the right to stay; individual level

	M1		M2		M3	
Control variables						
Sex (ref.: male)	0.06*	(0.02)	0.07**	(0.02)	0.05**	(0.01)
Age (by 10 years)	-0.04	(0.03)	-0.07	(0.03)	-0.07	(0.04)
Age (by 10 years, squared)	0.00	(0.00)	0.01*	(0.00)	0.01	(0.00)
Contact with foreigners (ref.: no)	0.16***	(0.02)	0.12***	(0.02)	0.06***	(0.01)
Migration generation (ref.: no migration background)						
First generation			-0.07*	(0.03)	-0.07*	(0.02)
Second generation			0.05	(0.02)	0.03	(0.02)
Structural cleavages						
Level of education (ref.: tertiary)						
Non or primary			-0.16*	(0.06)	-0.11*	(0.04)
Secondary			-0.13***	(0.02)	-0.06**	(0.02)
Occupational class (ref.: upper class (I))						
Upper middle class (II)			-0.01	(0.02)	-0.03	(0.02)
Centre middle class (IIIa)			-0.03	(0.02)	-0.03	(0.02)
Lower middle class (V & VI)			-0.12**	(0.03)	-0.12**	(0.03)
Self-employed (IVab & IVc)			-0.12**	(0.03)	-0.10**	(0.03)
Routine non-manual (IIIb)			-0.04*	(0.02)	-0.05*	(0.02)
Unskilled manual workers & agriculture (VIIa & VIIb)			-0.13**	(0.04)	-0.11**	(0.03)
Unemployed (ref.: employed)			0.03	(0.05)	0.02	(0.04)
Household income			0.05**	(0.01)	0.03*	(0.01)
Cultural cleavages						
Political placement (ref.: centre)						
Left					0.13**	(0.03)
Moderate left					0.13***	(0.02)
Moderate right					-0.09***	(0.02)
Right					-0.24***	(0.05)
Society: culture enriched by foreigners					0.21***	(0.02)
Identity: exclusively national (ref.: other)					-0.18***	(0.03)

Country differences

Country (ref.: Spain)					
Austria	-0.15***	(0.00)	-0.18***	(0.01)	-0.12***	(0.01)
Cyprus	-0.62***	(0.00)	-0.65***	(0.01)	-0.46***	(0.02)
France	-0.22***	(0.01)	-0.24***	(0.01)	-0.18***	(0.01)
Germany	-0.01	(0.01)	-0.06***	(0.01)	-0.06***	(0.01)
Greece	-0.35***	(0.00)	-0.36***	(0.01)	-0.24***	(0.02)
Hungary	-0.84***	(0.01)	-0.81***	(0.01)	-0.74***	(0.01)
Ireland	-0.16***	(0.01)	-0.18***	(0.01)	-0.13***	(0.01)
The Netherlands	-0.13***	(0.01)	-0.18***	(0.01)	-0.08***	(0.01)
Poland	-0.52***	(0.01)	-0.54***	(0.01)	-0.40***	(0.01)
Portugal	-0.13***	(0.00)	-0.10***	(0.01)	0.02	(0.01)
Slovakia	-0.69***	(0.01)	-0.67***	(0.01)	-0.53***	(0.02)
Sweden	-0.05***	(0.01)	-0.07***	(0.01)	-0.06***	(0.01)
Constant	3.50***	(0.08)	3.39***	(0.12)	2.85***	(0.11)
R^2	0.145		0.167		0.283	
AIC	19,911.0		19,686.7		18,247.4	

Source: TESS 2016, own calculations.

Notes

$n = 9{,}535$; Unstandardised coefficients from pooled OLS regression with robust standard errors (clustered by country), *$p < 0.05$; **$p < 0.01$; ***$p < 0.001$, standard errors in parentheses.

confirmed the country-by-country differences already discussed above and upheld that respondents from the Visegrád countries were the strongest opponents to refugees having the right to remain.

Let us now turn our attention to the factors that could generate cleavages. The results from model M2 show that, in line with our hypotheses, people from the lower occupational classes, from poorer households, and/or with lower educational backgrounds were more likely to be against refugees coming to their country. Contrary to our expectations, unemployment did not have any effect on people's attitudes. As for the effects of a migration background, only first generation migrants were less likely to approve of accepting refugees, with this effect continually levelling out with each generation thereafter. In M2, the explained variance grew meagrely by just 2 percentage points compared to the base model. Such low levels of explained variance by structural variables on attitudes towards migration in multivariate regression models were also found by Crawley and colleagues (2013) using British survey data.

The results changed somewhat when we factored in the particular characteristics that are capable of forming a cultural cleavage. In line with our assumptions, we found a significant and strong effect on attitudes towards refugees in all the magnitudes taken into account (M3). Compared to the people who described their political orientation as centrist, left-wing individuals were more in favour of taking in refugees, while politically right-wing people were generally against it. A significant gradation was evident between centre-right and far-right people. It was further evident that the people who saw their culture as endangered by migrants and refugees, whom we have labelled as national communitarians, tended to be against taking in refugees. Finally, the hypothesis that stated that having an affectual tie to the nation state would considerably weaken solidarity with refugees was also confirmed. Compared with M2, however, the explained variance of above 12% highlighted the exceptional explanatory power of the cultural variables.[14] When we incorporated them into the model, the strength of the effects of country variables fell compared to the base model. Indeed, the variations between countries persisted, albeit at a reduced level. Some of the country variations were due to the significant overrepresentation of people with certain cultural characteristics in some countries; this was the case for Cyprus, Poland, Slovakia, and Hungary in particular.

Altogether, the results indicate that the potential for conflict on the question of solidarity with refugees is first and foremost culturally motivated, and structurally less so. Yet, as we argued in Chapter 2 based on Aubert's theory of conflict, cultural conflicts are more difficult to resolve than conflicts of interests, because the object of the argument cannot be easily negotiated, thereby making it difficult to find a compromise.

In the next step, we tested our three macro-level hypotheses. The top left corner of Figure 6.6 shows the correlation between the strength of the welfare state and the average approval rate for accepting refugees controlled for by the individual characteristics. Our expectation that a stronger welfare state would be

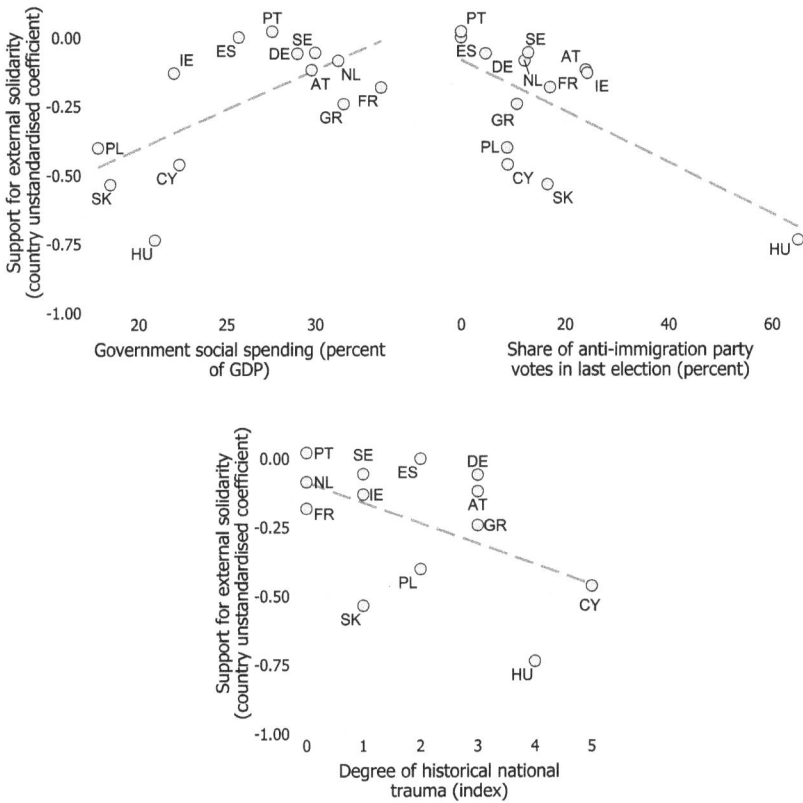

Figure 6.6 Social cleavages regarding granting refugees the right to stay; country level.

Source: TESS 2016, own calculations.

capable of absorbing the population's potential anxieties and that, correspondingly, approval for the right to asylum would correlate with the strength of the welfare state was generally confirmed. This correlation also held when we factored in the country's economic strength (measured as GDP; these results are not depicted in the figure). The influence that the strength of a country's welfare state had on attitudes towards refugees was therefore independent of a country's economic power.

In the top right quadrant of Figure 6.6, we tested the extent to which the controlled average rate of approval for the right to stay would be influenced by the strength of right-wing, anti-immigration parties. We argued that the strength of parties would have an impact on the public discourse and thus on the ways in which political topics are interpreted. The result shows that willingness to express solidarity with refugees in a country decreased as the strength of anti-immigration parties' representation in parliament increased. However, when interpreting these results, we must consider that we were unable to make assumptions on the direction of causality. We assumed that anti-immigration parties would inform citizens' attitudes towards refugees and that, accordingly, the degree of rejection would increase with the strength of anti-immigration parties. In this context, Liesbet Hooghe (2007) has spoken of a top-down process of elites influencing the attitudes of regular citizens. However, this could also occur as a bottom-up process. The strength of anti-immigration parties would then result from the proportion of citizens who were predisposed to reject refugees and who voted for anti-immigration parties precisely for this reason. We assumed that both of these theories are correct and that this thereby constitutes a dynamic, self-reinforcing process, even if we were unable to verify this empirically.

As the graph at the bottom of Figure 6.6 shows, there was a negative correlation between the historical experience of losing national sovereignty and the acceptance of refugees. The more severely and frequently a country has suffered from loss and conflict in its history, the lower its national approval rate was in terms of willingness to express solidarity. The past loss of national sovereignty has led to a new form of national consciousness in the present, which in turn goes hand in hand with a tendency to exclude foreigners.

Considering all three macro factors altogether, we could confirm another finding from the descriptive analysis: the post-socialist countries of Poland, Slovakia, and Hungary formed a cluster in which the rejection of solidarity with refugees was particularly strongly pronounced. Conflicts due to the uneven rate of welfare-state development can be resolved politically, for example via transfer payments. In contrast, conflicts resulting from the strength of anti-immigration political parties and from the historical experience of sovereignty loss are a considerably greater challenge for politicians interested in establishing a common refugee policy.

As a last point, we come to the results of the cross-level analysis. We did not find indications that socio-economically vulnerable people were more strongly against refugees when they lived in a country where the government spent a low share of the GDP on social spending. However, we confirmed some of the hypotheses concerning macro cultural factors. People who strongly identified with their nation state and lived in a country that has experienced the loss of sovereignty in the past were more likely to reject refugees' right to stay than people with the same affectual ties to their nation but who lived in a country that had not experienced a comparable loss of national sovereignty in their history (see Figure 6.7). In contrast, our hypothesis that the degree of historical national trauma would influence the effect of citizens' right-wing political orientation on external solidarity could not be confirmed (results are not depicted).

Altogether, our analysis in this section shows that a majority of citizens in Europe and in the 13 countries featured in our study supported refugees having

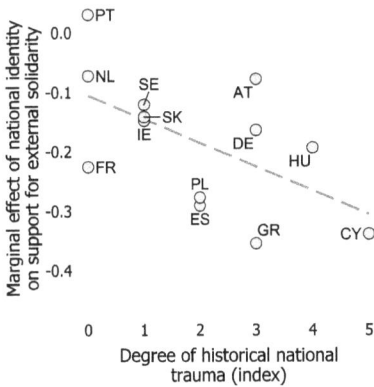

Figure 6.7 Social cleavages regarding granting refugees the right to stay; cross-level effects.

Source: TESS 2016, own calculations.

the right to remain, albeit not equally so for every group of migrants. At the same time, we found a minority who reject the right to remain and who thus possess considerable potential for the formation of social cleavages. Their opposition is primarily motivated by cultural and not by structural factors. Opponents of refugees having a right to remain were generally right wing in terms of their political convictions; they do not regard refugees as any sort of enrichment but rather as a danger to their own culture, and they feel strongly bonded to their nation state emotionally. Such individuals are heavily overrepresented in countries characterised by processes of renationalisation due to the historical experience of losing national sovereignty and also in countries where anti-immigration political parties are particularly strong. Because these described factors apply to several eastern European countries, it is in these places where the greatest percentage of opponents to solidarity with refugees are to be found.

6.2.7 Results on the political cleavages

Social cleavages can become political cleavages when citizens articulate discontent in a coordinated way. Here, just as in the preceding chapters, we also investigated whether people who display a lack of solidarity with refugees systematically vote for certain political parties. In the process, we particularly focused our attention on right-wing populist parties because of their exceptionally strong opposition to accepting refugees. The Hungarian prime minister, Viktor Orbán, is doubtlessly the most prominent political figure demanding restrictions on the number of migrants and refugees; in this, he stands alongside the Polish and Slovakian governments, which likewise believe that refugees represent an eminent danger to public safety in his country. They speak of an elevated terror risk and also warn against national and European culture being overwhelmed by foreign cultures brought in by refugees from a Muslim religious background. By positioning himself in this way, Orbán has found support among other right-wing populist parties across Europe. An analysis of the European Elections in 2014 and the general elections of recent years has shown that right-wing populist parties have succeeded in significantly raising their vote share and establishing the topic of 'immigration' (and their clear stance against it) as the most important reason for voting for them (Hobolt and de Vries 2016).

As has been elucidated in the preceding chapters, Sara B. Hobolt and Catherine de Vries (2016) split Eurosceptic parties into four different groups along two dimensions. We presumed that opponents of solidarity would be more inclined to give their vote to right-wing Eurosceptic parties as these parties opposed the intake of refugees in their manifestos (Steinmayr 2016). As solidarity with those in need and the idea of international solidarity are constituent parts of left-wing parties' ideologies, we did not presume that opponents to the intake of refugees would vote for left-wing parties.

In order to measure the voting intention of respondents, we asked them about which party they would vote for if the national general election were held tomorrow. Following Hobolt and de Vries' suggestions, we then grouped the parties into four distinct groups.

In each quadrant in Figure 6.8, the likelihood of voting for a Eurosceptic party was calculated and placed on the chart depending on the respondents' degree of agreement with accepting refugees. For reasons of clarity and comprehensiveness, and because we were primarily concerned with the opponents of

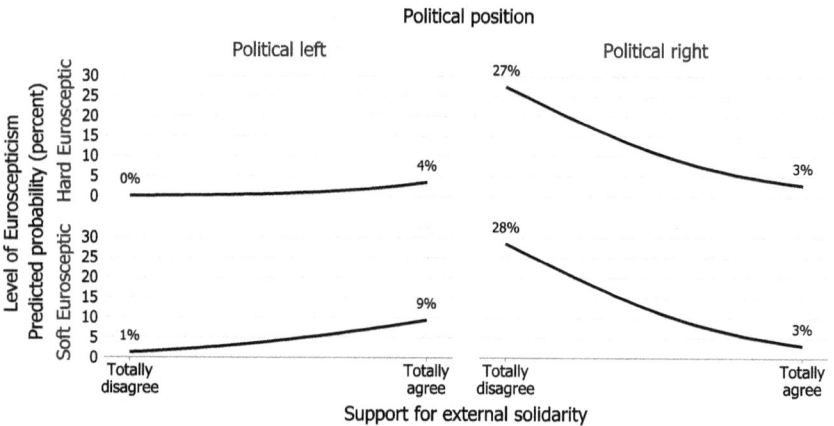

Figure 6.8 Support for external solidarity and political position of party voted for.

Source: TESS 2016, own calculations.

solidarity, we chose not to portray voters who said they would cast their vote for one of the moderate parties. The probability estimations were carried out by using a bivariate multinomial regression model.[15] The graph depicting the results should be interpreted as follows (top-right quadrant): someone who fully and completely declined all solidarity with refugees was given a 27% likelihood of voting for a hard Eurosceptic and right-wing party. If the estimated probabilities for all the values were of the same size on the refugee index, then this would indicate that attitudes on the taking-in of refugees had no influence on voter behaviour.

The results in both of the right-hand quadrants show that willingness to vote for a right-wing party clearly increased in line with the rejection of refugees. Our hypothesis that right-wing Eurosceptic parties provided a political home for opponents of solidarity was thus confirmed. Particularly people who described themselves firmly against refugees' rights tended to vote disproportionately for right-wing Eurosceptic parties.

The results from both of the left-hand quadrants meanwhile show that the probability of voting for a left-wing Eurosceptic party slightly increased in line with advocacy for solidarity with refugees. As usual, international solidarity seems to be a shared value among the voters for left-wing parties. But, because of the fact that left-wing parties represent the interests of the lower social classes, who in turn may also feel threatened by refugees (see above), it would also be plausible to expect opponents of refugees' rights to be voters for left-wing political parties. This prediction, however, could not be confirmed in our analysis.

In summary, we determined that attitudes towards refugees structure the voting behaviour of citizens. At almost 60%, the probability of voting for a right-wing Eurosceptic party, either hard or soft, was ten times higher for people who fully rejected granting refugees the right to stay than the rate for individuals who favoured international solidarity. Opponents of taking in refugees can find their political home in right-wing Eurosceptic parties and thereby translate their viewpoints and attitudes into the political process.

6.3 Sharing the burden in the refugee crisis

With the influx of refugees into Europe, the question of their allocation, and hence the associated financial costs to the member states became a controversial political topic. As explained in the introduction to this chapter, the number of refugees taken in has varied greatly from member state to member state. In order to address this asymmetry, the European Commission suggested to the Council of the European Union that around 160,000 refugees be allocated from the heavily burdened countries of Italy, Greece, and Hungary to other EU states. From the very beginning, the public discourse on this quota was connected with the debate on whether and to what extent the EU and its individual member states should be taking in refugees in the first place. Thus, the heads of state who were most ardently in favour of closing state borders and securing the EU's external border were, at the same time, the main opponents of the refugee quota. They feared foreign infiltration, i.e. that immigrants would overwhelm their national culture, and that these EU measures related to the refugee crisis would threaten their national sovereignty. As the debate on accepting refugees became entangled with the argument over their allocation, we expected that the attitudes towards external solidarity would also influence attitudes towards internal solidarity and that the differences in approval rates between countries would be similar for both domains of solidarity. So, what other factors could influence people's attitudes towards the question of how the refugees should be allocated between countries?

First, we expected self-interested motives to also play a role here. Citizens from countries that have already taken in an above-average number of refugees would thus express their preference for a more uniform allocation. This should apply to the Mediterranean states, for instance, Greece and Italy, who have taken in the largest number of refugees as a result of the Dublin Regulation since most refugees reach the EU by arriving in these countries first. We expected precisely these countries and their citizens to have a special interest in a fairer distributive system. However, with the direct entrance of refugees into the countries at the end of the Balkan route since 2015 (Germany, Austria, Sweden), the circumstances surrounding the interests of these countries and their citizens changed as well. Therefore, we expected citizens of these countries to also be in favour of a uniform allocation scheme.

Nevertheless, it could be the case that for some people the issues of national self-determination and the protection of their country's cultural and ethnic homogeneity are more important than any advantage of being able to transfer refugees to another country. The prime minister of Hungary, whose country could transfer 54,000 refugees to another member state if the quota were passed, justified his rejection of an equal allocation scheme for refugees with the statement that 'deciding whether to accept migrants is a matter of national sovereignty' (Than 2016). For this reason, the Hungarian government initiated a national referendum against the European allocation quota and additionally justified their dismissal of a quota regulation by referring to the supposed dangers that could arise from refugee and migrant populations (BBC 2016). In the discussion on the quota, Hungary put forward an alternative proposal with the collaboration of Poland, the Czech Republic, and Slovakia (Visegrád Group 2016). According to this, every member state should be able to decide for itself whether, in what ways, and with what resources it is able to support member states hosting large numbers of refugees. In their understanding, support also means providing resources to reinforce the external border in order to stem the further influx of refugees.

Finally, we can assume that, alongside a country's vested interests and the defence of national sovereignty, considerations of justice would also have an influence on attitudes towards the allocation of refugees. The EU sees itself not only as a community of shared interests, but one of shared values too. This includes the idea that justice and parity ought to prevail between the member states and that problems pertaining to the shared external border should also be managed in common. Among the advocates of this position is the former president of the EU Parliament, Martin Schulz. In the face of the uncooperative stance taken by some of the member states he claimed, 'We are not dealing with a failure of the EU, but rather with a glaring failure of some governments who don't want to take any responsibility and are thereby impeding a joint European solution' (Carrel 2015). In making this claim, he was aware that a sizeable section of the European population was firmly on his side. An example of this support was shown in Spain, where, in response to their government's failure to comply with its commitments – it had only taken in 1,100 of the agreed 17,000 refugees – several hundred-thousand demonstrators took to the streets of Barcelona on 18 February 2017 and called on their government to take in more asylum seekers (Deutsche Welle 2017).

What do we know empirically about the willingness of citizens to reciprocally support taking in refugees? To date three recent publications have addressed this issue. One of them, a study by Catherine de Vries and Isabell Hoffmann (2016) titled 'Border Protection and Freedom of Movement', is particularly noteworthy. The authors concluded that a clear majority of European citizens were in favour of redistributing asylum seekers based on data from an EU-wide survey carried out in December 2015. At the same time, though, significant differences between the member states became apparent in their study. While citizens from western member states were in favour of redistributive measures and were supportive of the use of penalties for countries that refuse to help, the rate of agreement in the eastern member states was substantially lower. In these countries, penalties were also dismissed by a majority (de Vries and Hoffmann 2016). Another piece of research on this topic, an article by Kirk Bansak and colleagues (2017), is also worth highlighting, as it presented the results from a multiple-country survey. The investigation focused on which refugee allocation policies the citizens of Europe preferred. The authors ascertained that considerations of both the utility of and the fairness of the policies played an important role in the selection of a preferred allocation method, provided that the considerations of fairness proved to be decisive in cases of conflict. In 12 of the 15 survey countries, they were able to find a large majority in favour of redistributing refugees in proportion with the size and economic strength of the receiving country. Majorities in favour of the status quo could only be found in Poland, the Czech Republic, and Great Britain. Most recently, Philipp Genschel and Anton Hemerijck (2018) conducted an online survey on supporting other EU countries in times of crisis. Among other scenario items, they asked whether respondents would support requiring member states to help other EU countries who are under pressure due to a great influx of refugees. Overall, 55% of the respondents approved of helping countries in such a case. However, they found no majorities in Poland, Lithuania, France, and the UK. Our findings show higher approval, which might relate to the fact that we did not openly suggest a 'don't know' answering category.

6.3.1 European citizens' attitudes towards burden sharing

According to our understanding, solidarity could only be considered to exist between the EU member states in the managing of the refugee crisis if both the majority of citizens across Europe as a whole as well as in each country separately agreed to the proposal that every country should commit to taking in refugees in equal measure. In our survey, we gathered data on this understanding of solidarity and a second variant of internal European solidarity, namely the attitudes of people towards the Visegrád states' proposal that countries that take in fewer refugees should be subjected to compensation payment. We obtained the approval rates for both of these suggestions to manage the refugee crisis with the help of a four-level Likert-type scale by posing the following questions:

> Recently, many refugees came to the European Union. I will now read out to you some statements about how the EU countries could tackle the refugee problem together. Please tell me to what extent you agree or disagree with the following statements.
>
> Each EU country should be required to accommodate refugees.
>
> If an EU country does not want to let refugees in, it has to pay compensation to other countries that take them.

The first statement asks for the participant's point of view on a quota regulation, while the second one operationalises their standpoint towards one of the suggestions by the Visegrád countries. Figure 6.9 sets out the approval rates sorted by country for the suggestion of a distributive system resembling a quota.

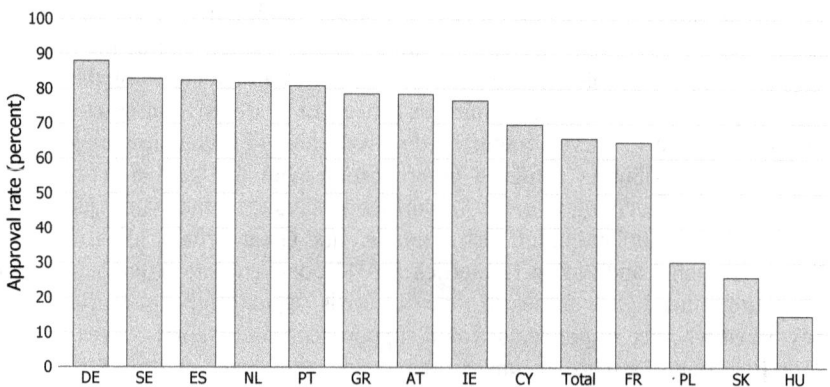

Figure 6.9 Average approval rates of the proposal that every country must accept refugees by country.

Source: TESS 2016, own calculations.

On average, nearly two-thirds of the respondents agreed with the suggestion that every country should take in refugees. At the same time, however, majority approval was not present in each of the individual countries; thus, the first criterion for the existence of European solidarity has not been fulfilled. The approval rates between the countries diverged by up to 70 percentage points and thus varied at a greater rate than they did on the question on the rights of refugees. Making up one side on the allocation issue were the northern, western, and southern European states, in which at least two-thirds of survey participants supported the allocation measures. On the other side of the schism, there were the post-socialist countries; we did not find a majority in favour of an equal distributive system in any of these. The split between the countries was even more pronounced than in the above-mentioned study by Catherine de Vries and Isabell Hoffmann (2016).

How can we interpret the large differences between the countries? Self-interest would dictate that citizens who are from countries situated at the southernmost part of the EU's external border (e.g. Greece, Cyprus, Portugal, Spain, Hungary) should support a fairer allocation of refugees; this applies to countries already burdened by the euro crisis and therefore with no means to take on another financial burden (e.g. Greece, Cyprus, Portugal, Spain, Ireland) and citizens from countries who took in above-average numbers of refugees (e.g. Austria, Germany, Sweden). Indeed, the approval rates reflected these self-interest-guided attitudes to a certain degree. Approval rates for allocating refugees were very high in Greece and Cyprus. In Spain and Portugal too, where a below-average number of refugees have been taken in as a proportion of their total population, approval rates were over 80%. In contrast, while Hungary should have a high interest in a more equal allocation of refugees, it had the lowest approval rates.

Opposing the self-interest argument, there are two reasons why citizens should be more likely to oppose a fairer allocation of refugees. On the one hand, countries might generally perceive redistributive measures first and foremost as a restriction on their national self-determination. This should be especially true in post-socialist countries, and such a consideration was reflected in the low approval rates for the allocation of refugees there. The majority of Visegrád citizens seemed to share the same perspectives as their governments and regarded the compulsory intake of refugees as an imposition on their national sovereignty (see discussion at the beginning of Section 3.1). Apart from respondents from Hungary, less than 30% of respondents from Poland and Slovakia agreed with an equalisation of the burden between EU countries.

On the other hand, cultural motives and generally negative attitudes could also drive individuals to reject allocating refugees. Therefore value-oriented and affectual motives may be stronger than the short-term interest in divesting themselves of refugees they have taken in via allocation. The approval rates in both Slovakia and Hungary indicated that such an argument was valid.

Lastly, it is interesting to see how these arguments manifested for a given country. In Greece and Cyprus, the approval rates for distributive measures were higher than the approval for whether refugees should be able to gain the right to remain (compare with Figure 6.2 in Section 6.3), which suggests that their self-interest was considerably stronger than their aversion of accommodating people with various backgrounds in their own country. Similarly, in Spain and Portugal, the approval rates were at the same level for both internal and external solidarity. In Hungary, in contrast, value dispositions and the fear of different cultures, as well as the question of national sovereignty, seemed to play a stronger role. Thus, this again indicates that the national public discourse is an important factor in shaping citizens' opinions about prominent issues. For example, the exceptional rejection of allocation in Hungary may be attributable to two special local circumstances at the time, namely the plebiscite initiated by the Hungarian government and the immense state public relations campaign against the EU's refugee quota, both of which were going on at the time when our survey's fieldwork was conducted there.

The citizens' attitudes towards the second proposal, namely that compensation be paid by countries that refuse to take in any refugees, are sketched out in Figure 6.10. As can be seen, the results were quite similar to those from Figure 6.9. Once again, the citizens of Poland, Slovakia, and Hungary starkly differed from citizens from the other surveyed countries. The correlation between the two proposed solutions was rather strong, from which we can conclude that the respondents' opinions on the two proposals did not differ strongly. Behind both proposals there was clearly a general, firm point of view on solidarity between the EU's member states. One of these positions is that the allocation of refugees is a task for the entirety of Europe to deal with and that it should thus be solved in solidarity with all the countries (regardless of how this solution may actually be implemented). Another viewpoint is that the EU has no right to force its

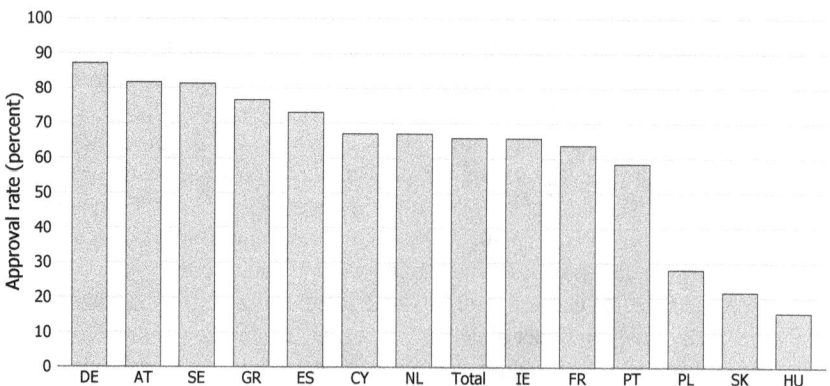

Figure 6.10 Average approval rates regarding the proposal about financial compensation for refusing burden-sharing by country.

Source: TESS 2016, own calculations.

member states to apply any particular solution, because the decision on whether to take in refugees is one for each of the nation states to make themselves.

Altogether, the evidence shows that the European population is divided on the subject of the allocation of refugees. In the Visegrád countries of Poland, Slovakia, and Hungary neither of the two proposals on how to share the burden met with majority approval, while in the other surveyed countries, both proposals met with majority approval. A central, uniting condition for the existence of a European solidarity is therefore not fulfilled due to the great divide between citizens from the post-socialist countries and citizens from the other EU countries.

6.3.2 Supporters and opponents of sharing the burden

As with the analysis on attitudes towards the right to stay, we were also interested in the question of whether supporters and opponents of allocation of refugees were divided by social and political cleavages.[16] As the questions of whether to take in refugees and how their allocation ought to occur are for the most part not separated in European public discourse, we predicted based on the descriptive analysis that being against refugees' right to stay would be related to respondents' stances on their allocation among member states. We expected the question of allocation to be superimposed on whether refugees should be allowed to stay in Europe in the first place. In order to test this hypothesis, we calculated the correlation of the two solidarity variables. With a Pearson's rank correlation of 0.53, the relationship was moderate, with a tendency to be strong. The correlations were also similarly strong when the two variables were calculated separately for each country. This means that the citizens from countries against the acceptance of refugees are highly likely to also be against any distributive measures. We take this amalgamation of external and internal solidarity into account in the following analysis, in which we adopt the measurements for external solidarity as an additional control variable in the calculations for assessing whether and to what extent there are cleavages.[17] The effects of the independent variables can thereby be interpreted as a 'pure' measurement for cleavages in the debate on the allocation of refugees.

Not all the variables that we theoretically deduced beforehand and took into consideration for solidarity with refugees in the preceding section were relevant for explaining attitudes towards allocation. In the following section, we will elucidate which factors should be taken into consideration theoretically for this particular issue.

6.3.3 Structural cleavages

Because we presumed that the structural aspects of individuals would not have an influence on attitudes towards allocation of refugees independent of the macro conditions, we started with a hypothesis concerned with the macro level.

Following the logic of our argumentation that self-interest influences willingness to engage in solidarity, we can assume that citizens from countries that have taken in a higher number of refugees would on average be more in favour of a more equal allocation scheme because this might lessen the load placed on their own country. In return, citizens from countries that accepted a considerably lower number of refugees should be against such allocation measures. We measured the rate at which a country was actually burdened by the refugee crisis by determining the ratio between the number of applications for asylum made in the year 2015 and the total population size. While the descriptive evidence initially suggested that this argument would not prove relevant, we still tested this hypothesis against more restrictive modelling, albeit without much expectation that it would be confirmed.

If we follow the hypothesis on threat levels, which we have already formulated in Section 6.3, then the respondents who found themselves in socio-economically precarious situations and who lived in a country that had taken in a large number of refugees in relation to the EU average would surely be the ones in favour of a more equal allocation because they might have perceived the presence of refugees in their country as a threat to their status. In contrast, we expected the variables indicating a socio-economically precarious situation to have the opposite effect in countries that had not taken in a high number of refugees. These individuals, we assumed, would be less likely to support the allocation of refugees, as they perceived the influx of refugees in their own country as a threat. Correspondingly, we predicted an interaction effect between the size of the burden borne by a country and the structural characteristics of the respondent (income, education, employment status, and occupational class).

6.3.4 Cultural cleavages

While we did not expect an impact to occur independent of context for attitudes towards allocation concerning the respondents' structural characteristics, we did predict that their cultural characteristics would have such an impact. We theorised that politically left-wing people would tend to agree with the allocation between countries because the values of equality and international solidarity are a core component of leftist values. In contrast, politically right-leaning respondents and people who identified exclusively with their nation would be strongly attached to their national community. For these people, sovereignty should possess greater importance, and they should hence perceive equal allocation measures as an affront to their national sovereignty. In this regard, we expected that these respondents would be more inclined to be against the proposal of allocation schemes.

The allocation of the burden is always bound with questions of justice as well. Hence, we gauged the respondents' general positions on justice by asking them to respond to the statement 'the distribution of wealth and income should be as equal as possible in society' and building their answer into the analysis as an explanatory variable. We assumed that people whose ideas of justice were formed by the principle of equality would be more likely to be in favour of distributing the means and responsibilities for mutually dealing with the refugee crisis than people for whom an equal allocation of resources was not such an important issue.

Much like the case of external solidarity, we theorised that political parties' constructions and interpretations of problems would shape citizens' attitudes towards them. In public debates, anti-immigration parties always underline the significance of their country's solidarity whenever and wherever possible. Accordingly, we expected the approval for a fair allocation of refugees to be low in countries where anti-immigration parties were strongly represented. Finally, we assumed that interaction effects would occur between the strength of anti-immigration parties within a country and the cultural characteristics of its people. We hypothesised that people who identified exclusively with their nation state and described themselves as on the right politically would oppose redistributive measures with particular strength when they also resided in countries where anti-immigration parties were especially strong.

6.3.5 Results on the social cleavages of internal solidarity

Table 6.2 presents the results for the regression analysis. The rate of agreement with the proposal that every country should commit to taking in refugees served as the dependent variable. The base model M1 only contains the controlled variables and the dummy countries. On this question, it is visible that women were more willing to display their solidarity than men were. It is evident, furthermore, that attitudes towards the allocation of refugees were influenced to a very significant degree by attitudes on the acceptance of refugees. The data on country variables show that respondents from post-socialist countries particularly rejected distributive measures. The explained variance for the base model was very high at 43%. A large part of the variance in the approval of allocation measures was explained by the respondent's attitudes towards solidarity with refugees and nationality.

In addition to the control variables, model M2 contains the structural and cultural characteristics of the respondents. Here, it was apparent that socio-economically vulnerable people, i.e. people with a low education, low household income, and low occupational class, were more likely to reject distributive measures. However, the influence of structural characteristics was still very low compared to the impact of cultural characteristics. As already formulated above, we theorised that the structural characteristics of individuals would not have an effect independent of the macro conditions. We will come back once more to the significance of the structural characteristics accordingly in the analytical section dedicated to the macro effects.

With respect to respondents' cultural characteristics, our hypotheses were confirmed. People who described themselves as politically right wing and who

Table 6.2 Social cleavages regarding approving the proposal that every EU country must accept refugees; individual level

	M1		M2	
Control variables				
Sex (ref.: male)	**0.08***	(0.03)	**0.09***	(0.03)
Age (by 10 years)	0.06	(0.04)	0.03	(0.04)
Age (by 10 years, squared)	−0.00	(0.00)	0.00	(0.00)
Right to stay for refugees[a]	**0.61***	(0.04)	**0.55***	(0.04)
Structural cleavages				
Level of education (ref.: tertiary)				
Non or primary			0.03	(0.05)
Secondary			**−0.06***	(0.02)
Occupational class (ref.: upper class (I))				
Upper middle class (II)			−0.00	(0.02)
Centre middle class (IIIa)			0.00	(0.02)
Lower middle class (V & VI)			**−0.09***	(0.03)
Self-employed (IVab & IVc)			−0.07	(0.05)
Routine non-manual (IIIb)			**−0.05***	(0.02)
Unskilled manual workers & agriculture (VIIa & VIIb)			**−0.11***	(0.04)
Unemployed (ref.: employed)			−0.03	(0.04)
Household income			**0.06***	(0.01)
Cultural cleavages				
Political placement (ref.: centre)				
Left			**0.21***	(0.04)
Moderate left			**0.21***	(0.04)
Moderate right			**−0.13***	(0.04)
Right			**−0.34***	(0.08)
Justice: equality matters			**0.07***	(0.02)
Identity: exclusively national (ref.: other)			**−0.41***	(0.04)
Country differences				
Country (ref.: Spain)				
Austria	0.00	(0.01)	**0.07***	(0.02)
Cyprus	**−0.38***	(0.01)	**−0.25***	(0.02)
France	**−0.54***	(0.01)	**−0.48***	(0.01)
Germany	**0.15***	(0.01)	**0.19***	(0.02)
Greece	**0.06***	(0.00)	**0.15***	(0.01)
Hungary	**−1.81***	(0.01)	**−1.60***	(0.03)
Ireland	**−0.17***	(0.01)	**−0.05***	(0.02)
The Netherlands	**−0.05***	(0.01)	**0.09***	(0.02)
Poland	**−1.20***	(0.01)	**−0.99***	(0.03)
Portugal	**−0.05***	(0.00)	**0.05***	(0.01)
Slovakia	**−1.52***	(0.01)	**−1.33***	(0.02)
Sweden	**0.11***	(0.01)	**0.24***	(0.03)
Constant	**3.11***	(0.11)	**2.59***	(0.18)
R^2	0.434		0.448	
AIC	24,295.3		24,071.2	

Source: TESS 2016, own calculations.

Notes
$n = 9,530$; Unstandardised coefficients from pooled OLS regression with robust standard errors (clustered by country), *$p < 0.05$; **$p < 0.01$; ***$p < 0.001$, standard errors in parentheses.
a Dependent variable in Table 6.1.

identified exclusively with their nation state rejected the measures for redistributing refugees significantly more strongly than people who described themselves as moderate or who had a European or world citizen identity. The more politically left wing a respondent was, the more he/she was inclined to approve of the allocation of refugees. The respondents' preference for a specific principle of justice also played a significant role: those who advocated for an equal distribution of resources in society were also more likely to support the more equal allocation of refugees between EU countries.

All in all, however, adding the individual variables only improved the explained variance by around 1% compared to the base model. The social cleavages regarding the question of the allocation of refugees thus appear to be very weakly pronounced. Indeed, note that we used attitudes towards refugees' right to remain as the control variable in our analysis and only measured the 'pure' cleavages, as it were, on the question of allocation.

As attitudes towards the acceptance of refugees and attitudes towards their allocation were closely intertwined, both in the public discourse and in citizens' consciousness, we could thus assume that the strong cleavages on the question of the right to stay would also play an important role in terms of the allocation issue.

Let us now turn our attention to the findings regarding the influence of the macro factors on citizens' attitudes towards the allocation of refugees. The left-hand graph in Figure 6.11 depicts the correlation between the burden borne by a country (the number of asylum applications in the year 2015 as a percentage of the total population) and the country-by-country differences in the rejection of measures for distributing refugees. There was no discernible correlation between

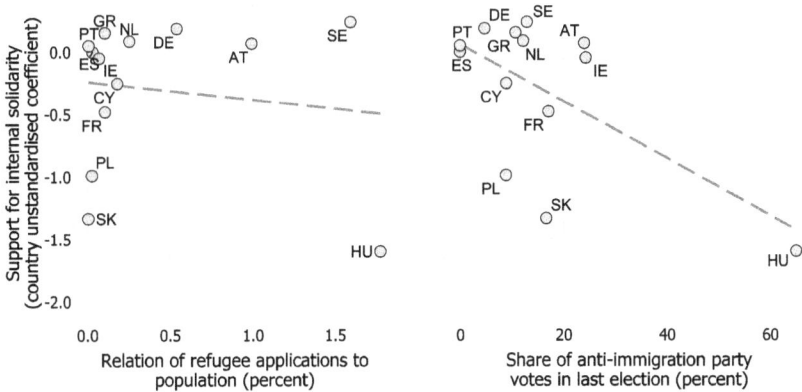

Figure 6.11 Social cleavages regarding approving the proposal that every EU country must accept refugees; country level.

Source: TESS 2016, own calculations.

the two factors. The right-hand graph shows that there was a strong negative correlation between the electoral success of anti-immigration parties and the approval rate regarding the allocation of refugees. Despite all this, we need to be cautious when ultimately accepting the direction of causality between the two factors here, because there is still a possibility that citizens' attitudes against an allocation of refugees may have led some of these people to vote for anti-immigration parties, which would then influence citizens' views due to the position of authority they gain as a result. In order to more accurately determine the direction of causation between the two factors, we would have needed to use panel data.

Figure 6.12 portrays the final results from the analysis of the interaction effects between the individual level and the macro level. In keeping with our theoretical predictions, it was apparent that unemployed people living in countries with an above-average number of refugees were markedly more in favour of redistributive measures than the unemployed in countries with fewer refugees (Figure 6.12, top). The higher the number of refugees that a country has taken in, the more probable it was that these people would express their preference for a more equal allocation scheme.

Contrary to our expectations, the strength of parties expressing anti-immigrant sentiments in a country did not strengthen the effects of the individual characteristics, either for 'identification with the nation', nor for 'political right-wing orientation' (for greater clarity we have not displayed these panels in the book). Interestingly, however, we were able to establish a correlation between the strength of political parties expressing anti-immigrant sentiments within a country and views towards the allocation of refugees among citizens who classified themselves as 'slightly left wing' or 'left wing' politically. As we have already analysed in the above section, left-leaning people should be more inclined to support a fair allocation of refugees. This tendency, however, increased as the strength of parties with anti-immigrant sentiments in their country grew (compare with Figure 6.12 centre and bottom). It is quite apparent that the strength of such political parties in a country has a polarising effect, whereby an antagonistic dynamic motivates leftist-oriented people to position themselves more strongly in opposition.

Let us now weigh up the results in the conclusion of this section: on first glance, opponents to the allocation of refugees among the individual EU member states appear to exhibit characteristics that would make the emergence of a social cleavage not especially probable. Indeed, it turns out in fact that people who were politically right wing, who had a strong bond with their nation state, and who lived in countries where parties communicated strong anti-immigrant sentiments were also significantly more likely to speak out against internal solidarity. The statistical correlations were not strongly pronounced overall. However, this can be attributed to the fact that these people's attitudes towards a redistributive system were superimposed on top of their attitudes towards refugees' right to stay. Even if it makes sense methodologi-

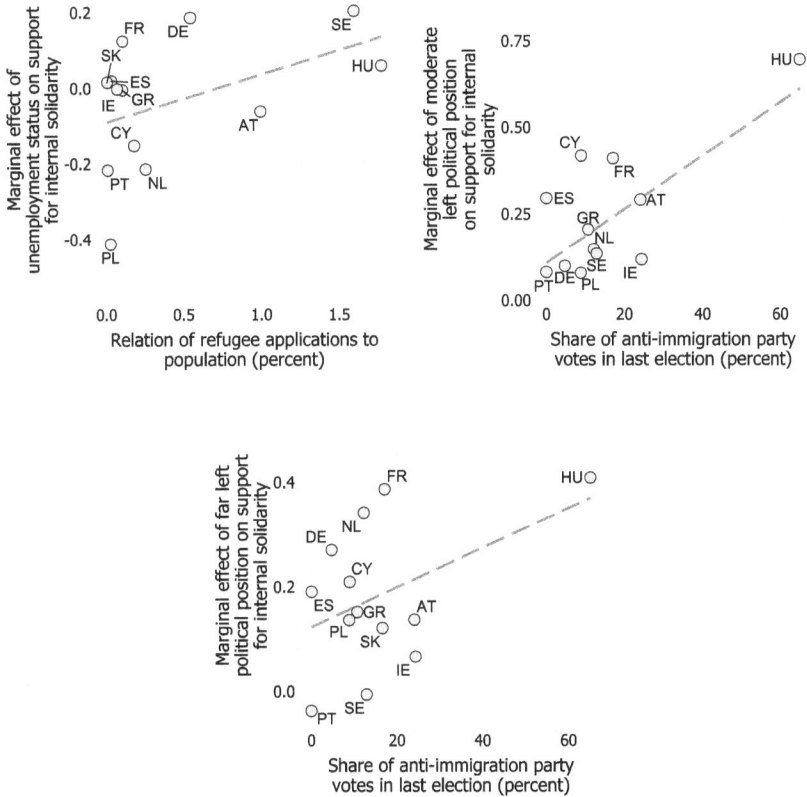

Figure 6.12 Social cleavages regarding approving the proposal that every EU country must accept refugees; cross-level effects.

Source: TESS 2016, own calculations.

cally to control for the influence of perspectives on refugees' right to remain when analysing the emergence of cleavages around the issue of allocation, in practice this process leads to a significant underestimation of the potential for cleavages to form around this topic.

6.3.6 Results on the political cleavages

In the final section, we wished to test whether those who opposed European internal solidarity on the question of a fairer allocation possessed a clear political party preference and thereby ensured that their concerns would be politically articulated. We expected opponents of redistributive measures to prefer to vote for right-wing Eurosceptic parties, because these parties insist on the right of national self-determination and oppose any increase in cooperation of EU member states. Right-wing parties all over Europe supported Hungary and Slovakia in their cases before the European Court of Justice against the quota on accepting refugees. Alexander Gauland, a leading politician for the German right-wing Eurosceptic party the Alternative für Deutschland (AfD), commented on their defeat at the European Court of Human Rights by saying 'Hungary, and Slovakia must now remain steadfast and may not bend to the Brussels dictatorship' (Tagesspiegel 2017).

As we did in Section 6.2 and the other chapters of this book, we measured the citizens' voting intentions by asking them which party they would vote for if there were a general election tomorrow. The parties were in turn assigned into groups in line with the suggestions proposed by Hobolt and de Vries (2016). In Figure 6.13, a bivariate multinomial logistic model depicts the estimated probabilities that the respondents would vote for a Eurosceptic party depending on their stance on the allocation of refugees. The results confirmed our hypothesis: right-wing Eurosceptic parties offered opponents of redistributive measures a political home. The more strongly opposed a person was to a fair allocation scheme, the more likely it was that he/she would vote for a right-wing Eurosceptic party. In total, 42% of unequivocal opponents of measures for the allocation of refugees stated that they would vote for a right-wing Eurosceptic party.

Left-wing Eurosceptic parties, in contrast, appeared to be unattractive to opponents of European solidarity in the face of the refugee crisis. Those who favoured redistributing refugees even had a slight tendency to vote for a soft-Eurosceptic left-wing political party.

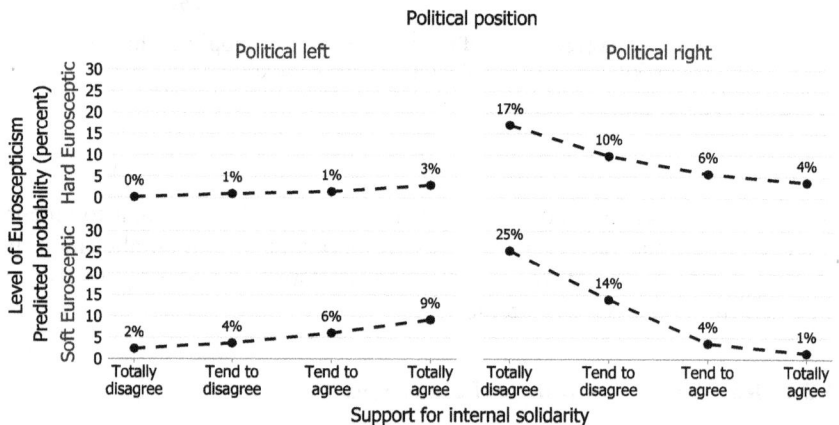

Figure 6.13 Support for internal solidarity and political position of party voted for.

Source: TESS 2016, own calculations.

6.4 Conclusions on refugee solidarity

This chapter has been dedicated to the analysis of European solidarity in the refugee crisis. To do this we first differentiated between two different domains of solidarity: (1) the willingness of European citizens to offer refugees the right to stay in general (external solidarity), and (2) their willingness to distribute the costs that arise from taking in and accommodating refugees between the member states (internal solidarity). For both domains of solidarity, we tested the extent to which the criteria for the existence of a European solidarity, which we formulated in Chapter 2, were met. We found the following regarding the existence of a European solidarity in the refugee crisis:

1   Nearly four out of five respondents were in favour of accepting refugees. Refugees who have fled from war or civil conflict, from persecution after having campaigned for human rights, or for persecution because of their Christian beliefs received especially high levels of approval from our respondents. Lower approval rates were evident when the refugees in question were persecuted because of their homosexuality or their Muslim religious convictions. In addition, a majority of citizens were in favour of granting asylum to refugees in each of the different countries in our survey separately. In 11 of the 13 surveyed countries, the majority amounted to approximately two-thirds of respondents, while in the other two countries (Slovakia, and Hungary) we found a mere simple majority. Still, with majority approval among all EU citizens for taking in refugees in general, the first criterion for the existence of a European solidarity is fulfilled. Nevertheless, this majority approval does not apply to all groups of refugees in the same way, as persecuted Muslims in particular are singled out, with approval rates for their right to asylum in the EU recorded at below 50% in Cyprus, Poland, Slovakia, and Hungary.

2   The proposals for sharing the burden of taking in and accommodating refugees between member states also found majority approval overall. However, a closer look at the approval rates reveals there to be a clear divide in opinion on these issues between EU countries, a tendency that the approval rates for the taking-in of Muslim refugees already hinted at: while both the proposals for distributing the burden had strong approval in ten of the countries, citizens in the post-socialist countries (Poland, Slovakia, and Hungary) rejected them significantly, thus aligning with the political standpoints pushed by their governments. Hence, the second criterion, which we formulated for proving the existence of a European solidarity, in terms of internal solidarity was not met.

3   For both domains of solidarity in this domain, we tested whether social and political cleavages exist around this issue and how pronounced they were. Without elaborating on any of the details here, it was apparent that opponents of solidarity with refugees were most distinguished by their cultural

characteristics; therefore we can observe cultural cleavages. These opponents are people who position themselves on the political right, who display a strong identification with their nation state, who perceive foreigners and immigrants more as a threat than as a source of cultural enrichment, who live in countries where the historical experience of losing their national sovereignty is deeply embedded within the collective memory and where there is also a strong presence of anti-immigration political parties.

Similar features characterise the opponents of a fair allocation of refugees among member states, even if the social cleavages here are somewhat weaker. That said, in the investigation into the cleavages surrounding internal solidarity, it was evident that the two domains of solidarity interlocked in various ways. Those who expressed their opposition to taking in refugees also tended to be against the establishment of a uniform distributive system. Somewhat curiously, the real, objective measurable ways in which a country was affected had no discernible influence on the attitudes of citizens. The values held by citizens, the fear of losing their national sovereignty, and the mobilisation of anti-immigration political parties were the main motives behind the opposition to distributive measures expressed by people in several eastern European countries.

4   The social cleavages regarding taking in refugees and allocating them among the EU member states also translated into political cleavages. The analysis of respondents' party preferences for the next election showed that opponents of both domains of solidarity have a markedly higher propensity to vote for right-wing Eurosceptic parties.

All in all, the analysis shows that the criteria for the existence of an internal European solidarity have not been fulfilled: the majority rejected a common allocation scheme and the allocation of refugees among European countries in several eastern European countries. What's more, this dismissal was (a) culturally rooted, as the opponents of distributing refugees between EU countries are distinguished by cultural characteristics and clustered within certain countries, and (b) politically relevant, because the rejection of internal solidarity went hand in hand with the propensity to vote for right-wing Eurosceptic parties. The results regarding external solidarity – that is, the willingness to take in refugees – are slightly better. Surprisingly, we found a distinct majority of citizens in favour of humanitarian solidarity with refugees in this case; they thus adhere to the values to which the EU has legally committed itself. Nevertheless, the minority of people who rejected taking in refugees comprise a culturally determined cleavage, which is capable of mobilisation, and that also translates into votes for right-wing Eurosceptic parties through the political process.

To some extent, we were also surprised by the high degree of willingness to take in refugees, because this does not conform to our perception of the public discourse on this issue. Since 2015, refugees have been a dominant issue in the public debate in many EU countries. The topic has been and continues to be discussed controversially, with many powerful actors speaking out openly against the taking-in of refugees (Czymara and Schmidt-Catran 2017). For citizens as well, the subject of refugees and migration are among the most important political issues. In Germany, for example, the group of themes tying into the central migration and refugee debate have continually been of much greater relevance than all other political issues (Forschungsgruppe Wahlen 2017) and the public discourse has been very volatile (Vollmer and Karakayali 2018). The Eurobarometer surveys, which cover all EU member states, have reached a similar conclusion as well. European citizens see 'migration', together with the issue of terrorism, as the greatest challenge of the EU currently (European Commission 2017b). Alongside the increase in the number of refugees in Europe, the number of attacks carried out on asylum centres has also continually increased.[18] Populist parties with anti-immigration policies have gained traction in many European countries and have used their new-found influential position to determine the direction of public debate. So just how does this image fit in with the high approval rates for taking in refugees, which our analysis has uncovered?

The opinions that are published in the media often do not match identically with those held by members of the general public. We have observed that the people who reject taking in refugees, despite making up a mere minority, do at the same time constitute homogenous social and political groups. People who are against taking in refugees are able to find representation for their views in the right-wing political parties in particular, which have in turn shaped the public debate in many European countries with their actions, political soundbites, and public statements. This may have subsequently led to the public discourse on refugees, and the opinions that get published on the topic on the one side, shifting away from the (silent) majority opinion held by the total population on the other side.

Furthermore, when interpreting the high approval rates for accepting refugees, it is just as valid to consider the ways in which we measured this approval rate. We asked about several groups of refugees, and emphasised for each of them respectively the fact that they had been persecuted in their home country. By using the word 'persecuted', we invoked an objective emergency. In the public debate on the rights of refugees to be accepted into Europe, the fundamental question of whether persecuted peoples should be taken in does not tend to be touched upon for the most part; instead it is one of the neighbouring themes. At the centre of these debates lies the question of whether the refugees we are dealing with are people who have been persecuted in their home country or 'normal' migrants who are seeking refuge in Europe because of their dissatisfaction with the economic situation in their home country. The second topic concerns the question of the extent to which refugees' identity had been sufficiently and reliably screened upon entering Europe and whether several (potential) terrorists may have taken advantage of the poor controls and lax identity checks at the borders in order to get into the EU in the period between 2014 and 2016. A third debate touches upon the question of whether the countries that have taken in refugees can send them back to their countries of origin once their reason for seeking asylum has become invalid. Fourth and finally, the public discourse has concentrated on criminal offences committed by some small number of refugees. It is right-wing populist parties and social movements who have transformed these four outlined issues into subjects of public discussion and have thereby caused them to be perceived as considerably more important than they actually are.

In doing this, these parties can count on the support for citizens, as people tend to have very pronounced viewpoints on each of these four issues described above. Citizens neither want migrants who have moved for economic reasons to be acknowledged as refugees (for comparison with empirical evidence in Germany, see Jürgen Gerhards and colleagues (2016)), nor do they wish for the identities of people who have immigrated towards Europe to have been incorrectly checked. Additionally, citizens would like people who are granted asylum to be made to return to their country of origin when the terms of their asylum have expired and for refugees to adhere to the laws of the host country.

The opinions of citizens on taking in persecuted people have not exactly remained untouched by the four highlighted subject areas. Yet a study by Christian S. Czymara and Alexander W. Schmidt-Catran (2017) has shown, with a focus on Germany, that these issues have in fact not led to citizens rejecting the taking-in of refugees. However, this will not necessarily remain so. The turning of these four described issues into topics of public discussion is plainly a political communications strategy executed by right-wing populist movements as a way of reducing the degree of acceptance for taking in refugees in general. If politicians wish to ensure the support for citizens for humanitarian solidarity at the level shown by our study, then this will depend on finding practical political solutions to these problem areas as a direct path to securing the long-term legitimacy of the universal human right of abode that asylum seekers, refugees, and persecuted peoples are entitled to claim.

Our final reflections on this matter are backed up by research on the welfare state. In this research, it has likewise transpired that people are especially ready and willing to help others who are in need (with these findings once more confirmed by our results in Chapter 5). Such a willingness to help, however, does not come unconditionally. The need must be a genuine one and may neither be fabricated nor attributable to a lack of adequate effort on the part of the person in danger (Fong, Bowles, and Gintis 2006). If citizens ever get the impression that measures for institutional solidarity have been abused, then this will undermine their belief in the integrity of these institutions and, in turn, their support.

Notes

1 Mengozzi's proposal would allow victims of persecution to submit an asylum application by applying for a visa that could be obtained from EU countries' embassies, thus preventing them from having to take their chances on illegal and dangerous escape routes. In the corresponding negotiations before the European Court of Justice, a Syrian family of five from Aleppo claimed that their visa application had been rejected by the Belgian embassy despite the father of the family having officially documented evidence that he had been kidnapped and tortured. Despite this, however, the judge ultimately ruled against their claims.

2 Paragraph 1 from Article 21 of the Lisbon Treaty stipulates that:

> The Union's action on the international scene shall be guided by the principles which have inspired its own creation, development and enlargement, and which it seeks to advance in the wider world: democracy, the rule of law, the universality and indivisibility of human rights and fundamental freedoms, respect for human dignity, the principles of equality and solidarity, and respect for the principles of the United Nations Charter and international law.
>
> (The Treaty of Lisbon 2007)

3 Through a series of vignettes carried out in 15 European countries, the authors systematically sketched out the varied characteristics of asylum seekers and gathered evidence on respondents' willingness to take in refugees of all different combinations of these aspects. This showed that migrants with Muslim beliefs are 11% less likely to be accepted than Christians, even when all other factors that could otherwise influence attitudes towards refugees were controlled for.

4 The index expresses the overall attitudes towards refugees as a composite measure and averages the responses to the five groups of refugees. This index is a continuous variable. In Figure 6.3 for the sake of comparability with the Likert-scale items (first five categories), we adjusted the depiction of the index (bottom category). The index here represents the rate of responses in each answer category (i.e. fully agree, tend to agree, tend to disagree, fully disagree) for all five items across the total number of responses for all five items. For example, 81% of responses fell into the category 'fully agree' or 'tend to agree' for all five items.

5 In the study by Jürgen Gerhards and colleagues (2016), the respondents were not just allowed to agree or disagree with the refugees being granted the right to stay, but were also allowed to express their indecision with 'not sure'. For this reason, the approval rates in our survey were around 10 percentage points above the levels given in that earlier study.

6 A recent survey by the Pew Research Center (2016) reached the conclusion that in the eastern European states, which are still considered to be young historically, religion plays a more important role in social cohesion than it does in the 'established' nation states of western Europe.

7 The approval rates for non-heterosexual refugees were also lower in the post-socialist states than in the other EU countries.

8 Although we use causal rhetoric throughout the book, our analysis is not a causal analysis in the narrow sense. For a strict causal analysis, a randomised trial (Hernán 2018) or panel data (Morgan and Winship 2015:363–91) would be more appropriate. Unfortunately, our cross-sectional survey data cannot be categorised as such. Nonetheless, we share the opinion of Miguel A. Hernán who argued that 'without causually explicit language, the means and ends of much observational research get hopelessly conflated' (Hernán 2018:617).

9 Esping-Andersen developed the concept of different welfare state regime types, which are a good approximation for different decommodification levels. Unfortunately, the

original types excluded the large number of the eastern and southern European countries in our sample. As an alternative, it would have been nice to have an absolute index based on citizens' rights to social insurance for all our sample countries. This would have come closer to the concept of decommodification than the amount of money spent on social insurances. However, such an effort would have gone beyond the scope of our research project. Other authors (Allan and Scruggs 2004; Palme and Korpi 2003; Scruggs 2014; Stephens 2010) have built such an index. However, their results are mostly outdated and do not cover all of our surveyed countries.

10 Aside from this, attitudes towards migrants are also influenced by the public discourse on the nation's economic situation. Anabel Kuntz and colleagues (2017), for example, demonstrated that perceived changes to a nation's economic status were more likely to influence attitudes on migrants than any actual change to the economic situation.

11 The interaction effect that we speak of refers to the interplay between individual structural characteristics and macro-level cultural characteristics generally, and here specifically to the interpretations of an issue by political actors. Since the hypotheses regarding cultural cleavages have not yet been discussed, we have no choice here but to elaborate on the details in the next section somewhat prematurely. In this next section, we will illustrate the ways in which we have empirically operationalised the construction of the refugee issue by political parties.

12 In the TESS, the respondents were able to declare their identity as a national, European, or world citizen. They were also permitted to name more than one of the above.

13 With five points, Greece possessed the highest point value in our sample. On the other end of the scale, there were the Netherlands, France, and Portugal, all with zero points.

14 We carried out the same analysis with the dependent variable 'attitudes towards taking in Muslim refugees' added in. Though the calculations reached some quite different conclusions, the influence of cultural variables was indeed more distinct.

15 When we extend the bivariate models by including other variables influencing a person's political party preference, then the impact of attitudes towards refugees remained in place for the most part. The influence on voting for hard Eurosceptic right-wing parties was especially robust.

16 Both items that measure internal solidarity showed the same effect patterns in the multivariate analysis. Therefore and for simplicity, we only discuss the results of the item that asks about respondents' opinion on the actual allocation of refugees.

17 Since we included external solidarity as an independent variable, the regression estimators of the variables that were included in both models of refugee solidarity tended to be biased in the model of internal solidarity because they influence the dependent variable directly and indirectly through their effect on external solidarity. In order to obtain unbiased results, we applied an auxiliary regression of all the variables that appeared in both models on the refugee index. Subsequently, the residuals of this auxiliary regression were included as unbiased measures of external solidarity in the internal solidarity model.

18 For statistics on this in Germany, see Bundeskriminalamt 2016.

References

Allan, James P., and Lyle Scruggs. 2004. 'Political Partisanship and Welfare State Reform in Advanced Industrial Societies'. *American Journal of Political Science* 48(3):496–512.

Allport, Gordon W. 1979. *The Nature of Prejudice*. Reading, MA: Addison-Wesley.

Associated Press: Dailymail. 2016. 'The Latest: Slovak Leader Says Migrants Can't Be Integ-rated'. *dailymail.co.uk*, 7 January. Retrieved 6 August 2017 (www.dailymail.co.uk/wires/ap/article-3388441/The-Latest-Norway-received-31-000-asylum-seekers-2015.html).

Bansak, Kirk, Jens Hainmueller, and Dominik Hangartner. 2016. 'How Economic, Humanitarian, and Religious Concerns Shape European Attitudes toward Asylum Seekers'. *Science* 354(6309):217–22.

Bansak, Kirk, Jens Hainmueller, and Dominik Hangartner. 2017. 'Europeans Support a Proportional Allocation of Asylum Seekers'. *Nature Human Behaviour* 1(133):1–6.

BBC. 2015. 'Migrants Crisis: Slovakia "Will Only Accept Christians"'. *bbc.com*, 19 August. Retrieved 20 June 2017 (www.bbc.com/news/world-europe-33986738).

BBC. 2016. 'Hungary PM Claims EU Migrant Quota Referendum Victory'. *bbc.com*, 3 October. Retrieved 12 June 2017 (www.bbc.com/news/world-europe-37528325).

Blalock, Hubert M. 1967. *Toward a Theory of Minority-Group Relations*. New York: John Wiley & Sons.

Bobo, Lawrence, and Frederick C. Licari. 1989. 'Education and Political Tolerance: Testing the Effects of Cognitive Sophistication and Target Group Affect'. *Public Opinion Quarterly* 53(3):285–308.

Bohman, Andrea. 2011. 'Articulated Antipathies: Political Influence on Anti-Immigrant Attitudes'. *International Journal of Comparative Sociology* 52(6):457–77.

Börzel, Tanja A., and Thomas Risse. 2017. 'From the Euro to the Schengen Crises: European Integration Theories, Politicization, and Identity Politics'. *Journal of European Public Policy* 54(1):1–26.

Bundeskriminalamt. 2016. *Bundeslagebild Kriminalität im Kontext von Zuwanderung 2015 [Federal Situation View on Crime in the Context of Immigration 2015]*. Wiesbaden: Bundeskriminalamt. Retrieved 31 January 2017 (www.bka.de/DE/AktuelleInformationen/StatistikenLagebilder/Lagebilder/KriminalitaetImKontextVonZuwanderung/KriminalitaetImKontextVonZuwanderung_node.html).

Callens, Marie-Sophie, Bart Meuleman, and Marie Valentova. 2015. 'Perceived Threat, Contact and Attitudes towards the Integration of Immigrants: Evidence from Luxembourg'. *SSRN Electronic Journal*. Retrieved 20 September 2018 (https://papers.ssrn.com/sol3/papers.cfm?abstract_id=2694572).

Card, David, Christian Dustmann, and Ian Preston. 2012. 'Immigration, Wages, and Compositional Amenities'. *Journal of the European Economic Association* 10(1):78–119.

Carrel, Paul. 2015. 'EU Parliament Chief Attacks "Cynical" States over Refugee Crisis'. *Reuters*, 29 August. Retrieved 27 April 2017 (www.reuters.com/article/us-europe-migrants-schulz/eu-parliament-chief-attacks-cynical-states-over-refugee-crisis-idUSKCN0QY0DQ20150829).

Ceobanu, Alin M., and Xavier Escandell. 2008. 'East Is West? National Feelings and Anti-immigrant Sentiment in Europe'. *Social Science Research* 37(4):1147–70.

Ceobanu, Alin M., and Xavier Escandell. 2010. 'Comparative Analyses of Public Attitudes toward Immigrants and Immigration Using Multinational Survey Data: A Review of Theories and Research'. *Annual Review of Sociology* 36(1):309–28.

Chandler, Charles R., and Yung-mei Tsai. 2001. 'Social Factors Influencing Immigration Attitudes: An Analysis of Data from the General Social Survey'. *The Social Science Journal* 38(2):177–88.

Citrin, Jack, Donald P. Green, Christopher Muste, and Cara Wong. 1997. 'Public Opinion toward Immigration Reform: The Role of Economic Motivations'. *The Journal of Politics* 59(3):858–81.

Crawley, Heaven, Stephen Drinkwater, and Rukhsana Kauser. 2013. 'Regional Variations in Attitudes towards Refugees: Evidence from Great Britain'. *IZA Working Paper* (7647). Retrieved 16 August 2018 (http://repec.iza.org/dp7647.pdf).

Czymara, Christian S., and Alexander W. Schmidt-Catran. 2017. 'Refugees Unwelcome?: Changes in the Public Acceptance of Immigrants and Refugees in Germany in the Course of Europe's "Immigration Crisis"'. *European Sociological Review* 33(6):735–51.

de Vries, Catherine E., and Isabell Hoffmann. 2016. 'Border Protection and Freedom of Movement: What People Expect of European Asylum and Migration Policies'. *Bertelsmann Stiftung, eupinions* 1.

Dempster, Helen, and Karen Hargrave. 2017. 'Understanding Public Attitudes towards Refugees and Migrants'. *ODI & Chatham House Working Paper* (512). Retrieved 18 June 2018 (https://euagenda.eu/upload/publications/untitled-92767-ea.pdf).

Deutsche Welle. 2017. 'Thousands Call on Spain to Welcome More Refugees'. *Deutsche Welle*, 18 February. Retrieved 27 April 2017 (www.dw.com/en/thousands-call-on-spain-to-welcome-more-refugees/a-37618207).

Dixon, Tim, Hans-Jürgen Frieß, Emily Gray, Robert Grimm, Stephen Hawkins, Marc Helbling, Miriam Juan-Torres, Katja Kiefer, Daniela Kossatz, Nicoleta Negrea, Alexandra Schoen, Liane Stavenhagen, Vincent Wolff, and Armgard Zindler. 2017. 'Attitudes towards National Identity, Immigration, and Refugees in Germany'. Retrieved 12 September 2018 (www.thesocialchangeinitiative.org/new-research-reports-on-attitudes-to-migrants-in-germany-and-france/).

Esping-Andersen, Gøsta. 1990. *The Three Worlds of Welfare Capitalism*. Princeton, NJ: Princeton University Press.

European Commission. 2015. *Managing the Refugee Crisis: Western Balkans Route: State of Play Report*. Brussels: European Commission. Retrieved 27 April 2017 (https://ec.europa.eu/home-affairs/sites/homeaffairs/files/what-we-do/policies/european-agenda-migration/background-information/docs/western_balkans_route_state_of_play_report_en.pdf).

European Commission. 2017a. *Report from the Commission to the European Parliament, the European Council and the Council: Fifth Report on the Progress Made in the Implementation of the EU–Turkey Statement.* COM (2017) 204 final. Brussels: European Commission. Retrieved 13 June 2017 (https://ec.europa.eu/home-affairs/sites/homeaffairs/files/what-we-do/policies/european-agenda-migration/20170302_fifth_report_on_the_progress_made_in_the_implementation_of_the_eu-turkey_statement_en.pdf).

European Commission. 2017b. *Standard Eurobarometer 87 – Public Opinion in the European Union.* S2142_87_3_STD87_ENG. Brussels: European Commission. Retrieved 15 December 2017 (http://data.europa.eu/euodp/en/data/dataset/S2142_87_3_STD87_ENG).

European Council. 2015. *Council Decision (EU) 2015/1601 of 22 September 2015: Establishing Provisional Measures in the Area of International Protection for the Benefit of Italy and Greece.* Brussels. Retrieved 10 October 2017 (http://eur-lex.europa.eu/legal-content/EN/TXT/HTML/?uri=CELEX:32015D1601&from=RO).

European Parliament, European Commission, The Council, and the Representatives of the Governments of the Member States meeting within the Council. 2008. *The European Consensus on Humanitarian Aid: Joint Statement.* 2008/C 25/01. Brussels: European Union. Retrieved 6 June 2017 (http://eur-lex.europa.eu/legal-content/EN/TXT/?qid=1431445468547&uri=CELEX%3A42008X0130%2801%29).

European Parliament, and European Council. 2011. *Directive 2011/95/EU of the European Parliament and of the Council: On Standards for the Qualification of Third-country Nationals or Stateless Persons as Beneficiaries of International Protection, for a Uniform Status for Refugees or for Persons Eligible for Subsidiary Protection, and for the Content of the Protection Granted.* 2011/95/EU. Brussels and Strasbourg: European Parliament and European Council. Retrieved 6 June 2017 (http://data.europa.eu/eli/dir/2011/95/oj).

Eurostat. 2017a. *Asylum and first time asylum applicants by citizenship, age and sex Annual aggregated data (migr_asyappctza): Eurostat – Data Explorer.* Retrieved 2 February 2017 (http://appsso.eurostat.ec.europa.eu/nui/show.do?dataset=migr_asyappctza&lang=en).

Eurostat. 2017b. *Population change – Demographic balance and crude rates at national level (demo_gind): Eurostat – Data Explorer.* Retrieved 2 February 2017 (http://appsso.eurostat.ec.europa.eu/nui/show.do?dataset=demo_gind&lang=en).

Eurostat. 2018. *Asylum and first time asylum applicants by citizenship, age and sex Annual aggregated data (migr_asyappctza): Eurostat – Data Explorer.* Retrieved 10 July 2018 (http://appsso.eurostat.ec.europa.eu/nui/show.do?dataset=migr_asyappctza&lang=en).

Fong, Christina, Samuel Bowles, and Herbert Gintis. 2006. 'Strong Reciprocity and the Welfare State'. Pp. 1439–64 in *Handbooks in Economics*, Vol. 23, *Handbook of the Economics of Giving, Altruism and Reciprocity*, edited by J. Mercier Ythier and S.-C. Kolm. Amsterdam and New York: Elsevier.

Ford, Rob, and Nick Lowles. 2016. *Fear & Hope 2016: Race, Faith and Belonging in Today's England.* London: HOPE not hate. Retrieved 18 June 2018 (www.barrowcadbury.org.uk/wp-content/uploads/2016/03/Fear-and-Hope-report-1.pdf).

Forschungsgruppe Wahlen. 2017. 'Politbarometer – Wichtige Probleme in Deutschland: [Politbarometer – Important Problems in Germany]'. Retrieved 10 December 2017 (www.forschungsgruppe.de/Umfragen/Politbarometer/Langzeitentwicklung_-_Themen_im_Ueberblick/Politik_II/#Probl1).

Fuchs, Dieter, and Hans-Dieter Klingemann. 1989. 'Das Links-Rechts-Schema als politischer Code: ein interkultureller Vergleich auf inhaltsanalytischer Grundlage [The Left–Right Pattern as a Political Code: An Inter-cultural Comparison Based on an Analysis of Contents]'. Pp. 203–34 in *Kultur und Gesellschaft: Verhandlungen des 24. Deutschen Soziologentags, des 11. Österreichischen Soziologentags und des 8. Kongresses der Schweizerischen Gesellschaft für Soziologie in Zürich 1988*, edited by M. Haller, H.-J. Hoffmann-Nowotny, W. Zapf, and Deutsche Gesellschaft für Soziologie (DGS). Frankfurt am Main: Campus Verlag.

Genschel, Philipp, and Anton Hemerijck. 2018. *Solidarity in Europe.* Policy Brief. Issue 2018/01. Fiesole: EUI School of Transnational Governance: School of Transnational Governance. Retrieved 20 December 2018 (https://stateoftheunion.eui.eu/wp-content/uploads/sites/9/2018/05/Policy-Brief-Solidarity-in-Europe.pdf).

Gerhards, Jürgen, Silke Hans, and Jürgen Schupp. 2016. 'Kant, das geltende Recht und die Einstellungen der Bürger zu Flüchtlingen und anderen Migranten [Kant, the Applicable Law and the Attitudes of Citizens towards Refugees and other Migrants]'. *Leviathan* 44(4):604–20.

Gerhards, Jürgen, and Holger Lengfeld. 2015. *European Citizenship and Social Integration in the European Union.* London and New York: Routledge.

Gilens, Martin, and Naomi Murakawa. 2002. 'Elite Cues and Political Decision Making'. Pp. 15–49 in *Research in Micropolitics*, Vol. 6, *Political Decision-making, Deliberation and Participation*, edited by M. X. Delli Carpini. Amsterdam: Jai.

Green, Donald, Bradley Palmquist, and Eric Schickler. 2002. *Partisan Hearts and Minds: Political Parties and the Social Identities of Voters*. New Haven, CT and London: Yale University Press.

Hainmueller, Jens, and Michael J. Hiscox. 2007. 'Educated Preferences: Explaining Attitudes toward Immigration in Europe'. *International Organization* 61(2):399–442.

Hainmueller, Jens, and Daniel J. Hopkins. 2014. 'Public Attitudes toward Immigration'. *Annual Review of Political Science* 17:225–49.

Hatton, Timothy J. 2016. 'Immigration, Public Opinion and the Recession in Europe'. *Economic Policy* 31(86):205–46.

Hernán, Miguel A. 2018. 'The C-word: Scientific Euphemisms Do Not Improve Causal Inference from Observational Data'. *American Journal of Public Health* 108(5):616–19.

Hiers, Wesley, Thomas Soehl, and Andreas Wimmer. 2017. 'National Trauma and the Fear of Foreigners: How Past Geopolitical Threat Heightens Anti-immigration Sentiment Today'. *Social Forces*:1–28.

Hobolt, Sara B., and Catherine E. de Vries. 2016. 'Turning against the Union? The Impact of the Crisis on the Eurosceptic Vote in the 2014 European Parliament Elections'. *Electoral Studies* 44:504–14.

Hooghe, Liesbet. 2007. 'What Drives Euroskepticism?' *European Union Politics* 8(1):5–12.

Hooghe, Liesbet, and Gary Marks. 2005. 'Calculation, Community and Cues: Public Opinion on European Integration'. *European Union Politics* 6(4):419–43.

Hooghe, Liesbet, and Gary Marks. 2009. 'A Postfunctionalist Theory of European Integration: From Permissive Consensus to Constraining Dissensus'. *British Journal of Political Science* 39(1):1–23.

Hopkins, Daniel J. 2010. 'Politicized Places: Explaining Where and When Immigrants Provoke Local Opposition'. *American Political Science Review* 104(1):40–60.

Index.hu. 2015. 'Orbán: Gazdasági bevándorlóknak nem adunk menedéket [Orbán: We Do Not Give Asylum to Economic Refugees]'. Retrieved 12 February 2018 (https://index.hu/belfold/2015/01/11/orban_gazdasagi_bevandorloknak_nem_adunk_menedeket/).

Ivarsflaten, Elisabeth. 2005. 'Threatened by Diversity: Why Restrictive Asylum and Immigration Policies Appeal to Western Europeans'. *Journal of Elections, Public Opinion & Parties* 15(1):21–45.

Juncker, Jean C. 2015. *Conclusions of the European Council Meeting of 15 October 2015 and the Leaders' Meeting on Refugee Flows along the Western Balkan Route of 25 October 2015 – Speech by President Juncker at the European Parliament Plenary Session*. Brussels: European Commission. Retrieved 6 June 2017 (http://europa.eu/rapid/press-release_SPEECH-15-5935_en.htm).

Kallius, Annastiina, Daniel Monterescu, and Prem K. Rajaram. 2016. 'Immobilizing Mobility: Border Ethnography, Illiberal Democracy, and the Politics of the "Refugee Crisis" in Hungary'. *American Ethnologist* 43(1):25–37.

Knutsen, Oddbjørn. 2010. 'The Regional Cleavage in Western Europe: Can Social Composition, Value Orientations and Territorial Identities Explain the Impact of Region on Party Choice?' *West European Politics* 33(3):553–85.

Krăstev, Ivan. 2017. *After Europe*. Philadelphia: University of Pennsylvania Press.

Kreutz, Joakim. 2015. 'Human Rights, Geostrategy, and EU Foreign Policy, 1989–2008'. *International Organization* 69(1):195–217.

Kuntz, Anabel, Eldad Davidov, and Moshe Semyonov. 2017. 'The Dynamic Relations between Economic Conditions and Anti-immigrant Sentiment: A Natural Experiment in Times of the European Economic Crisis'. *International Journal of Comparative Sociology* 0020715217690434.

Lattimer, Charlotte, and Sophia Swithern. 2016. *Global Humanitarian Assistance Report 2016*. Bristol: Global Humanitarian Assistance. Retrieved 6 June 2017 (http://devinit. org/wp-content/uploads/2016/06/Global-Humanitarian-Assistance-Report-2016.pdf).

Marks, Gary, and Marco R. Steenbergen, editors. 2004. *European Integration and Political Conflict*. Cambridge: Cambridge University Press.

Mengozzi, Paolo. 2017. *Request for a Preliminary Ruling from the Council for Asylum and Immigration Proceedings: Jurisdiction of the Court – Article 25(1)(a) of Regulation (Ec) No 810/2009 Establishing a Community Code on Visas*. Case C-638/16 PPU. Den Haag: European Court of Justice (http://curia.europa.eu/juris/document/document. jsf?text=&docid=187561&pageIndex=0&doclang=EN&mode=req&dir=&occ=first&p art=1&cid=229935).

Merkel, Wolfgang. 2017. 'Kosmopolitismus versus Kommunitarismus: Ein neuer Konflikt in der Demokratie [Cosmopolitanism versus Communitarianism: A New Conflict in Democracy]'. Pp. 9–23 in *Parties, Governments and Elites: The Comparative Study of Democracy*, edited by Philipp Harfst, Ina Kubbe, and Thomas Poguntke. Wiesbaden: Springer VS.

Morgan, Stephen L., and Christopher Winship. 2015. *Counterfactuals and Causal Inference: Methods and Principles for Social Research*. New York: Cambridge University Press.

Newsweek. 2015. 'Austria to Build Fence on Slovenian Border to Control Flow of Refugees'. *newsweek.com*, 28 October. Retrieved 6 June 2017 (http://europe.newsweek.com/austria-build-fence-slovenian-border-control-flow-refugees-335563).

Nickerson, Angela M., and Winnifred R. Louis. 2008. 'Nationality versus Humanity? Personality, Identity, and Norms in Relation to Attitudes toward Asylum Seekers'. *Journal of Applied Social Psychology* 38(3):796–817.

OECD. 2008. *Jobs for Immigrants (Vol. 2): Labour Market Integration in Belgium, France, the Netherlands and Portugal*. OECD (http://gbv.eblib.com/patron/FullRecord. aspx?p=408011).

Palme, Joakim, and Walter Korpi. 2003. 'New Politics and Class Politics in the Context of Austerity and Globalization: Welfare State Regress in 18 Countries, 1975–95'. *American Political Science Review* 97(3): 425–46.

Pappi, Franz U. 2005. 'Cleavage'. Pp. 104–6 in *Lexikon der Politikwissenschaft: Theorien, Methoden, Begriffe [Encyclopedia of Political Science: Theories, Methods, Terms]*, edited by D. Nohlen and R.-O. Schultze. München: CH Beck.

Pettigrew, Thomas F., and Linda R. Tropp. 2008. 'How Does Intergroup Contact Reduce Prejudice? Meta-analytic Tests of Three Mediators'. *European Journal of Social Psychology* 38(6):922–34.

Pew Research Center. 2016. *Europeans Fear Wave of Refugees Will Mean More Terrorism, Fewer Jobs*. Washington, DC: Pew Research Center (http://assets.pewresearch. org/wp-content/uploads/sites/2/2016/07/14095942/Pew-Research-Center-EU-Refugees-and-National-Identity-Report-FINAL-July-11-2016.pdf).

Ray, Leonard. 2003. 'When Parties Matter: The Conditional Influence of Party Positions on Voter Opinions about European Integration'. *The Journal of Politics* 65(4):978–94.

Schlueter, Elmar, and Peer Scheepers. 2010. 'The Relationship between Outgroup Size and Anti-Outgroup Attitudes: A Theoretical Synthesis and Empirical Test of Group Threat- and Intergroup Contact Theory'. *Social Science Research* 39(2):285–95.

Schlueter, Elmar, and Ulrich Wagner. 2008. 'Regional Differences Matter: Examining the Dual Influence of the Regional Size of the Immigrant Population on Derogation of Immigrants in Europe'. *International Journal of Comparative Sociology* 49(2–3):153–73.

Scruggs, Lyle. 2014. *Social Welfare Generosity Scores in CWED 2: A Methodological Genealogy.* No. 1. Comparative Welfare Entitlements Dataset Working Paper. Retrieved 1 August 2018 (http://cwed2.org/Data/CWED2_WP_01_2014_Scruggs.pdf).

Semyonov, Moshe, Rebeca Raijman, and Anastasia Gorodzeisky. 2006. 'The Rise of Anti-foreigner Sentiment in European Societies, 1988–2000'. *American Sociological Review* 71(3):426–49.

Sides, John, and Jack Citrin. 2007. 'European Opinion about Immigration: The Role of Identities, Interests and Information'. *British Journal of Political Science* 37(3):477–504.

Steenbergen, Marco R., Erica E. Edwards, and Catherine E. de Vries. 2007. 'Who's Cueing Whom?' *European Union Politics* 8(1):13–35.

Steinmayr, Andreas. 2016. 'Exposure to Refugees and Voting for the Far-right: (Unexpected) Results from Austria'. *IZA Discussion Paper* (9790) (https://papers.ssrn.com/sol3/papers.cfm?abstract_id=2750273).

Stephens, John D. 2010. 'The Social Rights of Citizenship'. Pp. 511–25 in *The Oxford Handbook of the Welfare State*, edited by F. Castles, S. Leibfried, J. Lewis, H. Obinger, and C. Pierson. Oxford: Oxford University Press.

Tagesspiegel. 2017. 'Ungarn und Slowakei müssen Flüchtlinge aufnehmen [Hungary and Slovakia Have to Take in Refugees]'. *Der Tagesspiegel*, 6 September. Retrieved 8 November 2017 (www.tagesspiegel.de/politik/urteil-des-eugh-ungarn-und-slowakei-muessen-fluechtlinge-aufnehmen/20288244.html).

Than, Krisztina. 2016. 'Orban Says to Amend Constitution so EU Can't Impose Migrants on Hungary'. *Reuters*, 2 October. Retrieved 6 June 2017 (http://uk.reuters.com/article/uk-europe-migrants-hungary-referendum-idUKKCN1213Q5).

The Treaty of Lisbon. 2007. *Article 21.* European Union. Retrieved 5 March 2017 (http://eur-lex.europa.eu/legal-content/EN/TXT/?uri=OJ:C:2007:306:TOC).

Tseng, Huan-Kai, and Ryan Krog. 2014. 'No Strings Attached: Chinese Foreign Aid and Regime Stability in Resource-rich Recipient Countries'. *Working Paper.*

UNHCR. 2017. *Desperate Journeys: Refugees and Migrants Entering and Crossing Europe via the Mediterranean and Western Balkans Routes.* Geneva: UNHCR. Retrieved 28 March 2017 (www.unhcr.org/58b449f54).

Visegrád Group. 2016. *Effective Solidarity: A Way Forward on Dublin Revision (Non Paper).* Retrieved 2 May 2017 (www.statewatch.org/news/2016/nov/eu-council-slovak-pres-non-paper-dublin-effective-solidarity-11-16.pdf).

Vollmer, Bastian, and Serhat Karakayali. 2018. 'The Volatility of the Discourse on Refugees in Germany'. *Journal of Immigrant & Refugee Studies* 16(1–2):118–39.

Wintour, Patrick. 2017. 'Hungary to Detain All Asylum Seekers in Container Camps'. *Guardian*, 7 March. Retrieved 6 June 2017 (www.theguardian.com/world/2017/mar/07/-hungary-to-detain-all-asylum-seekers-in-container-camps).

Chapter 7

Conclusion – in search of Europe's futures

In this book, we have presented the findings of a survey on European solidarity conducted in 13 EU countries in late 2016. Our analysis has revealed quite surprising results. Overall, Europe's citizens exhibit a notably high degree of solidarity with citizens of other EU countries and EU states. At first sight, this result seems at odds with developments in the EU over the past decade, given that the number of actors opposing European solidarity has been rising rather than falling. In this final chapter, we discuss two questions: how do our results relate to recent political and social developments in the European Union, which are characterised by the growing importance of Euroscepticism? If we assume that our findings are trustworthy, what political conclusions can we draw from them? Before going into these two questions in Section 7.2, we will summarise the results of the previous chapters and discuss how valid and reliable our findings are (Section 7.1).

7.1 Summary of the findings

The starting point for our study was the various crises the European Union has had to face and to deal with over the last ten years. Each of the domains of European solidarity we identify is related to a different crisis. The financial and the euro crisis have revealed whether crisis-affected countries can expect help from the wealthier countries – a domain of solidarity we call fiscal solidarity. The economic crisis some member states have faced was a direct consequence of the financial and sovereign debt crisis; this involves two different domains of European solidarity. First, European welfare solidarity has become a relevant issue – a domain of solidarity that refers to supporting people in need who live within the territory of the European Union, regardless of which EU member state they belong to. Second, as the economic crisis fostered an increase in economic inequality between EU member states, territorial solidarity, defined as people's willingness to reduce inequality between poor and rich EU countries, has become an issue in the political debate. Lastly, the surge of refugees arriving from war-torn regions in the Middle East constituted the beginning of a third crisis, the refugee crisis. Regarding the refugee crisis, we distinguish between two different aspects of European refugee solidarity: the first refers to the extent to which European citizens are willing to accept refugees from third countries (external solidarity) and the second involves the extent to which Europeans support a fair allocation of refugees between the EU member states (internal solidarity). Figure 7.1 summarises how the different domains of solidarity are related to the three different crises.

In order to determine the strength of European solidarity, we defined four criteria and examined whether the four criteria were met or not for each domain of solidarity. As a starting point, we found it helpful to speak about the existence of European solidarity only if this idea was accepted by a majority of Europe's citizens. As European citizens have two roles in the constitution of the European Union – as citizens of the union and of one of the member states at the same time – we argue that having the support for the majority of all Europeans for the idea of European solidarity is not sufficient. The majority of citizens in each individual member state has to be in favour of the idea of solidarity as well.

Second, we distinguished between three spatial reference points for solidarity: solidarity with citizens of the same nation state, solidarity with citizens within the EU, and solidarity with citizens living outside the EU. To determine the existence of European solidarity, it is necessary to empirically demonstrate that European solidarity is distinct from other spatial reference points for solidarity. We therefore claimed that an independent European space of solidarity exists if European solidarity is stronger than global solidarity. However, due to the fact that the nation state is still the most important societal organisational form, we do not expect European solidarity to be stronger than national solidarity.

Third, it is difficult to determine with any certainty whether citizens' attitudes towards European solidarity are merely a form of a lip service expressed in a poll, without any behavioural consequences. Therefore, we aimed to investigate

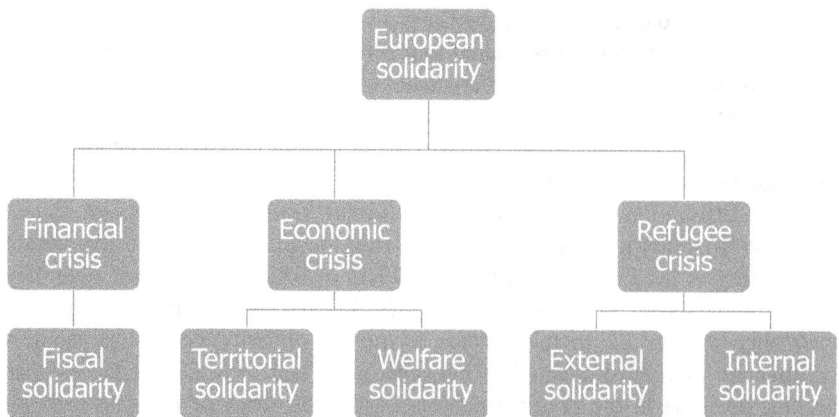

Figure 7.1 Different crises and different domains of solidarity.

whether citizens' attitudes towards European solidarity are resilient, meaning whether citizens are willing to stand up for their beliefs by paying higher taxes to bring about European solidarity. Due to time restrictions when conducting the survey, we could not measure citizens' resilience for all domains of solidarity.

Fourth, we argued that a solid European solidarity should not go along with strong social and political cleavages between proponents and opponents of European solidarity. We proposed that these cleavages are highly likely to emerge if citizens who reject European solidarity share common social characteristics. Therefore, we analysed the extent to which attitudes towards solidarity can be explained by respondents' structural and cultural characteristics and by the specific social features of the countries they live in, which can then lead to the emergence of socio-structural and cultural cleavages. We also tested whether these cleavages might translate into political cleavages if citizens plan to vote for Eurosceptic parties in the next election and thereby transfer their objectives into the political arena.

Table 7.1 summarises the results of the empirical analysis for all domains of European solidarity along the four criteria we distinguish. Not all of the identified criteria can be applied to all domains of solidarity. For instance, the term refugee refers to people coming from outside of Europe; accordingly, national solidarity cannot be operationalised in this case.

The first criterion for the existence of a European solidarity was met for nearly all domains of solidarity. For fiscal solidarity, the results showed that two-thirds of the respondents were willing to give emergency aid to EU countries in crisis. Even if differences in approval levels were apparent between the 13 countries, we found a majority in favour of European fiscal solidarity in all countries. For welfare solidarity, support rates were even higher. On average, more than 80% of respondents approved of support for socially vulnerable (unemployed, elderly, and sick) individuals and endorsed the redistribution of wealth between rich and poor people across the EU. Differences in approval rates by country were rather small. Moreover, a majority of EU citizens supported the idea of European territorial solidarity, as more than 70% of respondents were in favour of reducing spatial differences between EU member states. Regarding refugee solidarity, our analysis revealed a more differentiated picture. Overall, a two-thirds majority of the whole sample approved of accepting refugees in Europe. However, when it comes to granting asylum to Muslim refugees, the majority of citizens in Cyprus and in the Visegrád countries (Poland, Slovakia, and Hungary) were not willing to grant these refugees the right to stay in Europe. A similar picture emerged when we analysed attitudes regarding internal solidarity. While citizens in all western and southern European countries supported the idea that refugees should be distributed equally between member states, three quarters of Polish, Hungarian, and Slovakian citizens rejected this suggestion.

Another surprising conclusion relates to the question of whether European solidarity constitutes a specific space of solidarity, which differs from global solidarity. Support for European fiscal solidarity was somewhat lower than

Table 7.1 Summary of the results along the different criteria of the existence of European solidarity

	Double majority	Specific space	Resilience	Cleavages	
				Social	Political
Fiscal solidarity	✓	✓	✓	weak	moderate
Territorial solidarity	✓	✓	not measured	weak	moderate
Welfare solidarity	✓	✓	not measured	moderate	weak
External solidarity (refugees)	✓	not applicable	not applicable	strong	strong
Internal solidarity (refugees)	✓/–	not applicable	not applicable	weak	strong

support for crisis-affected regions within respondents' own nation states, but it was considerably greater than the support for crisis-affected countries that are not part of the EU. Similarly, European welfare solidarity represented a separate spatial sphere. Although support for European welfare solidarity was somewhat weaker than support for national welfare solidarity, it still ranked above support for global welfare solidarity. A similar picture emerged for the domain of territorial solidarity. While support for European solidarity was slightly smaller than support for equalisation measures within nation states, there was still majority support for European solidarity, which is not the case for a global redistribution scheme.

In the domain of fiscal solidarity, we additionally applied the criterion of behavioural resilience. It turns out that more than 60% of respondents were willing to contribute financial assistance to countries in need from their own pocket in the form of an additional tax. Here, country differences were rather low, except for France, where we did not observe majoritarian support. Hence, at least for one domain of solidarity, the criterion of resilience was also fulfilled.

Finally, we summarise results concerning the criterion of the emergence of social and political cleavages that could lead to a politicisation of European solidarity. In this regard, the results for fiscal and territorial solidarity, and to a lesser extent for welfare solidarity, were very similar: we found a weak to moderate indication of potential cleavages emerging. This was most evident between groups of citizens with different cultural and political orientations but was barely evident between citizens and countries with different socio-economic positions. In the case of European welfare solidarity, social cleavages were stronger than for national welfare solidarity, but at the same time, this was counterbalanced by high absolute support rates for this domain. Concerning political cleavages, our analysis showed that citizens who rejected fiscal, territorial, and welfare solidarity were at the same time more inclined to vote for right-wing Eurosceptic parties. However, the correlations were weak to moderate.

The picture was slightly different in regard to external and internal refugee solidarity, as social cleavages were more pronounced. Opponents of refugee solidarity were set apart by their specific cultural characteristics: they positioned themselves on the political right, had a strong identification with their nation state, perceived foreigners and immigrants more as a threat than as a source of cultural enrichment, and lived in countries where their historical experience of losing their national sovereignty is deeply embedded within the collective memory and where there is also a strong presence of anti-immigration political parties. Similar features characterised the opponents of a fair allocation of refugees among member states, even if the social cleavages here were somewhat weaker. Both solidarities were strongly interlocked, as those who expressed their opposition to taking in refugees also tended to be against the establishment of a uniform allocation system. We also found that these social cleavages translated into political cleavages: those opposing the granting of asylum to refugees were more likely to vote for right-wing Eurosceptic parties.

Overall and in terms of all criteria, European solidarity seems to be more pronounced than many observers have presumed so far. This especially applies to fiscal, territorial, and welfare solidarity, but to a lesser extent to the two domains of solidarity, which are related to the refugee crisis. Before we discuss how these rather optimistic results concerning the existence of a European solidarity relate to the more Eurosceptic perspective, which seems to dominate the public and intellectual discourse on Europe, we wish to reflect on the question of whether our findings may be methodologically flawed, i.e. whether and to what extent they are reliable, valid, and rest on a firm methodological foundation. For us, there are at least three potential objections to our findings from a methodological perspective.

(1) The European Union currently consists of 28 countries (most likely 27 countries after the UK has left the EU). Our study, however, only refers to 13 member countries. Given this, it is not possible to simply generalise our results to all EU member countries. However, as discussed in Chapter 2 and in the Appendix, we selected the 13 countries according to four systematic criteria, which enabled us to map possible variances between the member states. Whether we have really succeeded in this is unfortunately difficult to prove. However, we also have no reason to believe that the 13 countries do not reflect the range of possible country differences between the member states.

(2) Our survey is a snapshot of citizens' attitudes towards European solidarity during the summer and autumn of 2016. Since no panel data are available, we do not know whether citizens' attitudes are stable or volatile over time. If the latter is the case, then our results would not allow us to draw the conclusion that European solidarity is strong. This in turn would inhibit the development of future politics based on this. What makes us confident that people's attitudes will be relatively stable over time?

The questions we asked in our survey in order to operationalise European solidarity aimed at measuring generalised attitudes, which have the character of social values rather than citizens' attitudes towards specific policies. The differences between items that relate to general values and questions that relate to concrete policies are evident when referring to our study's questions. For instance, we asked respondents if they agree with the statement that 'the European Union should guarantee access to health care, a decent standard of living for the elderly and a decent standard of living for the unemployed in the EU'. Even if a respondent agreed with this, he/she nevertheless did not agree with a specific policy to protect vulnerable groups but only that these groups should be protected by the European Union. When seeking to protect vulnerable groups, different policies can be utilised. Whereas people's attitudes towards specific policy options are often volatile and context sensitive, research on values has shown that citizens' values are relatively constant and stable, even though there are slight changes in the course of life and after certain intervening events. In addition, differences in value stability depend on the type of value (Schwartz 2005). Overall, however, research shows that citizens' values are relatively stable (Milfont, Milojev, and Sibley 2016).

(3) Our analysis concludes that a majority of citizens support the idea of European solidarity. Critics might argue that we overestimated citizens' approval rates because respondents were being asked to respond to a value that is socially desirable. We cannot completely dispel this objection but can present a number of arguments in response. (a) If our survey had motivated socially desirable responses, then respondents who opposed European solidarity would have ceased answering the questions during the interview because they did not want to communicate their views on European solidarity. This would in turn have meant that those who were more likely to have a positive attitude towards European solidarity would be over-represented in our survey. However, our data do not confirm this assumption. Time-spell-related monitoring of the telephone interviews showed that only 1% of the respondents who originally agreed to be interviewed stopped the interview before completion. (b) Social desirability bias in surveys is more likely to arise when there is only one legitimate opinion in response to a specific question. Is this the case with our domains of solidarity? At least with regard to fiscal and refugee solidarity – and perhaps to a lesser extent with respect to territorial and welfare solidarity – there has been a broad and heated debate in many member states on both issues. For instance, questions have been raised on whether citizens should support other countries who are in financial need and whether to take in refugees and how to allocate them between EU member states. Many political actors have argued against fiscal solidarity and against the reception and allocation of refugees. From this, we conclude that the conditions for a strong social desirability bias that would lead to an over-reporting of positive answers are not given.

And yet there is a small indication that our survey overestimates the number of proponents of European solidarity. In a German survey from 2016, we measured citizens' attitudes towards fiscal solidarity using the same question we used for this study (Lengfeld and Kroh 2016). When we compared the results of the two studies, it turned out that the approval rate for fiscal solidarity measured in our study was somewhat higher. Juan Díez Medrano and colleagues (2019) also found less support for the notion of 'pooling national state funds to help EU countries having difficulties in paying their debts' (ibid.:145) than we have found in our survey. We do not know exactly why these differences exist. But even if we subtracted 10 percentage points from our approval rates, the criterion for the existence of European solidarity would still be clearly fulfilled.

7.2 The paradox: strong European solidarity on the one hand and the rise of right-wing nationalism on the other

Even if we have little reason to doubt the reliability of our results from a methodological point of view, our positive findings about the existence of European solidarity do not fit well with the public image of the state of the European Union. This image suggests that the European Union is deeply divided and that the future is more than uncertain. With the departure of the United Kingdom, an important member state is leaving the European Union. The Brexit negotiations have made the interdependence of European countries very clear; it is very difficult for a country to leave the EU and the costs are high for both sides.

At first glance, it may appear as if the European Union has overcome the major crises we have described: the euro still exists as a common currency, although some had predicted the collapse of the monetary union. Greece and other southern European countries have not become insolvent despite persistently high debt levels. Economic growth in the EU countries as a whole, and especially in the countries worst affected by the crisis, has again risen slightly (World Bank 2019a). At the same time, unemployment rate in Europe fell from 11.0% in 2011 to 8.2% in 2017 (World Bank 2019b), which means that, at the very least, social inequalities did not worsen any further. Finally, the number of asylum seekers in Europe has fallen dramatically since 2016 (European Commission 2017).

However, these developments cannot hide the fact that the EU is not adequately protected from renewed crises. Analyses show, for example, that the institutional reforms introduced to cope with future crises are far from sufficient. The euro crisis – and the debt crisis – originated in the banking crisis. Anat Admati and Martin Hellweg (2013, 2018) have shown that the institutional precautions necessary to prevent a renewed collapse of systemically important banks have not been put in place. Hence, a new crisis like the one that began in 2008 with the insolvency of Lehman Brothers cannot be ruled out. In Italy, the EU's fourth-largest economy, the national debt has continued to rise steadily while economic growth has been very low. Italy's right-wing populist government, elected in 2018, is not willing to use its economic and budgetary policies to counteract the country's increasing indebtedness; on the contrary, it has further increased the country's national debt and is thus violating European treaties. The consequences of this development may be unpredictable. According to many analysts, the European Financial Stabilisation Mechanism (EFSM) would not be able to cope if Italy became insolvent, because Italy's absolute degree of public debt is nearly seven times higher than that of Greece.

Likewise, the degree of social inequality between European countries offers little cause for comfort. There has been no major redistribution between rich and poor countries in the EU. Even though unemployment has fallen in the EU as a whole, it remains extremely high in some EU countries and especially among certain population groups. The youth unemployment level in July 2018 was 39.7% in Greece, 33.4% in Spain, and 30.8% in Italy; in Germany, by contrast, it was only 6.1% (Eurostat 2018). These figures indicate that inequalities between countries remain very high and show that the aftermath of the crisis hit vulnerable groups particularly hard. Finally, the conflicts associated with the immigration of refugees do not seem to have been overcome. There is no consensus among the member states on the allocation of refugees. Nor is it possible to calculate how the number of people seeking refuge in Europe will develop in future, even though the number has fallen significantly since 2014 and 2015. This is partly due to the fact that the political and economic crises outside Europe that prompt people to flee cannot be accurately predicted. In addition, attempts to safeguard Europe against immigration are standing on an uncertain foundation. This is particularly true for the agreement with Turkey on the retention of refugees. Turkey's foreign policy is unpredictable, and there is hence a possibility of termination of or non-compliance with the EU–Turkey deal if relations between the EU and Turkey continue to deteriorate.

For some political actors and member states, the various crisis management mechanisms do not go far enough; they will therefore not be able to prevent future crises. For other countries, the measures have already gone too far, because they restrict their national sovereignty too much. The crises and the policies to resolve them have further politicised the European project. The public's attention to and salience of European issues have increased significantly during the euro crisis (Drewski 2015; Grande and Kriesi 2015; Rauh and Zürn 2014) and the debate on Europe has become increasingly polarised.[1] Above all, the importance of actors that are critical or sceptical of the EU has increased. In some member states, nationalist parties are in government (Belgium, Finland, Greece, and Austria) or are supporting a minority government (Denmark); in other countries, they have even been appointed the head of government (Italy, the Czech Republic, Poland, and Hungary) and thus influence the future of the EU in the European Council. The conflicts between those who want to persist with the European project and who even want to deepen integration to some extent and those who explicitly favour a policy of renationalisation have grown. A changing global political constellation, with commensurate effects on the European Union and its member states, is exacerbating intra-European dissent. These include developments in the USA since the rise to power of Donald Trump, who has pursued a national-interest-centred policy. As a result, he has abandoned the previously close alliance between the USA and the EU and regards the EU more as a competitor than as a partner. This changing American position vis-à-vis the EU has led to intensified conflicts between EU member states. Especially those countries that have insisted on more national sovereignty and that have restricted rights that are central to the EU's identity, such as freedom of the press and the independence of the judiciary in their countries, such as Poland, Hungary and the Czech Republic, find in Trump an influential and eloquent ally who supports their anti-European course. Anti-European policies are also benefiting from an indirect tailwind owing to China's enormous economic success. The fact that China does not share the liberal and democratic principles that constitute the EU's DNA but is economically very successful at the same time makes the Chinese regime attractive to some critical European governments and strengthens their own authoritarian policies. And finally, the public discourse about the right way to organise society has shifted. Books with titles like *How Democracies Die* (Levitsky and Ziblatt 2018), *The People vs. Democracy: Why Our Freedom Is in Danger and How to Save It* (Mounk 2018), and *How Democracy Ends* (Runciman 2018), which have all become popular science bestsellers, all have a similar basic tenor: they are sceptical that the Western model of society, which also underlies the European Union, will continue to be successful in the future.

In our view, the developments briefly outlined here must be placed in the broader context of a reconfiguration of the political space through the emergence of a new cleavage structure. The literature seeking to describe the structure of this newly emerging conflict line contains quite different conceptual proposals and various empirical studies (Grande and Kriesi 2015; Hutter, Grande, and Kriesi 2016; Kriesi et al. 2012; Merkel 2017), which we cannot address in detail here. The new cleavage structure runs between a cosmopolitan and a communitarian (or nationalist) camp. This division simultaneously complements and is layered on top of the old line of conflict between politically left- and right-oriented actors. It results in four different camps that have developed different options for the future of Europe and different ideas regarding the necessity and feasibility of European solidarity (see Figure 7.2).[2] We first briefly present the four different camps and then interpret the results of our study by referring to the reconfiguration of the political space.

(1) Right-wing communitarians/nationalists: Political representatives of this camp include Viktor Orbán in Hungary, Matteo Salvini in Italy, Marine Le Pen in France, or Alexander Gauland in Germany. Their parties are in favour of a devolution of the European Union. Competences transferred to Brussels should be transferred back to the nation states, they argue. This applies above all to the

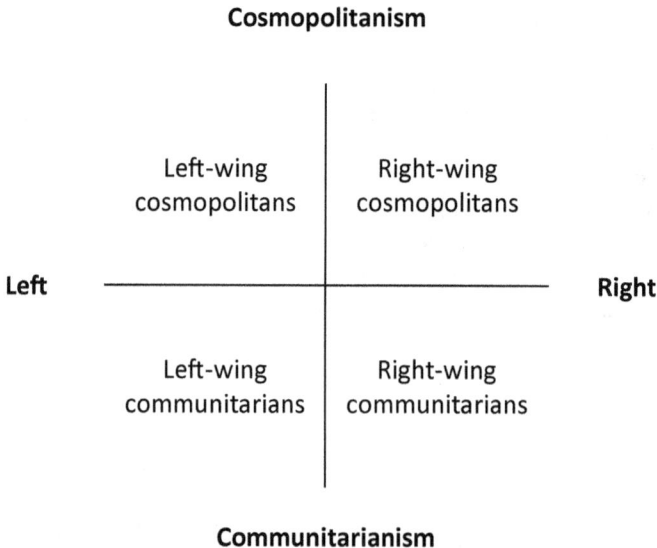

Cosmopolitanism

	Left-wing cosmopolitans	Right-wing cosmopolitans	
Left			**Right**
	Left-wing communitarians	Right-wing communitarians	

Communitarianism

Figure 7.2 The political space of new and old cleavages.

core areas of national sovereignty, such as defence and foreign policy, monetary policy, and border security, but also to economic policy. Some actors from the right-wing communitarian camp advocate for a dissolution of the EU or for the withdrawal of their own country from the EU. The technocratic argument for this policy option is that nation states can solve problems more effectively. Having their own currency makes it possible for countries to compensate for asymmetries in their economic performance by revaluing and devaluing the country's currency. The fact that nation states alone have sufficient police and military personnel puts them in a position to effectively secure their borders, e.g. against refugees. Yet the actual motives for right-wing nationalists' political orientations are less technical but more cultural in nature and relate directly to the question of solidarity. The nation state, so the assumption goes, is a community made up of citizens who are emotionally attached to each other and separate themselves from other nation states. Cultural elements, such as a common language, a common history, or the bonds of religion, serve as points of reference for the construction of national identity. Accordingly, the representatives of the right-wing communitarian camp also celebrate the rituals of national identity construction. These include singing the national anthem, publicly displaying the national flag, or placing an emphasis on national historical achievements. In their view, a European solidarity that transcends the national community is empirically impossible because the citizens of Europe have too few common characteristics and will therefore reject European solidarity.

(2) Left-wing cosmopolitans: At the opposite pole to the right-wing communitarians, we find left-wing cosmopolitans, represented above all by the green parties in Europe in the political arena. They are the strongest advocates of the European integration process. From their point of view, it will not be possible to cope with crises by having less European integration but by having more. For this to occur, however, the European institutions must be strengthened vis-à-vis nation state institutions. These institutions should be enabled to solve crises through a common European policy, for instance, by harmonising asylum policy at European level, sharing the burden equally between the member states, and developing a common European economic policy that also reduces social inequalities. The political measures also include democratising the European Union by strengthening the European Parliament: for instance, by transforming the European Council into a second chamber representing the member states. These political ideas, too, have their basis in assumptions about the nature of European solidarity. From the point of view of left-wing cosmopolitans, it is normatively necessary to think about solidarity in ways not restricted to the nation state. Solidarity is European and global because from an ethical perspective there is no good reason for favouring one's own citizens. Furthermore, left-wing cosmopolitans assume that citizens are also prepared to show European solidarity.

(3) Left-wing communitarians: Left-wing communitarians are weakly represented in the party spectrum of European countries. In Germany, for example,

this camp includes the cross-party movement *Aufstehen*[3] founded by the politician Sahra Wagenknecht, and in Italy – at least to some extent – it includes the Five Stars party movement. In addition, the established socialist and social-liberal parties contain currents that can be thought of as part of the left-wing communitarian camp. These actors are 'left wing' insofar as they put criticisms of neoliberal economic policy and of the banks and financial capital at the centre of the analysis and work for more social justice and social equality by redistributing resources. A neoliberal economic policy pursued not only by the member states but also by the EU itself has, this camp assumes, led to an increase in inequalities within and between the EU member states. The EU's crisis management policy has further increased inequalities, as the austerity measures imposed by the union have led to a shrinkage of national welfare states. More equality and justice can only be achieved if nation states are strengthened, because only the nation state and not the European Union is in a position to compensate for social inequalities (Streeck 2018). For example, Wolfgang Streeck advocates for the withdrawal of the economically highly indebted countries from the monetary union so that they can become competitive again by devaluing their national currency (Streeck 2014). A cultural argument complements the technocratic argument for strengthening the nation states and paring back the EU. From the point of view of left-wing communitarians, the foundations that would be necessary for European solidarity are not currently in place. Only the nation state has the institutional foundations for a community of solidarity. This foundation includes a common language, common collective memories, and experiences with the specific national institutions of a society (Streeck 2018). Accordingly, left-wing communitarians are primarily concerned about socially disadvantaged people in their own country. They fear that a redistribution of resources between poor and rich countries in Europe will come at the expense of low-skilled people in their own country. In contrast to the right-wing communitarians, however, they are less attracted to national-communitarian positions, because, as leftists, they also feel committed to the principle of international solidarity. The same applies to their position on refugees. Thus, left-wing groups do not reject taking in refugees in their own countries, because they are also committed to the idea of internationalism; at the same time, however, they fear that the immigration of refugees will increase competition on the labour market and, above all, that low-skilled workers in their own countries will suffer due to immigration. Accordingly, left-wing communitarians advocate limiting the immigration of refugees, albeit very cautiously.

(4) Right-wing cosmopolitans. Some conservative parties in Europe have changed their political orientation from a right-wing communitarian to a right-wing cosmopolitan orientation. An example of such a change is Germany's CDU party under the leadership of Chancellor Angela Merkel, which has played a major role in shaping EU policy in the various crises. Right-wing cosmopolitans continue to be right-wing oriented, in that their economic policy orientation is market oriented. They are in favour of strengthening the European economic and

monetary area. Questions of social inequality, on the other hand, do not play any particular role for this camp. At the same time, its representatives have a moderate cosmopolitan orientation; for instance, they seek to take responsibility for a global environmental policy, want to strengthen international institutions at the expense of those of their own nation state, and campaign for respect for human rights and equal rights for men and women. The right-wing cosmopolitan orientation sketched out here also applies to European policy. The creation of the European Stability Mechanism, for example, was primarily intended to save the currency area and thus the single European market. Welfare state measures to protect vulnerable groups in crisis-affected countries were largely absent from this mechanism because increases in social inequality between EU countries and the social upheavals within crisis-affected countries are not seen as a danger to the integration process. In contrast to right-wing communitarian parties, however, a desire to achieve a solidarity transcending the nation state also plays a role for right-wing communitarian parties, at least as a secondary motivation for political action. The refugee crisis has made this particularly clear. Political actors classified the plight of refugees as so grave that they put aside national interests and felt obliged to take in refugees, above all from the civil-war-stricken country of Syria. This normative orientation formed the basis for the decision of the German chancellor in 2015 to allow refugees stuck in Hungary to enter Germany.

The poles of 'cosmopolitanism' versus 'communitarianism/nationalism' have thus given rise to a new line of conflict, which has had especially negative implications for the traditional people's parties. Parties from the right-wing camp that have opened themselves to cosmopolitan issues have thus opened up a gap in the political space that is now being filled by new right-wing communitarian parties. And the left-wing social-democratic/socialist parties that have opened themselves to cosmopolitan issues have opened up space for the emergence of both right-wing and left-wing communitarian parties.

When we apply the results of our study to the above-described changes in the political space and to the four different political camps, it is evident that our empirical results support the position of the left-wing cosmopolitans above all, because citizens' attitudes are more compatible with the left-wing cosmopolitan position and less with the positions of the three other camps. This especially applies to issues of fiscal, territorial, and welfare solidarity. These three domains of solidarity are about redistributing resources to create more social equality, whether by supporting socially needy individuals or by redistributing resources to poorer or financially destitute EU countries. Support for more social equality and redistribution is a genuine left-wing political issue. At the same time, it is a cosmopolitan issue because the recipients of the resources are not the citizens of respondents' own countries but the citizens of other EU member states. Our results show that the majority of EU citizens support fiscal, territorial, and welfare solidarity, that they are willing to pay more taxes for it, and that the potential for conflict is rather weak.

The question of solidarity in the refugee crisis deviates from the context described. Admittedly, the majority of citizens are also in favour of accepting refugees in Europe and distributing them fairly among the member states. However, the majority of citizens of Cyprus and the Visegrád countries (Poland, Slovakia, and Hungary) disagree with this idea, at least with regard to Muslim refugees.

But how do these results fit in with the impression that the right-wing communitarian camp is gaining importance? There are two plausible reasons for this difference.

(1) In the 1970s, the German communication studies scholar Elisabeth Noelle-Neumann developed a theory of public opinion: the 'theory of the spiral of silence' (1974). This theory distinguishes between 'public opinion' and 'published opinion', i.e. the opinion published in the mass media. According to Noelle-Neumann, only published opinion can be perceived by the people. In contrast, the opinions of citizens, which can be reconstructed through surveys, are private, invisible, and inaudible to the public. This can give rise to the following situation: a minority opinion that is expressed loudly in public and is communicatively supported by the media appears stronger than it actually is. Conversely, the actual majority opinion, which consists of the uncommunicated opinions of citizens, seems much weaker than it truly is.

Our suspicion is that the actors from the right-wing communitarian camp have succeeded in shaping published opinion and imposing their concerns on it. To achieve this, they have, on one hand, drawn on a repertoire of protest forms formerly used by left-wing political actors (Hutter and Borbáth 2018). On the other hand, they have drawn on the mobilising power of social media – Facebook, Twitter, blogs. At the same time, actors from the other three political camps have unintentionally contributed to the increasing visibility of right-wing communitarian positions in public because they have made this new competitor in the political arena the subject of media debate. This development has contributed, we assume, to the drifting apart of published opinion and public opinion, as manifested in the results of our survey.

One example of this process is the public attention that the party 'Alternative für Deutschland' (Alternative for Germany, AfD) receives in Germany. This party is the only one in the German parliament to speak out decisively against all types of European solidarity. It won 12.6% of the votes in the last election to the German Parliament (The Federal Returning Officer 2017). This means that 87.4% of voters did not support this party. In the public discussion, however, the AfD is accorded much greater importance than its share of the vote and its influence on federal politics would merit.

(2) In our survey, we measured citizens' *basic* consent to various domains of European solidarity. We did not survey whether and to what extent citizens agreed with the process of implementing concrete political measures to achieve European solidarity. However, it is in the implementation of European solidarity via specific policies that a range of problems have emerged. We suspect that the

right-wing communitarian social movements and parties are supported by the citizens because, among other things, they make these problems an issue and generate controversy around them. Yet the support they receive from citizens is probably not related to a general rejection of European solidarity to any significant extent. Citizens support communitarian actors because they disagree with certain policies for *implementing* European solidarity. We illustrate this argument using the example of refugee policies.

Whether someone is entitled to asylum or subsidiary protection must be legally examined. In addition, the right to asylum is limited in time. It expires when persecution no longer exists in the country of origin or when the war has ended. When either an application for asylum is rejected or when the reason for asylum ceases to exist, the person in question must leave the country. Citizens support this legal position, as we can show with our data. Although a large majority of citizens support the right to asylum, 68.3% of the respondents say that asylum seekers should be sent back to their home country when the situation has improved and the reason for asylum no longer exists (Gerhards et al. [unpublished]).

In practice, administrative bodies and courts reject the majority of asylum applications. Across Europe, asylum is granted in almost a third of cases (Eurostat 2019). Assuming that the procedures for determining asylum are generally carried out in a legally correct manner, we can conclude that many applicants try to gain access to Europe through the asylum procedure, even though they are not, in fact, being persecuted in their home country. This can give citizens the impression that the right to asylum is being abused, which, in turn, can increase citizens' dissatisfaction with governments' inability to limit immigration to those who are actually persecuted. And this dissatisfaction can lead citizens to support political actors from the right-wing communitarian camp, because they focus on the abuse of the asylum procedure and accuse governments of not solving this problem. Citizens' support for right-wing communitarian actors therefore does not necessarily mean that citizens are fundamentally opposed to the right to asylum. They are only against its abuse.

A similar situation prevails when it comes to the repatriation of failed asylum seekers. We do not have data on this for all EU countries, but we do have data for Germany (Deutscher Bundestag 2018). As of 30 June 2018, there were nearly 235,000 people in Germany whose asylum applications had been rejected by several authorities and mostly also by the courts. These people are, in principle, obliged to leave the country. Of these 235,000 people, however, only 27,000 could be deported, for a variety of reasons. These include, for instance, people who have committed crimes in Germany and whose criminal proceedings have not yet been concluded. Even members of a terrorist organisation cannot be returned to their country of origin if there is reason to fear that they will be subjected to torture there. People who do not have identity papers or who have intentionally destroyed them cannot be returned either, because their identity must first be established and this is very often not possible. Although these reasons for why rejected asylum seekers cannot be returned to their countries of origin are legitimate from a constitutional perspective, the fact that only a small proportion of those who are obliged to leave the country can actually be returned runs contrary to citizens' convictions. We suspect that some citizens support right-wing communitarian actors because these actors address and generate controversy around the low rate of repatriation and not because they are fundamentally opposed to accepting refugees. A final example can help to illustrate our argument. Particularly in 2014 and 2016, many people succeeded in immigrating to western European countries via the Balkan route without their identity having been fully verified. This opportunity was also used by members of radical Islamist groups. In Germany, for example, the proportion of people belonging to Salafist groups rose from 7,000 in 2014 to 9,700 in 2016 (Bundesamt für Verfassungsschutz 2019). Possibly this increase is causally related to immigration during this period. This, too, is an abuse of the right to asylum, which European citizens not only reject but also fear. Since right-wing communitarian actors address this problem and at the same time exaggerate its significance, citizens support these parties, not because they reject legitimate asylum claims in principle, but because they reject the abuse of asylum law.

Very similar arguments can also be formulated for other domains of solidarity. We have seen, for example, that citizens are highly willing to support member countries in fiscal distress. At the same time, they do not want the money sent to support these countries to be badly administered by recipient countries' state administrations or to be misappropriated. If the impression arises that state administrations in the recipient countries are misusing the aid money, citizens become sceptical as to whether the aid payments and the solidarity they express make sense. According to the Corruption Perception Index, which determines perceived corruption in the public sector and is compiled and published by Transparency International, Greece ranked 60th in 2017, below the average of many other EU countries (Transparency International 2018). The criticism by right-wing communitarian actors of the Greek bureaucracy, which does not manage these funds well, is therefore not entirely empirically unfounded.

Let us summarise our arguments: the strength of the right-wing communitarian camp is being overestimated for two reasons. Because right-wing communitarian actors have succeeded in determining published opinion in relation to their issues, they sometimes appear stronger than they – as measured by the public opinion – actually are. In addition, some citizens do not support the right-wing communitarian camp in elections because they approve of its rejection of European solidarity. They support these actors because they are dissatisfied with some political measures to implement European solidarity and because these problems are being addressed by the right-wing communitarian actors. Of course, it is not easy to precisely determine the actual extent of problems (e.g. in the form of the abuse of asylum) as opposed to the problems defined by political actors. In a competitive democracy, the actors who expect to gain more support from the citizens – e.g. in the form of votes – will dramatise and scandalise problems such as asylum abuse.

What conclusions emerge from our results regarding practical action by European institutions? The observed high willingness of citizens to show solidarity creates a space of opportunity for the EU to take political measures to implement European solidarity. This does not mean that every form of concrete EU policy is justified from the citizens' point of view. When it comes to the concrete implementation of policies, new questions and problems arise, such as the design of the process for implementing a measure, the semantic framing of the measure, or the particular constellation of actors that must be taken into account when implementing a measure. We do not want to and cannot give any concrete policy recommendations here. We can, however, point out certain conditions that should be considered when seeking to strengthen European solidarity.

The public's willingness to show solidarity is a kind of *conditional solidarity*. If citizens have the impression that the measures to achieve European solidarity are not achieving the real objective, this will have a negative effect on their willingness to show solidarity. This not only applies to European solidarity, but also to citizens' support for their national welfare state, as Christina M. Fong, Samuel Bowles, and Herbert Gintis have shown: 'people are willing to help the poor, but they withdraw support when they perceive that the poor may cheat or fail to cooperate by not trying hard enough to be self-sufficient and morally upstanding' (2006:1442).

From our point of view, three conditions of European solidarity are important and should be taken into account by European political actors:

1   Limit free riders: the EU and its member states should ensure that aid measures that operationalise European solidarity are not exploited by those who do not need them and make certain that they reach those for whom they are intended. If citizens get the impression that solidarity measures are being exploited by third parties who, from the citizens' point of view, are not among the intended recipients, this leads to a reduction in their willingness to show solidarity. The case of the refugee crisis in countries such as Finland, Sweden, Germany, Austria, and the Netherlands has shown what happens when governments are, at least temporarily, unable to distinguish between asylum seekers with legitimate reasons to flee and those with other reasons not recognised by asylum legislation. In all these countries, right-wing populist parties have become very popular. Of course, it is not easy to prevent abuse. In our view, however, it is a decisive weakness of the left-wing cosmopolitan camp, which is most strongly committed to European solidarity, that it does not sufficiently recognise the problems in implementing solidarity or often trivialises problems that have arisen. This may increase the influx of citizens into right-wing communitarian organisations that address the arising problems. The further promotion of European solidarity goes hand in hand with referring to the problems and grievances and the attempt to remedy them.

2   Ensure more fairness in burden sharing: the majority of citizens want those who are better off to be more involved in implementing solidarity than those

who are socially weaker. As far as fiscal solidarity is concerned, we have shown that EU citizens do not want socially weaker people in crisis-affected countries to be burdened by additional cuts in social benefits. Instead, the majority of citizens argue that the wealthy should be made to pay higher contributions through wealth taxes. Elsewhere, we have referred to further studies that show that citizens support linking the levels of solidarity contributions to individual prosperity (Gerhards and Lengfeld 2015:177ff.). A large majority of citizens are of the opinion that the upper social classes should be made more accountable in crisis situations such as the sovereign debt crisis. Those actors who, in the opinion of the citizens, are joint instigators of the crisis and who have an exorbitantly high income should not only be more closely monitored, but should also pay higher taxes for the common good.

A new, trans-European cleavage is emerging here that does not run horizontally, i.e. between the nation states, but vertically between the upper classes on the one hand and the not so privileged majority of European citizens on the other. If EU institutions want to strengthen citizens' support for European solidarity, then they need to make greater efforts to introduce a financial transaction tax and other measures that would especially target the rich and large companies, even if this means going against the will of individual member states' governments.

3   Do not create new European institutions: citizens are sceptical about the creation of new European institutions because they believe that these institutions are too far removed from the democratic control and influence of their own nation state. An example can illustrate this thesis. The so-called troika – consisting of the European Commission, the European Central Bank, and the International Monetary Fund as well as the newly created funds ESM and EFSF – was intended to overcome the financial crisis. However, these institutions were and are very controversial, not only in crisis-affected countries, but also among the citizens of the creditor countries. One of the arguments advanced by right-wing and left-wing political actors is that the institutions are not legitimised by national parliaments and thus not linked to the will of the citizens.

We suspect that the EU will be able to implement the citizens' desire for solidarity more successfully if it does not create new supranational institutions but makes use of existing European and national institutions. For instance, in the field of welfare solidarity, EU actors should refrain from creating a European welfare state or from intervening directly in national social security systems through European legislation. It would be better to help the nation states with the greatest social problems to develop effective social policy measures by financing earmarked measures from the EU budget. The implementation of these measures would be undertaken by the respective nation states. Here the establishment of the European Pillar of Social Rights is a clear example. Another example of a

European directive on social policy that leaves responsibility for implementing the details to national-level actors would be the EU-wide minimum wage that Emmanuel Macron prominently mentioned in his Sorbonne address. The establishment of funds could be another tool to engender European welfare solidarity and constitute the 'golden mean' between European and national responsibilities. In this scenario, historically grounded national social security systems would still remain the key instrument for distributing resources and would not be replaced by a new supranational insurance system for all Europeans. Instead, all member states would finance a backup budget that could be used when short-term shocks arise in national social security systems, e.g. due to unemployment. This would even make it possible to accurately recreate the financial transactions that would occur under a uniform European insurance system. This form of support for Europeans in need will find greater support among citizens than the construction of a European welfare state.

Notes

1 The literature assumes that a politicisation of the EU would take place when the public's attention to and awareness of European issues increases and the number of collective actors (parties and interest groups) expressing opinions on European issues in an increasingly controversial and polarised way expands (de Wilde 2011; de Wilde, Leupold, and Schmidtke 2015; Rauh and Zürn 2014; Risse 2015; Statham and Trenz 2015).
2 In the literature, quite different interpretations of the empirical findings of an increasing polarisation of the European project and the formation of a new cleavage structure can be found. While Thomas Risse (2014), for example, interprets the increase in controversy about the future of European integration as a process of normalisation and as constitutive for democratic systems, other authors – including Edgar Grande and Hanspeter Kriesi (2015) – are much more sceptical and see the polarisation as linked to the danger of a break-up of the EU.
3 'Stand up' in German.

References

Admati, Anat, and Martin Hellwig. 2013. *The Bankers' New Clothes: What's Wrong with Banking and What to Do about It*. Princeton, NJ: Princeton University Press.

Admati, Anat, and Martin Hellwig. 2018. 'Risks Grow as Reform Resolve Disappears'. *Global Public Investor*. Retrieved 12 February 2019 (https://admati.people.stanford. edu/sites/g/files/sbiybj1846/f/admati-hellwig-omfif-2018.pdf).

Bundesamt für Verfassungsschutz. 2019. 'Salafismus in Deutschland [Salafism in Germany]'. Retrieved 12 February 2019 (www.verfassungsschutz.de/de/arbeitsfelder/ af-islamismus-und-islamistischer-terrorismus/was-ist-islamismus/salafismus-in-deutschland).

de Wilde, Pieter. 2011. 'No Polity for Old Politics? A Framework for Analyzing the Politicization of European Integration'. *Journal of European Integration* 33(5):559–75.

de Wilde, Pieter, Anna Leupold, and Henning Schmidtke. 2015. 'Introduction: The Differentiated Politicisation of European Governance'. *West European Politics* 39(1):3–22.

Deutscher Bundestag. 2018. 'Abschiebungen im ersten Halbjahr 2018: Inneres und Heimat/Antwort – 14.08.2018 (hib 591/2018) [Deportation during the First Half of 2018: Internal Affairs and Community/Answer]'. Retrieved 12 February 2019 (www.bundestag.de/presse/hib/-/566394).

Díez Medrano, Juan, Irina Ciornei, and Fulya Apaydin. 2019. 'Explaining Supranational Solidarity'. Pp. 137–70 in *Everyday Europe: Social Transnationalism in an Unsettled Continent*, edited by E. Recchi, A. Favell, F. Apaydin, R. Barbulescu, M. Braun, I. Ciornei, N. Cunningham, J. Díez Medrano, D. Duru, L. Hanquinet, J. S. Jensen, S. Pötzschke, D. Reimer, J. Salamonska, M. Savage, and A. Varela. Bristol: Policy Press.

Drewski, Daniel. 2015. 'Has There Been a European Public Discourse on the Euro Crisis? A Content Analysis of German and Spanish Newspaper Editorials'. *Javnost – The Public* 22(3):264–82.

European Commission. 2017. *Report from the Commission to the European Parliament, the European Council and the Council: Fifth Report on the Progress Made in the Implementation of the EU-Turkey Statement.* COM (2017) 204 final. Brussels: European Commission. Retrieved 13 June 2017 (https://ec.europa.eu/home-affairs/sites/homeaffairs/files/what-we-do/policies/european-agenda-migration/20170302_fifth_report_on_the_progress_made_in_the_implementation_of_the_eu-turkey_statement_en.pdf).

Eurostat. 2018. 'Euro Area Unemployment at 8.2%: EU28 at 6.8%'. Retrieved 12 February 2019 (https://ec.europa.eu/eurostat/documents/2995521/9105310/3-31082018-AP-EN.pdf/772f2449-74be-415d-b4b0-351f31982720).

Eurostat. 2019. 'Final Decisions on (Non-EU) Asylum Applications: Table: migr_asydcfina'. Retrieved 12 February 2019 (http://appsso.eurostat.ec.europa.eu/nui/show.do?dataset=migr_asydcfina&lang=en).

Fong, Christina, Samuel Bowles, and Herbert Gintis. 2006. 'Strong Reciprocity and the Welfare State'. Pp. 1439–64 in *Handbooks in Economics*, Vol. 23, *Handbook of the Economics of Giving, Altruism and Reciprocity*, edited by J. Mercier Ythier and S.-C. Kolm. Amsterdam and New York: Elsevier.

Gerhards, Jürgen, and Holger Lengfeld. 2015. *European Citizenship and Social Integration in the European Union*. London and New York: Routledge.

Gerhards, Jürgen, Holger Lengfeld, Marta Soler Gallart, Zsófia S. Ignácz, Florian K. Kley, Maximilian Priem, and Raúl Ramos. [unpublished]. *Transnational European Solidarity Survey [Codebook]*.

Grande, Edgar, and Hanspeter Kriesi. 2015. 'The Restructuring of Political Conflict in Europe and the Politicization of European Integration'. Pp. 190–226 in *European Public Spheres: Politics Is Back*, edited by T. Risse. Cambridge: Cambridge University Press.

Hutter, Swen, and Endre Borbáth. 2018. 'Challenges from Left and Right: The Long-term Dynamics of Protest and Electoral Politics in Western Europe'. *European Societies*. Online first publication.

Hutter, Swen, Edgar Grande, and Hanspeter Kriesi, editors. 2016. *Politicising Europe: Integration and Mass Politics*. Cambridge: Cambridge University Press.

Kriesi, Hanspeter, Edgar Grande, Martin Dolezal, Marc Helbling, Dominic Höglinger, Swen Hutter, and Bruno Wüest. 2012. *Political Conflict in Western Europe*. Cambridge: Cambridge University Press.

Lengfeld, Holger, and Martin Kroh. 2016. 'Solidarity with EU Countries in Crisis: Results of a 2015 Socio-Economic Panel (SOEP) Survey'. *DIW Economic Bulletin* 6(39):473–9.

Levitsky, Steven, and Daniel Ziblatt. 2018. *How Democracies Die: What History Reveals about Our Future*. München: Deutsche Verlags-Anstalt.

Merkel, Wolfgang. 2017. 'Kosmopolitismus versus Kommunitarismus: Ein neuer Konflikt in der Demokratie [Cosmopolitanism versus Communitarianism: A New Conflict in Democracy]'. Pp. 9–23 in *Parties, Governments and Elites. The Comparative Study of Democracy*, edited by Philipp Harfst, Ina Kubbe, and Thomas Poguntke. Wiesbaden: Springer VS.

Milfont, Taciano L., Petar Milojev, and Chris G. Sibley. 2016. 'Values Stability and Change in Adulthood: A 3-year Longitudinal Study of Rank-order Stability and Mean-level Differences'. *Personality and Social Psychology Bulletin* 42(5):572–88.

Mounk, Yascha. 2018. *The People vs. Democracy: Why Our Freedom Is in Danger and How to Save It*. Cambridge, MA: Harvard University Press.

Noelle-Neumann, Elisabeth. 1974. 'The Spiral of Silence: A Theory of Public Opinion'. *Journal of Communication* 24(2):43–51.

Rauh, Christian, and Michael Zürn. 2014. 'Zur Politisierung der EU in der Krise [On the Politicisation of the EU in the Crisis]'. Pp. 121–45 in *Krise der europäischen Vergesellschaftung? Soziologische Perspektiven [Crisis of the European Socialization? Sociological Perspectives]*, edited by M. Heidenreich. Wiesbaden: Springer VS.

Risse, Thomas. 2014. 'No Demos? Identities and Public Spheres in the Euro Crisis'. *Journal of Common Market Studies* 52(6):1207–15.

Risse, Thomas, editor. 2015. *European Public Spheres: Politics Is Back*. Cambridge: Cambridge University Press.

Runciman, David. 2018. *How Democracy Ends*. London: Profile Books.

Schwartz, Shalom H. 2005. 'Robustness and Fruitfulness of a Theory of Universals in Individual Human Values'. Pp. 56–95 in *Values and Behaviour in Organizations* [in Portuguese], edited by Á. Tamayo and J. B. Porto. Petropolis, Brazil: Vozes.

Statham, Paul, and Hans-Jörg Trenz. 2015. 'Understanding the Mechanisms of EU Politicization: Lessons from the Euro-Zone Crisis'. *Comparative European Politics* 13(3):287–306.

Streeck, Wolfgang. 2014. *Buying Time: The Delayed Crisis of Democratic Capitalism*. London: Verso.

Streeck, Wolfgang. 2018. 'Taking Back Control?: The Future of Western Democratic Capitalism'. *Efil Journal of Economic Research* 1(3):30–47.

The Federal Returning Officer. 2017. 'Bundestag Election 2017'. Retrieved 14 February 2019 (www.bundeswahlleiter.de/en/bundestagswahlen/2017/ergebnisse/bund-99.html).

Transparency International. 2018. 'Corruption Perceptions Index 2017'. Retrieved 12 February 2019 (www.transparency.org/news/feature/corruption_perceptions_index_2017).

World Bank. 2019a. *GDP Growth (Annual %): Indicator: NY.GDP.PCAP.KD.ZG*. Retrieved 18 February 2019 (https://data.worldbank.org/indicator/NY.GDP.MKTP.KD.ZG).

World Bank. 2019b. *Unemployment Rate (Percent): Indicator: SL.UEM.TOTL.ZS*. Retrieved 19 February 2019 (https://data.worldbank.org/indicator/SL.UEM.TOTL.ZS?view=chart).

Data set, variables, methods

The empirical findings of this book stemmed from the *Transnational European Solidarity Survey (TESS)*. The TESS was commissioned as part of a joint venture between two research groups: (1) the international research project *Solidarity in Europe: Empowerment, Social Justice and Citizenship* (SOLIDUS) which is funded by the European Commission through the Horizon2020 research programme (Grant Agreement n. 649489), and (2) the German DFG Research Unit *Horizontal Europeanization* funded by the German Research Foundation (FOR 1539). The TESS was conducted in 13 EU countries in 2016: Austria, Cyprus, France, Germany, Greece, Hungary, Ireland, the Netherlands, Poland, Portugal, Slovakia, Spain, and Sweden. We were responsible for the conceptualisation of the survey. *Kantar TNS* (formerly known as *infratest dimap*) Berlin, a public opinion research company specialising in electoral and political research, carried out the survey in the 13 countries in collaboration with national, affiliated institutes belonging to the TNS group. Jürgen Hofrichter, Michael Kunert, and Anja Simon from *Kantar TNS* were in charge of the fieldwork and data collection process. The information presented in the following is partially based on the methodological report provided by *Kantar TNS*.

A.1 Technical background information about the survey

A.1.1 Country selection

Unfortunately, we were not able to survey citizens from all EU countries due to limited financial resources. Thus, we selected 13 EU member states for the analysis. Our country selection aimed to reflect the diversity of all EU countries and their different positions in regard to factors relevant for the four domains of solidarity. Thus, we took into account the following criteria for our country selection (see Table A1 for an overview):

1   Whether or not a country received financial assistance from an international fund or facility during the euro crisis;
2   Whether or not the country is part of the Eurozone;

Table AI Country selection rationale

Country	Situation in financial crisis	Part of Eurozone	Type of welfare regime	Pro-European vs. Eurosceptic
Austria	creditor	yes	conservative	Eurosceptic
Cyprus	debtor	yes	Mediterranean	Eurosceptic
France	creditor	yes	conservative	Eurosceptic
Germany	creditor	yes	conservative	pro-European
Greece	debtor	yes	Mediterranean	Eurosceptic
Hungary	neutral	no	post-socialist	Eurosceptic
Ireland	debtor	yes	liberal	pro-European
The Netherlands	creditor	yes	conservative	pro-European
Poland	neutral	no	post-socialist	Eurosceptic
Portugal	debtor	yes	Mediterranean	Eurosceptic
Slovakia	creditor	yes	post-socialist	Eurosceptic
Spain	debtor	yes	Mediterranean	pro-European
Sweden	neutral	no	social democratic	pro-European

3   What kind of regime the country's welfare state belongs to (liberal, social democratic, conservative, Mediterranean, post-socialist);

4   Whether or not the country's population is in general more pro-European or more Eurosceptic based on the most up-to-date Eurobarometer at the time of country selection.

A.1.2 Basic population, survey technique, and sampling

The population for the survey were those nationals eligible to vote in the national parliament elections of the respective survey country living in private households. The target size for the net sample was 1,000 interviews per country (500 in Cyprus due to its smaller population size).

The survey was conducted by means of computer-assisted telephone interviewing (CATI). For the sampling this poised two major constraints. First, the fact that a large share of households did not have a landline phone these days. Therefore, relying only on landline sampling would have possibly caused selective coverage biases. Thus, *Kantar TNS* Berlin deployed the standard proportions of Eurobarometer Flash surveys from 2016 with varying land-line/mobile phone quotas per country. For example, it was sufficient to conduct 10% of all interviews via mobile connections in Germany, whereas 50% needed to be conducted in Poland. Table A2 shows the applied quotas.

Second, to prevent oversampling of certain regions of each country, the number of contact attempts in the gross sample were stratified regionally by using the NUTS II regions (Eurostat 2015). The gross sample was allocated to cells representing the NUTS II regions according to their share in the population. Within each cell, the dialled numbers were selected randomly. In landline households with multiple members, the interview partner was identified using the last birthday method.

Table A2 Dispersion of landlines and mobile phones by country

Country	Landline (percent)	Mobile (percent)
Austria	49	51
Cyprus	90	10
France	90	10
Germany	90	10
Greece	80	20
Hungary	52	48
Ireland	70	30
The Netherlands	90	10
Poland	50	50
Portugal	70	30
Slovakia	30	70
Spain	70	30
Sweden	60	40

A.1.3 Survey instrument: the questionnaire

We developed a German and English bilingual master questionnaire. The questionnaire consisted largely of standardised closed-ended questions in order to operationalise concepts related to the different domains of solidarity. Subsequently, the bilingual master questionnaire was translated into local languages by a professional translation office familiar with survey research and was then cross-examined by a second translation company. Finally, native speakers of respective languages from the social science field reviewed each national questionnaire. These national splits have been adjusted for country specifics (e.g. region names or currencies mentioned in the survey text (see Table A3)).

In order to test and validate our questionnaire, pre-tests were conducted with samples of 50 interviews from each surveyed country from 27 April to 4 May 2016. Automatic time measurement of the interview duration was also part of the pre-tests. As the average length of the interview was more than 30 minutes, we were concerned about how interviewee cognitive fatigue could undermine the validity of our results. Hence, we revised the master questionnaire and the translations again: questions were partly simplified or amended, others were completely dropped. With this, the average interview time was reduced to less than 30 minutes.

Table A3 Country-specific variation in TESS questionnaire

Country	Currency	Name of regions	Country-specific value of currency		
			3%	2%	0.5%
Austria	euro	Bundesland	60	40	10
Cyprus	euro	Επαρχίες (eparchies)	30	20	5
France	euro	Department	50	30	8
Germany	euro	Bundesland	50	30	8
Greece	euro	περιφέρεια (periferia)	15	10	3
Hungary	Hungarian forint	megye	4,000	2,500	600
Ireland	euro	regional authority region	50	30	8
The Netherlands	euro	provincie	50	30	8
Poland	Polish złoty	województwa	60	40	10
Portugal	euro	região	15	10	3
Slovakia	euro	kraji	15	10	3
Spain	euro	comunidades autónoma (CCAA)	30	20	5
Sweden	Swedish krona	län	600	400	100

A.I.4 Fieldwork

The fieldwork was coordinated and conducted by *TNS Triple C Centre* in Brussels from 6 June to 15 November 2016. Table A4 summarizes the information about the interviews. The average interview lengths ranged from 23 minutes in Cyprus to 32 minutes in Sweden. Given the fact that there was no differences between countries related to filtering or questions, the difference in length resulted from differences in local languages. Table A4 also shows the total number of realised net interviews per country. In order to reach the intended sample size, up to 293,000 telephone numbers per country were randomly drawn. The majority of these numbers led to neutral non-responses (e.g. unused numbers, numbers of fax machines, or non-private households). Deducting these non-responses from the gross sample leads to the adjusted gross sample, which is the reference for the net response rates of the national surveys. Almost all non-responses can be traced back to unanswered phone calls or participation refusals before the interview started. The dropout rates during the interview were below 1% of the adjusted gross samples in all countries. Overall, net response rates (share of completed interviews of the adjusted gross sample) ranged from 1.3% in Austria to 9.5% in Hungary.

A.I.5 Weighting

All surveys face the issues of sampling errors from random sampling and selectivity caused by non-response. In order to correct for them, *Kantar TNS* Berlin calculated two weight variables using an approach introduced by Edwards F. Deming and Stephan F. Frederick (1940; see also Cochran 1968) for national representative statistics (national weights) and one for ensuring representative statistics over all 13 countries (sample weights). The weights took into account the national landline/mobile ratios, but factored in the possible response selectivity. The sample structure was compared to the actual population structure along age, gender, labour market status, regions (NUTS II), employment status (known from Eurostat and the Statistics on Income and Living Conditions (EU-SILC) database), and the highest level of completed education (measured with the ES-ISCED 2010–2014 scale from the European Social Survey (ESS Round 7: European Social Survey 2016)). *Kantar TNS* added the corresponding weighting factors to the TESS data set (population weight: PFAKT; national weights: GEFAKT). In the analysis, we highlighted whether we applied weighting.

A.2 Variables

In the following we describe those variables of the TESS that are used in the analysis of this book. The wording of variables excluded from our empirical analysis can be found in the TESS codebook (Gerhards et al. [unpublished]). Table A5 lists the exact wording of the items from the English master questionnaire, which served as the basis for the national splits. Table A5 is divided into

Table A4 Information on fieldwork by country

Country	Fieldwork period	Number of net interviews	Average interview length (minutes)	Gross sample	Adjusted gross sample	Response rate (in percent)
Austria	6 June to 6 July	1,010	30	293,214	76,849	1.3
Cyprus	7 June to 22 June	500	23	122,976	18,395	2.7
France	10 October to 5 November	1,002	27	63,097	18,965	5.3
Germany	6 June to 1 July	1,001	28	177,333	33,569	3.0
Greece	9 June to 1 July	1,000	24	48,118	19,455	5.1
Hungary	6 June to 30 June	1,001	29	30,804	10,566	9.5
Ireland	10 October to 14 November	1,000	25	131,267	38,369	2.6
The Netherlands	6 June to 5 July	1,000	29	54,807	18,188	5.5
Poland	6 June to 1 July	1,000	27	83,147	22,842	4.4
Portugal	6 June to 1 July	1,000	27	85,266	13,001	7.7
Slovakia	6 June to 5 July	1,000	29	86,011	13,200	7.6
Spain	6 June to 6 July	1,001	26	99,512	43,656	2.3
Sweden	7 June to 13 July	1,000	32	59,281	16,459	6.1

Table A5 Variable wording and values

Variable	Range in analyses	Original item wording
A. Domains of solidarity		
A1. Fiscal solidarity		
Support for fiscal solidarity		We have learned in recent years that regions within countries as well as entire countries can fall into a severe debt crisis. Please tell me to what extent you agree or disagree with each of the following statements. (1 totally agree, 2 tend to agree, 3 tend to disagree, 4 totally disagree) *Recoded to: 1 = 4, 2 = 3, 3 = 2, 4 = 1*
National fiscal solidarity	1–4	[Q11A] In times of crisis, the better off [GENERALREGIONNAME]s in [COUNTRY] should give financial help to other [GENERALREGIONNAME]s facing severe economic difficulties.
European fiscal solidarity	1–4	[Q11B] In times of crisis, [COUNTRY] should give financial help to other EU countries facing severe economic difficulties.
Global fiscal solidarity	1–4	[Q11C] In times of crisis, [COUNTRY] should give financial help to other countries outside of the European Union facing severe economic difficulties.
Decision question for fiscal solidarity	1–3	[Q12A] Assuming a decision about priority has to be made: in your opinion, where should financial support be provided to first? 1 To a [GENERALREGIONNAME] within [COUNTRY]. 2 To another country in the European Union. 3 To another country outside of the European Union.
	1–3	[Q12B] And where should it be provided to second? 1 To a [GENERALREGIONNAME] within [COUNTRY]. 2 To another country in the European Union. 3 To another country outside of the European Union. *Remark: answer in B) had to vary from A)*
Austerity measures		There are certain measures countries in crisis have to take in order to get financial support from the European Union. Please tell me for each measure to what extent you agree or disagree that countries in crisis should take them in order to get financial support from the EU. (1 totally agree, 2 tend to agree, 3 tend to disagree, 4 totally disagree) *Recoded to: 1 = 4, 2 = 3, 3 = 2, 4 = 1*

Variable	Range in analyses	Original item wording
	1–4	[Q16A] Increase value-added tax.
	1–4	[Q16B] Raise wealth tax.
	1–4	[Q16C] Cut social spending.
	1–4	[Q16D] Raise the retirement age.
	1–4	[Q16E] Reduce the number of employees in the public sector.
Establishment of EU fund to fight debt crises		And now imagine the following situation. To fight against future debt crises, every Member State of the European Union has to contribute to a European solidarity fund. This money will only be used to fight economic crises in EU countries with severe financial problems. (1 yes, 2 no) *Recoded to: no = 0, yes = 1*
	0,1	[Q14A] Would you personally be willing to pay 3% of your income, but at least [COUNTRYSPECIFICCURRENCYANDVALUE1] per month to this fund?
	0,1	If respondents didn't want to pay 3% of their income, they were furthermore asked: [Q14B] And what about 2% of your income, but at least [COUNTRYSPECIFICCURRENCYANDVALUE2] per month?
	0,1	If respondents didn't want to pay 3%, nor 2% of their income, they were asked: [Q14C] And what about 0.5% of your income, but at least [COUNTRYSPECIFICCURRENCYANDVALUE3] per month? *Remark: All country-specific currencies and their values are listed in Table A3.*
Support for country-specific fiscal solidarity		I will now read out a list of EU countries. Please tell me for each country whether or not it should receive financial support in times of crisis. What about ...? (1 yes, 2 no) *Recoded to: no = 0, yes = 1*
Group 1	0,1	[Q13_01] Cyprus
	0,1	[Q13_02] Greece
	0,1	[Q13_03] Ireland
	0,1	[Q13_04] Portugal
Group 2	0,1	[Q13_05] Hungary
	0,1	[Q13_06] Poland
	0,1	[Q13_07] Slovakia
	0,1	[Q13_08] Spain
Group 3	0,1	[Q13_09] Germany
	0,1	[Q13_10] Austria
	0,1	[Q13_11] United Kingdom
	0,1	[Q13_12] Sweden

Continued

Table A5 Continued

Variable	Range in analyses	Original item wording
	0,1	[Q13_13] The Netherlands *Remark: The item battery was randomised for each interview. Each respondent randomly received 6 items from the 13, 2 from each income group. France was not included in the battery.*

A2. Territorial solidarity

Variable	Range in analyses	Original item wording
Support for territorial solidarity		There are differences between rich and poor regions in a country, between countries, and also between countries in the world. Please tell me to what extent you agree or disagree with the following statements. (1 totally agree, 2 tend to agree, 3 tend to disagree, 4 totally disagree) *Recoded to: 1 = 4, 2 = 3, 3 = 2, 4 = 1*
National territorial solidarity	1–4	[Q17A] Differences between rich and poor [GENERALREGIONNAME]s in [COUNTRY] should be reduced, even if wealthier [GENERALREGIONNAME]s have to pay more.
European territorial solidarity	1–4	[Q17B] Differences between rich and poor countries in the EU should be reduced, even if wealthier countries in the European Union have to pay more.
Global territorial solidarity	1–4	[Q17C] Differences between EU countries and poor countries outside of the EU should be reduced, even if EU countries have to pay more.
Decision question for territorial solidarity	1–3	[Q18A] Assuming a decision about priority has to be made: in your opinion, where should the differences be reduced first? 1 Between rich and poor [GENERALREGIONNAME]s in [COUNTRY]. 2 Between rich and poor countries in the European Union. 3 Between EU countries and poor countries outside of the European Union.
	1–3	[Q18B] And where should they be reduced second? 1 Between rich and poor [GENERALREGIONNAME]s in [COUNTRY]. 2 Between rich and poor countries in the European Union. 3 Between EU countries and poor countries outside of the European Union. *Remark: answer in B had to vary from A.*

Variable	Range in analyses	Original item wording

A3. Welfare solidarity

Variable	Range in analyses	Original item wording
Support for national welfare solidarity		People have different views on what the [NATIONAL] government should be responsible for. Please tell me for each of the following statements whether you totally agree, tend to agree, tend to disagree or totally disagree. (1 totally agree, 2 tend to agree, 3 tend to disagree, 4 totally disagree) *Recoded to: 1 = 4, 2 = 3, 3 = 2, 4 = 1*
Support for national social security	1–4	[Q01_1] The [NATIONAL] government should guarantee access to health care for everyone in [COUNTRY].
Support for national social security	1–4	[Q01_2] The [NATIONAL] government should guarantee a decent standard of living for the elderly in [COUNTRY].
Support for national social security	1–4	[Q01_3] The [NATIONAL] government should guarantee a decent standard of living for the unemployed in [COUNTRY].
Support for national income redistribution	1–4	[Q01_4] The [NATIONAL] government should reduce income differences between rich and poor in [COUNTRY].
Support for European welfare solidarity		Now please don't think about [COUNTRY], but about the European Union in Brussels and its responsibilities. Please tell me for each of the following statements whether you totally agree, tend to agree, tend to disagree, or totally disagree. (1 totally agree, 2 tend to agree, 3 tend to disagree, 4 totally disagree) *Recoded to: 1 = 4, 2 = 3, 3 = 2, 4 = 1*
Support for European social security	1–4	[Q02_1] The European Union should guarantee access to health care for everyone in the EU.
Support for European social security	1–4	[Q02_2] The European Union should guarantee a decent standard of living for the elderly in the EU.
Support for European social security	1–4	[Q02_3] The European Union should guarantee a decent standard of living for the unemployed in the EU.
Support for European income redistribution	1–4	[Q02_4] The [NATIONAL] government should reduce income differences between rich and poor in [COUNTRY].
Decision question for welfare solidarity	1–3	[Q03A] There are people in need not only in [country] and in the EU, but all over the world. Assuming a decision about priority has to be made: in your opinion, where should people in need be helped first? 1 In [COUNTRY]. 2 In other countries in the European Union.

Continued

Table A5 Continued

Variable	Range in analyses	Original item wording
		3 In other countries outside of the European Union.
	1–3	[Q03B] And where should be helped second? 1 In [COUNTRY]. 2 In other countries in the European Union. 3 In other countries outside of the European Union. *Remark: answer in B had to vary from A.*
Uniform social welfare system in the EU	1–4	[Q04] Please think now about the possibility of a social welfare system in the EU and tell me for the following proposition to what extent you agree or disagree. There should be a uniform social welfare system for everyone in the EU, even if this leads to an increase in taxes and social spending in [COUNTRY]. (1 totally agree, 2 tend to agree, 3 tend to disagree, 4 totally disagree) *Recoded to: 1 = 4, 2 = 3, 3 = 2, 4 = 1*

A4. Refugee solidarity

Variable	Range in analyses	Original item wording
Support for external solidarity		People have different reasons for coming to the European Union. Please tell me to what extent you agree or disagree with granting the right to stay for people who … (1 totally agree, 2 tend to agree, 3 tend to disagree, 4 totally disagree) *Recoded to: 1 = 4, 2 = 3, 3 = 2, 4 = 1*
	1–4	[Q09A] … are persecuted because they campaign for human rights.
	1–4	[Q09B] … are persecuted because they belong to a Christian minority.
	1–4	[Q09C] … suffer from war.
	1–4	[Q09D] … are persecuted because they are homosexuals.
	1–4	[Q09E] … are persecuted because they belong to a Muslim minority. *Remark: The composite index used in the cleavage analysis was the mean of items Q09A through Q09E.*
Support for internal solidarity		Recently, many refugees came to the European Union. I will now read out to you some statements about how the EU countries could tackle the refugees problem together. Please tell me to what extent you agree, or disagree with the following statements. (1 totally agree, 2 tend to agree, 3 tend to disagree, 4 totally disagree) *Recoded to: 1 = 4, 2 = 3, 3 = 2, 4 = 1*
Sharing the burden	1–4	[Q08A] Each EU country should be required to accommodate refugees.

Variable	Range in analyses	Original item wording
Compensating for the burden	1–4	[Q08B] If an EU country does not want to let refugees in, it has to pay compensation to other countries that take them.

B. Social cleavages
B1. Structural cleavages

Occupational class	1–7	[S07A] What is your current occupation? 1 Employed professional (employed doctor, lawyer, accountant, architect). 2 General management, director or top management (managing directors, director general, other director). 3 Middle management, other management (department head, junior manager, teacher, technician). 4 Employed position, working mainly at a desk. 5 Employed position, not at a desk but travelling (salesmen, driver, etc.) 6 Employed position, not at a desk, but in a service job (hospital, restaurant, police, fireman, etc.). 7 Supervisor. 8 Skilled manual worker. 9 Other (unskilled) manual worker, servant. *Recoded to: 1,2 = 1 Upper class, 3 = 2 Upper middle class, 4 = 3 Centre middle class, 7,8 = 4 Lower middle class, 5,6 = 6 Routine non-manual, 9 = 7 Unskilled manual workers & agriculture* *Recodes refer to Erikson-Goldthorpe-Portocarero-class-scheme (EGP)* *Remarks: The category "Self-employed (5)" was defined by another variable indicating the respondent's employment situation (see below); If respondent was currently not part of the active labor force, we asked them a similar question to indicate their prior occupation.*
Unemployed	0,1	[S06] Which of the following applies to your current employment situation? Are you ... 1 Full-time employee (30 hours a week or more). 2 Part-time employee (less than 30 hours a week). 3 Self employed. 4 Retired/pensioned. 5 Housewife, doing housework or otherwise not employed. 6 Student. 7 Unemployed. *Recoded to: 1–6 = 0, 7 = 1*

Continued

Table A5 Continued

Variable	Range in analyses	Original item wording
Household: number of children		[S03] How many of these people are under the age of 14?
Household income		[S08A] Could you please tell me what the total monthly net income of your household is? I mean the amount remaining from salaries, pensions and other income after taxes and other compulsory deductions like social security contributions. If you don't know the exact figure, please give an estimate. *Recoded: The values are equalised according to the modified OECD-scale. Values are in euros (purchasing power parities, logarithmised).* *Remark: If respondent did not indicate their exact monthly net income of the household, they were kindly asked to name the income bracket in which their household income falls. They were read out ten hierarchical income brackets adjusted to the country's income distribution. If they did so, we approximated their household income by the bracket's mean. For details please refer to TESS codebook.*
Level of education	1–3	[S05] What is the highest level of education or vocational training you have achieved? 1 No formal qualification, only primary education. 2 Lower secondary education. 3 Upper secondary vocational education. 4 Upper secondary education. 5 Post secondary education, advanced vocational education below bachelor's degree level. 6 Medium duration higher education at university or polytechnic college. 7 Long higher education at university or polytechnic college. 8 Other. *Recoded to: 1 = 1, 2–5 = 2, 6,7 = 3* *Remark: The labels are adjusted to the country´s education or vocational training schemata and terms. For a full list of countries see TESS codebook.*
Migration generation: first generation	0,1	[S13] Were you born in a foreign country? (1 yes, 2 no) *Recoded to: no = 0, yes = 1*
Migration generation: second generation	0,1	[S14] Was your mother or father born in a foreign country? (1 yes, 2 no) *Recoded to: no = 0, yes = 1*

Variable	Range in analyses	Original item wording

B2. Cultural cleavages

Political placement 1–5

[Q23] In political matters people talk of 'the left' and 'the right'. How would you place your views on a scale from 0 to 10, where 0 means the left and 10 means the right?
Recoded to: 1,2 = 1 'Left', 3–5 = 2 'Moderate Left', 6 = 3 'Centre', 7–9 = 4 'Moderate Right', 10–11 = 5 'Right'

Society: culture enriched by foreigners

I will now read to you several statements about society. Please tell me to what extent you agree or disagree with the following statements: (1 totally agree, 2 tend to agree, 3 tend to disagree, 4 totally disagree) ´
Recoded to: 1,2 = 1, 3,4 = 0

0,1   [Q20A] [COUNTRY]s cultural life is generally enriched by people coming to live here from other countries.
Some people think of themselves as [NATIONALITY], others as Europeans, and others as citizens of the world. What about you? (1 yes, 2 no)
Recoded to: no = 0, yes = 1

Identity: national   0,1   [Q19A] Do you feel [NATIONALITY]?
Identity: European   0,1   [Q19B] Do you feel European?
Identity: global   0,1   [Q19C] Do you feel you are a citizen of the world?
There are different ways income and wealth in a society can be distributed. Please tell me to what extent you agree or disagree with the following statements. (1 totally agree, 2 tend to agree, 3 tend to disagree, 4 totally disagree)
Recoded to: 1,2 = 1, 3,4 = 0

Justice: equality matters   0,1   [Q22A] The distribution of wealth and income should be as equal as possible in society.
Justice: basic needs   0,1   [Q22C] Income should be distributed in a way that ensures everyone's basic needs are met.

C. Political cleavages

Party preference

[Q24] If the [NATIONALELECTION] were held tomorrow, which party would you vote for?
Remark: Respondents could only choose among parties eligible to run in the next national election. For a full list of countries see TESS codebook. See Tables A6 and A7 for details about the categorisation of each party for Euroscepticism and political orientation.

Continued

Table A5 Continued

Variable	Range in analyses	Original item wording
D. Control variables		
Sex	0,1	[S01] Self-generated by interviewer (1 male, 2 female) *Recoded to: male = 0, female = 1*
Age		[S04] Can you tell me your year of birth, please? *Recoded as: 2016 − year of birth*
Contact with foreigners	0,1	[S09] Do you have regular contact with people from other countries in your circle of friends and acquaintances? (1 yes, 2 no) [S10] Do you have contact ... 1 Only with foreigners living in [COUNTRYOFRESP] 2 Only with foreigners living abroad. 3 With foreigners living in [COUNTRYOFRESP] and to foreigners living abroad. *Recoded to [S09]: 2 = 0* *Recoded to [S10]: 2 = 0, 1,3 = 1* *Remark: Question [S10] was only asked if respondents had indicated that they have regular contact with people from other countries (asked if S09 = 1).*
E. Macro-level variables		
GDP per capita (in 1000 USD)	0–100	The gross domestic product (GDP) is the sum of gross value added by all resident producers in the economy plus any product taxes and minus any subsidies not included in the value of the products (without making deductions for depreciation of fabricated assets or for depletion and degradation of natural resources). This sum is later divided by midyear population so that it is equally distributed to the population (per capita). Data are in 1,000 US dollars. Data are from 2015 in the analyses. (Retrieved on 11 October 2016). Data source: World Bank – World Bank national accounts data, and OECD National Accounts data files (Indicator: NY.GDP.PCAP.CD)
GDP growth rate (percent)		The growth rate of the gross domestic product (GDP) per capita is calculated annually on the basis of local currency from the previous year and shown in percentage. Data are from 2015 in the analyses. (Retrieved 11 October 2016). Data source: World Bank – World Bank national accounts data, and OECD National Accounts data files (Indicator: NY.GDP.PCAP.KD.ZG)

Variable	Range in analyses	Original item wording
Rate of government debt (percent)		The ratio of government debt outstanding at the end of the year to gross domestic product at current market prices. For this calculation, government debt is defined as the total consolidated gross debt at nominal value in the following categories of government liabilities (as defined in ESA 2010): currency and deposits (AF.2), debt securities (AF.3) and loans (AF.4). The general government sector comprises the subsectors of central government, state government, local government. and social security funds. Data are from 2015 in the analyses. (Retrieved 12 December 2016). Data source: EUROSTAT – General government gross debt (table: sdg_17_40)
Unemployment rate (percent)	0–100	A person is unemployed if she or he is without work but is actively seeking for employment and available to work (e.g. not chronically ill). The unemployment rate refers to the percentage of unemployed people compared to the total labour force (modelled ILO estimate). Data are from 2014 in the analyses. (Retrieved 11 October 2016). Data source: World Bank – International Labour Organization, ILOSTAT database (Indicator: SL.UEM.TOTL.ZS).
Income inequality (Gini index)	0–100	With the measurement of the Gini index it can be shown to which extent the income distribution (or, in some cases, consumption expenditure) among individuals or households within an economy diverge from a perfectly equal distribution. Primarily the Lorenz curve is calculated by plotting the cumulative percentages of total income received against the cumulative number of recipients, starting with the poorest individual or household. Accordingly the area between the Lorenz curve and a hypothetical line of absolute equality is measured. That is expressed in the Gini index. Its scale starts with 0 (= perfect equality) and ranges up to 100 (= perfect inequality). Data is from 2015 in the analyses. (Retrieved 11 October 2016). Data source: World Bank – Development Research Group. Data are based on primary household survey data obtained from government statistical agencies and World Bank country departments (Indicator: SI.POV.GINI).

Continued

Table A5 Continued

Variable	Range in analyses	Original item wording
Government social spending (percent of GDP)		Expenditure on social protection contain: social benefits, which consist of transfers, in cash or in kind, to households and individuals to relieve them of the burden of a defined set of risks or needs; administration costs, which represent the costs charged to the scheme for its management and administration; other expenditure, which consists of miscellaneous expenditure by social protection schemes (payment of property income and other). Data is from 2013 in the analyses. (Retrieved 3 April 2018). Data source: EUROSTAT – Expenditure on social protection (table: tps00098).
Share of anti-immigration party votes in last election (percent)		Building on Sara B. Hobolt and Catherine de Vries' (2016) suggestions for party movements in combination with the qualitative analysis of party manifestos at the time of election, the authors identified parties who were evidently positioned as anti-immigrant. The following parties were labeled as anti-immigrant: See list in Table A6. Data source (results of last elections): www.parties-and-elections.eu/
Degree of historical national trauma (index)	0–6	The authors Wesley Hiers, Thomas Soehl, and Andreas Wimmer (2017) developed an index based on the 'historical, geopolitical fate' of nations, incorporating a country's historical experiences of shocks such as the loss of national sovereignty, the loss of a part of the state territory, as well as external and internal conflicts. Every nation is ascribed an index score according to the intensity and extent of the experience, varying on a scale of zero to six (with 0 being the lowest level of geopolitical threat and 6 the highest). Theoretical source: Hiers, Soehl, and Wimmer 2017 Further information on https://muse.jhu.edu/article/668088
Relation of refugee applications to population (percent)		The relation of refugee applications to population in each country was calculated with the EUROSTAT data on country population in 2015 and the number of asylum and first-time asylum applicants in the respective countries in 2015. Population numbers and application.

Variable	Range in analyses	Original item wording
		Data are from 2015 in the analyses. (Retrieved 7 December 2016). Data source: EUROSTAT – Population change – Demographic balance and crude rates at national level (table: demo_gind) and Asylum and first-time asylum applicants – annual aggregated data (rounded) (table: tps00191)

Note
Original values 'don't know' and 'no answer' are treated as missing values.

Table A6 Classification of anti-immigrant parties

Country	Classification based on election of the year	Anti-immigrant party
Austria	2013	Freedom Party (FPÖ)
		Alliance for the Future of Austria (BZÖ)
Cyprus	2016	National Popular Front (ELAM)
France	2012	Rassemblement National (RN)
Germany	2013	Alternative for Germany (AfD)
		National Democratic Party (NPD)
Greece	2015 II	Popular Association – Golden Dawn (Xrusi Augi)
		The Independent Greeks (ANEL)
Hungary	2014	Hungarian Civic Alliance (Fidesz)
		Movement for a Better Hungary (Jobbik)
Ireland	2016	Soldiers of Destiny (Fianna Fáil)
The Netherlands	2012	Party for Freedom (PVV)
		Reformed Political Party (SGP)
Poland	2015	National Movement (RN)
		Kukiz'15
Portugal	2015	National Renovator Party (PNR)
Slovakia	2016	Slovak National Party (SNS)
		People's Party – Our Slovakia (ĽSNS)
Spain	2016	
Sweden	2014	Swedish Democrats (SD)

Source: own classification.

Table A7 Classification of parties regarding their political position

Country	Political left – hard Eurosceptic	Political left – soft Eurosceptic	Political right – soft Eurosceptic	Political right – hard Eurosceptic
Austria	–	Alliance for a different Europe (ANDERS)[a]	Alliance for the Future of Austria (BZÖ)	Freedom Party (FPÖ)
Cyprus	–	Progressive Party for the Working People (AKEL)	–	National Popular Front (ELAM)
France	Left Front (FG)	New Anticapitalist Party (N.P.A.)	–	Rassemblement National (RN) France Arise (DLF)
Germany	–	Left Party (Die Linke)	–	Alternative for Germany (AfD) National Democratic Party (NPD)
Greece	Communist Party of Greece (KKE)	Coalition of the Radical Left (SYRIZA)	Popular Orthodox Rally (LAOS)	Popular Association – Golden Dawn (Xrusi Augi) The Independent Greeks (ANEL)
Hungary	–	–	Hungarian Civic Alliance (Fidesz)	Movement for a Better Hungary (Jobbik)
Ireland	People Before Profit Alliance (AAA-PBP)	We Ourselves (Sinn Féin)	–	–
The Netherlands	Socialist Party (SP)	–	Christian Union (CU)	Party for Freedom (PVV)
Poland	–	–	Law and Justice (PiS) United Poland (SP)	Congress of the New Right (KNP)
Portugal	United Democratic Coalition (PCP–PEV)[b]	Left Bloc (BE)	–	–
Slovakia	–	–	Ordinary People and Independent Personalities (OLANO) New Majority (NOVA) Freedom and Solidarity (SaS)	Slovak National Party (SNS)
Spain	–	United Left (IU) We Can (Podemos)	–	–
Sweden	Left Party (V) June List (jl)	Feminist Initiative (FI) Pirate Party[c]	–	Sweden Democrats (SD)

Source: Adapted from Hobolt and de Vries (2016).

Notes

a Alliance consisted of the Communist Party of Austria (KPÖ), Pirat Party (Piratenpartei), The Change Party (Der Wandel), and independents.

b Coalition consisted of the Portuguese Communist Party (PCP) and the Ecologist Party 'The Greens' (PEV).

c Party is difficult to classify as either left- or right-wing.

The complete overview of political parties is available in the TESS codebook.

five main sections. The first section describes the item wording for the domains of solidarity. The second describes the structural and cultural variables, which are applied in the analysis of the social cleavages, the third section is devoted to the relevant variables of the analysis of the political cleavages, the fourth section displays the wording of additional individual-level control variables, while the fifth section contains a description of the macro-level variables.

A.3 Methods

In the empirical chapters (Chapters 3 through 6) we employed an array of bivariate and multivariate methods to analyse European solidarity. In our multivariate analysis of the social cleavages, we identified effects that shape the respondents' attitudes towards the respective domains of solidarity at the level of the individuals, the countries, and the interaction of these two levels. Throughout the analysis we treated our items measuring European solidarity as continuous variables. The TESS is a stratified sample and the survey data are nested in countries. To test hypotheses on nested (or hierarchical) data, scholars, in particular economists and sociologists, usually apply hierarchical linear models (HLM). Even though we apply HLM as robustness checks, we considered the current state of statistical research. Mark L. Bryan and Stephen P. Jenkins (2016:19–20) concluded that HLMs require at least 25 cases at the second level in order to not reject the null-hypotheses at a premature stage. In our case, we have only 13 cases at the second level. Alternatively, Bryan and Jenkins recommended an effective alternative to use in cases when there is not enough cases on the second level: two-step approaches. We followed their recommendation in our book. Thus, our methodological approach is a combination of OLS regression and its multi-group extension: the two-step regression approach. The applied methods are described briefly in the following.

A.3.1 Ordinary least squares regression

Ordinary least squares (OLS) regression is a widely used statistical method to detect correlation patterns between selected variables. OLS estimators are determined in such a way that the sum of squares of the difference between the estimated outcomes and the true values of the dependent variable is minimized (Wooldridge 2013:27). We used it as a cornerstone of our cleavage analysis in order to estimate linear relationships between the respective domains of solidarity (as the dependent variable) and various explanatory variables both at the individual and the country level.

We employed pooled OLS regression to identify cleavages at the individual level. We also had to account for the fact that all participants are nested in their respective countries and that observations within a country are not independent of one another. Therefore, we applied cluster-adjusted standard errors in our pooled OLS models (Angrist and Pischke 2009:312–13). Variables capturing social and structural cleavages were our main independent variables and we also controlled for various individual factors, as well as country context (with country dummies). The received regression coefficients are the average individual effects of the structural and cultural cleavage variables on the attitudes towards solidarity.

A.3.2 Two-step regression approach

As its name suggests, a two-step regression (TSR) approach consists of two regression steps; the first step conducted at the first (individual) level and the second at the second (country) level. The (unstandardised) coefficients from the first step constitute the dependent variables in the second step. The TSR approach connects results from different OLS regressions. Note, however, that the unit of analysis changes from individuals in the first step to countries in the second step.

As the second step is at the country level, this had consequences for the models. The degrees of freedom are usually low in these country-level OLS regressions because of the low number of countries in the sample. Thus, in our case, with 13 countries, we decided to include a maximum of two explanatory variables in the second step. Additionally, the probability of rejecting the null-hypothesis is low with such a low number of cases. So, we raised the alpha-error to a level of 10% in the second step of the TSR approach.

To assess the country-level effects, in the first step we ran a pooled OLS regression. The model included dummy variables for all countries (Spain as reference category), as well as the previously specified indicators for structural and cultural cleavages, as well as the control variables from the individual level. The country dummies represented country fixed effects. In a second step, we took the values of the unstandardised coefficients of the country dummies from the pooled OLS regression as the dependent variable and macro indicators as independent variables and ran OLS regressions at the country level to test hypotheses on the effects of country characteristic.

We also applied the TSR approach to test our hypothesis on cross-level effects, albeit slightly differently. We no longer relied on country fixed effects, because we wanted to allow the individual effects to vary across countries. These model specifications are called random intercept and random slopes in the HLM equivalent. By applying a TSR approach to a random slopes model, we risked a loss in efficiency compared to random-intercept and random-slope HLM models. But considering again the relatively small number of countries, the TSR approach is the most reliable approach to gain unbiased estimators for our cross-level analysis (Heisig, Schaeffer, and Giesecke 2017). So, as a first step, we first estimated separate OLS regressions with identical specifications for each country. The model specifications were the same as for individual-level analysis: we ran models where cleavage variables and control variables were independent variables. This meant that we had the unstandardised coefficients for each independent variable in all countries. As a second step, we took these coefficients as dependent variables and macro indicators as independent variables in order to estimate the effect of country characteristics on individual-level cleavages structures.

A.3.3 Multinomial logistic regression

Multinomial logistic regression (MNL) is from the family of general linear models, where the dependent variable is nominal. MNL can be considered a set of binary logistic models, where each of the categories of the dependent variables are compared to one another. MNL models are estimated with maximum likelihood estimation and the main value for the fit of the model is the likelihood value of the model. MNL can be seen as a probability model, in the sense that the coefficients of the model express the probability of respondents falling into a specific category compared to the chosen reference category (Long 1997). These probabilities are dependent on the explanatory variables in the model. MNL can be used in both bivariate and multivariate cases.

In our case, MNL is the main method to analyse political cleavages and understand how the degree of solidarity influences voting behaviour. Since the distribution of the data across the five categories of the dependent variable is strongly skewed, as too many answers fall in one category, we only conducted bivariate MNL analysis. In the empirical chapters we show predicted probabilities stemming from bivariate multinomial logistic regressions.

References

Angrist, Joshua D., and Jörn-Steffen Pischke. 2009. *Mostly Harmless Econometrics: An Empiricist's Companion*. Princeton, NJ: Princeton University Press.

Bryan, Mark L., and Stephen P. Jenkins. 2016. 'Multilevel Modelling of Country Effects: A Cautionary Tale'. *European Sociological Review* 32(1):3–22.

Cochran, W. G. 1968. 'The Effectiveness of Adjustment by Subclassification in Removing Bias in Observational Studies'. *Biometrics* 24(2):295–313.

Deming, Edwards W., and Stephan F. Frederick. 1940. 'On a Least Squares Adjustment of a Sampled Frequency Table When the Expected Marginal Totals Are Known'. *The Annals of Mathematical Statistics* 11(4):427–44.

ESS Round 7: European Social Survey. 2016. *ESS-7 2014 Documentation Report. Edition 3.1*. Bergen (www.europeansocialsurvey.org/data/conditions_of_use.html).

Eurostat. 2015. *Regions in the European Union: Nomenclature of Territorial Units for Statistics; NUTS 2013/EU-28*. Luxembourg: Publ. of the Europ. Union. Retrieved 18 February 2019 (https://publications.europa.eu/en/publication-detail/-/publication/a4f9243e-fa53-4798-90f4-bb51cb355a3a).

Gerhards, Jürgen, Holger Lengfeld, Marta Soler Gallart, Zsófia S. Ignácz, Florian K. Kley, Maximilian Priem, and Raúl Ramos. [unpublished]. *Transnational European Solidarity Survey [Codebook]*.

Heisig, Jan P., Merlin Schaeffer, and Johannes Giesecke. 2017. 'The Costs of Simplicity: Why Multilevel Models May Benefit from Accounting for Cross-cluster Differences in the Effects of Controls'. *American Sociological Review* 82(4):796–827.

Hiers, Wesley, Thomas Soehl, and Andreas Wimmer. 2017. 'National Trauma and the Fear of Foreigners: How Past Geopolitical Threat Heightens Anti-immigration Sentiment Today'. *Social Forces* 96(1):361–88.

Hobolt, Sara B., and Catherine E. de Vries. 2016. 'Turning against the Union? The Impact of the Crisis on the Eurosceptic Vote in the 2014 European Parliament Elections'. *Electoral Studies* 44:504–14.

Long, J. S. 1997. *Regression Models for Categorical and Limited Dependent Variables.* Vol. 7. Thousand Oaks, CA: SAGE Publications.

Wooldridge, Jeffrey M. 2013. *Introductory Econometrics: A Modern Approach.* 5th ed. Mason, OH: South-Western Cengage Learning.

Index

Page numbers in **bold** denote tables, those in *italics* denote figures.

For Product Safety Concerns and Information please contact our EU
representative GPSR@taylorandfrancis.com
Taylor & Francis Verlag GmbH, Kaufingerstraße 24, 80331 München, Germany